Sovereign Intimacy

Sovereign Intimacy

Private Media and the Traces
of Colonial Violence

Laliv Melamed

UNIVERSITY OF CALIFORNIA PRESS

University of California Press
Oakland, California

Portions of chapter 1 were previously published as Laliv
Melamed, "What is a Girlfriend? Toward a Political Concept
of the Girlfriend," *Discourse: Journal of Theoretical Studies
in Media and Culture* 43, no. 3 (Fall 2021): 421–46.

Portions of chapter 2 were previously published as Laliv
Melamed, "Seeking an Advice: A Political Economy of Israeli
Home Videos," in *Global Perspectives on Amateur Film Histories
and Cultures*, ed. Masha Salazkina and Enrique Fibla-Gutiérrez
(Indianapolis: Indiana University Press, 2021), 95–111.

Library of Congress Cataloging-in-Publication Data

Names: Melamed, Laliv, author.
Title: Sovereign intimacy : private media and the traces of colonial
    violence / Laliv Melamed.
Description: Oakland, California : University of California Press,
    [2023] | Includes bibliographical references and index.
Identifiers: LCCN 2022029931 (print) | LCCN 2022029932 (ebook) |
    ISBN 9780520390287 (cloth) | ISBN 9780520390294 (paperback)
    | ISBN 9780520390317 (ebook)
Subjects: LCSH: Bereavement—Political aspects—Israel—
    20th century. | Social media—Israel—20th century.
Classification: LCC BF575.G7 M445 2023 (print) | LCC BF575.G7
    (ebook) | DDC 155.9/37095694—dc23/eng/20221017
LC record available at https://lccn.loc.gov/2022029931
LC ebook record available at https://lccn.loc.gov/2022029932

32   31   30   29   28   27   26   25   24   23
10   9   8   7   6   5   4   3   2   1

For Hedva Melamed
For Jonathan Kahana

Contents

Prologue

"OUR SONS"

Sovereign Intimacy is not about forms of political resistance leading us towards a hopeful horizon. It is about a pervasive, even passive, compliance. It tackles the paradoxical relationships in liberal and neoliberal politics between kinship and sovereign power, paradoxes that the book seeks to articulate rather than resolve. While *Sovereign Intimacy* is not about resistance, I want to begin by recalling a moment when these paradoxes crystallized, simultaneously provoked and reaffirmed.

In February 1997 four Jewish-Israeli women founded what would become the most popular and successful anti-occupation movement in Israel. The women, all living in the north of Israel, all mothers of soldiers who served on the northern front, initiated a local protest following a disastrous event in which two helicopters carrying seventy-three soldiers across the northern border crashed, leaving no survivors. Their activities took place under the name Four Mothers. For Jewish-Israeli society these were years of constant unrest, when a chain of occupied posts in southern Lebanon termed a "security belt" by the Israeli military yielded daily casualties. The helicopters' crash was described as an event whose ruinous aftermath touched every part of society, and for days, the media streamed images of broken families mourning their loved ones. The Four Mothers' protest, calling the government to immediately withdraw from southern Lebanon, soon became a nationwide popular movement with unprecedented success. Thousands joined their call for the sake of lives, mostly the lives of Israeli soldiers, "OUR

SONS." The movement call was taken up by the political leader of the Israeli center-left at the time, the former general Ehud Barak, who assimilated the cause into his electoral campaign. In May 1999, Barak was elected as Israel's prime minister and in May 2000, the Israeli Defense Force (IDF) pulled out from southern Lebanon, ending almost two decades of occupation.

The Four Mothers movement's oppositional position against the Israeli security regime—its claims on the political—emanated from its appropriation of the voice of maternal care. To speak from a place of care turned out to be the key for mobilizing public opinion and the motor for the movement's substantial popularity. An important landmark in undermining Israeli militarism and the pact between patriarchy and nationalism so essential for Israeli statehood, the Four Mothers movement belongs to a national and international tradition of feminist movements. Jewish-Israeli feminist anti-war movements such as Women in Black (initiated in 1988, a few months after the eruption of the first Intifada) and Checkpoint Watch (initiated in 2001 following the eruption of the second Intifada) have to negotiate their place and legitimacy to speak out against occupation in a society governed by militancy, securitism and chauvinism.[1] Predictably, populist discourse in Israel dismisses feminist activists as collaborators, traitors, or as irrationally emotional, thus still bound to a binary metaphorism of either clueless or promiscuous social danger. Women's movements, shows Diana Taylor, have questioned state sovereign power precisely by performing the gendered politics of motherhood.[2] Re-appropriating the maternal position as a form of citizenship was a strategic decision for Four Mothers, partly led by the movement itself and partly applied by the public discourse around it and its supportive or less supportive media coverage.[3] Indeed, regardless of the movement's investment in an informed critique, what popularized it and paved the road for its success was the call on family love and the soldier's life as a way of undermining the military imperative.

While the movement contributed to the gendering of citizenship by legitimizing maternal affinity as a political position and was able to disarm national securitism, it also had the effect of excessively infantilizing the representative of state power, the soldier, now seen as an endangered son. Negotiations have a flip side. While kinship potentially introduces a different discourse to the dominance of militarism and security, it also speaks its language. Kinship plays into a fraught bio-political and affecto-political power, where it can quickly be used as a strategy for containing militarism and colonization rather than rupturing them. Whereas the call on kinship emerged as a critical stance, it ended up either being assimilated into the state's own mechanisms of administrating and governing life, or sentimentalizing the very forms of power it sought to dismantle. Consequently, the movement's call for geo-political re-strategizing (military withdrawal) made for the sake of "our sons" shifts the aim: from justice and rights for those subjugated by occupation, to withdrawal for the sake of domestic unity and the well-being of the family—and the nation.

This book's topic, families' homemade videos commemorating their loved ones, soldiers who died as part of Israel's long-running regime of security and military aggression, encapsulate the same paradox. Initially a challenge to the state-run memory in their call on intimacy as a mode of labor and production that prioritizes love over death (or money), they ended up, or maybe were to begin with, at the very core of sovereign politics. To end occupation and violence for the sake of "our sons" stays within the discourse of security, the only difference being that what is protected is not territory, wealth, or the population at large, but kinship. Calling upon kinship exposes the price of loss, but does not imagine life outside or beyond the colonial military state.

In the discourse of liberalism, the sovereign subject—a self-sufficient, self-governed figure of liberalism, our son or their parent—is situated as the vector for everything which is just and right, and needs to be defended. As a citizen, our son or their parent validates a system of normative, indeed gendered and racialized, social values, with the family as its ultimate symbol. In order to unlearn a social logic so total as the logic of militarism in Israel, there are some attachments, some sentiments, we will have to let go. Nevertheless, a critique of the inside of that social logic, its intimacy, is meant not to further normalize or sanctify it, but to insist on citizenship as the space for political action and resistance.

When I have presented this research in international conferences, or discussed it with my professors at New York University, or with colleagues in the United States and later in Germany, I have had to translate the videos. This was a practical necessity: the videos, produced by families for their own use with a limited circulation in the Jewish-Israeli public sphere, are in Hebrew, and my work and research has taken place in the English-speaking academic world. My pragmatic attempts at translating them became a difficult, yet illuminating experience. To translate these videos was to move them into a different language: from their subjects' very private expression of loss to the analytic and public sphere of academic knowledge; from intimate family attachments to a systematic thinking-through of media and the political economy of production and circulation; from a sphere of naturalized values and codes to a language that is foreign to them. It is striking how repeating something in a different language unnaturalizes it. Translating the videos forced me first and foremost to reflect on my own position in relation to my object of research as the one who knows the language and all its nuances. To know a language—to know its codes, slang, cliches, dialects, and biases—means to be articulate, to be part of its very order, to be shaped by it. It is an intimate position, and this intimacy is not comfortable. In my analysis of the videos, I try to reproduce this position of uncomfortable intimacy, meaning I try not to shy away from their affect and to be explicit about the stakes, because I believe this is the only way to learn and unlearn how intimacy, as part of the state mechanism, operates.

Working on intimacy, sometimes ends do not meet. When trying to gather information on a video in memory of Eliav Geffen, a soldier who died in 1975 in a fire exchange across the northern border, I found very little about the video itself, which was made in 2011 by a semi-professional local production studio. In my research I discovered, however, a news item in the press from 2006 that mentions Geffen's father. Upon receiving the Memorial Day letter written to bereaved families by the Ministry of Defense, Geffen's father sent the letter back to the Ministry with a poignant letter of his own. The father writes: "I sadly return your generic condolences. . . . The letter has no substance and it is full of cliches. Our damn aggression killed my son, Eliav, for nothing. . . . You kill and eliminate and cannot realize that war, hatred and death will stay with us until we will grant our neighbors minimal autonomy and dignity."

Eliav Geffen's father joined the Israeli-Palestinian Parents Circle-Families Forum, an anti-occupation, bi-national organization that mobilizes mourning and kinship as means of recognition. He did not appear in the 2011 memorial video. Geffen's mother did appear, and in one of the more excruciating scenes, she walks to the place where, thirty-five years earlier, her son was killed, a spot she can clearly see from her home. Ends do not meet not because the information I gathered was partial, which is mostly the case when working on autonomous media made outside industrial matrixes. It is also not because of the tension between the video's special circumstances and its being part of a consistent mode of production, a tension held by all videos as expressions of personal mourning. It is because there are systems of proximities here that are hard to cohere. What does it mean to want to distance yourself from loss's very mechanisms, yet to live so intimately *with* the space of loss? I share the story of the video in memory of Eliav Geffen precisely because I could not make meaning of it and believe this is an important position to hold in relation to these materials. This does not mean that I am hesitant in my critique of the overall mechanism that the videos eventually serve, but that I acknowledge that mourning often resists meaning, or stays utterly opaque, that there are contradictory vocations like rejecting the state's cliches and seeking other channels to articulate your loss, and that complicity is a complex and not straightforward position. In this book I try to represent intimacy in its nuances, yet to be clear about what is at stake for the oppressed. By articulating the multiple ways in which citizens attached themselves to the state and its violent endeavors I hope to open up a path for refusal: to object to being a citizen of an intimate sovereignty.

A Note on Sources

All videos discussed in this book were broadcast on Israeli television during the National Memorial Day. After failed attempts to gain access to them through television archives, most of them were accessed via VHS recordings of the television programming in the years 2008–2012, which are now in the author's personal collection. In the second decade of the 2000s many of the discussed videos were uploaded on YouTube or other online platforms, such as personal commemorative websites. A few of the videos were accessed after directly contacting families and/or producers.

FIGURE 1. Recordings of the National Memorial Day Programming, author's personal collection.

Acknowledgments

As someone interested in how institutional constellations cater to affective registers of kinship, I am an avid reader of acknowledgments. Perhaps this is why writing my own was a difficult task. This book, which took some time to bring to a completion, started as a dissertation at NYU under the supervision of Anna McCarthy and Jonathan Kahana. Both played an important role in my formation as a thinker, and I thank them for their generosity, support, and friendship. Brady Fletcher, Hadi Gharabaghi, Ramesh Kumar, Debashree Mukherjee, Cortland Rankin, Priyanjali Sen, and Paulina Suárez Hesketh were a supportive cohort whose astute feedback helped me get this started. I also wish to thank Dana Polan, Zhen Zhang, Robert Stam, Ken Sweeney, Liza Greenfield, and Melanie Daly for making my time at NYU possible and wisdomfull. NYU's Provost's Global Research Initiative fellowship in Berlin was crucial to realize this project and the time there a precious haven for writing and thinking. I would like to thank the SCMS dissertation award committee members for granting this project an award. It helped me gain confidence in a world that often felt foreign to me.

A number of invitations provided the opportunity to revisit my ideas and put them in conversation with a variety of disciplines, from law to philosophy, politics and the Middle East. The "Specters of Justice" conference at the Philipps-University Marburg, the Political Lexicon workshop dedicated to kinship at the Minerva Center at Tel Aviv University, and a talk at the Department of Modern Culture and Media at

Brown University, supported by a Salomon Grant for Guest Lecturers, enabled such fruitful exchange. The Interdisciplinary Memory Studies Group at the New School for Social Research was likewise a stimulating arena. I'm particularly thankful for Yifat Gutman, Lindsey Friedman, and Benjamin Neinass for our many discussions and the collaboration that ensued.

At Goethe University, Frankfurt, I wish to thank the members of the DFG-funded Configurations of Film graduate research program and the members of the cluster of excellence ConTrust: Trust in Conflict—Political Life Under Conditions of Uncertainty. Vinzenz Hediger, Verena Mund, and Kalani Michell actively listened to me speaking about this project on a number of occasions. Rembert Hueser and Philipp Dominik Keidl read chapters of the manuscript and offered helpful comments. The Forschungszentrum Historische Geisteswissenschaften (FzHG) PPD grant assisted in the final polishing of the manuscript. My research assistants, Fabian Wessels and Marie Malina, put in essential labor. I am especially thankful for Marie Malina, who proofread the final manuscript in a highly professional manner while teaching me valuable lessons on backups and other stuff. I joined the department of Art, Culture and Media at Groningen University while at the very final stage of the book. I thank my colleagues there—Miklos Kiss, Julian Hanich, and Annie van den Oever—for making it a soft start, giving me time to bring the process to its end.

I feel fortunate to have Raina Polivka as my editor at University of California Press. She immediately recognized what the book is about and where I can do better, and I am grateful for the trust she had put in this book and in me. Madison Wetzell, Sam Warren, Jeff Anderson, and Jon Dertien, also at UCP, made the production process smooth and manageable. I would like to thank my copyeditor Catherine Osborne. When I approached Tamie Parker Song and asked her if she was willing to help me shine my ideas, she wrote back saying that the manuscript was in her area of "care," and care she did. I cherish what I learned from her, as well as the friendship that was formed.

Two short meetings, probably less memorable for my interlocutors than for me, were key moments. I thank Marita Sturken, who met me in her NYU office and gave me vital advice, and Rami Elhanani, who met me in a Jerusalem café and gave me hope.

I would like to express my gratitude to Pooja Rangan. Her thorough reading and astute comments helped with putting things in their right place on so many levels. Yaron Shemer provided me with valid feedback that tightened my perspective. John Mowitt was a generous reader of chapter 4. I would also like to thank Marianne Hirsch, Rebecca Schneider, Ruthie Ginsburg, Jennifer Horne, and Caren Kaplan for a number of eye-opening conversations. I couldn't (or wouldn't) think without a community. Visible Evidence was the first academic conference where I had such a feeling. I would like to thank especially Alisa Lebow, Malin Whalberg, Michael Renov, Brian Winston, Patricia Zimmemann, and Joshua Malitski for making this a place I am always excited to go back to.

I loved pitching ideas to Adam Ross Rosenthal and Paige Sarlin. Paige always sent me back to the page with a renewed enthusiasm. Jason Fox, Toby Lee, Pooja Rangan and Tess Takahashi helped me nurture some potent ideas and took me swimming. Paul Fileri, Ohad Landesmann, Kathrin T. Model, Neta Alexander, Kartik Nair, Asaf Harel, Julia Schade, Hanna Pfeifer, and Sonja Simoni provided readership, nuance, and mostly friendship. Benjamin Schultz-Figueroa and I exchanged chapters while I was developing the book's final version. It was something to look forward to in a pretty hectic period for both of us and I learned a lot from him. Daniel Mann was/is a close interlocutor and I appreciate his knowledgeable, bright, and curious notes. I thank Diego Semerene and Jaap Verheul for their girlfriendhood, or rather, their counter-institutional kinship. It was a gift to share a library hall and then the world with Paulina Suárez Hesketh, who is the sharpest observer I ever met, and Debashree Mukherjee, who constantly makes me look at things differently, mostly while laughing.

Lastly I would like to thank my family: my siblings Harel and Sivan Melamed and my parents Uri and Nurit Melamed, who supported me endlessly even when what I had to say was uneasy. I dedicate this book to my grandmother, Hedva Melamed, who instigated in me the passion to learn, and to Jonathan Kahana, who nurtured that passion. They both died in the final stages of the book and I will think of them when it returns to me as an object in the world. I could not have done all of this without Yossi Capua. Yossi, Mila, and Yuli—thank you for taking me away from my desk and asking me to redefine, time and again, life.

Introduction

During the early 1990s, the recently privatized Israeli television started allocating a special slot during the National Memorial Day programming schedule for homemade soldiers' memorial videos. After suffering loss, individual family or friends have made the videos, drawing on their innermost registers of mourning and extending a gesture of love for personal, private kin. It is not quite clear how these videos get to television in the first place. They are neither produced nor commissioned by any formal media body, but are an eclectic amalgam of materials, formal structures, and styles, emanating from a range of access to film knowledge and means of production, supported by community outreach, personal initiatives, and voluntary work. In parallel to their broadcasting, or as a result, this mode of homemade commemoration increasingly became a trend and has been supported by a growing semi-official production infrastructure in the private media market. Their gradual standardization notwithstanding, the videos have persisted at the very margins of the National Memorial programming day, almost outside the institutions of television and memory. Late into the night and early in the morning, at the cusps of a state-orchestrated day of monumental grief, the Israeli televisual public sphere is populated by a plurality of singularized, uncanny manifestations of the intimacies of love and loss.

The mediated ghosts of dead soldiers, Benedict Anderson tells us, are leading actors in the communal national imagination.[1] Yet, with mandatory recruitment for every one of its citizens, militarism in Israel is not an abstraction in the social imagination, but a familiar practice and a citizenry common-sense. An infrastructure of Zionist securitism and domination, the military, it can be argued, is also key to Israeli social-ism, an internal structure of radical equality through which every citizen takes an active part in society. Concurrently, a well-established and well-maintained tradition of commemoration has existed in Israel since its earliest decades.[2] Specific to media, this was manifested in the form of films produced either by public television, the Ministry of Defense, or the Israeli Defense Force (IDF). These officially produced visual memorials mobilized the life and death of a particular figure to create a national mythology of heroism, to write a collective biography, to produce a sense of necessity, and to justify the ongoing militarization of Israeli society through the rhetoric of survival, protection, and shared ideals. These formal media pieces take place within a clear hierarchy of memory-production sites and subjects. Yet, the aforementioned homemade videos are nowhere to be found in the national archives or national canon. Did they mark a break from the recruitment of death by the state project? Calling upon the price of loss, the videos differ from, and even seem to undermine, the spectacle of military and memory quintessential to Israeli national ideology. For these memorials and their producers, video has been a means of healing—and the military not a social meta-structure or a necessity for national resilience, but a trivial element, engrained in the most mundane, most prosaic aspects of everyday life.

The cultural artefacts this book investigates are a seemingly haphaz-ard and insignificant assemblage of media productions, prompted by loss. The videos paste together family pictures, home videos, letters, and text messages. These are poor images: marked by VHS interlacing distur-bances, sometimes ornamented with tacky 1990s video effects, imbri-cated with poorly-lit interviews recorded impromptu with the camera's microphone, often including makeshift thematic montages organized to popular music—a video clip parlance. They are neither a product of a consistent plan nor do they follow a particular production scheme, but are rather arbitrary and relational both in the ways they came into being and their approach to videomaking. The book is populated by an eclectic milieu that leads us down a variety of paths: upon the death of a childhood friend and teammate, one soldier borrows his father's cam-corder and starts interviewing the people surrounding him; following the death of her son, a mother studies basic editing software with which she composes a fairytale-like memorial video; a successful television producer learns that her friend's son died and recruits a shooting team to work pro-bono; a sympathetic television director receives a call asking him to support and program a short video by a young film student about the loss of her boyfriend.[3] Film schools, military alumni associations, and local production studios likewise lend a hand and help families make their own memorials. Programmed as they get, loyal to mundane intimacy, the videos' material texture is melancholic, rudimentary, and inchoate, articulating a sequence of banal transmissions: a jumpy video of a school end-of-year celebration, souvenirs from a family trip, a message on an answering machine discussing plans for the weekend, or a laconic text message: "See you soon."

What are we to make of these private media when they are shown on television? How do we reconcile these pleas with their context, nearly a century of colonial violence?

Video articulates a new claim, a claim for the right to love. This is allegedly a universal right for all, yet as with all rights, while it is granted to the individual, it simultaneously affirms and conforms to the sovereign who grants it. The video memorial contains the fractures of love and life, but it also perpetuates and is compliant with Israeli sovereign power and its pervasive form of authority over its citizens and noncitizens, regardless of the position of individual producers. The claim for the right to love and the desire for a restorative mourning work is not the excess of such power, but its form of maintenance. By its circulation, formation, and standardization, video produces self-sufficient citizens whose right to a private life separates them from those lives taken in their name. In *Sovereign Intimacy* I show how love and loss are conditioned by an autonomous, expressive, and embodied medium that simultaneously articulates an intimate subject and state-mandated violence. Family mourning imagines a space of love outside sovereign politics. Yet love is not outside militarism or colonization, but at their very core. Israeli settler colonialism, I show throughout this book, permeates and seeks to naturalize place, time, labor, and language itself. Moreover, it imbues the most intimate registers of love, life, and desire. The homemade video memorial's modes of production and circulation carve an entangled scene of social reproduction precisely because they are divorced from institutional memory productions and cater to different channels of creation and contacts. Here the state military project passes as normal, mundane, part of a familial affectionate exchange; the sovereign becomes intimate.

PRIVATIZATION TENDENCIES

In 2006, a coalition of bi-national organizations co-founded the Israeli-Palestinian Memorial Ceremony, a shared gathering that ritualizes loss not as an instrument of national enmity, but as a platform of recognition and reconciliation.[4] The ceremony, now produced by a vast anti-occupation organizational alliance, endorsed by public figures and intellectuals, and attended by a growing audience, echoes what Judith Butler theorizes as a politics of loss grounded on mutual precarity.[5] Since its initiation, the ceremony regularly links to a controversy. In 2019, for instance, a few hundred vocal right-wing protestors tried to block the entrance for the thousands of participants who attended, accusing them of betrayal, provocation, and sacrilege. As a narrative structure, a scandal represents an instance when a specific social pact becomes visible. Most directly, the controversy around the annual ceremony exposes how Jewish-Israeli memory culture is rooted in an ethno-centric perception, where vital memory is predicated on blunt forgetfulness. Implicitly, the ceremony challenges the long-term bracketing of memory from what Jewish-Israeli society deems "politics." The scandal of politicizing loss—making it a condition of living together—not only surfaces the uneven distribution of mourning in Israel-Palestine, but discloses how Israelis got accustomed to placing memory in an "apolitical," consensual locus of privacy. It is not the direct enmity I seek to explore here but the tenants of the liminal sphere of privacy.

Other small-scale scandals flesh out the bracketing of memory from politics. On May 5, 1984, the Israeli daily newspapers reported in their mid-sections that a controversy had erupted during the Memorial Day ceremony in the city of Tel Aviv. Asher Ben-Natan, a bereaved father who was assigned to speak at the event, allegedly voiced criticism in his public address. The context was the aftermath of the 1982 Israel-Lebanon War, a highly disputed invasion of Israel's neighbor that was presented to the Israeli public as a way of securing the state's northern border. The invasion aimed to crush structures of exiled Palestinian leadership, culture, and resistance, and led to an eighteen-year-long occupation of southern Lebanon. In his speech, Ben-Natan said that unprecedently, the Lebanon war revealed "a growing gap between the frontline and the home."[6] A point that seems trivial at first sight struck a chord, triggering post-war sensitivities for an audience still agitated by the fragmenting consensus. Some members of the audience got on their feet and interrupted Ben-Natan's speech, others hushed the objectors and for a few moments, it seemed that the ceremony would be terminated by the heated debate. Those who reproached Ben-Natan did so not necessarily so much because they disagreed with his comments, but because he brought what they perceived to be a political dispute into the sphere of commemoration.

In July 2011, at a ceremony held in memory of soldiers who died during the 2006 iteration of the Lebanon conflict, a scandal once again erupted when a bereaved father verbally attacked the wartime Chief of General Staff, Dan Halutz, who was in attendance.[7] The father, Yoav Tzur, objected to the ex-general's presence, claiming it was meant to promote his political aspirations. While the father echoed criticism shared by the war's bereaved families and a large sector of the Israeli public, he was quickly silenced by others. Hagit Rain, who also lost her son in the war, argued that Tzur should have withheld his criticism out of respect for the ceremony and the memories it evoked. When reporters at the event asked for Halutz's reaction, he said: "I respect this place, the event and the families. I do not wish to argue with a family who lost its dearest."[8] While their interpretations of the event varied, all sides seemed to agree: criticism or debate were deemed scandalous in the context of the memory of the dead. The gap between the front lines and the home should remain intact, and in the scene of memories, family is sacred while politics (or aspiring politicians) need to keep silent.

While these instances put pressure on the purity of memory as coherent or inert, what is being articulated here is a collective common sense regarding what memory or politics is—or rather what it is not. There seems to be a displaced logic: the memory of the dead—even, or especially, when they have died in a violent conflict which defines national sovereignty and territory—should be "politically neutral." Such memory, one of the signifiers of Israel's national narrative and sentiment, which marks the state's territory and is enshrined in its annual calendar, remains external to debates on the character of the state, its use of military power, and its relations with its citizens and Palestinian and Lebanese non-citizens. Although marked by a public gathering, memory is located in an imagined private sphere of family love and mourning, secured from political critique.

Another dispute reveals a slightly different allocational logic. On September 3, 2007 Israel's leading newspaper, *Yediot Achronot*, publicly apologized to a bereaved father for a column written by one of its journalists. The column referred to a correspondence the father had with the ministry of finance's office while trying to retrieve some funds withheld by the state after the passing of his son in the 2006 war. The journalist used the parents' bureaucratic ordeal to harshly attack the ministry Accountant-General's insensitive administration. Discovering this reference alongside his son's picture in the weekend newspaper, the father was outraged by what he later defined as a cynical use of his son's memory. Once again, the father did not reject the underlying criticism, but rather the exploitation of his son's memory in such a public affair. In that same year, a video the family produced in memory of their son was broadcast on Israeli television.[9] The family's conflict with the journalist on the one hand, and their production of the video on the other, reveals a tacit assumption about what constitutes privacy, legitimizing contexts, media and authors of memory. It also lays the groundwork for denouncing others as cynical or invasive.

As a shared cultural currency, memory maps, and is even an active catalyst in organizing the social. Marita Sturken differentiates official memory stored in institutional spaces such as libraries, museums, and national archives from private memories that belong at home, while designating cultural memory as what "is shared outside the avenues of formal historical discourse yet is entangled with cultural products and imbued with cultural meaning."[10] Sturken's notion of entanglement conveys memory as a vehicle that crosses social scales. Mediated through various institutions, technologies, and forms, memory mobilizes experience and feelings as public manifestations, pertaining to the private/public scheme that underlines the social structure of contemporary liberal democracy. Sturken herself indicates a separate domain of privacy: one's home, one's property, one's personal feelings are kept separate from the public sphere of social interactions. Yet, in the Israeli example, memory is programmed like a bracketed glimpse into a familial intimacy, guarded as such by the artificial separation between politics and loss, money and mourning.

This last controversy exposes more than the social rationale that distributes memory to different social strata: state level, cultural level, and so on. The actual glitch is that it exposes the technocratic management of memory by the state, an act of governance stored at home, hidden behind the public manifestation of personal mourning. Paradoxically, a bureaucratic appeal to a state entity belongs with the family, and a video containing the family's intimate memories, produced by and for the family, is made available for the public to watch. Feelings of loss become a kind of common currency, whereas calling upon the state's debt remains a private affair.

I use this set of examples to indicate some of the dominant social perceptions of memory in Israel. While the state has continuously drawn on family as a source of validation and authentication of national memory, this book focuses on the 1990s and early 2000s, when, rather than nationalizing family sentiment, the family became a vector in privatizing memory. This period marks a shift towards privatization evinced in changing ideological paradigms, the emergence of new political subjecthood, new media technologies, and most swiftly, the establishment of a privatized neoliberal statehood. Therefore, privatization is used to characterize a set of interconnected tendencies related to modes of governance, the position of the citizen vis-à-vis the state through the division of private-public, and the growing effect of a market rationale on politics and media production.

As Asher Ben-Natan rightly pointed out, the first Israel-Lebanon War (1982) marked an ideological crisis. The war engendered a movement of conscientious objection, mass anti-war demonstrations, and furious public debate. For Jewish Israelis, the Lebanon conflict and the first Intifada—a massive uprising of Palestinians in Gaza and the West Bank in 1987—were no longer conceived as "no-choice" wars of defense, a prevalent perception of previous wars. These were not delimited "events," but rather derailed and unending military conflicts, a perpetual war contributing to an ongoing state of exception. Media coverage presented the Israeli public with a popular resistance movement that was countered by disproportionate military force. The IDF's brutal response undermined Jewish-Israeli society's popular conception of a "moral army." It is important to note that what changed was not the form of power—the state deprivation and oppression of the Palestinian population goes back to 1948—but its visibility within Israeli society. With a constant stream of casualties in a perpetual war, the narrative of a heroic death justified by a greater cause lost its impetus. During the 1990s the debates around the Oslo accords (1993) and the assassination of Israeli prime minister, Yitzhak Rabin (1995) were another manifestation of this internal crisis of legitimacy. Recurring suicide attacks during the early 2000s brought violence into the heart of Israeli civil society, no longer confined to the fractured Palestinian and Lebanese territories. The attacks introduced a new sense of victimhood into the conflict, making the Israeli public even more fixated on its own share of suffering. As the events of war and conflict became more contested, the memory of the dead was detached from the political discord, and was guarded as a safe, consensual site of social unity. Conversely, both violence and memory became habitual and mundane.

Within the growing fracture between Israeli civil society and sovereign politics, the family emerges as a firm, continuous social institution. During the 1990s, a series of omissions, accidents, and fatal incidents contributed to a sense of growing mistrust between the public and the military. In the first and second Tze'elim incidents (deadly misfires during two military exercises that occurred in 1990 and 1992), the lack of accountability from the IDF high command created a sense of wariness among families whose sons served, or were about to serve, in the army. Controversies related to mishandling of soldiers' corpses and the withholding of information from families—for example, the scandalous deposit of soldiers' remains outside of caskets without the families being notified after a failed commando operation, or an affair involving the National Institute of Forensic Medicine and its withholding of body parts and tissues of dead soldiers—made the public mistrust the military's handling of soldiers' bodies and lives.[11] Military gravestones and soldiers' epitaphs, which according to a 1949 state law have to have a unified appearance and wording manifesting equality and unity, were highly contested sites during these years.[12] Families' appeals to the supreme court asking to revise the unified epitaph—to add names of the dead's siblings[13] or to change the terminology about the cause of death—were made as a claim on history, memory, and kinship. In the aftermath of the most disastrous event during the Lebanon period, the crash of two helicopters near the northern border that precipitated the Four Mothers movement (see prologue), the families appealed to the supreme court asking that the epitaph refer to the event as it was known in public: a disaster, rather than the state's terminology of "accident." In his ruling in favor of the families, Judge Yaakov Turkle wrote that the common phrase "has turned seventy-three families to *one family whose last name is now 'The Helicopter Disaster.'*"[14]

The ruling, and more so its prose, is worth pausing on, as it shows the power that the family gains and the affective terminology of kinship that Israeli law has adopted. Israeli sovereignty yields to the family. In the later Lebanon period, the scandal of the state's omission could not be covered by the glamorous cloak of heroism or the novelty of the cause: here, too, the national myth was undermined, challenged by the bereaved family. As the new political subject, the family is like a modern Antigone, whose call upon body and kinship—intimacy—challenges the sovereign.

These threads delimit a double movement: first, the crumbling of what stood at the heart of Jewish-Israeli society collectivism, namely, the narrative of defense and the persistence of the military as a popular social project; second, the rise of a new political subject, the kin. This double movement indicates a leaning towards a place secluded from the state intervention, a private space. That these movements organized around the notion of crisis or disaster—frequent terminology used by the media in covering the various military omissions and accidents— suggests a sense of fracture between Israeli civil society, represented by the family, and the state. The Four Mothers movement and the public outcries engendered by the above series of omissions stand for reclaiming the kin, still alive or already dead, from the state. Memorial videos, very much a product of the Lebanon period, are prompted by the same notion of privatization as a way of rebuking state-issued memory as an institutionalized building block in the project of nation formation.

However, in privacy, in the sphere of kinship, the centrality of the military in Israeli sociality was never challenged. Likewise, unlike in the court or the street, when families finally brought the kin back home into the family memorial, the scandal and controversy were omitted from the work of mourning. These overlapping motions—into the home, away from sovereignty—ostensibly depoliticize and privatize violence, as the violence is displaced from a demarcated military arena into a sphere of "private life." Social and geo-political shifts in the Israel of the 1990s demarcate the withdrawal from grand narratives into a site of injury: the home as bearer of loss. As a byproduct, it gives rise to a narcissistic politics of victimization, populated not by a representative of state power, but an individuated, personalized, and singularized figure of intimate love.

Another tendency is linked with the more common use of the term privatization to describe the effect of market rationality on contemporary statehood, where privatization stands for the move of national industries into the hands of private capital. The 1990s mark a decade of rapid privatization of state entities, from infrastructure to social services and cultural institutes. In the following chapters I show how, on the one hand, the privatization of Israeli television, its move from a state-owned public channel to a commercial multi-channel model, was a crucial catalyst for the emergence and formation of the homemade video memorial and its sphere of reception. On the other hand, the formulation of a rhetoric of service, a form of labor in the free market catering to the individuated customer that I thematize through the freelance filmmaker working with the family, provided the videos with their ultimate form as a standardized commodity.

For television, a medium historically connected to domesticity, the homemade memorial video—customized content made by private producers outside the network system—filled a gap in the programming schedule. They came to be programmed in a newly launched multi-channel system during the National Memorial Day, the one day of the year when content is dictated by public sentiment and a stricter regulatory code. The programmed videos met a particular social desire for an "authentic" personalized expression of consensual mourning. Nevertheless, it is important to stress that the homemade memorial video was, and still is, an obscure manifestation, existing on the margins of the televisual. The freelance filmmaker, working in between television and the private market, fits a hybrid mode of production, catering to the family's search for healing while carving a space for memory which is publicly private. These developing private sectors of cultural production and media services should be put on a continuum with other state mechanisms—specifically, in this context, those that govern life and death. The privatization of state agencies of care and support, the flourishing of non-governmental organizations that take upon themselves state functions, and the privatization of sectors of the military, reconfigure the state as a provider of services and orient the bereaved towards a privatized mode of memory production.

That something is private means it has no claims on the common. "The videos belong to the families," determines one head of the documentary section of a leading television network. In an email, she explains to me that the network broadcasts the videos "and then sends them back." As I proceeded with this research, I found that the videos are absent from national archives, public cultural funding schemes, and from the television apparatus itself: its commissions, production venues, broadcasting policies, popular television columns, and scholarly critique. Even the video memorials themselves often omit a gesture of disclosure regarding their source and makers. They persist as isolated expressions, obscured by their ephemeral airing. The logic that underlines such striking absence first maintains that the videos are the private property of the family: the commodity argument. It further implies that as a low form of production, privately consumed, they lack aesthetic and artistic value, and that dwelling in the anatomy of family feelings, they have no relevance for broader public debate: the intimacy argument.

A system of allocations attributes certain utterances to different spheres of life and action, and constitutes a politics of non-politics that dwell in privacy—the idiosyncratic versus social convention, individual feelings versus collective narrative, public interest versus private property and creative authorities as precursors for cultural values, mourning work versus statecraft, love versus occupation. Indeed, when private mourning can be detached from larger political formations, it constantly represses its primary scene: the Israeli colonial project. This system of allocations, their displacement and their interconnectedness are at the core of what I term here *sovereign intimacy*.

In their characterization of Israeli memory, Ilana Shamir and Matit-yahu Mayzel organize memory across the private-public divide.[15] Thinking with media as a habitual practice, I accentuate privatization as an active and dynamic process that constantly reformulates the social categories of private and public. I situate the homemade memorial video as intrinsic to the politics of Israeli neoliberalism and its means of governing as it emerged in the 1990s, tangling economic aspects with cultural and technological ones. As I will soon argue, not memory, but its media are determinant in shaping the video memorials' social place.[16] In the commodity market of media technology, the commercial distribution of digital video as of the mid-1990s catered to the private individual as both the consumer and producer of media content. Another tendency of technology, reflected by market sectors, is that it enables the formation of a "private" subject detached from grand narratives and ingrained in everyday practices. Moreover, linked with the family telecommunication media, video portrayed this subject as *intimate*.

As the anecdotes with which I open reveal, there are two social fantasies about intimacy that lie behind these privatization tendencies, tending towards private loss and private violence, towards private media and towards memory as a private property. The first understands intimacy as a social texture *separated* from the political meaning of the state. Here, memories, although collectively shared, remain sacred and are stored at home. The second, a fantasy fraught with paradoxes, understands intimacy as a queering of the state, that is, as *an alternative force* that alters sovereign logic or power. These imaginaries obscure the complex power of intimacy in the relations between the state and its citizens. The reading I work through hereafter is set in relation to these two social fantasies.

THE TECHNO-AFFECTIVE

The state itself has never commissioned, initiated, funded, or actively produced a personal video memorial. What, then, links spontaneous expressions of creativity and loss with statecraft? A 2010 booklet issued by the Families Section in the Department for the Commemoration of

Soldiers under the Israeli Ministry of Defense guides bereaved families on ways to privately commemorate their fallen loved ones.[17] When the Ministry of Defense released the booklet, it reflected an existing genre of private memorials—specifically video memorials, which were an already standardized mode of production, relying by that time predominantly on freelance video work. The state concerns itself with ways for its citizens to channel and incorporate their loss as a function of institutional care, yet it only advises on a set of techniques allegedly external to its operations. What the state advice articulates is a politics predicated on governing by methods of self-administrating, what Michel Foucault terms "technologies of the self," which translate society's disciplining institutions into modes of subjectivation and self-fashioning.[18] A project that involves the majority of the Jewish-Israeli population, Israeli militarism is predicated on state mechanisms of managing mourning as one of its outcomes. I discuss this booklet and the ways the state's logic of care plays into a private economy of affective production in chapter 2 of this book. The advice, with its soft address, refers to the state mandate of nurturing life, a flip side of the sovereign's sanction of death.

Foucault's theorizations of modern power are central for my contention that mourning videos are *a priori* features of governance. First and foremost, Foucault characterizes sovereign power as bio-political power, a power whose direct mandate is over life, holding the right to eliminate, manage, and control, but also to foster and better biological life. The advice booklet, however, indicates that a facet of the government's technocratic sector responds to needs, in this case, the need to heal from loss. Foucault separates a form of state power he terms governmentality from that of sovereignty. While the two forms of power are not contradictory, sovereignty is predicated on explicit dictions of law and domination, and governmentality centers an economy that Foucault defines as a form of home-keeping, that is, administrating a system of needs and dependencies.[19] The memorial video stands for a mediatized maneuver in which sovereign power is channeled through and displaced by the internal dynamics of governmentality and the state's biopolitical mechanism. It is then further distanced from the state through a privatized sector of producers engaging directly with the family. While Foucault designates governmentality as addressing different mechanisms than that of sovereign power, throughout this book, I insist that these mechanisms are continuous.

Placing video in acts of governance entails understanding it as a utility, without neglecting its aesthetic and embodied vocations. As I explore in the following section, video is a particular kind of technique that targets the psychic formation of the citizenry, enmeshing representation and communication, technologies and bodies, love and wage labor, institutional and personal media constellations. Video, and television as long as its operations prolong those of video, should be probed as technologies of intimacy, through which the autonomy of the subject and the sovereignty of the state are mutually reproduced.

The advice pamphlet assigns familial and habitual media to the technocratic level of the state mechanism. Or rather, a techno-*affective* level, where the explicitness of a ruling mechanism, represented through the suffix '-cratic,' is sublimated by affect, and where governance addresses the mundane and habitual. Relegating a social condition to an expertise-based solution, technocracy potentially surpasses ideological aspects related to sovereign power. Specific to the techno-affective, it is the very tension between the institutional allocation of techniques and the concept of expertise, between governing and a politics based on affect—on death and mourning, on the longing for physical presence or the reliance on physical potency—that make it so pervasive. Put differently, when it comes to the ways the privatized state attends citizens' affective life, institutions, professionalism and production modes are structured as a set of contingencies that substitute aspects of authority for personal utility, and can thus be located as an indirect means of regulating the subject through technique, advice, or services.

VIDEO, BIO-POLITICS, AND GETTING IN TOUCH

In her seminal study of family films, Patricia Zimmermann shows how amateur film technology was marketed, distributed, and practiced based on a constructed separation between amateurism and professionalism. Zimmermann traces the term "amateurism" back to nineteenth-century capitalism, when it designated a form of labor associated with passion, autonomy, creativity, imagination, and leisure, as against a rationalized, expertise-based, productive labor associated with the workplace.[20] Analyzing a much more saturated and ubiquitous media environment to hold this separation, Wendy Chun notes that digital media, likewise associated with personal use and creativity, seamlessly induces forms of political power and hegemonic control into our habitual life, where these are negotiated through the very ways we practice such media technology.[21]

My account of private media centers on video technology, its domestic use, and the embeddedness of everyday media practices in modes of self-governance on the one hand, and forms of political and domestic imaginations on the other. Expressed in terms of either transgression of, or in affinity to, hegemonic media, the history of video reflects on film and television's own status as established industries and cultural institutions. Distributed as a mass product for domestic use in early 1980s, video brought with it notions of de-centralization and individuation of distribution, production, and consumption. Video, designed as accessible and user-friendly, undermined existing hierarchies and formats of production, legal ownership, and artistic authorship linked to formal mastery.[22] Making content available for ubiquitous use transformed the singularity of experience associated with the cinematic spatial conditions of theatrical viewing, and the televisual temporal programming of content. Whereas film and television were predicated on the public sphere, as Peter Alilunas shows, the history of video is engrained in the realization of privacy, opening up new spaces for desire.[23] Additionally, in loosening institutional power, video was tied to a set of social and artistic practices that convey new politics of media based on notions of democratization, personalization, liberation, and creativity, very much in line with the ideal of the liberal subject. Potentially, video's attack on the sovereignty of narrative and form, deemed by Michael Newman video's revolutionary aspect,[24] brings with it an attack on political sovereignty. It is that very liberatory potential that *Sovereign Intimacy* problematizes. Despite the affordances of freedom and compactness, video was quickly instrumentalized in a growing mechanism of mass surveillance.[25] In light of these different genealogies, it is video's elasticity, pervasiveness, and usability that makes it a medium of simultaneous singularity and mass-reproducibility, intimacy and control.

In addition to its coinciding with the mass distribution of digital video technology,[26] the critical attention to domestic media as sites of knowledge and visibility signaled a growing interest in the humanities in the everyday and the affective as the basis for a new form of historicity. The notion of breaking away from hegemonic records underlined the excavation of homemade footage and its discursive appropriation as a marginal phenomenon where kinship, creativity, and amateurism (as non-professionalism) provides an alternative for the dominant discourse and its modes of production.[27]

Memorial videos made throughout the 1990s and early 2000s feature subjects who came of age in a videotaped era. Beyond its imbrication in an institutional production matrix, there is the question of how video is practiced at home. Home video's affectivity and closeness are not only a translation of its position of kinship, but stem from the idea that media is acted upon and is being put into use like a customary idiom. Video for the family is not only a means of representation—linked with visibility and recognition—but a means to "get in touch," extending image-making into modes of contact that substitute physical presence with a technological one. Through the prism of telecommunication, video is a medium of immediacy, relationality, duration—what James Moran defines as the anti-monumentality of video[28]—that pertains to love, desire and the longing for a physical presence, all means of realizing life. Within the framework of loss, video carries intimate resonances, relayed by its very banality, excessiveness, tackiness, or rawness as a form of exchange and usage. Such dynamism and desire notwithstanding, intimacy is not a condition localized to the privatized settings of the medium, but rather *a motion*, crossing and infecting different social scales. This condition is derived from the quintessentially porous aspect of media that video brings to the fore. Video's accessibility for habitual use and its practice outside institutional media, yet always in reference to it, its coinciding expressivity and standardization, yields to the complex distribution of citizenship and state power.

Here intimacy is thought of as a form that extends personal, even hidden attachments and routes into public ones, as sustaining particular submissions and jurisdictions. Lauren Berlant poses intimacy as a social state of synchronization and alignment.[29] I translate her proposition to material practices, thinking through the mediation and adjustment of different velocities, trajectories, rhythms, and locales enacted by private and domestic media—home video, marginal video productions and private media campaigns as well as television. Set within "zones of familiarity and comfort,"[30] intimacy communicates with minimal gestures and signs. Intimacy is a formation that sustains a politics that personalizes memories while disavowing conflict, that caters to a certain transparency, or "obviousness" of genres of love, and that connotes home video and its minimal formal and production standards as a medium of love.

I do not position intimacy and sovereignty as opposing spheres that are then blended in the homemade video, but rather, I claim that the very state of proximity and inchoateness of intimacy is what makes it a location into which sovereignty can be displaced. Berlant represents a strand of feminist political critique that situates intimacy within the politics of sovereignty and disrupts its grounding on a divide between reason and unreason (passion, longing, bodily attachments, and so on). Lisa Lowe's reading of intimacy as a circulation of commodities, labor and memories that transcends, and even bypasses, the articulated paths of the nation-state proposes a mode of in-between-ness and connectedness. It is a tricky alterity that does not counter but rather anticipates the more pronounced forms of statecraft.[31] Intimacy delimits psychic, temporal, and bodily fissures in the formation of subjecthood, indicating the implicit and obscure realms of political violence in which atrocities are assimilated and normalized. Violence is not only inflicted on subjects, but it is also (and mostly) done on behalf of or extended by subjects. Christina Sharpe utilizes intimacy to analyze the making and remaking of racialized subjects through notions of desire and cruelty injected into the domestic scene in narratives of slavery. In Sharpe's account, intimacy is the setting in which violence is encountered; in my account, intimacy is where violence is *repressed*, not a space of fracture but of comfort.[32] It might be a form of containment and attachment for the subjects entangled in it, but it is not necessarily a desired proximity, and what it buries under its affect is the very normal anomaly of systemic, racialized violence. To these formulations I add intimacy as a sphere of emergence, incipience, uncertainty, and interiority, a sphere where things can be left undetermined. Intimacy is a place with no didacticism, that does not produce any statements, where things are not yet committed to the public record or absorbed into historical narratives; hence its trickiness. Lastly, intimacy is a bodily condition that involves tactile submissions, a form of doing or crafting that relies on a condition of care—of practices of care and/or caring as a motivation for doing.[33]

As a techno-affective form, the homemade video invokes these notions of intimacy, self-formation, and interiority on the one hand, and state and media sovereignty on the other. Presented as a practice of care and healing, video is assimilated to an assemblage of institutions and techniques that are part of the state biopolitical power, its means of regulating psychic life and administrating death and mourning. In light of video's various histories, it is utilized not only as what Adi Kuntsman and Rebecca Stein characterize in the context of digital culture as an everyday practice of compliance with state militarism,[34] but as an affective technology that pertains to the very realization of life and death as constitutive elements of the sovereign power of the state. Being at once an expressive outlet in the hands of the individuated subject and a techno-affective technique of social reproduction, video is indeed a channel for the state to get in touch and be intimate with its subjects.[35] The state and its technocratic branches directly and indirectly shape loss, grief, memories, and even before death took place, familial modes of contact and media, their circulation, trending, and standardization in various ways that unravel intimacy and its "outside" violence. These unravelings can be found in various operations, from the airing of family videos on television to advising the family on how to commemorate their loved one. *Sovereign Intimacy* zooms in on and dissects these entanglements and convergences of specialist knowledge and amateur activities, the formal and the mundane, the body and the medium, technology and emotions.

THE INTIMATE SOVEREIGN

Sovereign politics are thematized in this book on two levels. The first is the level of media and its intricate relations to statehood, manifested not only through the direct institutional extension of the state into media (such as television), but also through questions of legitimacy, value, and utility of media. The second level is the specificities of a sovereign power whose very foundations asymmetrically allocate life and death as the terms according to which political subjectivity is defined.

Drawing on Foucault's formulation of biopolitical power, Achille Mbembe contends that Israeli colonial power over Palestine exercises the sovereign "right to kill," while Jasbir Puar eloquently formulates it as "the right to maim."[36] This form of sovereign power is constituted through a radical separation between the Jewish-Israeli citizenry whose privilege relies on ethno-nationalist conceptions, and the Palestinian other, deemed as already, or almost, dead. These accounts of Israeli sovereign power, although mostly dissecting the brutal forms of state violence inflicted on Palestinians rather than the inward-looking articulation of intimate citizenship, provide an analytical framework for examining the political content of Israeli private media. To be clear, I do not attempt to give a reading that subjects Israeli citizens to the same form of violence endured by Palestinians as a way of redeeming Israeli society, nor do I argue that the videos are direct statements on the right to kill or maim. As I demonstrate in the following paragraphs, Mbembe's genealogy of a political economy of death that he terms necropolitics, and Puar's drawing on sexuality and body-politics, explicate the very logic of a power forged through physical potency and morbidity, and the violence that this entails. Yet, it is that violence and its implication of the videos' subjects, the intimate citizens, that the videos *exclude*, an exclusion that is part of the very operation of such power.

Although the homemade video memorial refers to a personal pain that belongs with the family as an allegedly universally shared structure of feelings detached from the politics of state's violence, the videos are an extension of the Israeli military project. Legitimated through a rhetoric of emergency and the state of exception, Israeli military power, together with other state mechanisms such as state law and infrastructural control,[37] are instruments for sustaining Israeli colonial rule over occupied Palestine. Tracking the evolution of colonial violence, Achille Mbembe argues that Palestine exemplifies a space where sovereign power is manifested through the "forms of subjugation of life to the power of death."[38] Necropolitical power subjects the population to either homicidal or suicidal logic. According to Mbembe, in Israel-Palestine this is manifested through the logic of survival (homicidal) and the logic of martyrdom (suicidal). The survivor, the "still alive" subject, is the enactor of a deadly power in the name of historical and national exceptionalism. With a sense of uniqueness and security, they draw their subject position while constantly reproducing a social imaginary of enmity, and, in so doing, perpetuating their own position as a victim. The figure of martyrdom, on the other hand, annihilates their own body as their ultimate (or perhaps the only possible) act of signification. Subject to control, surveillance, separation, and seclusion, deprived of political status and bound to a negating form of signification that entails self-destruction and self-alienation, Mbembe describes the necropolitical subject as a phantom, a shadow, the "living dead."[39] Fictionalized through the survivor's imaginary of enmity, rendered dead, or nullified by markers of subjective agency, the Palestinian is rendered already-absent. The absence is complimented by the singularity and narcissism of survival and victimhood, supported by the liberal formulation of a sovereign subject who is free and self-governed.

Such constructed absence is concatenated to a strategy of elimination, expropriation, and the systematic and deliberated effacement of Palestinian presence that characterizes Israeli policy since 1948, and contributes to the destruction and instrumentalization of Palestinian bodies and spaces. In the Israeli sovereign intimacy, enmity, conflict, and occupation, not to mention Palestinian suffering, are utterly absent. Commemorative family media omit the violence that engendered them, bracket out what causes death and instead are dedicated to the lives lost. Omitting the violence, they omit the narrative of enmity and the sovereign power that organizes such narrative into patterns of domination, occupation, and the management of life and death. Omitting the acts of the sovereign, they also omit any recognition of those who are subjugated by this power. This is not only because the videos are confined to intimate memories of love and disavow any form of hostility, and even exclude the critical stances towards the state that some families did and do hold, but because they persist in a regime that actively produces forgetfulness and shortsightedness, resulting in mourning without reflection.

Jasbir Puar's proposition of the "right to maim" examines the contemporary liberal state's version of the biopolitical "right of death and power over life" in light of contemporary forms of capitalism and colonialism. Puar argues for a state power that subjects entire populations to injury and debilitation, controlling not mortality, or the sovereign right to kill, but rather multi-dimensional operations of debilitation and incapacitation. Spaces, infrastructures and bodies are taken over and reconfigured in order to demobilize, disable, and neutralize. This strategy lets violence fly under the radar of international intervention and criticism, maintaining Israel's façade of liberal democracy and keeping Palestine permanently on the verge of a humanitarian crisis, a political logic described by Puar as "will not let die."[40]

Puar's intervention expands the biopolitical binaries of life and death, offering a radical reading of the politics of disability and debility by examining the more tacit rhetoric of sovereign power. Appropriating the right to maim, sovereign operations are extended to an affective sphere through targeting mobility, debility, sexuality and reproducibility. Puar's project is one of analyzing the fraught colonial and military mechanisms from the perspective of the colonized. Without claiming a symmetrical or comparative frame of analysis, I ask how the modulations of colonial power designed by the regime also reflects on the sovereign subject. While Israel inflicts a status of debilitation and chronic injury or incapacity on the Palestinian population, the Jewish-Israeli population is organized around an omnipotent and hyper-reproductive social body.[41] The permeation of biopolitical power beyond the formulations of "make live" or "let die"—what Puar brilliantly evokes through the right to maim— manifests also through the rehabilitated body, epitomized through the dead soldier, an eternally young and omnipotent figure.

In the Israeli political economy of life and death, the dead soldier is premium. In the closing chapter of this book, while considering other positions than the hegemony of intimacy, I cite a mother of a soldier held in captivity. The mother proclaims: "In this country the dead are sanctified rather than the living."[42] There is an investment on the side of the state in preserving the life of the already dead rather than those who are incapacitated, held captive, or disabled.[43] This mother's words reflect the differentiated logic that underlines the symbolic and real values of death, trauma, and injury that sustains Israeli militarism. It resonates with Puar's positioning of the sovereign right to maim as a byproduct of extractive capitalism that substitutes killing for what Puar terms attenuated death, or the slow extraction of life. The dead soldier is an emblem of the omnipotent and rehabilitated sovereign body as a site onto which national fantasies of reproduction and resilience—death that sustains life—are projected. Not a metaphor, the soldier is a vital part of the state's security apparatus, and a figure of familial intimacy which is in itself a national project. As argued earlier, with the privatized state, the latter had become the dominant paradigm, with the soldier cast as an emblematic son, and moreover, a future parent, a citizen in an intimate sovereignty.

The creation of an intimate sovereignty as a symptom of liberal statehood and liberal subjecthood, with its indices of privatization, individuation, and personification, provides Israeli society with a scheme of disassociation. This is what Lauren Berlant and Michael Warner characterize as a "familial model of society [that] displaces the recognition of structural racism and other systematic inequalities."[44] Their account of how such mechanisms of displacement work in the context of privatized constellations of sexuality, kinship, and citizenship attends the constructions that differentiate "personal life" from work and politics. Intimacy is mediated by heteronormative, and in the case of Israel hetero- and homonational, sexual institutions, such as the family, pertaining to a sense of normalization built around "non-political" sentiment. As Berlant and Warner write:

> Finally, those conventions [of heteronormative intimacy] conjure a mirage: a home base of prepolitical humanity from which citizens are thought to come into political discourse and to which they are expected to return in the (always imaginary) future after political conflict. Intimate life is the endlessly cited *elsewhere* of political public discourse, a promised haven that distracts citizens from the unequal conditions of their political and economic lives, consoles them for the damaged humanity of mass society and shames them for any divergence between their lives and the intimate sphere that is alleged to be simple personhood.[45]

As a genre of unconflicted citizenship, the family is the very instrument of social reproduction, of distribution and accumulation of capital and goods, the resource for the security regime, and the fabrication of sexual and racial/ethnic norms. As Elizabeth Povinelli shows, intimacy, which she formulates as love, sociability, and body, is the very foundation of the sovereign subject that habituates liberal settler colonies.[46] Crucial to this mechanism is its transparency: the universal right for intimacy, and kinship or love as its genre. The home video, certainly a genre of love, performs this annexing by convention. It is hegemonic because love and intimacy, ostensibly a universal norm and form, are beyond questioning. In its "obviousness" it eschews inequality, racism, violence, and the instrumentalization of subjects and feelings.

The idea of the sovereign state, an allegedly coherent social organization that rules by managing its subjects' lives and death within a more or less concise territory; and its predication on the idea of a sovereign subject, who consents to the rule by self-formation, agency and ethics—these ideas shape the utilization and realization of media. Practiced by the citizen, video is a way to imagine and reimagine love, life, and loss as abiding to the sovereign ideal. In that sense, media and its configuration of authority, either institutional, creative, or personal and self-containing, is a practice and a performance of sovereignty. Home video is a way to take in and intimate the state's manuals of death: its regulation, pedagogy, ways of remembering, and its incorporation or mourning. These are all rudiments of the overall political economy of death auctioned by the state and traded by commercial media outlets and the media arms of political organizations, with family mourning as its main currency. Examining the triangulation of the institutions of state, media, and family reveals these intricate policies and practices.

Yet the analysis I wish to offer is one that takes into account the specificity and affective intensity of love and intimacy, beyond their function as tools for a symbolic connection to the state. Media, particularly the homemade memorial video and its broadcast, not only reflect or represent these assemblages of regulation and subjugation, but condition them. Love, loss, and intimacy imply submission, which makes the question of sovereignty delicate. Attending personal loss demands elasticity and the ability of the sovereign itself to be consoling, supportive, and intimate.

The intimate sovereign is one for which biopolitical mechanisms are beneficial, restorative, and reparative. It persists in sites that are ostensibly removed from the formalities of statecraft, law, and discipline. It shares the secret of the obvious—a secret since this is something private, that circulates internally, implicit in the ostensibly immediate and non-reflective sphere of normativity. The sovereign is intimate because it provides the very conditions, material and symbolic, that form the norm and its implicated subject. Indeed, the sovereign is the source of life—killing the already dead, as Mbembe argues; or, according to Puar, sanctioning death without killing through systematic debilitation; or, when it comes to the sovereign citizen, keeping the dead alive. Life, not in the form of a ghost sustained by national ethos and collective memory, but life in its mundane, autonomous, and singular form: videographed life, intimate life. The specificity and uniqueness of this life, applied not only to those who have already died, but to those who will die or could have died under the norm of militarization, abstracts the biopolitical calculus at play.

LET ME TELL YOU AN ANECDOTE

In this introduction, I have offered two possible scenarios for the emergence of the homemade mourning video: one has to do with the figuration of a privatized political power and a privatized political subject, the other with the entrance of new media technologies that altered private media use. The first seems to be built as a historiography predicated on crisis (Israel during the 1990s), and the second as one based on progress (new habitual media technologies). While it is important to ground the memorial-video phenomenon in its historical context, I am careful about making claims for a linear and causal development, since these homemade objects were never a product of a stated, consistent, purposeful policy or movement. Trying to track a narrative of formation leads to fragmented and scattered traces: random decision-making, coincidental circumstances of production, spontaneous and immediate reactions to loss, hard-to-trace networks of personal ties, or an arbitrary yet resourceful and creative approach to film and video knowledge. The homemade memorial video circulated in what is not quite a business model, but "a labor of love," a form of productive work that is recompensed not by money but by "love." This has different forms, a range including intimate knowledge, solidarity formulated as voluntary work, pro-bono expertise, community projects, and pedagogic endeavors. Placing something outside politics, in a protective sphere of intimacy and love, results in archival lacuna, the absence of a paper trail or institutional acknowledgement, even after the fact. Due to the lack of material evidence, I approached television programmers, freelance filmmakers, support workers, and bereaved families. For all of them, the videos were anecdotal and exceptional. This is another aspect of intimacy: to render the utterance extra-territorial to historical discourse and in a constant state of formulation, an anecdote.

Against the decisive narrative of crisis, there is heterogeneity and indecisiveness; against the progressive narrative of technological development, there are sets of contingencies and anachronisms in which what we term digital culture and its ubiquitous production of singularity, personalization, and individuation is already materialized, or at least imagined, in earlier modes of video production and television broadcasting. I wish to think of the homemade video memorial as an instrument of emergence, a state of coming into being, unformulated, in-between one media regime and another. Intimacy is the relational mode that can sustain emergence and unformulatedness, positioning the homemade video memorial as a peripheral backlash of larger technological, institutional, and cultural shifts. Intimacy, not as a non-reflective attachment, but as a condition of embryonic entanglement, informs a reading that sustains ambiguities, complexities and the uncomfortable morbidity of the task of this book: to bring to the sphere of scholarly contemplation a form meant for affective consumption, to offer a political critique of what Israeli society, or Israeli individuals, might perceive as being beyond politics.

The book is structured in two parts. The first, "Sovereignty," is dedicated to the institutional locations of the private family media. These are delimited through reading the family video form as a way to negotiate state laws, military conduct, and broadcast media (chapter 1), analyzing the establishment of a privatized market based on freelance proxies, NGOs, and crowd sourcing (chapter 2), and mapping the concatenation of family videos within the temporal edifice of television programming (chapter 3). With that, chapter 1 demarcates settler colonial intimacies; chapter 2 probes private media of care; and chapter 3 investigates television's temporal regime as a way to excavate a chronology of privatization. The second part, "Intimacy," considers speech—the exercise of language, its address or listening to it—as the most subjective, and therefore ideological, register of a sovereign intimacy. The two chapters in this part zoom in on the Zionist left (chapter 4), and explicit or less explicit campaigns that provoke the national hegemony of intimacy (chapter 5). Centering the convention of message stories—the story of how one heard a loved one has died—chapter 4 asks: what does it mean to listen to the sovereign? What does it mean to then intimate the sovereign's speech, the message, and make it a family story? Chapter 5 broadens the book's critical perspective by looking at other related media campaigns in which the image of soldier or their kin, as a talking head, articulates an address. The talking head is a charged site of meaning and its address perceived as a gesture of referring to the other and calling upon shared ideals. Exposing the wider discursive realm and the productional conditions in which this address is made, the chapter delineates a political economy of life and death in a state of perpetual conflict and highly consensual militarism.

PART ONE

Sovereignty

CHAPTER I

To Keep in Touch

"You need to bring your *heart* into it."

—Hila Barel, Community Services, Reshet Television Network

Inquiring about "To Remember with Love," a community project initi-ated by the television network Reshet in order to assist families in com-posing their personal memorial videos, I was told a story. One day a woman arrives at the studios of the television network, holding a plastic bag with VHS cassettes in it. She asks to meet the network's chief di-rector. When the chief director, Benni Carmeli, meets her, she presents him with the bag of cassettes. She says that these cassettes are the only things she has left of her son, a soldier who died during his military service. She asks Carmeli to help her turn the materials "into a movie." This encounter, I was told, inspired Carmeli to conceive the project, as he realized that Reshet, a major media entity, could lend its production infrastructure and professional knowledge to bereaved families.[1] The in-formation related to the anecdote could not be verified; thus I will treat it figuratively, asking what can be learned from its aesthetic and dramatic structure: the woman on the doorstep, the plastic bag with videotaped remains, the promise of the composed "movie," the attuned CEO.

The anecdote illustrates a meeting point between the home (movie) and public media, or between love and a cultural institution. The woman appeals to a media authority—to television—in order to retrieve the memory of her dead son. In her appeal, even in her simply "showing up" at the studios, she overthrows television's cultural and institutional dictums and prioritizes the reading of television as a medium of pure transmission, reconnecting her with her private loss. She intimates

media. Her implied expectation is that via the professional intervention of the "television people," a plastic bag full of VHS cassettes will
transform into a movie (with its echoes of a public spectacle), will recover communication, if not reassemble and re-embody the memory of
the dead. The "story materials" of the anecdote are structured through
tensions: the anonymous woman and the television director, the irrational and the technical know-how, the dead son and his reincarnation
into moving images and sounds. Where do the two meet? What kind of
transformation takes place, what form of convergence? And why do we
need an anecdote to figure this out?

To begin unpacking these questions, the anecdote—its content and
its own materiality as a historiographic format—illuminates a certain
reciprocity between intimate relations, public representations, and state
authority. Walter Benjamin has noted the insurgent power of the anecdote, its undermining of official history and mass-mediated information. As he writes in *The Arcade Project*, "the constructions of history
are comparable to instructions that commandeer the true life and con-
fine it to barracks. By contrast: the street insurgence of the anecdote.
The anecdote brings things nearer to us spatially, lets them enter our life.
It presents the rigorous antithesis to the kind of history that demands
'empathy,' which makes everything abstract."[2] According to Benjamin,
the anecdote is unlike history, it does not abstract things, but represents
them in "our space," makes them step "into our life."[3] Benjamin articulates a sort of embodied velocity ("bring things nearer").

Reading Benjamin, Peter Fenves construes the anecdote as what is
"not given out," what "could not be made into the subject matter of 'eyewitness testimony.'"[4] For Fenves the anecdote is an unauthorized story, a
secret transmission, not confined by the order and evidential status of
history. It passes as a rumor, hearsay, or a piece of gossip; it embodies
singularity and refutes abstraction. Fenves's analysis demonstrates how
through both its format and content the anecdote unsettles notions of
authority—and by extrapolation, of sovereign law, history, and politics.
But the anecdote is not simply the alternative of history or law. Positioning the anecdote as what anticipates the literary, Fenves contends that
"as unauthored and unauthorized accounts of odd, unusual, or singular
events, anecdotes can serve as the link between 'lived' experience and
its literary representation, for they appear to give evidence of something *outside of or in between* solid systems of regulation, circulation,
and representation."[5] Therefore the anecdote is not simply antithetical
or "in contrast to," but it is the place where regulation, information,

circulation, and representation are anticipated, negotiated and formulated. Is that not precisely what the anecdote of the woman and the plastic bag of tapes is about—what is in between the raw videos and a movie, in between love and communication, in anticipation for a form, even an apparatus, of representation?

Writing about media appropriation of family footage, Michael Roth deliberates the fragile texture of everyday life and mundane interactions, a fragile texture he characterizes as "ordinariness."[6] Similar to the anecdotal, ordinariness conveys the singularity of transmission, mitigating over-banality and historicity. Reading home footage as history, Roth observes, risks turning the images uncanny, excessive, or melodramatic. Escaping the monumental, ordinariness is about "trying to find a way to make sense of something individual on its own, distinct, without erasing its individuality, its oneness, its distinction."[7] Roth's conceptualization of ordinariness echoes Benjamin's and Fenves's notion of the anecdote as distinct from the processes of abstraction and generalization necessary for public order of law and history; in other words, its intimacy.

In film and media studies, the rise of the home movie as an object of research indeed destabilizes questions of regulation, circulation, and representation, as well as production modes, usages, and canonization. Pertinent for discussions that emerged around preservation and archival practices of visual heritage, the home movie was often referred to through a rhetoric of excavation and recuperation.[8] As a category, the home movie displaces modes and spaces of production: from artistic authority to amateurism, from canon (mostly nationally defined) to materials that are eclectic and redundant, from profit-driven industry to the leisure economy or what I term a labor of love that traverses capitalist time-economy. In its marginality, usability, and multiplicity, the home movie was often read as a counter-historical, counter-hegemonic manifestation, allowing those not represented by hegemonic culture to negotiate the norm.[9] There are stakes involved in appropriating this form with its affective connectedness and singularity as a mode of social knowledge. Its obscurity, relationality—even emotionality—and its very normalcy imbue its images. The stakes are even higher when reading these images as counter-historical.

While the home movie seems to indicate an alternative to dominant modes of cultural production and representations, it is mostly defined in relation to two dominant forms: commercial media and the heteronormative family.[10] Commercial media haunts the home footage like a ghost, its tropes and conventions assimilated and repeated by everyday and familial actors. With the (heteronormative) family as what frames the scene, we can think of the home footage as a medium of recognition: a form through which people perform their social roles. From this standpoint, the home movie entails simultaneous assimilation and exclusion. Similar to Fenves's proposition, I situate the family/video as anecdotal to the state and media channels of reproduction. The home footage, I argue, offers an affective change of scale in which the state's military power and its necropolitical calculus are intimated.

A plastic bag with VHS cassettes, held by a woman standing on the threshold of television, a public medium. The woman's appeal places intimacy in the connective tissues that rearrange limbs and body parts, that seek to mend the fissures. However, when the cassettes are handed to the public medium to mend what was broken, they become something else. Intimacy puts forward attachments that are embodied, communicative, and enmeshed with a sort of practice or technique that organizes and materializes affinity. Intimacy is about getting closer, getting in touch: with the dead loved one, but also, indirectly, tacitly, with the state. In the following chapter families' claims on intimacy articulate a promise of life not lived, calls not answered, relationship not fully realized. Like the woman, these claims appear at the threshold of television—on its margins, not completely assimilated to its public platform—seeking to reconnect. Lauren Berlant understands citizenship, or the way individuals attach themselves to the state, as drawing from a promise of good life, the promise of happiness.[11] Counterpart to its infliction of violence and death, here the promise of citizenship is pinned to reproductive life, family life.[12] Per Berlant, the promise of happiness dwells in the private, following a liberal dream of economic flourishing detached from sovereign politics of colonization; nevertheless, it is that very insistence on the failed promise of happiness that subscribes citizens to state mechanisms. Neither intimacy nor love are antithetical to the state form or are an antidote to militarism and violence.

What I seek to explore here is a place of proximity, understanding the home movie as, paraphrasing Benjamin, actively "bringing things nearer to us." Adi Kuntsman and Rebecca Stein contend that habitual use of media helps Jewish-Israeli citizens create a surface of normalcy that abstracts militarized violence.[13] I add to their insight that in the case of personal commemoration, family media creates an affective membrane, organized around the liberal concept of the family as an allegedly individuated, non-political entity that in its intimacy nevertheless sustains the military state. Intimacy is complex, containing a dialectic of transgression and submission that assimilates the sovereign and, at the same time, displaces structures of domination into a remote elsewhere. I dissect these families' articulations of loss not to criticize their mourning but to reflect on the state form that organizes kinship while being mediated through it.

In what follows, love and intimacy put sovereignty into crisis but, at the same time, reaffirm it. Intimacy is affiliative, yet it is also exclusive, perhaps blind to what is not in its purview. In the videos discussed in this chapter there are tanks, soldiers training, heavy military boots thrown on the bedroom carpet, classified military maneuvers, ambush and war at the northern border. Yet all of these are assimilated into intimate transmissions, mediated by the "ordinariness" of family life. We see the tanks and the boots as objects associated with mundane and amorous transmissions. The perpetration of violence, the waging of war, the numerous civilian victims, the Lebanese and Palestinian dispossessed and displaced are completely absent from these claims. Instead, intimacy sterilizes categories of belonging and forms of attachments that are at the heart of settler colonial regimes. Channeled through a public medium, the families' search for a representation for their loss, for the right for love, appeals to a recognition that is discriminately distributed. It recognizes pain only if it is expressed within the exclusive consistency of sovereign citizens. Done by means of intimacy, this appeal is a channel for a secret and sacred attachment, not a medium of power or law, but merely anecdotal to those.

The chapter's first part thinks with the form of the anecdote by probing the metaphorical and legal status of the soldier's girlfriend and her video, as well as a television project that extends the institute into intimate realms. The second part analyzes the dynamics of family mourning within Israeli settler colonialism, arguing that even when loss is mobilized to criticize the state, as in the case of the Golan family, it is still contained within its militarized logic. The affiliative work of the home video, its predication on a dynamic set of proximities—*stepping into* our lives or a *step away* from formalities—and its parallel work of exposing the wound while covering the violence that caused it, is what this chapter seeks to explore as the core principle of a sovereign intimacy.

WHAT IS A GIRLFRIEND?

In February 1992, Eran Elquai, a twenty-four-year-old paratrooper company commander, died in southern Lebanon. Gaya Koren, who had been

FIGURE 2. Screenshot from *Things I Wanted to Tell You*, dir. Gaya Koren, 1992.

Elquai's girlfriend for seven years, was studying film at Tel Aviv University at the time of his death. Seeking a way to help Koren cope with her loss, her friends approached the Israeli television public channel and asked it to support the second-year film student in composing a short film about her dead boyfriend.[14] In the three months that followed, Koren used her unformulated knowledge of film and her intimate knowledge of her boyfriend to make him a commemorative video. In *Things I Wanted to Tell You*, Koren, mostly through voiceover, plasters a mix of still images and family videos of the dead Elquai, and reminiscences with his friends, family, and fellow soldiers to articulate a statement of longing. The video was broadcast on Israeli television on May 5, 1992, as part of the special programming schedule for the National Memorial Day. Its personal tone and its uncommon model of production—public television supporting an amateur filmmaker in her very private endeavor—stands out. The video had many reruns over the following years. Its time and circumstance of production make it a very early manifestation of the trend of personal video memorials, prompting others to likewise seek intimate ways to commemorate their loved ones.

In the following discussion love (girlfriend) and its form (personal video) are intricately tangled, transgressing industry and state's forms of representation. "What is a girlfriend?" is a question posed by the state when facing girlfriends' claims for recognition. For sovereign law, love—and loss—are represented through blood or money, biology or property.

For public media, modes of production are packed into professional categories, formulating media practices as art or work. A military colonel succinctly summarizes the problem: "[The army needs] a hundred percent certainty, because [what constitutes] a family is certain."[15] The sovereign cannot recognize what is not representable by the sovereign's own means of representation.[16] The law needs abstraction and generality to determine love, not singularity or the inchoate, still-formulating nature of intimacy. The figure of the girlfriend has connotations of ambiguity, immaturity, indecisiveness; thus, the girlfriend's love is a secret to the sovereign that can be disclosed only through the mediation of formalized kinship, or as the same colonel ponders: "What if there is a girlfriend and the family doesn't know?"[17] This is not to say that the girlfriend is necessarily hidden, but that this kind of intimacy entails instability, a promise of love.

To clarify, love here is an everyday relationality, not a love metaphorized to express fantasmatic desires towards national freedom or territory: the misogynic figuration of the nation through nurturing or rape. I use the girlfriend/video to show how intimacy carved a space at the heart of Israeli sovereignty and its bio-affective mechanisms, organizing love as a genre of the state, or rather, thinking the home movie as anecdotal to state sovereignty. As is mostly the case with intimacy, these lines are loose and indirect. Koren's *Things I Wanted to Tell You*—the girlfriend, her video—articulates the paradox that emerges between the two positions of intimate love and sovereign order.

Things I Wanted to Tell You opens with a few brief shots that show Elquai and his subordinates in the last stages of a sort of war game: a tiring fifty-mile march at the end of which the soldiers earn the paratroopers' iconic red beret. The footage is jumpy and rough. It was probably taken by one of the families whose son participated in the exercise. The soldiers seem exhausted while the sturdy-looking Elquai places the berets on their heads and laconically welcomes them into the corps. Like in graduation ceremonies or weddings, in this home footage a disciplining institute is imbricated into the family record, yet the military is a particularly lethal social institute. These roughly-shot images of inauguration cut to Elquai's funeral. The funeral images, of another red-berets gathering, were compiled from television news, as the watermark of Israel's Channel 1 on the top right corner discloses. The military funeral became a common news genre in 1990s Israel. Frequent casualties caused by the armed conflict between the IDF and the Islamist organization Hezbollah during the Israeli occupation of southern Lebanon

(1985–2000), incidents similar to the one in which Elquai was killed, represented the violence perpetuated in Lebanon mostly through the scene of (Jewish-Israeli) loss. Soldiers' funerals were a familial scene of departure and at the same time a performative mass event. With the family granting permission, television news often broadcast the funerals. A common sight on 1990s news and a procedure protocoled by the army, the family, and public media, the military funeral documentation likewise explicates a well-formulated social convention. While the video is devoted to a singular loss, in its outset it clearly gestures towards a recognizable narrative. The scenes are shot from afar, conventionality translated to a formal distance.

From this distance, the video cuts to a close-up of Koren, looking out of a car window that frames the passing view of a typical northern landscape, traveling to Elquai's military post. In the video's move from distance to intimacy, it is through Koren's eyes that we perceive the spaces of military conduct as spheres of love. Her conversations with the soldiers in the post, young recruits for whom Elquai was an authoritative company commander, bear little affect. One of the soldiers concludes: "He was strict, but above all, he was mysterious. This person—no one knew him." Being subject to his authority, a relation marked by formality, the soldiers have very little to add to Elquai's portrait as composed by his girlfriend. Her listening, recording, accumulating, and editing these recollections is what make them affective. Like the video, amorously employed to mobilize closeness, she too is a media, as well as a medium—a channel to speak to the dead. In voiceover, Koren describes the journey as something that always introduces distance into intimacy and intimacy into distance. She recalls: "Every visit to your post is like a test. Will you be there when I arrive or will you be out, training? Will you smile at me or pretend to be tough in front of the soldiers?" She continues, recalling how the first time she visited Elquai at the post it was in order to break up with him. Elquai's friends suggest throughout the video that his commitment to the army was something difficult for Koren to endure. She terminates the relationship, but later regrets doing so. The second time she visits, Elquai, in his role as company commander, withholds any affection in the presence of the other soldiers. Koren, as she herself describes it, needs to appear "pretty and distant" in front of her boyfriend's subordinates, so as not to compromise Elquai's display of authority. As intimacy undermines sovereignty, love is rendered a secret. Yet intimacy also ratifies authority, underlining its mystery.

Koren's trip to the post is a search for a closure. For her, this is the place where things ended—love, reciprocity and contact. Hagar Kotef argues that Israeli homeliness has in its foundations traces of expropriation and expulsion. She characterizes settler colonialism as transforming space through the layering of violence and domesticity.[18] Through the medium of the girlfriend, places of military conduct become spaces of intimacy and desire. In a later sequence, Koren brings us to the one-bedroom apartment she shared with Elquai. Starting at the door with the sign "Gaya and Eran," marked with two heart icons, the camera leads us into the apartment. It wanders across the living room, panning over a bookcase with a line of decorative articles and framed still photographs of Koren and Elquai. The following shot brings us to the bedroom, panning all the way to the couple's unkempt bed. Koren's voice hovers over the empty bed: "They say that if you dream about the dead and hold their hand, they will tell you everything you want to know." The video moves from the bed to what seems like an arbitrary zooming in on a telephone on the bedside table. She then cuts to a close-up shot showing heavy military boots lying on the bedroom carpet and a military jacket laid on a chair in the background. Koren speaks of how she used to get angry at Elquai for throwing his heavy boots on the carpet, adding that she no longer resents the boots' presence. The sequencing of the framed stills, the unkempt bed, the boots, the coat—all this portrays the apartment as a place where the ordinariness of living together is preserved, a still life. Koren ends the sequence by saying "Just come back already, come back so we can hug and fight and kiss again, so I can see your face again and caress you, so I can make you run back and forth when we play paddle ball on the beach, so I can tell you how much I love and how much I miss you." In this scene the military's presence passes as an everyday object, or a trigger for a quotidian fight. Threaded into intimate life, the military is the background of love, not the forefront of violence and of occupation that terminate other lives and loves. Just like the girlfriend is rendered a secret at the soldiers' post, at the lovers' home what is obscured is the military itself.

The video repeatedly accentuates the rupturing of communication. One of Elquai's former subordinates from his early days as a young lieutenant tells Koren that a week before he died, Elquai sent each one of them a personal letter, wishing them best of luck upon their imminent release from the army. The ex-soldier dwells on the sending of the letter and the signing of it with the inscription "yours, as a commander and a friend." Here too, formal hierarchies are mobilized into an affective position. The soldier ends his story by saying "I wanted to send him a response, but [pause] it got cut in the middle." Elquai's sister tells Koren that Elquai used to seek her advice on romantic gestures, and that each year on Koren's birthday, her brother asked her to send his girlfriend flowers and write a card on his behalf. The sister recalls that when Koren celebrated her birthday, a month after Elquai died, "I waited for him to call and tell me, Anat, send Gaya flowers. [pause] It was painful, but, I did it anyway." In another instance, one of Elquai's friends laments: "I didn't see him and didn't hug him one last time, and I didn't tell him I love him; he doesn't know, because I never actually said these words." The video leaves these transmissions scattered and open-ended. For the video memorial, or for the bereaved who employ it, love is quintessentially mixed with medium: intimacy is a condition of reciprocity.

Another trace that the video exhumes is the last message Elquai left for Koren, the night before he died. The sequence starts with an image of Koren sitting in front of a screen, watching an old video. The video shows Elquai dancing. It conveys a somatic scene with the body moving to the sound of loud music playing in the background. The video is paused, freezing the image of the dancing Elquai, and at the sound of a beep, an answering machine enters the frame.

> Gaya, I can't believe it! Where are you? I miss you so much! I love you! We have Katyushas [artillery rockets] here. . . . I might be home tomorrow, or not. If you hear something in the news, it's probably me. Be proud. That's it. I love you so much! I truly love you. Bye my beautiful one, see you. . . . I will call again to check if maybe you're at home and asleep and that's why you're not answering. Bye my love, bye.

Elquai's voice on the answering machine sounds very much alive: he speaks up-tempo, breathes heavily, and emphasizes his exclamation and question marks. The voice implication in a sequence of plans, correspondences, and time tables further attributes to the sense of aliveness: to get back home by tomorrow, to make arrangements for a vacation he and Koren were planning, as well as the stipulation of Koren's plans for the present, expressed in his wondering if she will be home later, or if she is asleep already. The message is an interlude for a meeting to come, an affirmation of love. Lastly, the message functions *retrospectively* as an announcement of his death: "If you hear something in the news. . . ." The present-absent body, the implication of the message in a stream of correspondences, and the loss or cut that haunts it, make the last message an epitome of a medium: carrying transmission, promising continuity yet devoid of presence. It is the ultimate message, an emblem of loss, precisely because it is the last one. The video joins the sequence of open-ended correspondences as much as it contains them. Following from its title, it provides a space, an open channel, and a means of recording things that wish to be told. Through this haunted address, Koren turns the video into a call-back, a channel for speaking to the dead. She recovers transmission, or rather frames its failure. Elquai's message, played again at the end of the video, is a phantom correspondence which is left unanswered. It enacts love with no reciprocity, and no authority, as Koren never answered the call.

Elquai's unanswered call is the ultimate message since the announcement of a soldier's death puts one in touch with the state, it is the state that enters the space of intimacy. This is where the sovereign—who has the power to determine life—and kinship literally meet. In cases of military death, representatives of the state appear in front of the family's doorstep and inform the family that their loved one has died, formally confirming the state's accountability for the loss. But for Koren there was no announcement, there was no founding momentum in which the army or the state yielded to her and incorporated her loss, there was no catharsis. In his message, Elquai casts Koren to play a symbolic role ("be proud"), but as far as institutional typology and bureaucratic attributions go, her status as Elquai's *girlfriend* did not grant her the kind of recognition and care materialized in the announcement procedure.

In a 2005 newspaper article, Koren describes the way she learned that her boyfriend had died as a non-event.

> On the day on which my entire world collapsed I was at the university. They may have taught a class on Pasolini. . . . I came home at five, exhausted. A few minutes later, the intercom buzzed. I was sure that Eran, my boyfriend, had come home from the army, but it was my dad. 'I have bad news,' my dad said, 'Eran is injured.' 'Injured? Injured how? What does it mean?' 'Badly injured.' 'How bad?' I continued. . . . For him [Elquai] I was the most precious thing in the world. For the army I was nothing. . . . The army wanted to announce his death in the news at noon, the same day, but his family pressured them to wait, until I got home, so I could receive the horrifying news face to face.[19]

Koren notes a lack of the crucial and defining exchange between the state and its subject. Recollection of the ways families received the message that their loved one has died—a key moment in video memorials discussed at length in chapter 4—works to render intimate the institution. In these scenarios love overshadows the work of the sovereign in determining life and death. Contrarily, in the recollection of a message that *did not take place*, the administration of death is highlighted, while calling on the non-recognition of love by the state and its institutionalized typology. The video serves a very intimate longing for communication, but could it also be a claim? What does the girlfriend, or the girlfriend's love, speak for?

Koren recounts her experience as a journalist, sympathetically covering the activities of an organization initially called "Non-Profit Organization for Emotional Support of Girlfriends (Fiancées) of Fallen Soldiers of the Israel Defense Force (IDF)." Founded in 1997 by a mother and a sister of a young woman whose boyfriend died, the organization's objectives are to petition for the institutionalizing of support venues for fallen soldiers' girlfriends, to represent them in front of the authorized entities, and to raise public awareness of what was until then mostly unacknowledged pain by the state-manifested care.[20] The organization's motivation was that whereas the state sponsors an entire mechanism of support—emotional, social and legal—it is only allocated to the bereaved family, and the girlfriend, who escapes the law's definition of kinship, is ignored. Back in 2005, the IDF's official response to Koren's article and to the claims raised by the organization was that "the IDF does not formally recognize fallen soldiers' girlfriends because it is difficult to define and establish criteria (for defining) *what is a girlfriend*."[21]

What is a girlfriend? The girlfriends ask that the state representatives appear on their doorsteps; they claim recognition from the sovereign. The difficulties faced by the state's formal mechanisms in recognizing or naming the girlfriend are echoed in the organization's internal terminology. In the translation of the group's initial name to English, the translator added the bracketed definition "fiancées"—missing in the original Hebrew title—in order to give the nebulous title "girlfriend" a semi-official seal. In the process of translation, the instability implied in the title resonates. Thinking about the organization's own terminology begs the question: is there a boyfriend? The "girlfriends organization"—an abbreviation applied by the organization itself—relays both the gender bias within the military in which the majority of combative roles are served by men, and the domination of Jewish-Israeli memory discourse by death in action. In interviews, the organization's CEO, Dina Cohen, and its founder Tamar Heimowitz declare their interest in breaking away from these gendered norms to include boyfriends in their activities. In a 2005 interview, they state that it is difficult to convince bereaved boyfriends to attend the organization's support groups, a refusal that Cohen and Heimowitz explain as a result of "the male ego."[22] Beyond the structured imbalance between male and female casualties, which is a result of gender-discriminatory constructions within the military, the organization seems to restrict itself within gender and sexuality biases, and admittedly fails to acknowledge non-heteronormative relationships.

Koren's videotaped lamentation clearly expresses everything that the state fails to recognize or authorize as kinship: a connection formed through reciprocity materialized in the numerous phone calls, messages, letters, birthday notes, and stills mentioned and captured in the video; a love that draws its force from cohabitation; and the symbolic capital of shared experience expressed through the anecdotal. The anecdote appears in the video—and in other videos, as we will see—as a form of currency that is essential to love, in its circulation and its ability to cross scales.[23] The anecdote is also a way to think about the video/the girl-friend as a medium, and their respective relations to sovereignty. Unrec-ognized by the state and the law, the girlfriend is a form of unauthorized intimacy, or a love that has not-yet been institutionalized. The girlfriend too is of an anecdotal order. She is that which is not (yet) formulated or named, but still resonates, that which sustains or circulates intimately.

The homemade video memorial, in its amateur, amorous making and its modes of communication, seems to be an apt channel to represent and contain intimacy. Girlfriends make a frequent appearance in video memorials, cast as a future of reproductive love, family, and home that the deceased should have had but will not live through. The horizon of a future is prominent as the dead are all rather young. In an untitled com-memorative video from 2001 that is divided into biographic chapters—childhood, adolescence, military and so on—one of the episodes is dedicated to the girlfriend. She tells the camera that whenever people asked her boyfriend "is this your girlfriend?" he would say "no, this is my future wife." Ten years later, the soldier's family decided to produce another commemorative video. The woman, who to the soldier's girl-friend at the time, had moved on. When the video was shot, she was pregnant and did not want to appear in the video at first, presenting the material presence of a reproduction with someone else. At the end, her short appearance is shot in a close-up from the shoulders up.[24] In another video, the dead soldier had started a romantic relationship with a woman just before he died. His friends assert that although the rela-tionship was young, "it seemed serious." The woman's appearance in the video is brief, she does not say much and seems to be perplexed by

FIGURE 3. Screenshot from *Things I Wanted to Tell You*, dir. Gaya Koren, 1992.

the symbolic weight, reluctant to embody the promise of a reproductive future.[25] In another case, the video makes an explicit gesture towards the status of the girlfriend as a legitimate family member and a future spouse. While the bereaved family members recall, over dinner, how it did not even cross their minds that the army would not notify their son's girlfriend that he had died, the camera cuts to the woman, sitting at the family table and maternally feeding the deceased's infant niece.[26] Configuring future plans and feelings that are so intense precisely because they were yet to be formally defined, the girlfriend's love is singular and at the same time a metaphor for the premature, unnatural death. The girlfriend is a promise, made through the medium of intimacy, not a formality; a medium which is generative, connective, but also primary and unformulated.

The reading I offer here is neither queer nor anti-colonial. Jasbir Puar identifies the vital, indeed visceral core of Israeli biopolitical power that directly draws on sexuality and reproductive love.[27] The challenge to the state recognition of kinship posed by the girlfriend notwithstanding, the girlfriend herself neither radicalizes nor resists heteronormative positions. On the contrary, she is locked in a gender-specific definition of the girl-friend and represents the imminent materialization of love into a hegemonic familial structure.[28] The girlfriend discourse necessarily assumes the ultimate institutionalization of intimacy, as one girlfriend says: "we already knew how we're going to name our kids and where we're going to live."[29] Glen Sean Coulthard notes that recognition is a core apparatus of the settler colonial state, instrumental to its means of assimilation and erasure.[30] The girlfriend's appeal for recognition does not provoke the state with its intimacy but intimates the sovereign. Through her promise of love, structures of sexual domination are separated from colonial ones. What is a girlfriend? Like the homemade memorial video, the girlfriend is a site where representation, regulation, information, and circulation are negotiated and then reaffirmed.

The girlfriend calls the sovereign recognition of love into question, and at the same time ratifies it. In the video, love permeates many realms and assumes many spaces, tying romantic intimacy to commitment towards the institution of violence. Elquai loved Koren, and he also loved the army. Elquai's friends assert that his "two loves" did not necessarily coincide, as one friend recalls: "He used to tell me: "I'm getting out [of the army], don't tell her, but I will. I love her, but don't tell her that as well." Elquai too was making promises for a future devoid of conflict and filled with love. As the video shows, the army prevails in every scene and every recollection. Although the army appears to be in contrast to intimate love, the army defines love, and defies the institutionalized confusion as to what is a girlfriend. Eventually, it is the loss of love, not the "ordinary" presence of intimacy, that pushes the girlfriends to claim recognition. The army is central for the secret of intimacy, and vice-versa, intimacy is central for the secret of violence. It sustains gender relations and makes longing and distance routine, which eventually leads toward securing love and commitment—to each other as well as to the army/state. What is a girlfriend? A girlfriend is a medium of intimacy. Koren's rough knowledge of video and her close knowledge of her boyfriend come together to produce an affective and radiating transmission. Her presence as a mere voice or behind the camera, scanning and zooming in on objects and pictures, freezing, replaying, cutting and enmeshing collected footage, makes her inseparable from the apparatus. Intimacy and sovereignty conflate: if the army is a channel of love for the girlfriend, the girlfriend becomes a redirected channel of intimate, secretive love for the state.

Things I Wanted to Tell You's ending sequence starts with Koren's and Elquai's families sitting together. The scene is haunted by romantic love's social convention of bringing the parents together as a step towards marital unification. In the case of Koren and Elquai this is a wishful manifestation, a "what if," or a probability, a "not-yet." Ultimately love was not formalized and Elquai died. From there, the video closes with the camera scanning a series of still photos of the couple: on a vacation, swimming, dressed up for an event, in one of the visits Koren paid Elquai when he was spending weekends in the army. Koren's voice enters the frame: "One evening I found myself sitting in the living room, begging you to give me a sign, to show that you're here, looking after me, . . . that you'll do something. I sat throughout the entire evening, staring. Nothing happened." The video is signed with the last message Elquai left her, played again while the video scans a bank check written by Elquai to Koren on the sum of "I love you!" numerously transcribed as a heart icon and XX/XX. It is a symbolic transaction, a humorous comment on the untranslatability of love to value, or the incommensurability of intimacy and the state's semiotics. The video's short credit sequence is accompanied by Phil Collins's 1984 *Against All Odds (Take a Look at Me Now)*, written for a blockbuster romantic drama with the same name.[31] The unformulated love is signed by the pseudo-authority of the last message and the bank check; the unformulated video is signed by the constitutive ghosts of commercial cinema. Both video and girlfriend are in proximity, a step away from authorized forms of kinship and production, both circulate and are constituted through intimate, even secretive, transmissions. The girlfriend is not-yet a wife; the videos' public exposure is restricted to the national Memorial Day in a late-night programming slot.

TO GET IN TOUCH

In 1998, allegedly following the meeting of the television director and the woman with the plastic bag, Reshet launched a community-service project titled "To Remember with Love." By 1998, sporadic productions of personal video memorials, like the one made by Koren, had gained some visibility, broadcast on television during the National Memorial Day, and attracting the attention of both bereaved families and industry. The project promised to provide professional input for families interested in commemorating their loved one in the form of a video. The Reshet project joined a gradually growing infrastructure supporting the production of family videos and in particular family video memorials (see chapter 2). Allocated as a community service, the project had no bearing on the network programming agenda and did not entail any commissioning or funding on behalf of the network. Families who wanted to join the project were assigned a meeting with a network representative, to which they were asked to bring the audio-visual materials they had at their disposal. The network did not produce any materials itself. In the meeting they decided on a list of emphases and cues that was then transferred, with the assortment of materials, to an editor in charge of assembling them. This was a *pro bono* project, and Reshet recruited mostly its less experienced and untenured personnel for this mission. Very little to no formal information is available on the process of editing or the identity of the editors, who were rarely credited as authors. When the video was completed, the network representative met the family again and showed them the finished product. The video was conceived of as the sole property of the family and the project itself was of modest scope, with the network producing several dozen videos from the day it was initiated through today. The videos were not broadcast on television until 2004; at this point they appeared in marginal time slots on the Memorial Day programming schedule, and only in those years in which Reshet was franchised to program.[32]

As the network states, the development of these videos does not engage the family in a creative process. In fact, there is something almost logistical in this sequence of transferences. In its protocoled workflow, the entity of love (the family) and the entity of technical expertise (the editor) never meet. The name of the project, "To Remember with Love," seems to suggest that remembering is not necessarily always on the order of love. In the context of Israeli memory culture, remembering is indeed a civic duty that is forged through the infrastructure of the state and its media. Central to the national ideology and narrative, television's production of memory corresponds with Israeli law, with broadcasting regulations, and with cultural formats associated with the nation's history and its ethos. All these, presumably, stand in opposition to love. The project's title casts memories of a different order as love draws directly from the family's own intimate transmissions. The project's premise also assumes that the family is the bearer of love, but lacks the means to perpetuate it, and that the network can provide the media platform for facilitating the family's work of *remembering*.

What is needed for television to remember with love? Television steps out of its usual framework. For example, the network becomes a provider of individualized and personalized services rather than a producer of public content; it valorizes materials not due to their informative or aesthetic value, but to the emotions they encompass. Lastly, although the network is a private commercial entity, it projects itself as a resource for the families. Hila Barel, the program's director since 2004, stresses that "this is not a therapeutic endeavor."[33] She emphasizes the professional input and disclaims any attempt on television's part to engage in what might be a process of mourning for the family. In another context she succinctly describes the nature of the network's collaboration with the family as technical enabling.[34] By this statement, she herself interprets television, stripped of its cultural and creative aspects, as a technology and a technique. However, she later says, "it's not a technical matter. You need to *bring your heart into it*."[35] The network's CEO, Yochanan Tzanagen, supports the notion that television, here, works outside of its own framework. He says: "we started the project not as a means of publicity or PR, but as a contribution to the community. . . . We know that if we hadn't *stepped into it*, the families would have no one to turn to. They have a lot of material, but lack the knowledge and the ability to do something with it."[36] While the project challenges some of television's features, it sticks to and forcefully reinforces television's role as a medium, as something that incorporates a transmission, a tool of communication.

In its mobilization as an intimate medium of love, television gains a body: it has a heart and legs ("step into it"), and its organs move.[37] Likewise, its source material—the family memorabilia manifested in the anecdote's detail of a plastic bag with VHS cassettes—puts forward media materiality while inviting a jarring bodily affect. One mother writes to the network: "my son will never come back, but the movie brought back some part of him."[38] Another letter says: "You revived Ari, and *every part of his body*, through his singing, his dancing and all the charm he had in him. . . . He *came out of the screen and connected* with each one of us in his own special way."[39] Writing to Reshet's Department of Community Service to thank them for their support in her family's video memorial, the bereaved sister Aliza Sari says that through the video she could "learn something new" about her brother, and that the video also sparked new interactions among his living family members. As Sari elaborates, the video is not just about recomposing the body, but an active process of recovering connectedness, generating new knowledge and ties. Sari seems to affirm Roger Odin's conceptualization of the home movie as something that actively forms the family through viewership and interpretation.[40] In this sense, video is not simply a record of the family but is constitutive to its communication and relations.

Media stands-in for the body, as another letter exhorts: "It wasn't 'about him', it '*was him*.'"[41] The same letter also expands on the connectable qualities of the video as a medium: "A movie is just perfect. . . . it has a video that shows who he was, and still pictures that show how he developed."[42] A letter sent to the network describes an expansive circle of affected viewers:

It's just unbelievable. . . . People stop my parents in the store, at the doctor's office, in the bank, at the crossroad, at work—they say they saw the movie. We received great compliments. They say they know more and feel more *connected*. . . . A neighbor that saw the movie said that after watching [it] she couldn't move for a few long minutes. She was paralyzed by crying and *her feet couldn't carry her*. . . . Among all these, a letter arrived, a little bit after Memorial Day, from people who we know nothing about, and they wrote to us. [The letter is attached]. Dad is about to call them now.[43]

Within this scene of radiating connectedness, once again the body appears ("her feet couldn't carry her"), and video seems to have a very touching effect.[44] Not only did the video spark new relations, and connect people, it also engendered possible relationships and additional modes of contact (in the form of the letter, the phone call). With the family's loss of reciprocity with the dead, intimate communication is redirected and affects a larger public. A form of attachment, they touch and connect others as well. Love for television, media for the family, are ways to gain a body and get in touch.

What is described here is a series of motions, things that are *entering our lives*, *appearing on the doorsteps*, *stepping-in* or *standing-for*. The Reshet project raises questions on the standardization and commercialization of the home video, and on the public-private role of television as a medium. These questions, important as they are, are addressed later in the book. Here I want to establish that these videos are a mode of communication which is intimate in its vital content as well as its very materiality and mediality. This very intimacy is a necessary precursor in incorporating a form of sovereign power constituted by necropolitical violence.

An open letter written by Ora Leffer-Mintz, a bereaved mother, was published in the newspaper on Memorial Day 2004. In the letter Leffer-Mintz suggests that the memory alliance of the family and the public is based on the call to keep in touch, and indeed, to remember with love:

Dear public, it is you that we need. . . . You promise the family and yourself that you'll keep in touch. But a day passes and another one, and you go back to your routine. And the bereaved family needs you so much. Every phone call is a source of light in a great darkness, your attention softens the hardest of all. . . . Some will say: I want to make this phone call, but it's too difficult, what will I say? Just say you called because you care. Even tell us you were embarrassed. Don't worry, the conversation will flow.[45]

In its quotidian yet affective transaction, the imaginary phone call described in Leffer-Mintz's letter is literal and metaphoric, it is left open (who is the generalized, anonymous figure of the caller?), and yet it answers a call of need. Through the inter-personal, two-ends medium of the telephone the public is encountered as a very intimate entity. Are the woman from the anecdote and the girlfriend from the video likewise petitioning for the public to get in touch? Like Leffer-Mintz, these women were also aiming at a purposeful use of a domestic technology of communication as a synecdoche for love, but also for social acceptance, care and acknowledgement. Here too, interpersonal and singularizing channels of communication cross paths with mass media—the phone call, the open letter, the newspaper that publishes it coalesce into an embryonic media sphere gearing towards a particular mode of contact.[46] In the Reshet project too, television steps out of its public institutional role to extend itself for the use of the bereaved. In that sense, the bereaved are an extension of the medium, sitting on its other end. There is, however, one major difference: television, although it is a domestic technology of communication, is not the same as the telephone. It is a non-reciprocal medium. Or is it? Through the home video, which is both a trivial way of communication among family members and a performative form that records and displays all other transmissions, television reaches out. Through the home video, television becomes a telephone, it answers a call.

When television is answering a call, it brings with it a different kind of framing. Going back to the anecdote of the woman appearing on television's doorsteps, although it tells us about an encounter which led to the public being touched, and being solicited to remember *with love,* the first to be reached out to, to get in touch with, is *the institution of media itself.* Per the anecdote, it is the anonymous, unauthorized, unedited that finds its ally in the institution, familiarizes it, gets in touch. For television the story reinforces its own altruism, its being touched and being in-touch. Moreover, when the anecdote is recounted and cited by the institution, it is in order to cast itself as an instrument of family transmission. Tzanagen's statement that "if we hadn't *stepped into it,* the families would have no one to turn to" assumes that authority is needed, someone should step in.

Tzanagen's words position television a step (away) from the state, what allows the alliance. The network is in affinity with the state, but distant enough from it to be intimate with the family. To be precise, television is a tool of sovereignty par excellence, but also as a medium it affords elasticity and different scales. What the anecdote illustrates is a reciprocal instance of gaining contact: with the lost son, with the public, and with the institution. This re-channeling and conflation take place through the technological and conceptual transformation of a consistency of feelings, embodied through "raw" VHS, into the fabricated and constructed form of a movie. Furthermore, these modes of contact prescribed in the anecdotal—family transmissions turned into home "movies"—are situated in proximity to authoritative forms of memory, media, and power. Therefore, if the anecdote is a mode of storytelling that opens up an in-between space where the illiterate steps towards the literate, where history steps into "our life," and where representation/circulation steps away from authority, then the home movie is not only a family expression to be later revealed to public eyes, *but a place where kinship, sociality, and state power are anticipated and constituted.* These moments of encounter, with all their polemics, open an intimate, unauthored, and unauthorized channel with the army and the media, through which sovereignty is incorporated.

That an account of the network community initiative slips into the realm of anecdote is perhaps key to understanding this entanglement. The anecdotal rejection of factual discourse—its historiographic alterity, its unauthorized characteristics as a story which is not exactly a history—turns the format to a statement of its own. The anecdote has something informal that redirects the institutional into the familial and that intimates, or even legitimates, what seems at first to be television's solely technocratic expertise. The anecdotal reflects memorial videos' own organization. Memorial videos evolve anecdotally, bringing stories, inside jokes, and ordinary interactions that produce intimate knowledge of the dead. They have a circumstantial quality that conveys the mundane and produces a single and singular tale, circulating at the margins like an obscure transmission that touches and embodies.

As these example show, sovereign power has embodied, informal, and amorous channels that are anecdotal to it and superfluous. The next two sections look more closely at the ways families incorporate the military. A necropolitical institute, predicated on death and injury as a marker of political life, the military too passes as essential to family intimacy.

"A ROCKET CRASHED INTO OUR HOUSE":
DISINFORMATION, DISEMBODIMENT,
AND DISINTEGRATION

On Thursday evening, September 4, 1997, Guy Golan, a naval commando combatant in the IDF's Shayete 13, called his parents and left the following message on their answering machine: "Hello my dear parents. It's Guy. I [pause] Good chance I will make it home only tomorrow.

Don't wait for me today. And [pause] that's it. I'm doing fine. OK. Bye."
His voice sounds casual and reassuring, a quotidian communication
alerting his family to a slight delay in an anticipated meeting. The message is played in a video titled *Guy Golan: A Touch of an Angel and His
Smile* (Reshet, 2007), just before Golan's friends and family recall how
they encountered the news of his death. The postmortem perspective
reads the message opposite to the information it transmits—there was
no homecoming. No longer a straightforward tool of communication,
the message amplifies what it failed to deliver and the family is left with
an excessive media form.[47] Golan never makes it back; instead come the
messengers, the military representatives who announce the loss to the
family. There is a morbid irony in the message, even before it is framed
by Golan's death. His calling home is not informing, but *dis-informing*,
even misleading. In contrast to the reassuring promise of the phone message and its bringing-closer despite the distance, Golan was on his way
to a top secret mission which had a fatal and scandalous outcome. Not
only does the message obscure the danger, it reorganizes family transmissions according to a military rationale that renders one's location or
actions a secret.[48] The banal, indeed singularized, communication coincides with and mitigates a routine of military occupation in southern
Lebanon constituted through inconspicuous military operations.

What has become known in Israel as the "naval commando affair"
(in Hebrew "Asson HaShayete," "the naval commando *disaster*") took
place during the night between September 4 and 5, 1997. A small team
of sixteen soldiers from the elite unit were on their way to a secret
operation in Ansariyeh, Lebanon. When the team crossed an orchard
on the outskirts of the town, a series of explosions, whose source has
yet to be fully determined, compromised the team and its mission. The
explosions led to a fire exchange with the Shia-Islamist paramilitary organization Hezbollah and resulted in the death of eleven soldiers, with
another casualty from the evacuation team, four wounded, and only
one soldier who remained unharmed during the event.[49] The failure
of the mission and its death toll occupied Israeli media and public for
many years. There is not much information on the non-Israeli casualties of the event. For Hezbollah, the event is mostly remembered trium-
phantly, showing their ability to compromise, even penetrate, the IDF's
operations.[50] A report by journalist Robert Fisk briefly mentions "a very
drunk 43 year old woman . . . and her Palestinian lover" as the event's
collateral damage. It's important to note the asymmetric account of death
as prerequisite for a legitimacy of mourning. The affair's unrecognized

death comes in the form of promiscuous love that happens in secret, then is caught and crushed by military fire and ultimately erased from all other accounts of the incident.[51]

The naval commando affair has put into crisis the channels of communication. First, both public and military investigations raised the suspicion that what caused the explosions was an ambush planed by Hezbollah, which meant that the organization had access to extremely classified information about the naval commandos' whereabouts. Second, more than a year after the incident, it was discovered that the state had withheld information from some of the families about their sons' corpses. Negotiating the return of the corpse of Itamar Eliya, a commando whose body was left in Lebanon, the IDF also received some body parts of two other commandos, Raz Teiby and Guy Golan. Those parts were secretly deposited in their graves by military officials without the families being notified.[52] What the affair surfaces is the scandal of secrecy, first in the form of information that leaked on undesired paths, not contained by the state and military operatives, and second in the form of information not disclosed by the state to its citizens. In fact, one journalist even argued that the recurring themes of betrayal and deceit in the naval commando affair disguised a more acute crisis: not the operational failure itself, but the state's lack of accountability for, misinforming about, and obscuring of the failure.[53] This lands us at the heart of sovereign politics, probing the delicate balance between the democratic state imperative of transparency, and the obscurity that is allegedly employed for the very sake of democratic transparency. Secrecy is a common modus operandi of sovereign politics, yet it is bracketed by the flow of information that facilitates accountability, reciprocity, and trust in modern statehood.[54]

The naval commando affair discloses not only on the sovereign politics of information, but its body politics, holding the state accountable for the soldiers and their bodies—alive, injured, or dead. Lastly, it is also about territory, framing acts done in secrecy outside Israel's sovereign borders. Information, bodies, and land are all disintegrated and in fragments.

Structured from an assortment of family stills and videos, news items, and interviews the family commissioned, Guy Golan's video manifests a work of assembling. What it omits quite masterfully, however, is the public scandal surrounding Golan's death. The family filed a legal suit against the army for withholding information about their son's body/parts, and the friction between the bereaved family and the state was well covered by mass media.[55] Why is this struggle absent from the video? Perhaps because the video is meant to *remember with love,* therefore omitting any conflicts.

The video is rendered anecdotal: an ordinary yet singular expression, close to the family yet disavowing its equal proximity to state affairs. Within the affair's scandal of transparency, the bereaved families play the most crucial role precisely because their demand comes from a place of intimacy rather than calling on the democratic contract. As one of the fathers bereaved by the affair explains: "the father is there, . . . he sees the child born. He wants to know, [especially] in incidents like this one, what happened at the end, to see, in spite of all, the end."[56] It is the loss of communication, the loss of touch, that pushes families to seek an answer. For the families, the state report is not just a procedural gesture of accountability. The state's relinquishing of information is perceived as a symbolic act that affirms the family's ownership of memories and loss. But most of all, as the father cited above suggests, families demand a report because it details the exact breakdown of their sons' final hours and serves the purpose of reassembling their sons' life stories. Such reconstruction is an important act of mourning that is performed by the commemorative video. While a memorial video is all about intra-familial transmissions of love, life, and relationships, something which is ostensibly independent from an official report, the body of memory cannot be recomposed and reintegrated without this information. The demand for transparency plays into the family's desire for closure, for collecting one more piece of information, one last picture, one last word, or one last signal.

"He had something in *his body*," recalls one of Golan's friends. Indeed, the video, as its title suggests, insistently equates life and closeness with the body. "It was as if he was *hovering* from one place to another." "When he showed up it was always with a *smile*, with this *face*, and with this *punch* that followed by a *hug*." "I miss the Karate jumps and the *pinching* and *high fives*, and the hugs, mainly the *hugs* [trails off]. I'm sure that each one of us would give everything just to get another *hug*." These recollections frame the unrecoverability of a bodily presence. Applying zoom-in to still pictures, or slow motion to videotaped gestures, the video rearticulates movement. Body movements and parts are captured, enmeshed, stretched, cut to pieces. The body is what the video aiming at, yet its haptic semiotics are a product of disjointedness, dismemberment, and disembodiment. Through the aesthetic of magnifying, freezing, punctuating, or isolating a detail, the recomposed body becomes a fetish.

While Golan's friends and family site intimacy in his body, the video renders visible the level at which Golan's body was shaped and instrumentalized by military training. Golan's service as a soldier in an elite unit included a constant challenge to the body. Images from his military service show Golan with his friends bathed in sweat and water, after exhaustive training or a diving exercise. The conflict with the state brings back the body in its disjointed form. The body-in-parts can expose the secret of a shattering violence that the work of memory—national and personal—seeks to suppress. The crisis of disinformation is echoed in the disjointed body. While the body was a source of miscommunication, discord, and friction, Golan's physicality is where longing lies. What becomes evident in the video's resurrections is how much the body is formed through communication and shaped by institution. A touch or a hug are now co-opted into the healing work of video. The state's transmission and its body politics come together in intimacy.

Home videos and still pictures, letters and phone messages, are tangled with news items and military-commissioned footage, rendering visible how both body and video are constituted by the prolongation of the military by the family, a proximity, not a division. As both soldiers and parents stated after the incident, although the unit is constantly involved in high-risk operations, its professionalism, the soldiers' training, the meticulous planning, and the secrecy of its operations created a feeling of safety.[57] A brief documentation from Golan's inauguration ceremony discloses how the military's display of discipline, effort, expertise, and brotherhood are assimilated into and reaffirmed by the family structures of support and care. Postmortem, a long sequence shows the erection/demolition of an underwater memorial, a sinking of a missile boat carrying twelve empty chairs into the depths of the Mediterranean. It shows a controlled explosion followed by the diagonal descent of the vessel underneath the waves, then cuts to a montage of stills and video of the monument that ends with a close-up of one of the empty chairs with a metal plate carrying Golan's name. Back to the surface, commando boats are circling the location of the now-invisible vessel, with family members observing the scene from a nearby boat. From there, the camera ascends and pans, showing the open sea, and filling the frame with luscious blue and turquoise. With the submersion of the boat, the recorded video becomes the monument itself. In the reintegration of memory and missing bodies, what emerges is not something tangible—a touch—but residue. In a different context, Catherine Russell describes the assemblage of footage associated with kinship and loss as a "montage of ruins."[58] The image of the sinking boat is one of destruction. The memorial was initiated by the bereaved families but realized by the military, and similarly, therefore, the footage. With this spectacular and spectral crash, it is almost as if the commandos reenact for the families the deaths of their sons. As most of the families affected by the incident attested: their sons loved the sea, which was why they joined the commandos. Implicit in this statement is the entanglement of love and violence, the secret of intimacy and the state's secret. While the Golan family struggled to withhold their son's body and his memory, the body is already marked, and then restored and embodied by the army.

In a book published by the Golan family, Guy's father Yoram speaks to the struggle of the family to retrieve information about their son's death and burial: "We, his parents, raised him for twenty one and a half years, and in one day, one second, it was as if he was expropriated from us, for good."[59] The father denounces the army's speech for being full of clichés. Following his line of argumentation, the cliché is in contrast to the state's transparency. He continues: "I didn't sacrifice my child, *I gave him life*. You [the army] took my child and killed him."[60] Facing cliché, the father speaks for the promise of life, but life as such is already at the sovereign disposal. He calls on the right for love and gives away the secret of violence ("you took my child"). The video omits the robbery. Can the family represent loss and destruction without falling back on the state cliché?

Yoram Golan writes to his dead son: "If we ever hurt you, I ask for your forgiveness. It was never intentional." Guy Golan's death and memory demonstrate how communication and embodiment are fraught with uneasy alliances, fractures and bypasses, yet the father's address encompasses a very intimate motion. His letter appears in the video twice. First it is read over the end of the ship-monument sequence by a female voiceover. Heard, not seen, and reading words it did not write, the voiceover introduces distance between body and speech. The body of the dead is marked by the empty chair; the body of the father, whose emotions are laid bare in the text, is disembodied by the voiceover; and the body of the boat, which used to carry the men, slowly becomes invisible, immersed under the surface. All these bodies are void and unrecovered. Necropolitics is fed by specters, and the family act of mourning is doomed to be assimilated by its logic. The second time the letter appears is as a digital scan in a makeshift memorial webpage built by Golan's younger brother. Scrolling down the page, the father's tidy handwriting, wandering slightly off the page's lines, indicates a body.

The written sign, "a text whose essence is irreducibly graphic," is a constitutive gesture where body, media and technique incorporate the relations between reason and experience, memory and perception.[61] These insights are important since much of the argument lies in the subjects' entanglement of intimate and sovereign life, their very bodies and the law. Double framed by the camera and the computer screen, scrolled down and pixelated, this body, like the body of the dead son, is highly mediated. The family's attempt at producing meaning or gaining contact is caught in the limbo of remediation: the frame within a frame, the body fractured by the military, the scandal, the loss.

"A rocket crashed into our house," recalls Tiki Golan, Guy Golan's mother. "The phrase 'putting together the pieces' is true. At that moment, I felt crushed."[62] Perhaps this crashing, the devastation and shattering—of coherency, of knowledge, and of a sense of one's fate and one's body—is what the video is about. The mother says that Guy was very discreet about the army. Loyal to his role, Guy withheld information. There were also intimate withholdings revealed to her after his death: the time he crashed a car, his occasional smoking. The mother found solace in collecting these anecdotes: "All I have left are stories." Unimportant cover-ups are tangled with other secrets that had a more devastating effect: the withholding of a true report about the circumstances that led to his death, the coherence of the body and its return to the earth, and mostly the public secret of perpetual violence, a violence rendered a secret since it is operative, mundane, and happening somewhere else, affecting someone else. Truth be told, what is far from being represented in all these accounts is Israeli colonial violence's collateral damage, a death anecdotal to, and more so unaccounted for by, the security mechanism. If the video is a translation of "putting together the pieces," of inscribing the parents' own report, disintegration is unavoidable. The video is a broken form, an account that lacks closure, an assemblage of debris.

The mother's appearance in the video conveys this sense of crashing. In the brief excerpt taken from television's Memorial Day special a year after the event, she speaks with great difficulty, stating: "There is no more joy in our home, everything just passes us by. I hope that with the years something in our heart will become numb, that we will grow a skin around the knife that penetrated our heart and something will be easier, but, as they say, 'Happy are those who believe.'" In all of her other appearances in the video she does not speak. The puncturing of life, the slicing of the heart brings the body back—this time, that of the mother. In the television show, as is also the case in other instances, tears

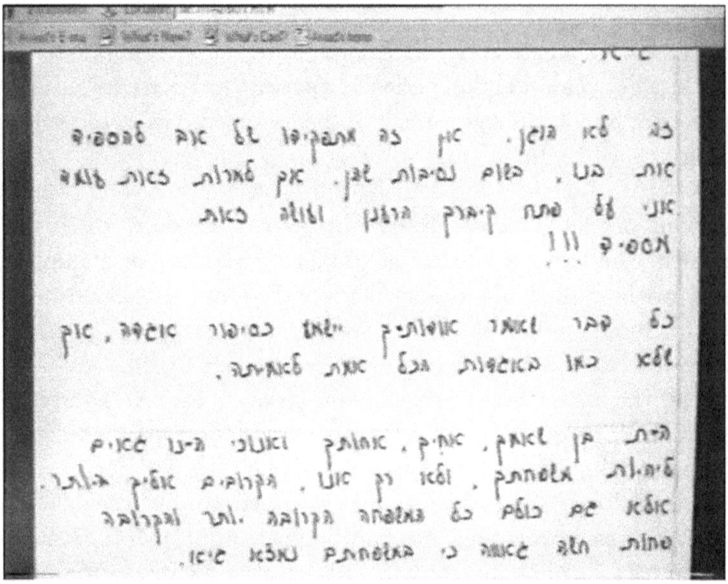

FIGURE 4. Screenshot from *A Touch of an Angel and His Smile*, dir. unknown, 2007.

are running down her face. Hers is a body that floods over itself, that has no writing, no language, no media or form to put it together. The disembodied body of the video configures a fracture, while her body bears the loss.[63]

FADE IN, FADE OUT: "I THINK I SAW YOU. . . ."

Going over my recordings of the National Memorial Day programming from 2008 I ran into an obscured video, nineteen minutes of an uncanny mash of raw footage underscored by Israeli folk music and a couple of cited poems. The programming schedule shows that the video was broadcast at 12:25 p.m. on channel 10, its title identical to its subject's name: *Tzur Zarhi*. The video has no paratext: no credits to disclose who made it and no content description on the television listing. This is not uncommon with family memorial videos. In its abrupt collection of found footage, a few pan shots stand out, showing the family house, a farm in Moshav Nahalal, founded in 1921 by Zionist immigrants near the Palestinian village Ma'lul.[64] The video lacks any narrative tropes; it has no interviews and barely any dialogue. Unlike in *Things I Wanted to Tell You,* its author makes no gestures towards an outside viewer. A few years later, when I met Zarhi's parents in their home in Nahalal, they said: "We wanted to keep it clean; we didn't want to make a show. [Interviews] are for people who didn't know him. We made our video for those who know the characters involved."[65] Zarhi died in the summer of 2007 in what is known in Israel as the Second Lebanon War, and elsewhere as The July War, or the Israel-Hezbollah War. Following his death, Nahum and Mina Zarhi sorted through a collection of videotaped records. Nahum Zarhi reached out to local archives, Mina Zarhi cued a list of musical themes[66]; they then transmitted the materials to an editor, who pasted them together. Here too, an assortment of VHS is given to a media expert to mend the pieces.

In one of the video sequences, we see a convoy of tractors "dancing" in a circle, with a waltz theme accompanying the images. The tractors' dance is followed by a bale-stacking competition. A green John Deere piling bales of hay is described by an announcer as "Tzur Zarhi, fourth generation in Nahalal, second generation in the armored corps." With a lack of context to anchor the display in a more intimate memory, what is left is the abstraction of these two identity categories: an agricultural one, related to life and growth, and a military one, related to death. The portrayal of Zarhi corresponds with the iconicity of salt-of-the-earth Zionism—he is shown riding his ATV (All-Terrain Vehicle) in the fields, inspecting the cows in the dairy farm, walking barefoot in the orchards, with his friends arranging white plastic chairs on the grass. These sentiments of communal life, of working the land and the visceral connections to landscape, resides at the core of the Israeli settler colonialism and its erasure of Palestine and Palestinians. Yet the video employs these markers trivially, their very mundane aspects underlining family life and neutralizing Israeli militarism. Zionism is referenced here not as a collective ethos, but through its filiality, what passes from a father to a son.

Footage of the family having dinner discloses that this is the last dinner before Zarhi joined the army. In the footage, Mina Zarhi expresses her concern. From there, the video sequences images of Zarhi in his military uniform and as a toddler held by his mother. Inserted in between is a brief image of Mina Zarhi talking on the phone—once again, communication as a synecdoche for love. In another mashup, footage of tank maneuvers is mixed with the audio transcription of Zarhi reciting encrypted commands on the military radio, an aerial shot, and maps with different markings. These are neither the product of the family's intimate transmission, nor do they belong to its vocabulary and lexicon.

These codes are available only to someone who is literate in the world of the armored corps. A series of still photos shows the father and son together in uniform. For the father, the military footage is not a spectacle, but a shared language and a shared experience that ties him to his son. That he can understand the encrypted language and read the aerial shots that explain the course of the events surrounding his son's death—events that the video leaves opaque—deems the operative language a shared, symbiotic one. The army is a carrier of intergenerational relations, constituting genealogical threads; it "stays in the family." Despite the video's introversion, its formal language can be described as a work of association: linking one image to another, linking music to the visuals, linking the biographic to the demographic. This associative mode is what guides a viewer not familiar with the intimate details. Finally, association is central to the father's mourning of his son, to the loss of linking, of lineage, of likeness.

Reflecting on her selection of songs for the video, Mina Zarhi says, "You can't write tears. [pause] I see movies. [pause] Words have no place." Zarhi lets the conventional (the all-familiar folk songs) contain her loss. The video's interlacing of life and death, childhood and fatal manhood, as if determinately destined to one another, recites a Zionist convention about the necropolitical relations between love and land. Boaz Neumann describes early Zionist attachment to land as constituted through physical energy, sweat and blood, conquering Palestine through vitality and desire.[67] While the Golan family associated cliché with the speech of the sovereign, sometimes cliché is the only viable means to convey the loss. The parents' refusal to make the video communicative to a larger public puts pressure on both intimacy and the performance of social norm. Filmmaker and writer Richard Fung shows how home movies created a normative display of what were essentially experiences of immigration, illness, and queer loss. He recalls the ritualistic family viewership of these films as involving the pleasure of "seeing ourselves like in the movies."[68] Fung brings to the fore the affiliative and self-regulatory aspect of domestic media, ascribing to a collective normative imaginary shaped by the iconicity of the filmic ideal. Marianne Hirsch notes that family pictures have an affiliative affect, their uncanniness mitigated by a sense of sameness.[69] Whereas specific actors or events are unknown to us, conventions of family life make them recognizable. Hirsch suggests that this puts the spectator in a position of interpretative investment in the footage.

Demanding investment, *Tzur Zarhi* traverses the abstraction with which ideology operates. Put differently, the video abides by the general rule by calling on arbitrariness and opacity that, in return, singularize and trivialize the rule, here a regime of colonization and militarization. The parents, sticking to their internal sense of knowing, surpass, even reject, the authority of "legitimate" media with its articulated narratives and subjects. At the same time, it directs the access of an outside spectator to the conventional, to knowledge gained through what is already known and immediately visible. What is intriguing about *Tzur Zarhi* is its uncanniness, portraying an odd familiarity, an unknowing-knowing, or unhomely homelessness. While Zionist ideology passes as intimacy, the video clearly expresses a settler colonial melancholia in its attempt to incorporate what was never at its disposal.

The melancholic attempt, an attempt to reclaim love, recompose the scattered limbs, and collect the last instances, is shared by all videos discussed in this chapter. For Nahum Zarhi this was a matter of mastering technique. After the first video was completed, he took two evening courses in video editing and videomaking, impressed, as he himself described it, by the affordances of video. As part of his coursework, he made a second video for his son and edited a number of short memorials for other families he got to know through his network of bereaved families in his area.[70] Acquiring editing tools, he started collecting multiple records of the days of the war in search of traces of his son's image. He reached out to the regional council, military intelligence, his son's military unit, and journalists who covered the northern border. He videotaped and scanned news reports and culled instructional videos of the ammunition manufacture that provides artillery for his son's armored corps battalion. He joined an amateur filmmakers' community and located a filmmaker who took images of tanks entering Lebanon across the northern border. In this stock, the father discovered images of Tzur Zarhi, near a tank, talking to his team. In some of the news footage he reviewed he thought he recognized a tank with the same chevrons as his son's. He retrieved the footage from the network and used his editing software to enlarge the image, then layered it on top of an image of the tank, realizing that it was not his son after all. He spotted images of his son/tank imbricated into a documentary that he recorded from television. The images were used to illustrate an unrelated eyewitness account. For the father, the illustrative use of images, a common practice in film editing, diminished or even violated his personal attachment to the image.[71] Videographics can bring together, uphold a final transmission, or encompass a trace, and at the same time can take apart, misrepresent, or disassociate. For Nahum Zarhi, video is not a fabricated mediation, but a work of love.

The father describes editorial skills as "*sensitivity*," which he explicates as the ability to identify, follow, and remember a figure in the frame.[72] Nahum Zarhi engages in a Barthesian investigation, searching for the image 'punctum,' a very visceral reaction, a shock or a pinch of recognition. Barthes, who is also approaching images from a position of love and loss, explains in the first few pages of *Camera Lucida* that what made him investigate photography was the inability to make desire and social knowledge commensurable on the surface of the photograph: "But an importunate voice (the voice of knowledge, of scientia) then adjured me, in a severe tone: 'Get Back to Photography. What you are seeing here and what makes you suffer belongs to the category "Amateur Photographs," dealt with by a team of sociologists; nothing but the trace of social protocol of integration, intended to reassert the Family, etc.'"[73] Barthes differentiates between the 'punctum' and 'stadium,' defining the latter as the cultural practice of "polite sympathy."[74] He elaborates: "The stadium is that very wide field of unconcerned desire or various interest, of inconsequential taste: I like/I don't like. The stadium is of the order of *liking*, not of *loving*."[75] Zarhi, like Barthes, like Benjamin, is after something different than sociological or historical episteme. He seeks a force that brings things nearer, touches, let them *step into* our lives. Through the techniques of exposure, disassembling, juxtaposing, magnifying, isolating a detail or zooming-in on an obscure cipher, techniques that digital video software affords, the father searches for an incidental, almost hopeless, presence of his son within the frame. The radiation of intimacy in these images, or rather in the way they are employed, displaces the war into the far background.

Materials collected and rescued by the father constitute his second video memorial, *Smoke Grenade*. This video is organized around a visit paid to the parents by one of Zarhi's tank team members, who tells them about their son's last days during the war. Images are interlaced swiftly, dominantly through the effect of either zooming or fading in and out. Images of the son and his team preparing the tank are superimposed on a televised interview of the father, telling the newsman that before his son left for war, the father, an alumnus of the armored corps, told his son to protect himself and not to enter an open field without some means of masking. In armored corps warfare, this effect, meant to obscure the tank's location, is achieved by a smoke grenade. A close-up of the father's talking head is placed over the war footage, then framed by a screen monitor and color filter; this fades out to an image of a tank maneuvering in action. The interlacing situates the father in between the techniques of war and media. The father's story is prolonged by the visitor's, sitting in the parents' living room. Images of tanks riding through a northern landscape are superimposed on the visitor's talking head, juxtaposing the home with the operative arena of battle. The visitor tells the father that while in the tank during the exhausting days of the war, they talked about the future and that Tzur was enthusiastic about living on his family's farm in Nahalal: "All he talked about was farm 16. I think [trails off]—was he in the process of taking your place?" The swift sequence pauses. An image of the northern border fades in and is superimposed on the father's image. The border, paved by tank treads, and the dairy farm: both places passed from father to son. The visitor's story culminates towards the morning when their tank is hit and Tzur dies. Images of war operations, pulled from commercial instructional footage, accompany the reconstruction of the chain of events: the view from the tank's periscope, the charging of explosives, a series of blasts, smoke rising in the distance. Is this smoke a sign of a hit or a rescue, its source an explosion or a technique of camouflage? Does it expose or cover? Kill or protect? It is these questions that attach the father's melancholia to the settler colonial affect where death, love, and land are already interconnected and predetermined.

In the video's climax the visitor tells the parents that a moment before the fatal hit, Tzur asked for a smoke grenade. The echoing of the father's advice within the stream of war recollections reorganizes the entire video around this transmission. While the visitor continues his story, an image of Tzur, sitting at the same spot, is superimposed on the visitor's image. The father admits that whenever Tzur's fellow-soldiers come to visit him, a thought sneaks in: "Why is he still alive and my son is not?"[76] The superimposition substitutes the living for the dead. A text message the father wrote to Tzur—"I think I saw you [standing] on the tank wearing a T-shirt, near Kfar Yuval"—fades in/fades out to an image of a figure wearing a white T-shirt, standing on a tank with the number 3 engraved on it. Whether or not this is indeed the dead son is left open to interpretation. For the father, every image possibly encompasses a last meeting, a trace. More than incorporating the loss, the father's use of video is a means to summon up ghosts. An image of three pillars of dust rising in the distance fades in and is then superimposed on an image of Tzur kneeling near his tank, smiling at the camera. The video does not foreclose, but this is the last image of Tzur, ultimately found in one of the father's relentless searches, an image of tanks on their way back to the northern border, one of them carrying his son's dead body.

Superimposition, or the placement of one image over the other and the overlapping of images through fade-in/fade-out, freeze-frames, and zooming are the dominant techniques the father deployed to produce a last transmission of love. They are palpable means for generating affinity and a sense of closeness. The layering of one image on another offers a dialectic: the living body of the loved one and the military machine, the grieving father and the battlefield, the dead son and his living counterpart. Superimposition and fade in/fade out present images as haunting one another, they project images onto each other. The visual elicits touch: images coalesce with each other, are laid onto one another. In the aftermath of the Lebanon war, harsh criticism was directed towards the military and the government for being ill-prepared, with some of the war's bereaved families taking a vocal position in the dispute. Like the war itself, with its death toll of more than a thousand people, the majority of them Lebanese civilians[77] as collateral damage of the Israeli bombing, the accusation of negligence or a lack of care on the side of the sovereign are ostensibly outside the video.[78] Or maybe not. Maybe the video is all about care. Heritage entails a promise: the promise of continuity. This promise manifests itself in the fabricated indigeneity of the first video and the entanglement of parental care and military conduct in the second. When his son left for war, the father, combining his military experience and his concerns as a parent, told his son to protect himself, to cover himself, to make sure he was not exposed. The father's video techniques are all about playing with levels of exposure and covering, laying his image over the battlefield in which his son's tank was dangerously visible.

The video is a labor of love. The father, worrying about his son's future, gave advice. The visitor, aware of his role in the family's reminiscences, arrives at their house to recollect past events. The editing closely observes the directive: the transmission is stretched, measured, doubled, and taken apart. The domestic record of the eyewitness account merges with television news, instructional footage mixes with the family album, the frame is doubled and layered. By so doing, the dead are imposed onto the living, past (a retrospective report) and future (a prospective advice) enmesh. In the video, the days of the war are compressed into nine minutes, the instants before the rocket hit the tank are dilated and recalled with minute detail, and the insurmountable, lifelong link between the father and the son is condensed into the moment when Zarhi

FIGURE 5. Screenshot from *Smoke Grenade*, dir. Nahum Zarhi, 2009.

echoes his father's advice by requesting camouflage. Gaining contact neither entails the embodied reconnection between a family member and a lost loved one, nor does it simply dispense with the video audience being touched or moved by it. Contact is translated to the transposition of intimate knowledge into technique, more specifically those video tropes that render the image's "touch" literal. These are practices of association and juxtaposition between and within shots, playing with levels of opacity and transparency, highlighting what passes from one image to another. More to the point, these are practices of contact and collision, amalgamating not only love and its object, but family life, media, and the military. We are introduced to sovereign military power through its "punctum," through its touching, visceral, affiliative form.

CONCLUSION: THE SECRET OF INTIMACY

What I term sovereign intimacy here is necessarily a mediated condition in that that it entails a negotiation between sovereignty and the citizens' right for love, calling on love's very means of representation and recognition, and the ability to articulate and disseminate it by their own means. This is not a claim on history, law, or even memory in its institutionalized and cultural forms, but intimate, rudimentary love which is allegedly not within the interests of sovereign power. Sovereign intimacy is necessarily a mediated condition as it is engrained in the very audio-visual syntax of the videos. Intimacy draws its force from the fractured, obscured, yet touching and singular form of the home video, and its split and broken channels of interpersonal communication on the one hand and representation on the other. Lastly, sovereign intimacy is necessarily a mediated condition, as it is the outcome of media capacity to cross scales from public to private. More specifically, it connotes the peculiar institutional location of these "home-movies" (or any home movie), manifested so bluntly in the hyphenated contiguity of the "home" to "movie," domesticity and public display. The anecdote that opens this chapter encapsulates this particular dynamic: prompted by the failure of domestic media to prolong interpersonal communication, loss brings the family to television's doorstep. Commercial television in the mid and late-1990s seeks reciprocity, steps away from the state to become "useable."

Sovereign intimacy upholds not only the intimate secret of love, but the secret of sovereign violence. The soldiers recalled in this chapter all died in Lebanon. Israel invaded Lebanon in 1982 after years of tense borders. It waged an active war on the country until the beginning of 1985, when it withdrew to its southern part, occupying what was termed "a security belt." During the Israeli occupation there were constant armed conflicts between the IDF and Hezbollah, occasionally escalating into short-term military operations which caused masses of collateral damage and forced displacement, disproportionally on the Lebanese side.[79] In 2000 the IDF withdrew from the south of Lebanon. In the summer of 2006, the tension erupted again in the form of a one month long full-fledged war. Nothing, or very little, of this history of violence appears in the videos. Occupation is a "secret" of sovereign power as it is extended beyond sovereign territory, by quasi-legitimate means, inflicted on non-sovereign-citizens, a form of oppression and dispossession excused under the rhetoric of security measures. Such secrets, their suppression practiced daily by the citizens of the colonial state, take shelter in the home.

The space of intimacy is revealed as fraught with the implications of war and violence. Loss calls state accountability into crisis, yet as much as each of the instances recalled here entailed a conundrum, the family's private media—and I leave each family's stances outside of the discussion here—is ordered as a means of mending. Video as a work of love, technique as fetish, and a "movie" as an intimate pursuit. Fathers,

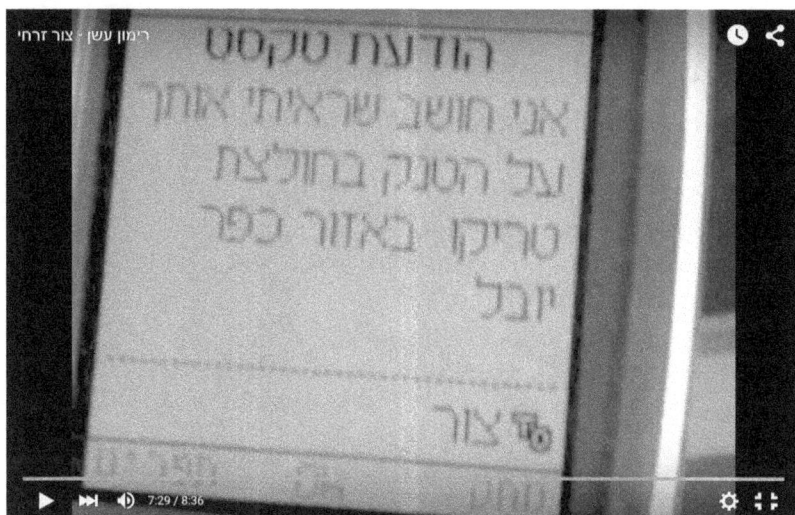

FIGURE 6. "I think I saw you on the tank in t-shirt around Kfar Yuval." Screenshot from *Smoke Grenade*, dir. Nahum Zarhi, 2009.

mothers, girlfriends, and their videographic mourning lay out the un-separated attachments, affinities, and dependencies that persist between intimacy and military. The family—its love, its media—is anecdotal to sovereign violence, yet not antithetical, rather a surreptitious conduit in which the state's institutional power of shaping, managing, or taking life is domesticated, internalized, and reaffirmed.

CHAPTER 2

Intimate Proxies

"Although there is a need for efficiency, and [in] a number of
formats and elements . . . personal movies cannot be turned
into a hamburger industry."

—Eytan Dotan and Udi Ben Dror, "A Proposal for Fallen
    Paratroopers' Memorial Videos Project"

RHETORIC OF SERVICE

In 2010, the Office of Families and Commemoration of the Israeli Ministry of Defense issued a booklet titled *Paths of Commemoration*. The booklet is meant to provide guidance for dead soldiers' families seeking to privately commemorate their fallen loved ones. Succinct, clear, and informative, it lists around a dozen activities, specifying preparations, timelines, professionals to consult with, and other considerations. Activities vary; authoring a commemorative book, organizing a sport activity, nurturing a garden, or making a video are among the recommended practices. The list was assembled through an "extensive survey," as the introduction states, in which various commemorative practices were "reviewed", "studied," "mapped," and "catalogued." *Paths of Commemoration* carefully maneuvers between matter-of-fact pragmatism and the family work of mourning.[1] Authored by the anonymous, neutralized voice of the state, such an address understands the state as counseling its citizen.

At face value, this is a matter of public mental health. The Office of Families and Commemoration, or any other state authority, has never produced, funded, or initiated the production of a personal commemorative video (what the booklet terms a "movie"). Ostensibly, making a video commemorating one's loved one, among other privately pursued commemorative activities, is offered by the Office of Families as something practiced by individuals according to their own interests and in order to serve their own individuated needs. Additionally, the office does not make the case for the family's engagement in private memory. Rather it is an underlining, unquestionable norm. Its stated non-involvement notwithstanding, the booklet provides a rare opportunity where private videotaped commemoration is scrutinized by the state, even if through the mere tentative form of advice. In this chapter, personal media production is understood as a matter of service and is analyzed through the medium of the document. A citizenry advice extended through a brochured guidance, a leaflet sent to bereaved families by a military alumni NGO, as well as application forms, contracts, vision statements, videomakers' portfolios, and a crowdfunding platform—all entail, often implicitly, a protocoled breakdown of visual templates, producers, funds, and distribution channels. Against a common approach in film and media studies that prioritizes creative processes and centers the visual medium, the document anchors what is perceived as a self-forming endeavor in a set of logistics. These entail policies, market dynamics, administrative affordances, legal rights, formats, and production standards.

Standardization is indeed what, in this context, the document tracks: namely the infrastructural norms and policies in which private processes of mourning and creativity persist. The standardization of personal video commemoration coincides with processes of privatization that affect the state's philosophy of governance, civil society's collective forms of organization, and labor settings in the changing media market. This is not about the family or its mourning gaining a unique intimate outlet through video, but about how different agents—the state's administration, NGOs, media entrepreneurs and producers in the free market, or crowdfunding platforms—understand themselves as providing services of care and support. All of these are the family's intimate proxies. The protocols analyzed in this chapter were not stored in proper archives—in fact, most of them turned out to be ephemeral, and many of the websites I consulted during my research are now offline—and do not point at a concrete fact sheet. They are suggestive, tentative, at times fictitious in the sense that they do not connect to a physical outcome and tend to say more through what they avoid saying.[2] Attending to sensitive matters of personal loss and bereavement, they address their readers softly: *advise, propose, direct, support*. Yet by so doing they adjure intimate mourning as a facet of the social organization that supports sovereignty in its now-private form: services of care advised on by the state and relegated to private professionals.

THE STATE LOGIC OF CARE

"A personal movie," the booklet explains, "tells [viewers] about your loved one and yourselves—his family—through stills, videos, interviews with family and friends, and the documentation of memorial and commemoration ceremonies."[3] The personal video/movie is defined, as always, in opposition to the commercial production of a documentary or a fiction film. The state authors describe the former as cultural texts that incorporate the individuated story into the narrative of historical events and involve a complex and expansive process done by professional production companies. The personal production, they note, is a common mode of commemoration today. The booklet summarizes the making of a personal commemorative video as collecting and organizing available footage, planning the shooting, putting together a script, editing and distributing the movie. A clause dedicated to distribution suggests screening the video to family members, friends, and acquaintances, as well as "targeted audiences," a term that refers to circles of membership or social groups related to the dead. If the family is interested in a wider distribution, the booklet mentions television and the internet as possible routes of circulation. Scriptwriters, camera operators, producers, editors, and distribution companies are listed as professionals that the family might want to consult. The double page dedicated to the personal video is, as with all other chapters in the booklet, straightforward and descriptive, highlighting efficiency and accessibility.

The different activities the booklet surveys are arranged according to the same formula: short description, professionalized help and a section titled "Preliminary Thought." This section aims at acknowledging the emotional labor, or rather emotional "investment," necessitated by the designated practice. In the part dedicated to video memorials, the authors warn that going over materials for the video might trigger difficult feelings, that the production process might be a prolonged one, and that production costs are varied and relatively high. "Preliminary Thought" reframes the information provided by the booklet as touching on practices of rehabilitation. Noting that some families prefer to start the process immediately, the authors stress the importance of time and perspective. In consideration of the prospective emotional tribulations, families are entreated to hand the work to "a person with some *affinity* to this field, who will be able to meet your expectations and who will know how to include *qualitative parts* and integrate them into the overall context." This will guarantee "true partnership in the work of commemorating your loved one."[4]

What do the authors mean by "a person with some affinity"? The prose of the booklet is strikingly suggestive, even enigmatic. Affinity to what: to the medium or to the care-work of the family process of mourning? What constitutes "qualitative parts" in a personal mourning work? Does quality imply an aesthetic caliber? What is "true partnership"? Is its status amiable or contractual? Is true partnership gained through co-creation, forms of support and containment, or maybe through fair compensation? Whether the booklet renders concrete categories of labor, investment, creativity, and knowledge, or rather leaves them in the abstract, within the rhetoric of service professionalization is only advised or informed on.

Michel Foucault tracks the ways methods of self-care and self-knowledge derive directly from the constitutive framework of power.[5] According to Foucault, in modern statehood sovereign power is gradually substituted by governmentality or the managing of the population's needs. In his writings, Foucault refers to those practices carved by the state but performed by individuals as "tactics" or "technologies."[6] Can we think of "paths of commemoration" as a set of tactics whose end is governmentality? The booklet underscores the intimate, haptic qualities of video, describing it as generating "a live and visceral documentation of the fallen soldier, [and] allow[ing] the family and the next generations to have a visual memory of their loved one, to hear his voice and experience feelings and descriptions told by his friends and acquaintances."[7] Video emerges as a technology that best configures the permeable nature of an expanded self, a subject which is individuated, embodied, and affective, yet at the same time formulated, reproducible, and scrutinized by the state. Video is a subjugating technic. The terminology itself, the choice of the word "paths," rather than the more literal "venues" or "practices," disassociates state power or utilitarian logic from one's own selfhood. The booklet's cautionary "Preliminary Thought" section demonstrates the meeting point between technic and subjecthood, mediating the apparatus to psychic life.

Institutes of care are a part of what is allegedly the state's "nonpolitical" institutions, assisting citizens to find way to cope with their loss. Nevertheless, issued by the Ministry of Defense to families whose dead were soldiers at the time of their death, such logic of care is also a matter of national endurance and a component of the sovereign tools of military power. It participates in the necropolitical imbalance in

Israel-Palestine in which only Jewish-Israeli lives are sanctioned by law, care, and symbolic or material capital. These direct links are obscured by the position of the state as a bettering system of governance rather than a sovereign. Published in 2010, with most of its listed techniques already formalized, the booklet seems to suggest that a certain conduct and a certain need had preceded the official response. As this book clearly shows, a decade into the new century the personal commemorative video was already a common format, broadcast on television and supported by a dynamic production infrastructure. Bureaucracy is never about inventing new paths, but about consolidating what is already out there and disciplining it through the form of the document. Indeed, the booklet does not open up new venues or advocate new techniques, yet it establishes those techniques as a standard and signals a process of institutionalization of certain "paths of commemoration."

While the state-issued brochure marks an institutional permanence, the emergence of video memorials was indirectly prompted by the Office of Families and Commemoration's continuing policy with regard to personal memory as the locus of the state's care work. The Office of Families and Commemoration[8] also now contains the Department for the Commemoration of Soldiers. Both are administrative branches of the state Ministry of Defense. In the past decade, this institutional complex rapidly shifted, reorganizing its operational foci and hierarchies. The Department for the Commemoration of Soldiers is a specialized unit with an extensive jurisdiction. It facilitates and finances the establishment and maintenance of military cemeteries, the erection of commemorative monuments, the publication of books, the uploading and maintenance of a web platform, and the observance of fallen soldiers' memory. The Office of Families and Commemoration houses these activities as well as financial and rehabilitating aspects related more specifically to bereaved families. Its realization of commemoration as something extended from the state level to civil society, to the level of the individual, is predicated on a stable division between private and public, and at the same time shows the contingencies of this very allocation. The office encourages and forms families' private initiatives via the intersecting channels of institutional and private commemoration, its counseling function, and its financial support, specifically through a "private commemoration grant"—amounting in 2020 to 7,803INS, equivalent to approximately US$2,300[9]—as well as loans and tax benefits. As part of these services, the office keeps itself informed of trends of commemoration, and is often addressed by families seeking advice. The latter triggered the writing of the booklet.

The space of private commemoration is therefore a category formed and designed by the state. Put differently, what is designated as private or personal is not *a priori*, but a sphere that is realized through the politics and policies of memory. In 1975, the Office of Families and Commemoration issued a booklet dedicated to personal memory with the same title as the 2010 version, *Paths of Commemoration*. Following the 1973 War, also known as the Yom Kippur War, the high numbers of the missing, wounded, and dead led the Ministry of Defense to radically revise its policy regarding the state's handling of bereaved families. With this organizational change it spotlighted the family's own mourning needs.

The 1975 survey of commemoration activities designates public commemoration as institutionally determined, practiced by municipalities, workers unions, youth movements, sport clubs, or schools, and as dedicated to a collective of soldiers. Personal commemoration, according to the booklet, centers a subject who is specific. The particularity of its subject notwithstanding, in 1975 personal commemoration is still geared towards civil society, whereas the family is positioned as instrumental rather than the subject of advice. In the 1975 booklet's opening essay, professor Efraim A. Auerbach writes:

> [The people] will not give away the greatest accomplishment of political independence and the people's freedom. The fallen had fallen for this, and their memory demands that we shall follow their ways. And it should be made clear: their memory does not grant us, those who remember—be it bereaved parents, widows or orphans—any special rights, but the right to remember more, and to be able to pass on this memory to those who owe gratitude for not being personally and intimately affected. . . . This memory, if perceived as right, can forestall hopelessness, weakening of the spirit, and provide our generation and the ones to follow a source of encouragement and faith.[10]

According to Auerbach, commemoration, even when personal, is a civic duty; memory is a national-spiritual asset pertaining to narratives of sovereign freedom; and the bereaved are cast in the role of those who secure the strength of national morals. In 2010, on the other hand, commemoration is rather a concern of private practices, serving self-healing and self-formation.

Auerbach was a professor of Judaism and a bereaved father himself. It is not specified in what capacity he was chosen to open the 1975 booklet. It is perhaps not by chance that the above statements were substituted in 2010 with a rather laconic introduction by an administrator, the head of the Office for Family and Commemoration, Mr. Arye Mu'alem. The 1975 booklet notes the spiritual rendering of personal expression, whereas in 2010 the rhetoric is one of management, measures, and outcomes. In 1975, the pain of loss is channeled to national ethos; in 2010 it is all about containing and buffering pain, transforming it into meaning and production, even a product. The state prompts the personalization of memory as of 1975, while the 2010 constellation reveals the effect of *privatization* of the personal. The 1975 booklet lists activities that stretch across the fields of leisure, culture, religion and science, such as beautifying outdoor spaces, editing an anthology of writings, holding scientific conferences, dedicating scientific publications, and launching educational programs, scholarships, and sport events. Here, the personal is not a mode of production, but rather a locus of social imagination. In 2010, personal memory is translated into a set of production niches that cater to a privatized economy of service providers—themselves, I will later show, actors in the free market and a direct product of privatization. While *Paths of Commemoration* (the 2010 version) is no longer available on the Ministry of Defense webpage, in the decade that has passed since its writing, the Office of Families and Commemoration public interface has adopted digital governance tools that highlight transparency, accessibility, and indeed services, while further toning down on the formal language that presents commemoration as a national-symbolic asset.

The state logic of care is grounded in the rise of the privatized state and its shift towards a privatized mode of production where the role of the state is mostly to advise, support, or facilitate; where media is modeled according to the free market and funded by private money. The rhetoric of the booklet positions the family as the unknowledgeable that needs to consult, highlighting questions of the family's investments and capacities as a matter of both material and emotional affordances. Most importantly, it positions the family as the one whose free choice and affordances lead the process of commemoration. This mix of nuanced sensitivity to the mournful family's emotional fragility on the one hand, and direct approach to matters of productivity on the other, and above all the delegation of choice, is what I term a *rhetoric of service*. It opens up a space for needs and at the same time delimits the contexts and conditions in which these needs are fulfilled. The 2010 booklet is designed to circumvent a top-down model that organizes memory into symbolic currency, and to underscore instead the agency of the bereaved. Its rhetoric of service carefully omits any implications of authority, designating private acts of creativity and mediation as beyond state regulation. Indeed, a rhetoric of service becomes a new lingua franca between the state and its citizens in the age of neoliberal governance, guiding rather than regulating citizens.

While the booklet carefully eschews any act of directing and uses self-help prose to establish a naturalized and neutralized position, it offers a glimpse into the ways in which the state perceives itself as assisting its citizens in implementing their roles as state subjects. Although the language is tacit and nebulous—that very tacitness being a defining aspect of the governance mechanism at play—what emerges is a structure of *affinity or proximity* between the family and non-state entities in the work of memory. In this scheme the role of the state is that of an uninvolved, uninterested party that expresses care by outsourcing the work to professional authority, a proxy. The family's proxy is assigned by or to the family, a media expert to whom the family expropriates the emotionally intense labor of commemorating: intimacy-by-proxy. The family's proxy is also a figure situated outside or at the periphery of commercial media, and it is from that very periphery that they can extend their services to the family: (mass) media-by-proxy. Although ostensibly self-used, these techniques are predicated on privatized professional labor in a systematic commodification of the family's memories and the de-regulation of the media market, an extra-state structure in which both work and professional knowledge are outsourced to the realm of the personal.

A consistent mode of production based on protocoled standards, contracted labor, investments and gains might feel alien to the personal video with its connotations of autonomy, creativity and idiosyncrasy— at least in media studies. To read the booklet's advice as policy entails traversing the rhetoric of service, reflecting not on the subject of address, but on the systematic rationale that positions the subject in terms of expertise, professionalism, and technique. The state indirectly regulates the subject's self-realization through making transparent the object of technology or expertise, and, in doing so, delimiting the subject's own sphere of autonomy, "the personal." But subjectivity, this chapter shows, is produced through infrastructural efforts, standards, private services and investments. Although ostensibly autonomous, the personal is at once stripped of its politics and controlled through the technocracies of mourning. This rhetoric reappears in the way private memory producers—NGOs, entrepreneurs, and freelancers—brand their practice, with a similar tacitness and circumvention. Tracing a protocol of

FIGURE 7. Screenshot of the Ministry of Defense's Families and Commemoration Office website, accessed on August 20, 2015.

production, even if through what is omitted or left as a blank space, explicates the work of these intimate proxies and their affinities to the family on the one hand, and to commercial mass media on the other.

NON-GOVERNMENTAL ORGANIZATION

The Paratroops Heritage Association was founded in 1993 by paratrooper alumni, all of whom had extended periods of service in higher command. The association is funded by donations and is supported mostly through volunteer work done by paratrooper alumni or bereaved families. Its activities include maintaining communal infrastructures of support and mentorship for injured paratroopers and the corps' bereaved families, caring for the paratroopers' commemorative sites, and giving lectures at schools and community centers about the corps' heritage. In 1999 the association launched a commemorative video project, ostensibly oriented towards the bereaved families. The video project was part of a larger vision held by the association about the potential of digital technology for memory practices and was conceived in tandem with the digitization of boxes full of ephemera—pictures, letters, and notes—that were found deteriorating in a storage space owned by the paratroops. Envisioning an interactive interface, the association was planning to use the digitized files and the videos for a new heritage museum, as of 2022 still unrealized.[11] The digitization campaign, and with it the video project, initially aimed at creating a digital memory for each fallen paratrooper. To date, the association claims to have produced more than four hundred videos.

The vision that induced the Paratroops Heritage Association's video project centers the relationship between memory and technology. With the launching of the video project, its advocates emphatically promoted what was back then a new technology as the remedy for a fading first-hand memory. Amir Keren, a former lieutenant colonel in the paratroops, stated provocatively:

> We, who had participated in these wars [1948, 1956, 1967, 1973], remembered each and every name. What is going to happen if the people don't remember their fallen? We made a movie on Yitzhak Ben-Menachem. Do you know him? Everybody called him Gulliver. He was killed at a position near the Sea of Galilee in the 'War of Independence' [1948]. . . . And there are no relatives. Our generation knows, but the kids don't. And here you go, you have a movie, and he's no longer anonymous.[12]

"This [video] is the best method to keep this material long enough and to present it in a way which feels alive," Tzila Halevi contended. Halevi, a volunteer and herself a paratrooper's widow, asserted: "In the future, few will search through the [cardboard] files, and I'm not sure if the next generation of families will keep all these cardboard boxes stuffed with materials like I do. These movies, I know they'll keep."[13] Both Keren and Halevi were armed with a discourse of rescue and preservation. Despite the association's recurrent emphasis that the project caters to the families, Halevi's comment seems to imply that the family is a container in which memory is stored and preserved, initially through the format of cardboard boxes, then through DVDs.

Mobilizing digital production formats to disseminate their causes, the association reflects a dominant mode of operation in late 1990s NGOs.[14] The rise of NGOs as a nexus of social activities external to the state is one of the defining characteristics of the neoliberal regime, delegating some of the state's economic, political, and cultural responsibility to the non-governmental.[15] Yet unlike the status of memory in the privatized state, per Keren, the affordances of digital technology—its impact on aspects of production, circulation and accessibility—are meant to support traditional codes of combative brotherhood, sovereignty in its most traditional form of fraternity. The association's video project merged different needs and aspirations.

Information about the internal administration of the Paratroops Heritage Association's video project is partial, and the project itself was contingent, with many discrepancies between what was planned and what eventually happened. These contingencies were manifested in the condition of the association archive when I visited there in the summer of 2013. The association's offices were housed in two cramped mobile units in the Ammunition Hill in Jerusalem and were maintained by a civilian volunteer. A small room in the association's offices hosted the video project in the form of DVDs, arranged alphabetically, alongside some commemorative books, stuck on dusty shelves. Also in the room, two computers served as viewing positions. My request to view documents that chronicled the production process, vision statements, or agreements with filmmakers and with families, was met with confusion. As in many other cases, the commemoration of a lost soldier is perceived as an emotional matter rather than a practice that deserves consecutive preservation. Recuperation pertains to the lost person rather than the means of reproduction. By chance, the association's retiring CEO, Ofer Kleifeld, was there that day to clean his office. He directed me to a pile of papers that he was planning to throw in the trash on his way out. The papers were contained in a single plastic folder, in no particular order. The folder included contracts, internal and external memos, consent forms, production notes, and filmmaker statements. All of these materials were in a state of flux. While the documents certainly suggest the protocol of a systematic production mode, their disposability and fragmentation attest the ontological instability of the quasi-institutional video. In what follows I use these traces found in the association offices as the basis of my analysis of the set of relations between the family, media professionals, and the association as an interested third party.

In its early years, the project was headed by Itzik Nadan, a paratrooper alumnus whose signature appears on most of the documents from that period. In 2000, a special steering committee was appointed.[16] Most of the committee's meeting reports at the outset of the project are about establishing a feasible funding scheme.[17] A year or two into the project, the committee was dealing with 210 videos in different stages of production and sought to produce a further 200, with priority given to fallen soldiers who had no kin to preserve their memory, whose parents had died or were aging. While some donation money supported the project, in planning its funding scheme the committee members counted on the commemoration grant given by the Office of Families and Commemoration. However, these funds are allocated to the family directly, and it is up to the family to decide whether and how it wants to spend them. The committee discussed how to inform families about their rights, and moreover, how to ensure that once families claimed the grant they would invest it in the video project. In the association's spirit of solidarity, the financial scheme is based on families making a general donation, with those who could afford it supporting those families lacking the means.[18] The paratroopers' fraternity dictates a sort of collective that muddies the demarcated sphere of the private.

Initially, decisions related to form and representation were also taken collectively. Leveraging its buying capital, the association approached a number of production companies[19] and asked them for a sample video. According to information provided by a letter to the families, the sample videos were screened to the paratroops' bereaved families in assemblies held by the association across the country. Responses were collected and reviewed by a committee comprised of family representatives, members of the association, and "professionals." The category of professionalism, originally mentioned in the letter, remains vague; the documents do not explicate whether they are professional in the field of mental support, army representatives, or media experts. Being self-appointed and volunteer-based, the committee could have used any of these consultations. The budget limitation and the scope of the production—a video for each one of the 1200 fallen paratroopers—necessitated a rather uniform format for the video. The association restricted the length of the videos to between seven and twelve minutes.

An internal memo titled "The Production of a Memorial Video—The Paratroop's Association Working Process" describes the measures taken by the organization in the production of a single video.[20] The first section, dedicated to the initiating party, proposes two scenarios in which either the family or the association initiate the video. The following sections list costs, bookkeeping, paperwork, and the logistics of handling the completed video. This last section concerns copies and media formats. The distribution of formats—DVD, mini DV, video flash file—correlates with the distribution of memory and media across different social sectors. The question of format encompasses a typology that stabilizes industrial protocols and indicates usability, mode of address, and affinity: DVD for the family, mini DV for the association's own stack, and so on. The memo attests to how a third party administrates the video, an object of which it is neither the producer nor the primary consumer. Another form is meant to regulate communication with the families. This form is composed of a series of blank spaces to be filled out by the family: the name of the deceased and the date they died, the applicants' contact details, date of application, and then, for the administrator, the filmmaker's contact date and the date a script was approved. The sequence of blank spaces creates a template into which singular information can be inscribed, rendered standard. Unlike general communication sent to the paratroops' bereaved families about the project, the application form is a direct form of exchange between parties, with the blank space being bureaucracy's most sincere gesture towards its subject. In the form, under the box titled "payment," an extended blank space is opened for transgressions; below that, another cavity under the prompt "additional comments." Literally and figuratively, these blank intervals leave a space on the surface of the protocol to single out and disrupt the prevailing unity, to make explicit the financial binding, and to make room for exceptions.

What was this blank space left for the individuated family in the association's mass production project? The project is predicated on a certain duality, positioning the family as the project's addressee on the one hand, and its resource on the other. In 1999, with the initiation of the video project, the association sent a letter to the paratroop corps's bereaved families detailing the steps leading to establishing the project media contractor. It invited families to join the project by filling out a form that they could send to the general address. This application form was absent from the copy I found. Two almost identical letters, one dated May 28, 2007, and one April 2013, however, are more explicit in their prodding of families to cooperate with what is designated as a benign service for them.[21] The letters describe the resulting video as "a personal and vivid documentation of each and every one of the fallen soldiers" and the overall project as "short videos that include chapters (bits) of the son's life and the circumstances of his falling."[22] The letters stress the association's commitment to the memory of the dead and disclose its possible use of the video for its own aims. The letters also assert that the videos are made by professionals—here explicitly media professionals—and indicate the potential for public exposure. Both letters end with recognizing the emotional difficulties that the process might entail for the bereaved and assure that the association will accompany the family throughout.

Taking upon itself the counseling mandate, the paratroops NGO extends the private channels of what Michel Foucault has famously termed "governmentality," linked with the economization of political life.[23] Foucault's formulation elucidates the political logic underlining the state's advice, echoed here by the private association. Governing, according to Foucault, is a way of managing the population through means that are essential and vital to it, with the goal of maintaining the population's wealth. Foucault notes that "the population is the subject of needs, of aspiration, but it is also the object in the hands of the government, *aware, vis-a-vis the government, of what it wants, but ignorant of what is being done to it.*"[24] Later in his lecture, Foucault describes the governmentalization of the state as "at once internal and external to the state, since it is the tactics of government which makes possible the continual definition and redefinition of what is *within the competence of the state and what is not, the public versus the private and so on.*"[25] According to the logic of governmentality the state advises on, provides, or offers solution to needs; however, the structures of control and management that underline such forms of response are obscured. Here the obscurity is doubled by these services' relegation to the non-governmental, a privatized governing entity that mimics (at times replaces) the state mechanism.

At this point Foucault differentiates sovereignty and governmentality. Sovereignty preserves power through the direct infliction of authority via concrete laws and institutions, while governmentality assures the survival of the state precisely because it is not linked to the centralization of power. Rather, it is concerned with making things available, with employing tactics which serve a "plurality of specific ends."[26] The plurality of ends—or even, the plural singularity of the dead—highlights personalized needs and choices. Providing advice, securing benefits, offering solutions, negotiating collective buying capital, mediating between personal wellbeing and the media industry, all of these services are offered by state or its substituting private entities. Indeed, the rhetoric of service is salient for the way different organs of memory production, working in the private sector, introduce themselves to the family. The market of private services and governmental or non-governmantal care coincide. Personal memory, though still concatenate to aspects of sovereignty, irrevocably departs from the state form and, outsourced to the private sector, reintroduces itself as a practice of self-care and the creation of an everlasting memory.

In line with the circumventing semantics that matters of care seem to necessitate, another address to the bereaved families brings up the issue of payments. Tackling this sensitive matter, this letter uses the euphemism "bumps in the road"—bumpy because, as the address acknowledges, the family needs to pay for a formation of feelings of loss, something that can be perceived as beyond exchange value.[27] In a performative self-reflection, the letter addresses "those who promote the project," suggesting that variations to the video's unified format can be introduced if the ordering family covers the additional costs. These "bumps" the letter wishes to circumvent might indicate more substantial issues compromising the association's vision. In addressing the families, the association's terminology contains an intriguing mix of emotional accountability and managerial rationalization. Didacticism on the process of administration or production and precautionary acknowledgement protrude as rhetorical means of carefulness, buffering complicated feelings. Beyond their careful phrasing these documents do not address this complexity directly, apart from those places in which potential feelings, mostly negative, are regarded as something to be avoided.

Its cause of catering to bereaved families notwithstanding, the project was premised on massification and formatting. The association's location in an institutional matrix, drawing on the families in relaying matters of national heritage, yet situated outside the state, partly lead to such plurality of singularization. Another factor was media access. Drawing on a collective mandate, the project was predicated on equal access to the means of production and consequently an individual token for each and every family. Facilitating equal access necessitates uniformity. Yet, that very access was mobilized as a way to call on individuality. The project is predicated on a confusing mix of idiosyncrasy and reproducing collective ethos.

This dualism is salient in the association's different addresses to the families. The open letter extends an invitation to the family while softening uneasy truths, namely, that what is for them an articulation of irrevocable loss is for others a matter to administrate or a source of livelihood. Another form, an untitled templated document, adds a logistical perspective, parsing responsibilities and outcomes.[28] The form provides "definitions" (that is, it establishes the entities partnering in the making of the video: the association, the family, and a videomaker), as well as "emphases" (that is, the nature of the partnership), and specifies the ultimate usages of the final product. It is the association that assigns a videomaker to the family; the family is responsible for all source materials and for clearing copyrights on materials it has not authored. The family also needs to grant its consent for the final video. The form seems to stand for a contractual abidance, officiating the relationship between the family and the association. When it comes to the mechanisms of video production, the association leaves things unspecified, providing a short description of the video length and general idea. In that same pile of papers, there was also a template of a work agreement with a videomaker, outlining timelines, outputs, terms of compensation, and formal standards.[29] In fact, the video project was managed with very little understanding of media, and the technological, aesthetic, and financial aspects of video production were its ongoing blind spot. In the aforementioned family form, the association requests that no credits appear in the video besides its own logo, shown at the video's opening and end. Not only the intimate singularity of loss is diminished in the association's project, but the uniqueness as well as authority of artistic practice, since this is, after all, about uniformity-as-equality and mass production.

An internal memo from Memorial Day 2006 surveys the following distribution of produced content in mass media: Channel 10 bought three hours of broadcasting material for the sum of US$3000, which consisted of a total of eighteen videos; Channel 1 broadcast seven videos out of the nine ordered, and all of these orders were per families' requests and therefore with no cost involved; an overseas broadcaster targeting the Israeli diaspora aired five videos and made a 550NIS donation; the educational television broadcast ten videos; Channel 48, a local cable channel and subsidiary of the TV network HOT, received thirty-eight videos, but broadcast only twenty-nine due to technical problems. The videos were broadcast in one set that was re-run four times across the day and the channel, in return for the content, displayed a slide with the association's logo and contact information.[30] "The internet," notes the memo, should be the association's next targeted distribution platform. It details that fifty-two videos were sent to YNET, an online news platform run by the media conglomerate Yediot Achronot, out of which forty were put online with a link to the association's webpage. As the memo discloses, not all videos programmed were distributed by the association. Some were sent by the families, some were broadcast on more than one channel, some broadcasters paid for the content, but agreements and exchanges are varied. The internal survey frames the instrumental role played by mass media, and more specifically television, in prolonging the video project. However, the document lacks a consistent strategy of distribution. It seems like the association simply took what it could get, without too much leveraging of its production volume. Nevertheless profits were never its objective.[31] When it comes to video memorials, both the NGO and television have had malleable policies of exclusivity and profit-making. Television needed the association's video production to populate its programming schedule; the association needed the exposure.

The association's video project necessitates a rationalized and pro-tocoled set of standards. Formats, costs, production, and aims—all these must be discussed, systematized, and communicated to families, to video-makers and, as a consensual measure, among the association members. Between the association's vision of a videotaped beacon for every dead paratrooper to be stored in a commemorative hall and what eventually took place, schisms prevail. The association's heritage objective did not necessarily coincide with the families' own vision of their commemora-tive video, or with material conditions and artistic visions inflicted by videomakers. Even the aforementioned commemorative hall is still a 3D-rendered architectural model on the association's website, pointing to a grandiose plan that did not materialize—not yet. The survey of the project itself draws on future oriented genres: statements of *purpose*, letters of *invitation*, empty templated forms *to be filled in* by family members, anticipating a future commitment and attempting to prevent a future conflict.

Handwritten notes attached to the forms, marked at the margins or on the backs of pages, disclose the gap between a statement and its realization, formal and informal channels of communication, or the splitting of addressees and interests. On the back of a copy of "letter to the families" dated May 1999, a note directed to "Ofer" (probably Ofer Kleifeld, the association's CEO from 2006–2013) orders that in the up-coming Memorial Day a video dedicated to Aharon Gordon and one dedicated to Ya'akov Sofer will be broadcast.[32] Appearing on the other side of the homogenizing format, the comment makes room for priori-tization and signaling-out. A note attached to a letter to the families from 2007, addressing Kleifeld and signed by videomaker Eytan Dotan, provides a short explanation about preparatory steps for the produc-tion of a video with the following observation: "Generally in documen-taries you use the narrator to tell the facts and the interviews provide the emotions, [and add] perspective, and personal experiences."[33] While the letter to the families positions their memory at the center, the added note delimits it as an emotion underlining "the facts," a formal convention. A certain duality translates into the graphic layout of the official form with its penned afterthought. As in any mass project there is the ideal and then there is what is actually happening.

As this bundle of documents clearly indicates, the family was the owner of the source material but not quite the author of its formulated memo-ries; videomakers were expected to negotiate between singularity and mass production; and the association was a mediator between families

העמותה להנחלת מורשת הצנחנים

תאריך: ....

נוסח הסכם פרט פורטרט

בין:
העמותה להנחלת מורשת הצנחנים ("העמותה"), עמותה רשומה מס' 580225753
כתובת: גבעת התחמושת, שד' אשכול ת.ד. 18580, ירושלים 91183
E.mail: prtropgt@internet-zahav.net .02-5327421 פקס .02-5326291 טל'

לבין:
מס' זהות........ ("המפיק")................
כתובת: .... טלפון: .... E.mail: ....

1. העמותה מזמינה מהמפיק לבצע הפקת פרט דיוקן והוצאה עבור החלל-.
שם פרטי: .... שם משפחה:............
2. המפיק מצהיר בזאת שהינו בעל ידע מקצועי וביכולתו לזכות את הסרט לשביעות רצון העמותה ומשפחת החלל.
3. הסרט יבוצע תוך תאום עם המשפחה.
4. רכות פרודיקט הסרטים בעמותה תיעזר את הקשר בין המפיק למשפחה וחיא תסייע למיני בעשר עם המשפחה במהלך הבנת הסרט.
5. המפיק יבצע את כל העשי/לית הנדרשות לביצוע הסרט כולל, מפגש עם המשפחה, תחקיר, איסוף חומר, הכנת תסריט, העברת התסריט לאישור רכות הסרטים והמשפחה, ביצוע שינויים לתסריט, צילום, עריכה, הגשת הסרט למשפחה ולרכות הסרטים, ביצוע תיקונים ועריכה סופית, אישור עריכה סופית ושיכפול עותקים של הסרט הסופי.
6. המפיק יס יום את הפקת הסרט (הגשת העתקים הסופי-ים) תוך 3 חודשים מחתימת הסכם זה.
7. במידה ותעורר קשיים ו/או עידוד תסופת זמן לסיום הסכת הסרט, יפנה המפיק לרכות הסרטים/גוהל העמותה ויקבל אישורים בכתב. פנית המפיק תתבצע לא פחות מ- 15 ימים מתום המועד הראשון שנקבע לסיום הסרט. המפיק יצין בבקשתו את סיבת הדחייה ומשך הזמן הנוסף שידרש לסיום הסרט.
8. המחיר עבור ביצוע הסרט היו 5,000 ₪. לסכום יתוסף מע"מ כחוק.

בכבוד העמותה/המשפחה, שד' אשכול ת.ד. 18580, ירושלים 91183
E.mail: prtropgt@internet-zahav.net .02-5327421 פקס .02-5326291 טל'

FIGURE 8. The Paratroops Heritage Association, "Agreement for the Production of a Portrait Film" (generic form), found document.

and video, or feelings and technics. The association passed information, DVD copies, ephemera and funds from families to filmmakers to broadcasters. It negotiated salaries and timetables amid a sensation of excruciating mourning and the singularity of loss. The protocols were composed of internal memos, handwritten notes, meeting minutes, application forms, contracts with authors, broadcasting records, and addresses to the family, each one of which possesses a different conception of the project. This play of dispositives configures the institutional and ideological complexity of the family media proxy.

STANDARDS

Among the documents found in the Paratroops Heritage Association's offices is a fourteen-page proposal written by Eytan Dotan together with Udi Ben Dror, under the brand name Tzelem Enosh ("A Human Image").[34] The proposal, addressed to the paratroops organization, provides a full breakdown of production costs and tasks. Attempting to streamline what is planned to be a mass production project, Dotan and Ben Dror offer what they term "standards." "One cannot escape the use of certain templates and genres and styles," they write. "Obviously, each movie will be different due to its protagonist and his story, but each will be packaged by pre-conceived patterns of directing and editing."[35] The standard, according to Dotan and Ben Dror, is a productional necessity that bridges the custom-made and the generic, between the singularity of loss and a reproduced template. For media, standards are stabilizing measures that pertain to the category of format or genre. Whether a material container that dictates the way information is arranged and delivered[36] or a formal foundation that indicates cultural and industrial modes of production, standards are prerequisites of media's institutional consistency.[37] For institutions of governing, the standard transforms life and death from particular singularities into something administratable.

Dotan, who seems to be the main author of this document, is a man of unique style. He describes things excessively and tends to get into the heads of producers, "customers," and viewers alike, stipulating their assumed perception of the video and its process of production. The proposal's grandiloquent prose and its status *as* a proposal—an outline of the tentative, even the ideal—makes this protocol a blueprint of the social dynamics and desires around the so-called personal family production. In particular, the notion of standards encapsulates the set of tensions involved: between the family mourning and managing loss, between artistic expression and operational logistics, between a more traditional model of media and memory production and a free market economy, between different agents and interests involved in the reproduction of Jewish-Israeli military loss.

At the outset of the proposal Dotan pitches his readers six formulas. "Standard A: A Story of Words" is built around a formal element. Dotan describes a potential flow: a smooth camera movement panning over inscriptions in memorial books, newspapers, and monuments, which then cuts to stills of the deceased; it might include archival audio of the deceased's relatives, but no interviews. It ends, according to Dotan, with "a final image that tells a lot about the character, fade-out, and a line or a sentence from a poem which is related to memory."[38] In "Standard B: The Story of a Battle," a linear tracking shot chronicles the events that resulted in the death of the video's subject. This dramatic sequence is embedded with what Dotan terms "windows" to the deceased's life-course. In "Standard C: Friends Tell," Dotan draws on testimonials. "This format might be weighty and slower," he warns. "The stories are fresh and in cases in which the surroundings are themselves fascinating characters, this format can prove to be very effective. Of course, you need to add to it all the usual elements."[39] Dotan does not explain what he means by either "effective" or "usual elements." "Standard D: A Life's Project" focuses, like standard B, on one particular aspect or event in order to portray the lost loved one. The last formula remains rather open and enigmatic. Standard E, "Reenactments and Illustrations," is associated with soldiers who practiced art, photography, or painting. Dotan suggests that in such cases, the artistic practice should become "meaningful for their story."[40]

Packaging personhood into standards is part of the pragmatism of mass reproduction. It is also the outcome of a form of representation that seeks parallel channels, some more intimate, some allegorical. Dotan's standards establish different epistemologies of subjectivity. Standard A understands subjectivity as a discursive construction, standard B seems to formulate the subject as historically determined, standard C constitutes the subject through performative speech, standards D and E read the subject as a metonym of desire or aesthetic expression. At the end of the section, Dotan adds a clause entitled "Beacons" where he formulates an additional standard, pertinent to unusual stories that might draw wider attention and be of interest for television broadcasters as full-length documentaries. This retrospective standard forges the subject as a public subject. It reminds us that television and mass media are always in the prospect of the personal family video.

Dotan and Ben Dror designate families, visitors to the Paratroop's commemorative sites, students, tour guides, and teachers as the videos' audiences. The latter, they add, can use the video as a resource in their teaching. Dotan and Ben Dror qualify themselves by highlighting their professional skills and background, but also their attention to the families who carry possible feelings of "frustration, anger, rage and disappointment." They never address what might cause these difficult feelings. On their approach to the medium, they write: "the cinematic aspect, unlike the book or the written word, suffers a certain flatness, generalization, hastiness, and an overload of details which can at times make a quasi-boring statement. On the other hand, the cinematic aspect can touch life, activate our emotions, feelings, make closer, illustrate, engulf."[41] The statement is confusing as it seems to diminish Dotan and Ben Dror's own medium, describing it as flat, generalizing, and even boring. Perhaps this is meant to indicate that video can "touch" and "activate" only if handled by the right person.

Dotan's résumé, found on an industry database in 2015, demonstrates extensive experience in commercial and industrial filmmaking.[42] His profile designated film production according to the professional-private dichotomy and was organized according to the categories of "television," "PR work," "industrial filmmaking," "electoral and municipal videos," "commercials," and "personal films," followed by the description: "to touch people's truth. Simple, clean, no effects and other noises."[43] Dotan, and other filmmakers surveyed in the following section, belong to a sector of producers situated at the periphery of commercial media. Working for the private sector, their body of production can be defined through what Haidee Wasson and Charles Acland term "useful cinema," putting forward utility and disciplining functions of film and video.[44] Dotan's work with the Paratroops Heritage Association appears in a separate paragraph in which he is described as one of the video project's key figures, having promoted the production of dozens of videos and, in special cases, expanded them to television documentary work. A closer look into his filmography discovers mostly private commissions and marginal production jobs in the mass media industry. There is no indication as to how instrumental he was for the paratroops' association project. The résumé, like the proposal, are documents that entail factual aspects as well as performative and tentative elements.

"Standards" or "Beacons"—thinking through the conundrum of containing personhood in ready-made templates lead Dotan and Ben Dror to develop what they term "the other way." Labeled as *other*, this production protocol is meant to digress practices associated with mass-produced media and to promote a closer collaboration between producers and subjects. Instead of a technical outsourcing rendered to the family, in this alternate mode the videomaker, teamed up with "researchers" (also termed "hosts"), editor, cinematographer, and an animator, meet with the family in a neutral location and embark on an intense day of brainstorming, workshopping, and mutually leading the creative process. Here, videomaking, though still related to constrains of time and budget, evolves by creating intimacy between makers and family members. In a carefully phrased passage Dotan offers a method that will buffer the family's "very understandable frustration." The model he develops assumes a preliminary conflict of interest between a rationalized and professionalized agent and what Dotan approaches as eruptive feelings, embodied by the bereaved family. "The other way" means to form close collaboration, or rather, to create intimacy in order to better control a potentially escalating situation. Placed in a monitored and sterilized environment, the family's feelings and the anticipated conflict can be contained. Even if as a model "the other way" was never implemented, it forecloses the presuppositions that guide Dotan in approaching the production of personal video memorials and is predicated on the binary between the two entities entering this partnership, the family and its proxy. Reading through his ambitious vision, I was left wondering: Is a videomaker the qualified person to mend difficult feelings?

"A few brief moments of touch, of a glance, a few stories, images, voices which will momentarily surface characteristics, thoughts, dreams and doings, [which will] screen and illuminate a few lines[,] which [will] draw a figure, animate a portrait, enable knowing, facilitate an encounter," poeticize Dotan and Ben Dror.[45] Their descriptions are uncanny. On the skill of navigating between the procedural and the singular they write: "although there is a need for efficiency, and in a number of formats and elements . . . personal movies cannot be turned into a hamburger industry."[46] In contrast, their job description is as follows: "touching the most sensitive nerve in the Israeli being" and "paying our debt to the bereaved family" while "uniting and strengthening" the "extended family."[47] Such prose appears in the proposal whenever its authors attend the role of the family. The style abstracts aspects that a proposal needs to make concrete: timelines, plans, and costs. Even before the video, the style itself is a manifestation of authority, already doing the work of organizing what is postulated to be the family's feelings into aesthetic form. With this, Dotan understands his task not as merely producing a video, but working on behalf of something or someone. The proxy's task, as we come to understand, is to translate mourning work into production work and to negotiate family feelings with the pragmatics of money, schedules, labor, and technology. What the proxy provides to the family is not only video-knowledge, or the video itself as an artefact, but the services of mediating production pragmatism and feeling, performed here through such verbal maneuvering. The paradox is that the very function of the proxy understands the family as separated from these sites of value, knowledge, and reproduction.

The rhetorical juggling is not only a translation of different interests—that of the family versus the producer, for instance—but is directly linked to different business models, one predicated on a free market of privatized service providers catering to individuals, the other assuming radical equality as an expression of the common. The latter is the model guiding the paratroops' organization, the former was becoming the prevalent mode of production when Dotan wrote his proposal. The different perceptions are manifested most obviously in the proposal's budget breakdown. The budgeting is a collective calculus based on a number of videos per month. Most likely written in the early 2000s, a sum of $38,400 US would purchase the production of fifteen to twenty videos a month, lasting five to ten minutes each, including the work of a researcher, a cinematographer, an editor, a producer and a director, and the costs of an editing studio, music, narration, mix, offices, meeting rooms, equipment, archival footage, computer, and graphics.[48] "The other way" also includes budgeting for an artistic director, production manager, logistics, hosting, and decoration which, along with the basic costs, adds up to a total of $47,400. Dotan presents a financial model according to which, in order to eliminate class-distributed access, families make a general donation, rather than a per-video payment. He also postulates that this way will generate families' commitment to the overall project. He makes a counter-proposal for a privatized process for the sum of $1000–1500 per minute of video. It should be noted that the scale and scope of production Dotan is proposing is larger than what a project of family commemoration can ever provide.

Dotan's proposal is intriguing and deserves a closer look precisely because it is a transitionary manifestation. Once the privatized mode takes over, there will be no more proposals and vision statements, since the video becomes a service tailored to each family's size, where services are determined based on direct and discrete communication. Overtly poeticizing the family's pain might come across as poor judgment or charlatanism—Dotan's vision is contaminated with both—but it is also a product of the uneasy reconciliation of discourses of care or solidarity and the commodity form. The proposal is an articulation of trying to satisfy subjectivity, both as individuated or agential and as a standard. It brands the videomaker in between an intimate-by-proxy and a mass-manufacturing professional. Moving between production niches, Dotan represents the free market while still leveraging the symbolic capital of national ethos (the sovereign's tools).

This is, too, a proposal for a form-to-be, a preliminary and speculative formation that discloses a certain social imagination of the place and functions of the personal memorial video. In the Paratroops Heritage Association documents there was no indication regarding to what extent Dotan's proposal was implemented and with what scope. Like the grand memorial hall in which a video for each fallen paratrooper is presented and all memory comes to life through digital tools with nothing left for oblivion, the megalomanic vision of "the other way" is left as a blueprint for a certain social potential. The plan, the vision statement, and the advice are all tentative, thereby leaving room for memory to remain unique and singular while already repurposing it for other social currencies. What the protocol strives for is managerial. The sovereign aims of militarism and colonial control are utterly repressed and the maintenance mechanism that reassures the value of lost life and the families' feelings is pushed forward.

THE FREE MARKET OF THE FAMILY VIDEO

With the privatization of the Israeli media market—a privatization marked by the launching of commercial television and cable television in the early nineties—freelancing became a common labor setting in the Israeli media industry. This ultimately shifted film and television production infrastructures and market from centralization and state regulation to ubiquity. In the era of state media, film and videomakers had a more or less stable relationship with the state broadcasting entity or the state film fund, whereas in the new economic model of privatization and deregulation, filmmakers work per project, stretching their qualifications and protocols to a maximum range of commissioned work. Here the state is twice removed. First, its sphere of control is traversed by the private market and sovereign power is substituted, as in the Foucauldian model, by governmentality as economics. It is then removed again through the bracketed category of personal services provided to the family by the producer. The former refers to the nature of the work, the latter to its market location. The precarity and adaptability of freelancing is symptomatic of the instability of capitalist media markets and moreover of the all-encompassing and amphibious nature of media—and capital—today. Although precarious, the emergence of freelancing appears as a balancing mechanism in a deregulated private market, one that opens up more spheres for production and employment, thereby sustaining corporate media.

In its first appearances in the media sphere, the personal video memorial emerged as a sporadic amateur engagement with video, with the voluntary assistance of occasional expertise: an insight here and there, provided as a labor of love by friends or kin who had some access to the field. "Labor of love" refers to work done by professionals outside a capitalist economy that translates expertise, time, and energy into material value. More specifically, it refers to media professionals and quasi-professionals who provide input for a video production because they care about the dead person, their family, or what they stood for.[49] As the state-authored "advice to the bereaved" shows, the system that was eventually established is one predicated on the private market of freelance services. Families reaching out to a techno-aesthetic authority that would assist them in putting together a video for their loved ones indicates the establishment of a production niche in a pre-packaged set of commemorative outlets, a conventionalization and professionalization of form. Here, I would even argue that although as a rubric of investment and knowledge a labor of love subverts the place of work in the political and economic framework of the modern capitalist state, it sets the ground as a preliminary model for the freelance filmmaker in the free market. Throughout the different protocols analyzed in this chapter, the definition of work as paid labor versus a form of giving is elastic, even consciously elusive. The economy of death and care work that assigns material value to either loss or mourning is the ongoing conundrum against which the different protocols are written. The outsourcing of the family's affective processing is part of the branding of family emotions and memories, which includes a growing and thriving market of wedding videos, Bar/Bat Mitzvah videos, and memoirs, created by freelance filmmakers and media entrepreneurs. The free market of freelance producers of family memories is nevertheless predicated on labor done intimately with the family in question, abstracting paradigms of mass consumption by valorizing singularity.

The proxy economy utilizes video-as-technique. The freelance filmmaker realizes video not as a tool of social mobility or community building but simply—although there is nothing simple here—as a commodity. Such processes of standardization of production and consumption materialize a private model in which one party provides services and the other pays, with a concrete product—a video—as a sign of labor on the one hand and value on the other. Nevertheless, within the neoliberal capitalist system the location of creative labor, and with it models of production or employment, change. With freelancing, the relations of work-product-value are rarely defined and stable. This is evidenced, as we will see, first, in the obscurity of work processes and rates; second, in the ambiguity or the strategic positioning of work in/out of professional media production or family intimacy; and third, in the description of the final product not as an artefact but as a lasting affect. Indeed, what the freelance filmmaker and the free market often sell is the *experience* of creativity, self-expression, and healing, as well as their own attentiveness and care. When the work of mourning enters the equation, or pertains to a system of production (even more so a model of mass-production), the instability of work-product-value relations further aggravates.

Freelance filmmaker Tzvia Keren's homepage organizes her oeuvre using the tabs "private customers," "business customers," and "documentary." A click on "private customers" leads to a page reading: "Grandpa is 70? Mum or Dad have retired? 25 years of marriage? There are more and more reasons to commemorate the personal or familial story in a movie that can be the center of an event or an original token of a life story or a story of a place. . . ."[50] Keren pitches her work with the family as "preserving" the family story by turning it into a "memory for the next generation." She does not list the memorial video as one of the family stories to be preserved, for obvious reasons: this is not a happy memory and not an event one would like to have in mind while browsing through web pages selling family memory services. According to Keren's webpage, her family videos are "engaging, moving and thorough," and are the product of "a gradual and collaborative process that will match the customer's expectations and budget."

Another media entrepreneur, Chen Shelach, highlights his "sensitive and sensible" treatment of the video and its subjects.[51] He stresses that the work "will progress gradually and in full coordination with the family" and details his services: "The production entails in-depth archival and human [social] research, conversations with family, friends and acquaintances, [and] putting together a manuscript that corresponds with the budget [.] [This] is [also] the case with [selecting] shooting locations which corresponds with the expectations and possibilities of those who initiate the production." Shelach designates private video work under the sub-section of "commemorative work and life-stories," yet he specifically avoids calling the family a customer. Instead, he uses euphemisms such as "ordering party," or "those who initiated the production." In both Keren and Shelach's professional profiles the customer or initiator are represented through their expectations, to be fulfilled or responded to, always signed with the gentle reminder that such expectations are framed within an agreed-upon budget. Shelach, unlike Keren, stresses the empirical work of research he conducts for the video. As he, Keren, and others, highlight, the work is gradual, collaborative, their approach is "sensitive" and the product is "engaging," "moving," "sensible,", and memorable.

Although these and similar websites contain preliminary (tentative) statements designed to sell services that would hopefully lead to a negotiation and an agreement on concrete investment, efforts, and outcomes, they are not a production protocol. Further investigation into what would be pre-set terms, working protocols, rates, or a sort of contractual engagement leads to inconclusiveness and ambiguity. Freelance filmmakers deliberately avoid stating terms and rates due to the nature of their services and their own work constellation, which is adjustable. In the specific case of the video memorial, a consensual subtext that we see throughout is abstaining from equating intimacy with money or assigning death a material compensation. Freelance filmmakers and entrepreneurs accustom themselves to the needs and dynamics of the individual family, aspiring to an organic production process. Both Keren and Shelach argue that the criteria, values, and rules of production are set according to the family and what it can afford, leaving the terms of engagement and even the actual product loose and elusive. Perhaps this is key to distinguishing *services* from a *job*. The family is being perceived as an individuated and private entity for whom there are no rules, only exceptions.

When the Ron family hired Chen Shelach to produce a video about their deceased brother, Shelach, who had extensive experience and personal ties in the television industry, identified Avner Ron's story as one of public interest. Ron was a soldier in an IDF elite commando unit whose team was sent, in the midst of the 1973 war, to rescue a pilot who had been captured by Egyptian troops. The operation failed, Ron died, and months later the pilot was returned to Israel as part of a post-war prisoner exchange. Shelach approached the public broadcaster Channel 1 and pitched the project to the channel's documentary unit.[52] He formulated the personal video-turned-documentary around a meeting, almost forty years after the events, of Ron's teammates and the ex-captured pilot. The dramatic failed-rescue story, together with the teammates' and family members' recollections, provided the project with a mix of history and affect, proper to the neoliberal character-driven TV documentary (see chapter 3).

The documentary, titled *When Jabel Fell* (Jabel was Ron's nickname among his teammates), was broadcast as a prime time program during Memorial Day 2008. For the Ron family, however, the video did not answer their needs and expectations of intimate remembering. They wanted a recollection of a private loved one, not a national hero. Shelach, accordingly, used footage from the television documentary combined with interviews with the family to make an additional video. This video was broadcast as part of a Channel 10 domestic productions slot in 2012. It is by the proxy that the two production modes—the personal homemade video memorial and the TV documentary—intertwine. As this example shows, the categories of family video and documentary might seem fluid or arbitrary. The programming schedule, with its division of broadcasting slots, and crucially, the family and its internal rationale of intimate memories, draw the line that parts the two.

What happens when the heterogeneous mix of family history and feelings meets the amphibious, all-serving production niche of the freelance filmmaker? What can be made of the home video which is not homemade, but also not a product of what we perceive as industrial or commercial production processes? In film and media studies, the allocation of cultural production corresponds with its institutional location (in that regard, the family is an institution as well), its channels of distribution, the kind of labor put into it, and the emotional and financial investment; but here, these tend to be ambiguous and indeterminate. There is a certain uncanniness to the mass-produced family video. The family is the commissioning party, the video's subject, and, to a certain extent, its co-producer, and yet the video is never a singular artifact. The freelance filmmaker in the free market has an analogous and similarly intricate relationship with corporate media. Occupying what can be broadly termed peripheral filmmaking, freelance filmmakers' peripherality is constituted by constantly traversing what is construed as center, or alternately, margins. Much of the free media market, with its mobility and plurality of outlets, persists within a particular structure of sociability, where work is generated through personal ties, favors, and coincidental encounters. Such an affective-economic model is a challenge for empirical scrutiny or critique. Although non-exhaustive, what follows attempts to provide a few sample genealogies.

Shelach worked for the television industry as a documentary editor and producer, his work being mostly project-based. While working for the television network Reshet, he was asked by the network's CEO to edit a homemade video memorial that was part of the network's community service project in which it offers bereaved families assistance in producing a video memorial (see chapter 1). Editors assigned to the project by the network were mostly junior and less experienced. The CEO asked Shelach, who was already senior in the field, to work on the video as a personal favor to him, as he wanted to make sure that the family, his close friends, were in good hands. Those were Shelach's first steps into this media niche. When he decided to start an independent career as a freelancer, and to leave the center for the north of Israel, he reached out to Keren, who already established herself as a northern media professional. While the two had no official work as co-directors, they had a good personal and professional relationship. With his still new business, Shelach took on mostly local work, including a number of commemorative videos. Today, most of his projects are feature documentaries.[53] Like Shelach, Keren had also zigzagged between the family market, work commissioned by the industrial sector, and television.[54] She worked mainly with the cable TV station Hot and produced television documentaries on themes related to regional history,[55] folklore,[56] and populist themes related to the military, such as battle stories, bereavement, and war.[57] Keren's television work is peripheral, in the sense that it takes place in the margins of the television industry, producing commissioned local documentary, and is geographically situated in the north, away from the cultural and economic center.

Similar to Shelach and Keren's professional portfolio, media entrepreneur Nissan Katz's filmography includes commissioned work and documentaries. Katz, however, provides no section on his official website for personal/private family productions. Instead, information was listed on Katz's Wikipedia page (and was later edited to omit these works), and his company's logo appeared on the videos he produced.[58] Gil Mezuman, a graduate of the religious-oriented film school Ma'ale, has directed acclaimed documentaries related to Jewish-religious-nationalist themes.[59] On an online industry platform he presents himself as a cinematographer and filmmaker who worked extensively with television and the industrial market.[60] Mezuman and his brother are credited as directors and producers of a video in memory of Shay Bernstein titled *From Me to Command*. The video was commissioned by Bernstein's girlfriend and was broadcast in 2009 in a programming slot mostly designated for personal commemoration. Although it did not broadcast outside the periphery of the Memorial Day programming schedule, its production values meet those of television documentaries, and its author, the girlfriend, promotes it as a public manifestation that portrays social ideals.[61] Similar to other cases of homemade video memorials, questions such as who financed the production, for how much, and to whom the money was paid, are not traceable. Another graduate of Ma'ale, Nurit Jacobs-Yinon, runs a production company under the brand name Aluma Films. Mezuman is credited as an editor and co-producer in a few of Jacobs-Yinon's early productions. Among the company's productions, all directed by Jacobs-Yinon, are documentaries, video art installations, commissioned work, PR work, and family or personal video work.[62] A close reading shows that the categories on her webpage are rather hybrid and fluid.[63] Especially intriguing is what she terms "microcommemoration," housed under the documentary tab. Her website also promotes lectures and events.

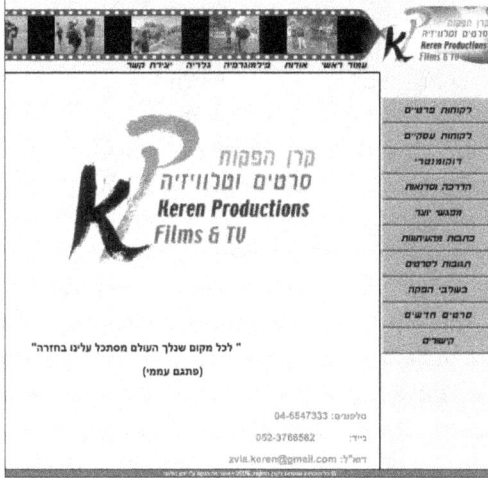

FIGURE 9. Screenshot from Keren Productions, the website of freelance filmmaker Tzivia Keren, accessed April 13, 2015.

These threads demonstrate the overlaps that characterize the work of peripheral filmmaking, as well as the coalescence of a number of networks or affinity systems that tie together people, practices, forms, and contents. The mobility of the freelance filmmaker within the free media market serves all sides. Their relationship with mass media is a crucial selling point that demonstrates their professionalism and attracts families who aspire to gain acknowledgement by distributing the memory of their dead in more resonating contexts and on high-profile platforms. Filmmakers, meanwhile, leverage their work with the private market and, when the story wields such potential, pitch it as a source of public interest to commercial media venues. These genealogies expose not only the essential elasticity of what constitutes a videomaker or videomaking, but also the categorical fluidity of every work of film/video. Such categorical fluidity is not only the product of the economic system, that is, the Israeli free media market, but the political mobility and hybridity of memory within Israeli sociability. The ultimate proxy, the freelance filmmaker in the free media market, is an emblematic agent of governmentality. Advised by the state commemorative manual, the proxy is external to sovereignty, yet close enough. As "a person with some *affinity*" to video-making, the proxy is a processing outlet. Their professionalism has a delimited authority; they merely *serve* the family. Aspects of class divide, colonial dispositions, and population control—all coming to bear on questions such as who is commemorated, by whom, and at what cost—are being suppressed by the rhetoric of services. Lastly, the free media market catering to private families can be understood as an aspect of contemporary capitalist settler colonialism: an economic sector that through liberal discourse normalizes and whitewashes Jewish-Israeli political violence.

Described by the Ministry of Defense as adding "qualitative parts," the proxy is designated as the one who transforms loss into containable, perspectival stories. With this mechanism at work, feelings of pain are treated, supported, and tamed. Moreover, the terminology of "affinity" proposed by the Ministry of Defense implies that these services are never merely technical or "qualitative," but involve intimate and affective attachments. Such practice is defined by its individuation, indefinability, exteriority to official mechanisms of control, and its mobility within production niches. Thus, the proxy is an attributive agent in a typology that separates the family from the state and the homemade video memorial from corporate media, while at the same time keeping them close to each other. The proxy mediates techno-aesthetic knowledge to the family and by so doing approximates institutional/corporate media and its ideological and juridical relations to the state. The proxy delimits an intricate set of affinities between the self and mediation, between subject and power, between consumer and producer, between work and love.

CROWDFUNDING: AN AFTERTHOUGHT

Luciana Parisi and Steve Goodman demarcate forms of power which are inflicted through embedded mechanisms that they term mnemonic control. They write: "Here, living labor becomes mechanic, consumers become producers, and everyone designs their own products through self-organizing networks of spontaneous creativity."[64] This is the very end of governmentality. Portraying an economy in which markets and creativity are inseparable and distributed through affective and sensational networks, Parisi and Goodman are interested in the impact of branding as what dictates, as they formulate it, a memory of the future of the unlived. Branding, they contend, is about what was yet to be actualized or experienced. Their critique addresses what they designate as affective and cognitive capitalism. Once the work of commemoration becomes a personalized commodity, once the product and the venues to produce it are branded, what kind of distribution does it have? Bringing their analysis closer to the case studied here, is it possible that through the contagious power of branding, it produces what Parisi and Goodman might call an affective and cognitive memory of the un-lost, or not-yet to be lost.

The constant mutability of media platforms, production protocols, distribution outlets, creative forces, and aesthetic formats, moved from a unity of production and expressions to individuation and privatization, brings with it an abstraction of value, labor, class and sovereign politics. As an afterthought, a look into a future production protocol (already manifesting itself in our present) brings back the common and its symbolic capital as a branded fantasy.

In the summer of 2014, a crowdfunding campaign titled *Eytan's Beach* was launched on the Israeli crowdfunding platform Headstart. The project was described as a commemorative documentary project dedicated to Eytan Barak, who died in 2014 during the Israeli invasion of Gaza. When Barak died, his friends wanted to name a beach strip in the south of the city of Herzeliya after him. To do that, they needed to re-inscribe Barak as a resonating public figure who served his country, and for that, they needed a video as an affective and circulating format, and Headstart to help fund it. The campaign listed Iris Ben Moshe, a recent graduate of Tel Aviv University Film Department, as the video's director. It described the video as a documentation of "a journey of commemoration . . . vis-a-vis getting to know Eytan through stories and images."[65] The project developers noted that "professionals"—once again a nebulous category—had expressed their support for the project's cause and have already agreed to collaborate. Later, under "professionals," the developers list the popular Israeli singer Rita, the Instagram phenomenon turned businesswoman Natalie Dadon, and Avia Shoshani, a finalist in the Israeli reality show *The Next Star*. Yet, voluntary work put in by celebrities (defined in the blurb as professionals) was not the project's main selling point, but the fact that Barak sacrificed his life as a soldier. The authors appealed to potential investors, writing: "Eytan left to protect us and never came back, the least we can do is to commemorate him. If you believe that Eytan deserves this *modest gift* after everything he sacrificed, support us."[66] The 40,000 NIS that was listed as the project's funding goal was collected in three days. By the time the funding campaign was over, the funds collected had reached 64,920 NIS, contributed by 325 people.

Platforms like Headstart, which allow individuals to develop their own projects, to pitch them to investors while maintaining control over the project, are part of what Michel Feher would refer to as "investee activism."[67] Feher contends that neoliberalism has brought with it speculative capitalism, that is, an economic model based on investment. For him, investee activism is a way to oppose the neoliberal model from within, to challenge investors and to use the sharing economy to name or shame. In short, it is to appropriate the investee role as the collateral and to alter the system by acting continuously, therefore reducing risk. Crowdfunding draws on symbolic (and concrete) capital and offers a program of wealth redistribution. The platform imposes a number of preconditions for creating a risk-free model.[68] A project can receive investment only if the funding campaign reaches its goal, collecting the amount it asked for within its set timeframe. This policy assumes that project creators will keep campaigns within their reach, base their goal on numerous small contributions, and appropriate the social economy of sharing in order to reach a wide audience.

When it comes to use a crowdfunding platform to produce a personal commemorative video, the case of Eytan Barak is, for now, a rare example. What kind of proxy relations does the platform materialize? Crowdfunding designates a place of production outside institutional or commercial media, and is in common use as an alternative source of funding for independent documentaries and vernacular media production. Despite its reliance on the common, it is still a private platform in a privatized market. In the world of interested investors, crowdfunding draws back on collective capital and, in this case, valorizes sacrifice as currency. Furthermore, here its redistribution of wealth applies to the one who is already inscribed in a matrix of political and symbolic capital: a dead soldier.

Loyal to notions of solidarity and commonality, investments—the donations at the crowdfunding platforms, or even the "investment" of one's life—are initially termed "gifts" by the project initiators. The Headstart interface, like other crowdfunding platforms, has a section where the campaign creators detail contributors' future benefits once the campaign is successful and the product is out. This is a contract of sorts, not one that outlines labor and compensation, as in liberal capitalism, but one that assigns value per investment, part of the collective imaginary in the branding economy. In the campaign for *Eytan's Beach,* a contribution of 25 NIS yields a personal thank-you letter signed by the family and producers; 50 NIS gives a letter and a link for streaming the film; 100 NIS provides all the above and the name of the contributor in the film's credits, and so on. For an investment of 5,000 NIS the investor is credited as co-producer. On top of the various merchandise, shares, or credits, each investment is rated using military ranks: sergeant for an investment of 25 NIS, staff sergeant for 50, first lieutenant for 100, major for 200 and so on. Those who invest 5,000 NIS get the highest rank, chief of staff.

In the age of social media, power is granted back to a transformed conception of the common. Family production, as a venue of memory, relied on an intimate proxy, whose aesthetic-technological knowledge and institutional knowledge made them the nexus of the private and public. In an age of mnemonic control, this version of memory and militarism, with death as its outcome, embodies a self-sufficient mechanism, funded by civil society. Here, it is all about making concrete a protocol that assigns capital to life, commodifies forms of solidarity and care, and promotes self-formation through branding.

Much of the sharing economy is about translating social capital into concrete capital. Social values and social leveling are woven into marketability and branding, the imperative to give back to the one who gave is leveraged to collect funds, while military ranks become a means of economic labeling. Social consciousness of a particular stream becomes investment, and the investors buy their way into structures of sociability. Beyond the dominance of branding as a selling practice—which guarantees that the product is at once unique and reproducible, as we saw with other proxies—branding is central to a crowdfunding project because it feeds the creation of different levels of investment. The humorous, slang-like gesture of labeling investment according to military ranks appears here as a kind of fraternal wink, and exposes, once again, how militarism has become naturalized in Israeli society, with its social stratification signaled in the campaign as levels (ranks) equated with brand names. The crowdfunding project surfaces how sovereign power and structures of affinity built around the symbolic capital of loss in Israel are intertwined. Personal attachments and affectivity are selling points, or even a share one can purchase (the personal thank-you letter signed by the family), and are framed by the gestural sponsorship of the celebrity, the ultimate figure of the branded self.

For Feher, crowdfunding is an insurgent model within contemporary neoliberal economy because, drawing on communal networks, it offers endurance and commitment in a market shaped by risk. Is crowdfunding a risk-free model? In the case of *Eytan's Beach*, risk, like the loss of life, is exactly what the video's branding promotes (selectively, as it nowhere mentions the horrendous scale of loss that the Gaza invasion caused). The film, according to what I could find, was never completed, like other projects reviewed in this chapter. However, branding is not necessarily about the completed artefact, but about the social imagination and desire of privately reproduced mourning. Contributing to a project of commemoration guarantees the continuation of a social commitment to remember, it is a mutual agreement. You pay to acknowledge someone else's loss, and someone else will support yours, an agreement of an affective and cognitive "memory of the unlost." As a technique of forming a socially recognized subject, one whose loss is acknowledged, crowdfunding and branding are based on an economy in which sociability yields to commodification, colonialism passes under self-care dictums, and militarism is a rising trend.

CHAPTER 3

Scheduled Memories, Programmed Mourning

"It was television on its 'best behavior.'"

—Sinai Abt, former director of Hot Cables Channel 8

Published in the back pages of the daily newspaper's entertainment section, the television listing for the Israeli Memorial Day of 2001 indicated
that the cable TV Channel 8 would dedicate its programming that day
to "personal soldiers' commemorative videos." Those browsing through
the entertainment section on April 26 that year would most likely have
paid little attention to this agenda. The daily summary of television
programming is a pedestrian document, lacking the kind of historical
consciousness that underscores news material. One uses it, but is rarely
mindful of it. For the newspaper reader, television programming on that
particular day would have attracted less attention. The Israeli National
Memorial Day subsumes television under a national project of mourning, aligns programming with a daunting public sentiment. It suspends,
or rather slows down, television's flow of new sensations, new formats,
or new episodes. More prominent television channels programmed live
broadcasts of the state official memorial ceremony, Memorial Day
specials, or local documentary productions. Within this programming
scheme, Channel 8 was certainly not a main player, but rather a special-
content channel in a plethora of broadcasters on the private television
market. In fact, the newspaper's television listing in 2001 could barely
contain the multiplicity of channels and programs within its pages. In
a few years, the listings would gradually migrate to online news platforms; in a little more than a decade, streaming technology would transform television's viewing itineraries all together.[1]

It could also be that the reader would have brushed over the page without due diligence, as the broadcasting of personal video commemoration was not uncommon. In fact, the television programming agenda for the National Memorial Day featured personal video commemoration in a seemingly open "broadcast yourself" model since the mid-1990s. This particular programming schedule, however, is the first one to tag them as a defined production form and a programming niche—that is, the first time television states, through the programming schedule, personal video commemoration and its operations as concatenated.

The television programming schedule is emblematic of contemporary temporal regimes, enmeshing law, power, media and markets to synthetically produce social rhythms. The Israeli Memorial Day stands for what sociologist Eviatar Zerubavel delineates as collective memory's time map, or rather the outlines through which memory affects a sense of historicity and shapes a common perception of time.[2] It is a day of highly regulated public feelings. Personal loss is institutionalized and collectivized through cultural reproduction, only to then be injected back to the private sphere through temporal sanctioning. During the course of the day, shops and restaurants close early; government offices, industry, and the corporate sector work in reduced capacity; street movement decelerates, while the state public sphere orchestrates acts of remembering. Israeli television, whose very first broadcast was the Independence Day parade in 1968, and which, per the regulator's order, evacuates its agendas during the National Memorial Day to program the day's themes and sentiments, accords with the state. But as much as television is adjacent to sovereign law, it also maintains a fantasy of intimacy and domesticity. As a cultural institute, television provides a prism that distills the settler colonial state's synthetic formations of time and space. Yet, the rather nebulous category of "personal video commemoration" does not come across as a national program. If anything, it highlights television's capacity to be personal and private.

Launched in 1996 by Hot cable TV and designated as the network's documentary channel, Channel 8 withheld its programming during the National Memorial Day in prior years and went back on the air once the day was over. From 1999–2002 it had a relatively compact programming schedule, populated mainly with personal videos and frequent reruns, until it expanded to other formats of production that stretched across a full programming day.[3] Channel 8's gradual and modular programming paradigm for the National Memorial Day reflects modes of conduct that were the norm on Israeli private television during the 1990s and early 2000s. Its program of "personal soldiers' commemorative videos" in 2001 entails an extremely sporadic, inchoate, and inconsistent mode of production of home videos commemorating personal loss. "At the time it was television on its 'best behavior,'" says Sinai Abt, Channel 8's director in the years 2001–2009, reflecting on programmers' decision to allocate time on the television's schedule for families' videos.[4] This statement is powerful yet suggestive. What is television's *best behavior*?

The homemade video memorial represented original content with no production costs. Its airing allowed networks a way out of content quotas for local productions imposed by the regulator. Associated with the personal, the homemade video memorial promoted memory devoid of criticism, complying with social sensitivities and resonating with the public demand for a consensual space during a national day of remembrance. Its programming accommodated such memories without falling back on the state's commemorative dogmas. It corroborated television's public mandate through the private sector. But, most importantly, airing the videos was perceived as a direct gesture to those who suffered loss, an act of institutional care. "It felt as if this was something we could *give* to the families," Abt asserts. Therefore, television's "best behavior" has to do with satisfying convergent needs: negotiating economic imperatives with the norm, mediating institutional ideology to common sentiments, and *giving*. What is the *gift* offered by television, a gift that intimates family and the media? Drawing from Abt's statement, television's gift to the family is that of time.

In this chapter I contend that in the last decade of the twentieth century and the first decade of the twenty-first century, Israeli television went through a series of technological, political, economic, and cultural transformations and moved from the locus of sovereignty to that of privacy. As part of these processes, television became personalized. This meant that the memory of national loss—the core of Israel's ethnocentrism and separatism, and a self-excuse for its colonial violence—relocates into the habitual realm, domesticated and intimated. More broadly, my argument is that television is the state's medium of privatization (the latter being understood as an active process that happens over time), a medium that displaces political structures and subjects while shifting from the centralized power of the state to private actors such as the market, the family, the individual. Writing from a point in time when networked media have rendered television's programmed itineraries irrelevant, I understand television not as a predecessor for the current era of personalized media, but rather as its embryonic phase.

In these decades of mutation, while its infrastructures, operations, and place within the social organization change, television needed to form a new institutional ideal, asking itself what it will or should be, what its *best behavior* entails.

The dominant model for television, introduced in Israel as well as in other social states around 1990, and prevailing to a certain degree to this day, is based on a commercial entity regulated by the state. Prior to that, Israeli television was essentially a state institution. Implemented as part of a larger political shift, this model stems from the breaking of the state monopoly and the privatization of the Israeli market. In the transition, with an all-at-once multiplicity of channels, creative entities were pressured by the regulator to produce new content to stock the new television programming schedule. The emerging commercial television negotiated economic imperatives with the state's program, statistics (ratings) with preconceived notions of popular sentiment; these were active considerations in shaping state-of-the-art formats. Such factors are heightened in what the local television industry dubs "special days broadcasting," programming for days singled out as bearing cultural and historical meaning, such as the National Memorial Day. A ritualistic pause in the yearly pace, the television programming schedule for the National Memorial Day captures the social imaginary of the state, its media and its ideal citizen-subject, as these paradigms shift across the course of the day (vertically) or throughout the years (horizontally).[5] Tracking those shifts in a kind of time map, television's programming schedule is also a blueprint for television's work of programming memories and forging time (or gifting time). Reproducing the programming sequence in this chapter, I ask: why is an ephemeral production done outside the institutional frameworks of television, aired by nascent channels or at the edges of the programming day, described as television's mastering of its social decorum?

Television's best behavior, Abt's notion of a televisual ideal, surfaces key characteristics of the medium that deserve some articulation. Per Abt, it seems that television's best behavior is its ability to bring closer, to reach out, to keep in touch. Programmers were guided by the perception of extending a platform of memory to contain families' intimate loss beyond the forms and formats of national ideology. For some viewers, for whom death is not an intimate fact, the family video memorial facilitates a "personal" encounter with the deceased and with those who suffer loss. The intimate video was conceived as authentic and is attended to with a special care. Another way of understanding television's authenticating touch is as "touching the real." 1990s television scholarship, in particular in the writings of Mary Ann Doane and Patricia Mellencamp, described the medium's impression of "real time" and its registers of the catastrophic and the instantaneous.[6] In the face of horror and death, television's touch of the real was about being in-sync and being on time—noted as television's attraction by Mimi White[7]—producing an absolute experience where urgency is responded to with continuity of visibility and transmission. For liveness theory, a popular branch of television scholarship at the turn of the century, real-time and crisis were television at its best, extremely potent in an age of constant trauma where crisis is an ongoing ontological condition. As this constellation teaches us, when television reached out to touch, calling upon rupture and loss, its features of containment, organizing the fractures into a continuous narrative, were at their prime.

"To be there" for mourners, an ideal predicated on the interface between loss and synchronicity, assumes reciprocity on behalf of television. First, giving back stands for giving something to the families that gave their children to the state. Here television is reciprocal in virtue of its reinforcing of certain social contracts. Giving something directly to the families, television positions itself as facilitating an exchange in which time as currency lies beneath the symbolic value of cultural significance. A second premise of reciprocity has to do with traversing the stream of information and affect as well as the hierarchies of production and reception, since it is domestic individuals ("families") who become the source of content. This traversal expands our understanding of television, from a medium which is a one-way channel for perceiving and imagining the social to one which is constituted by participation. Aspects of participation have been present in television discourse from an early stage, in the form of writing letters to the network or calling a TV show to vote for a favorite candidate. However, the kind of participatory model and the specific time frame in which it appears—mid-1990s and first decade of the 2000s—situates reciprocity in structures of production and distribution, recalling a near future of user-generated content platforms. Reciprocity with the family perhaps encapsulated television's hopes for a democratic utopia, or the personalization of media as means of individual reform, both echoing the preliminary excitement about the potential of these technologies. Yet, at the hands of corporate, quasi-national media, settler colonial ideology was not dismantled but privatized, further engrained in individuated bodies and allowing not memory, but rather amnesia to prevail.

Encompassing capital, law, and political power, but also embodying a meeting point of outside and inside, public and private, television can be characterized by the plurality and malleability of its operations. Television's elasticity, its ability to extend, does not apply only to its channeling of decoded cultural transmissions, but translates into television's modus-operandi, into programming itself as a work of sequencing, segmenting, and stretching. Progressing across the course of a day, television scheduling moves through different scales and brackets attention: there are times when one views like a citizen, times one views like a consumer, and times one views with care. Abt articulates the above televisual logic with a degree of morbid irony. Tracking the content he commissioned during his time as broadcaster, it seemed that he envisioned the channel as a critical haven of high quality documentary that would expose, time and again, the forms of occupation, apartheid, and genocide practiced by Israeli governments.[8] Nevertheless, this is neither about his nor the families' potential acts of resistance, but about pointing at a cohesive formation that organizes a variety of different vocations to comply with the national itinerary and its dictated consensual norms. It could be that the broadcaster's irony emanates from the discrepancies of seeing "the large picture," being the one navigating the entirety of intricacies and inconsistencies of television. For the broadcaster, television is a complexity of policies, infrastructures, formats, and ideas. In a sense, irony is integral to operating simultaneously on a number of social and organizational scales, a dynamic that certainly describes the television complex.

And still, television's best is on its margins, and the programming schedule is itself the news's rear part. Its mundanity and triviality is also what allows television to be private. The margins are where family-made memories could be perceived intimately. Their bracketed reception was also echoed by television's own logic: although homemade memorial videos were part of the television programming schedule as early as the mid-1990s, they remained mostly, if not completely, obscured from television's production structures, criticism, and archives. As the programmers and television officials with whom I talked all concluded, this was a "family thing." Perhaps it is the alleged exteriority of personal video commemoration to the project of national memory and to television programming that, in a time of transition, brought both some relief: television and sovereignty alike were sustained by becoming private.

Thinking television as orienting a common itinerary of mourning, one that makes time for intimacy, is reading television as chrono-specific. Here I take my lead from Anna McCarthy, whose work on television's site-specificity observes how "the diffuse network of gazes and institutions, subjects and bodies, screen and physical structures" concretize space.[9] "Time is television's basis, its principle of structuration, as well as its persistent reference," writes Mary Ann Doane.[10] According to chrono-specificity, television is both time-made and time-making. Media critics have revisited the molding of social rhythms by everyday media, conceptualizing it as a key apparatus in modern chronography. Traditional television, in this debate, was conceived as a medium that regulates time, bracketing rupture from routine,[11] whereas new digital media, with its constant updates, unleashed time, effecting a sense of perpetual crisis.[12] Turn-of-the-century television already entails the means of personalization, individuation, and ubiquitous communication that the digital unleashing puts forward. While memorial videos started trickling into social media and content sharing platforms relatively late, television was their main sphere of circulation and emergence precisely because, through its temporal design ordered by the state agenda, it made the audience concrete. Media temporality, whether its paradigms are unified or undifferentiated, contributes to "the annihilation of the singularity of place and event,"[13] its rhythms synthetic and homogenizing, carefully coordinated and at the same time indistinctive, collectivizing yet isolating. Indeed, time is television's gift, as it is no longer at our disposal or for us to govern.

In sum, television on its best behavior is about being in touch, about extending and reaching out, forming attachments but also bracketing and segmenting various social niches. It is about being in and on time, being personal and being "real," being in-sync and being attached, being "private" and "public" at once.[14] It addresses its viewer both intimately and, simultaneously, as part of a cohesive homogeneity. While my question is about what happens when television becomes private, it is only as one articulation sequenced with others, and in its specific location within the general scheme, that the broadcasting of families' videos was deemed television's fantasmatic epitome, its "best behavior."

TELEVISION TIME

The programming schedule for Memorial Day 2008 lists the following sequence.[15]

Channel 2, programmed by the subsidiary, *Keshet*:

P.M.

07:30: News, followed by a live broadcast of the opening ceremony in Jerusalem

08:30: Live broadcast of the Memorial Day gathering in Rabin Square in Tel Aviv

10:30: *Uvda, Investigative journalism: Summer Seeds* (documentary special, rerun)

11:00: *A Prince on a White Horse* (documentary, rerun)

A.M.

12:00: News

Programming after midnight was not detailed, although broadcasting continued overnight. The following day's broadcast was under the channel's subsidiary *Reshet*:

A.M.

06:00: *Remember With Love*

06:43: *The World This Morning* (news magazine)

09:00: *Remember With Love*

10:00: *Soon We'll be a Poem* (Memorial Day special, produced by *Galey Tzahal,* the military radio station, rerun of the 2007 special)

11:00: Live broadcast of the state official ceremony for fallen soldiers

11:35: *Heymish,* in memory of Amir Zimmermann

P.M.

12:05: *Sixty, Seventy, Eighty* (educational)

01:00: Live broadcast of the state official ceremony for victims of terror attacks

01:40: *Remember with Love*

02:00: *In Their Memory* (The Paratroops Heritage Association video productions)

02:30: *Not to be Lost* (Memorial Day musical special, rerun)

03:00: *Paper Squares*

04:00: *Remember with Love*

04:30: *His Spirit: In Memory of Dror Vienberg*

05:00: News

05:05: *Not to Be Lost* (Memorial Day musical special, rerun)

06:00: Six With. . . (news magazine)

Channel 10:

P.M.

07:45: Live broadcast of the state official opening ceremony

08:30: News

09:00: *Our Brother, We Cried* (documentary)

09:45: *I'll See You Tomorrow, My Child* (documentary)

10:35: *Sparrows in the Net* (documentary)

11:30: *The Price of the Body* (documentary)

A.M.

12:25: *Hero in Heaven* (documentary)

06:00: *HaReshut Netuna* (religion)

06:40: *Every Morning* (news magazine)

09:00: News

09:02: *Tzur Or, RIP*

09:15: *In Their Memory* (The Paratroops Heritage Association video productions)

11:00: Live broadcast of the state official ceremony for fallen soldiers

11:30: *David Iluz* (documentary)

P.M.

12:25: *Tzur Zarhi, RIP* (documentary)

12:45: *Oren Lifshitz, RIP* (documentary)

01:00: Live broadcast of the state official ceremony for victims of terror attacks

01:30: *In Their Memory* (The Paratroops Heritage Association video productions)

02:35: *The Days of Yotam* (documentary)

03:00: *Oz* (documentary)

03:15: *Aviho* (documentary, rerun)

03:45: *Uti* (documentary, rerun)

04:40: *Flew Away Forever* (documentary)

05:45: *Through Me to Control* (documentary)

06:30: *Zionism, No Quotation Marks. Yaron Amitai*

07:00: News

The 2008 schedule was published in the leisure section of the daily newspaper. In that year, one could also access it via online news platforms. On the news website *Walla*, small caricatured icons next to the program titles were used to articulate a taxonomy of content and audiences: an owl for documentaries, a miniature anchorman for news and public affairs, and an icon of a smiling man, woman and child to signal family content. Clicking on programs marked in blue would open a window with a short blurb. In the newspaper, dense blurbs contained in small boxes and imbricated in the running columns highlighted specific programs. In print and perhaps more so on the web, an indexical topography separated entertainment from more sober forms, and a dynamic architecture moved us across descriptive scales, from title to blurb.

Following the temporal patterns of Jewish holidays, Memorial Day runs from sunset to sunset. In 2008, it began on Tuesday evening, May 6, and concluded on the evening of May 7. Transitioning to and from the day is clearly marked in the programming schedule, with the 8:00 p.m. ceremony in Jerusalem positioned as a vector for the observance of the holiday. In fact, three state-produced commemorative ceremonies, transmitted live across all channels, can be found on the schedule. Ordered as permanent programming slots, repetitive and simultaneous, they correspond with the state dicta, a time designated as nation time. The evening news, attached to the live broadcast, prolonged the formal ritual with television's own quotidian ritual. It is from this point on that programming proceeds, splitting to a variety of formats that convey television's prime, or prime time. In 2008, documentary was the main format of social remembering. Personal commemorative videos are not marked as a concrete broadcasting category, as was suggested by channel 8 in its 2001 programming schedule. Although they are relatively obscure, two programs stand out: *Remember with Love* on Channel 2, a family commemorative project facilitated by Reshet TV, and a collection of videos produced by the Paratroops Heritage Association, programmed by Channel 10. Assimilated into the sequence of documentary content, personal commemorative videos can be located at the day's peripheries, as the broadcast drifts from prime time into late night or early morning. In the sequence presented here, programming gradually diverges from the formal staging of collective memory and into the unmarked and multiple realm of personal memory.

FIGURE 10. Screenshot of the programming schedule on the popular news platform Nana, Memorial Day 2008.

Side by side with television's rhetoric of variation, its main operation is in creating a continuous perceptual simulation. Raymond Williams perceived television programming as "necessarily abstract and static," locating its effect not in the scheme, but precisely in the liquidation of time slots and social codes, its flow.[16] With flow, hierarchies and locations of memory further enmesh. Television time is thus laboriously structured, yet seamless. Timelines, contend historians Daniel Rosenberg and Anthony Grafton, are coded graphic representations supported by underlying conceptualizations of continuity, simultaneity and rupture.[17] I draw on this cartographic terminology to deliberate the double work of reduction and extension, flow and segmentation, the scheme versus the narrative that the programming schedule entails as a time map.[18] To read television time against the grain means to excavate the interplay of social, economic, and cultural powers that render memory a synchronized, collective experience.[19]

Basing the following analysis on the programming schedule means reading television through its own infrastructural schemes and its own logics. Each of the programming schedule's temporal nodes stands for coded coordinates of regulations, institutions, financial formats and creative manifestations organized into time, or time slots. The tags of different programming formats, the indications of reruns in the newspaper, or the iconic signs in the website schedule, are compressed signals through which television communicates with the viewer. The programming schedule can be read literally—as exactly what it is, an index of cultural interests—yet it also encapsulates a claim on a historical narrative, a scheme of social temporalities and spaces, and a diagram of political agents in a dynamic sphere.

NATION TIME

P.M., 07:30–08:30, News and Live Broadcast
of Memorial Day Opening Ceremony

A mechanical sound, bearing the affect of agonizing wails, howling ambulances, or whistling bombs marks the opening of the National Memorial Day. At 8 o'clock in the evening, a minute-long flat siren orders a complete halt of all routine activities. For the duration of the siren, citizens of the Jewish-Israeli nation state stop their cars, pause their conversations, all movement is brought to a standstill. The sound comes from an infrastructure of speakers placed by local municipalities and broad transmission through radio and television, a combined system originally set to sound alarms in a state of war or impending threat.[20] An engulfing sound, a disruption that transgresses inside and outside, occupying the sensory and merging broadcasting and civil infrastructures, the signal creates a media environment of total synchronization, a zero-point for a collective day of mourning. The siren is an astonishingly effective device of interpellation, circumscribing those who listen to it under its affect. Permeating, the sound is not contained within the ethnocentric national space it aims to mark, but can cross over to Palestinian villages and cities or reach non-Jewish populations, affecting also those not targeted by its hail. The siren is not on the schedule, although television is part of its amplifying mechanism. Instrumental to what follows, the siren marks a shift and redirection of social rhythms. The 8:00 p.m. siren and another one at 11:00 a.m. the following morning are the opening signs of the state's official commemorative ceremonies, and concomitantly, their live broadcasting on television.

Launched with the siren, nation time is defined by its simultaneity and totality of operations. The Israeli Broadcasting Authorities, the governmental entities in charge of regulating public and private media, implement the live broadcast of the official state ceremony across all channels. The recording and live transmission of the ceremony are external to network operations, its production facilitated by a company commissioned by the state. In parallel to the state's ritual, municipal authorities hold local ceremonies; these reproduce the canonical pattern offered by the state. Unchanged, well-rehearsed, and neatly cued, the ceremony's setting is a minimalist stage with state leadership to the right, a military guard to the left, confronted by a crowd of invited guests. A speaker's stand, the state's blue and white flag, and a commemorative torch crowned by more soldiers are the common setting of the ceremonial stage. Every year, state leadership approaches the stand and recalls the memory of the dead as a model of citizenry behavior,[21] collective accountability,[22] and continuity.[23] While they speak, the camera moves or cuts to the audience, most of them members of bereaved families. Through its framing and editing, the live audience is portrayed as an element of the national *mise-en-scène* rather than the ceremony's actual addressees. The broadcast stands for a well-established tradition of televisual spectacle that Eliyahu Katz and Daniel Dayan termed a "media event."[24] More than a happening occurring to its live attendees, the ceremony is meant to be televised, with its overall arrangement designated for the television screen. The setting and the formal choreography replicate the aesthetics

of the state, creating a play of sentiment, authority, and power, and mobilizing memory from its individuated agents into national myth.

The ceremony is continuous with Israeli law and its temporal directives. In 1963, the Israeli parliament passed the "Remembrance Day
Law," or "Memorial Day for Fallen Soldiers Law," ordering that a day of
remembrance of the nation's fallen soldiers should take place seven days
after the Holocaust memorial day, and foreseeing the National Independence day.[25] More than a decade earlier and three years after the dec-
laration of statehood, in 1951, the Israeli legislature engraved memory
in its laws when it constituted the "Martyrs and Heroes Remembrance
Day Law" (today referred to as "Holocaust Memorial Day"). The 1963
Memorial Day law reads:

> On Remembrance Day there shall be, throughout the state, a two-minute
> silence during which all work and all road traffic shall be suspended. Flags
> on public buildings shall be flown at half-mast. Memorial functions and
> public rallies shall be held. Commemorative ceremonies shall take place in
> camps of the Defense Army of Israel and at educational institutions. Broad-
> casting programmers shall reflect the special character of the day.[26]

The law directs towards the ritualistic. In its generality, it infuses cultural activity, limits economic transactions and sanctions public entertainment. Can a law order memory? The law determines national ethos
on the level of state jurisdiction. It is a rather limited sphere of representation when it comes to the way memories are entrenched in the collective psyche, yet these laws form social temporality: they order a (causal)
sequence from Holocaust through heroism to national independence,
articulate a narrative, and *make time* for remembering.

James E. Young terms the scattering of spatio-temporal signposts that
produce common meaning "collected memory."[27] With its landscape
implanted with numerous monuments of military heroism, the memory
of the nation's dead is manifested in space in a way that concretizes the
affinity and historical right over territory, and that draws a continuous
line between the past and the present. Nadia Abu El-Haj demonstrates
how a similar "re-fashioning" of space and historical right takes place
through archeological sites that connect the modern Israeli state with
its ancient past.[28] Time and space formations are an essential and vital
component of settler colonialism synthetic indigeneity. Israel's ideological geography is grounded in a binary logic of presence and effacement,
the landscape marked by its combative history, and the traces of Palestinian villages and Palestinian lives covered and erased with the same

ferocious zeal. As I will later show, the spatial dualism of presence and absence is extended into the juridical temporality and its ordering of remembrance/forgetfulness. Together with the territorial fashioning, the calendric sequence establishes a causal relationship between life and death that follows the ideological syllogism of Jewish destruction, sacrifice and resurrection. It determines victimhood and survival as core component of the Jewish-Israeli national identity. Television's live transmissions of the official ceremonies during Memorial Day collide time and space under this narrative. In the evening, the official ceremony takes place at the Western Wall Plaza, the remaining wall of the ancient Jewish temple and a site of Jewish remembering. In the morning, the 11:00 a.m. ceremony takes place at Mount Herzl, also termed the Mountain of Memory, where the Holocaust museum and research center Yad Vashem neighbors the burial sites of Zionist leaders, the state's political leadership, and the military cemetery.

While the law implements a meta-narrative and a temporal pause, the state disciplinary institutions translate the general directive of the law into a coherent set of practices. Edna Lomsky-Feder shows how following the Ministry of Education directives for the National Memorial Day, schools in Israel implement memorial ceremonies as part of their nation-oriented educational program.[29] According to Lomsky-Feder, schools' own variations on the canonical ceremony—the state template described above—is where different social groups negotiate their own place in the collective national identity. Among the practices she describes are testimonials, makeshift commemorations of school graduates that build local mnemonic communities, or the translation of national ethos into performative arts (such as dance).[30] Such pedagogy of remembering processes the legal dicta into embodied, interpersonal experiences. The school, a representative of civil society, implements a didactic interpretation—ultimately an internalization—of state sanctioned memory. Broadcast media, like schools, are part of civil society's disciplining tools, its content and ways of operating succumbing to the day's principles of centralization and sober contemplation. But more than aligning itself with national agenda, the media (TV, newspapers, news websites, loudspeakers), by being ubiquitous and occupying the sensorial, converts the juridical into the habitual.[31] Moreover, by pacing everyday trajectories, media inject memory into all aspects of life.

Section 4 of the Remembrance Day Law orders the closure of government offices as well as cultural and commercial venues.[32] Municipal regulations dictate the shutting down of all venues of commerce, service, and entertainment in Jewish-Israeli locales. The law's limitations on commercial activity—targeting what can widely be referred to as the private sector—enacts a more pervasive mode of remembering, less explicit than the law's disciplining ramifications. Daily newspapers' coverage of Memorial Day during the 1980s continuously rebuked ice cream parlors, steakhouses, and kiosks in Tel Aviv for allowing customers in in the evening, after the day was already launched by the siren. Other items protested the inflated prices of flowers at the entrance to military graveyards during the day.[33] Not only the top-down structure of regulation and enforcement, but also the bottom-up implication of social shaming forges a time to remember. Law and taboo turn the Jewish-Israeli street into a sealed zone by prohibiting economic transaction and leisure activity. The summoning of the ceremonial on the one hand, and the restrictions over the banal on the other, implement an itinerary of memory.

As a public institution, television complies with the law by channeling the formal conduct of the day, epitomized by the ceremony. As a commercial establishment in the entertainment industry, the question of how to wield to the law is ambiguous. Reading through the regulatory documents of the Israeli Broadcasting authorities reveals that the generality of the law is maintained, with the documents leaving the live transmission of the ceremony as the only determined content.[34] The formula that was unanimously adapted by the different channels—the broadcasting of particular formats and local productions, the adoption of transitioning logo slides and musical notes to fit the mode and tone of the day, the banning of commercials and promos—emerges from the law's indirect diktats, its formation of a normative sphere. There is the abstract speech of the state, the regulator who listens, and the broadcaster that translates it to coincide with the social taboo. The shifting from the law to its administrative implications is replicated in the transition on the programming schedule from the ceremony to prime time. The ceremony and its broadcasting stand for an explicit diktat, while prime time programming attunes to the law's legal conscious, to its corresponding social sensibilities. Not its explicitness, but its implicit and pervasive layers make a law of remembering so affective.

As the 1951 and 1963 laws of remembrance show, the foundation of Israeli sovereignty was predicated on a call on collective sacrifice, populating its national calendar with ghosts and staging a call on loss as central to its nationhood.[35] A 1998 correction to the 1963 law expanded the definition of fallen soldiers to include what is termed "victims of terror attacks." The decision provoked bitter debates, with supporters arguing that collective memory should apply to all those who died as a result of national conflict, and opponents protesting the conflation of active defenders and helpless victims, reserving a special place for the soldier. The debate revolved not around legal rights or compensations, but rather around a symbolic position within collective memory. On the programming schedule the debate is evidenced in the temporal splitting of the morning ceremony into two events—one at 11:00 a.m. for fallen soldiers and one at 1:00 p.m. for victims of terror attacks.[36]

The 1998 provocation exposed the structured separation and discrimination in the Israeli law of memory. The law's positivist imperative of remembering entails a negative double, the ordering of forgetfulness. Such logic was revealed when in 2009, the Israeli Ministry of Education forbade the mentioning of the Palestinian Nakba (the Palestinian catastrophe of deportation, expropriation, and genocide that erupted in 1948 and continues to this day) in history textbooks used by the Palestinian sectors of the Israeli population. An additional law, passed in 2011, prohibits the marking of Israel's Day of Independence as a day of mourning.[37] The juridical scheduling of social epistemologies relays certain losses while censoring others, remembering Jewish-Israeli deaths and in doing so perpetuating the effacement of Palestinian lives. Achille Mbembe pungently describes the dynamic at play: "the two narratives are incompatible and the two populations are inextricably intertwined. . . . Violence and sovereignty, in this case, claim a divine foundation: peoplehood itself is forged by the deity, and national identity is imagined as an identity against the Other, other deities."[38] Collapsing all narratives under the dominance of triumphant national victory or monumental loss, and, on top of it, denying its victims and their disaster, these laws subsume all temporalities and all historical memories under the event of national formation. Ethnocentric at its core, such hierarchy of death is the line that parts sovereign citizens from noncitizens, and, as the 2009 and 2011 laws show, even within the community of citizens, draws a divide between Jews and Arabs. The basis of Israeli apartheid—a racially-based structure of separation engrained in state laws—deserves a deeper exploration than the one I can provide here, yet the double bind in which to remember means to forget, and in which to mourn particular losses means to perpetuate others, must be articulated. Such formation of sovereignty does not appear on the television agenda, though its absence also speaks. Censored, the occupation of Palestine and the Palestinian people have no representation on the Memorial Day programming schedule.

The sequence of the state ceremony and the news crystalizes the onto-logical and ideological paradigm underlying nation-time and is continu-ous with the synthetic rendering of settler colonial temporality. With this sequence, abstract and ritualistic notions of catastrophe are validated by news reports on actual crises; past deaths are highlighted by contempo-raneous death and performative gestures enmesh with mundane reports. The news inflates a national narrative of security with a populist sense of anxiety, making death both the result of a very urgent threat and an inevitable fate. While the siren permeates, the news is well confined within the spatiotemporal container of nation-time. Nation-time is a col-lision of myth and actuality, inducing memory with a sort of vigilance. From the perspective of television's own operations, the ceremony and the news coalesce two dominant approaches: liveness as spectacle and liveness as immediacy.[39] To borrow from Jane Feuer, the kind of ideologi-cal ontology produced here places on a continuum the state-orchestrated display of what is perpetual and symbolic with that which is ostensibly inevitable and factual.[40] Both temporalities, the eternal and the punctual, neutralize critical distance, being too imminent or too sudden.[41]

The above analysis assumes that the news is bad news—the onto-logical condition in a state of perpetual conflict—but the news is also an everyday ritual, a habit.[42] Here the sequence of ceremony and news tells us something about the 1990s television dispositive, being a social mechanism that mitigates different scales: between norms and excep-tions, from ritual to everyday, from the sovereignty of the state that or-ders the ceremony to the news that is a manifestation of the television's alleged autonomy. The ordering of a unicentric time, staged and dis-seminated by the state, reflects an older model of television as one of the state's cultural institutions. Moving to prime time introduces a different television that becomes prominent in the early 1990s: a multi-channel, commercial, privatized institution, a meeting point of sovereignty and market economy.

PRIME TIME

P.M., 8:30–11:00, Public Assemblies, Documentary

The centralized slot of ceremony and news, a ritualistic iteration on the schedule across the years and across all channels, shifts to a dynamic of formats and strategies. Moving from the unicentric towards that which stands for the people, even the popular, this slot is television's prime. The Second Authority, founded to regulate Israeli commercial television, broadly defines prime time as the time stretches from 5:00 or 7:00 p.m. until midnight.[43] Generally situated after the end of the workday and before bedtime, this is a time spent at home, a time of leisure, emblematic of a constructed notion of privacy—private space, private time, private choice. Targeting larger audiences, it is a carefully balanced programming category that conforms to a prevalent sense of social decorum, what television scholar Charlotte Brunsdon describes as "standards of taste and decency."[44]

Offering the highest viewing percentages, television's prime (time) stands for its peak revenue generation, when masses yield to advertisements. To maintain prime time's profit potential, networks compete for audience attention, offering elaborated high-budget productions, pushing programs' novelty or populism to their ends. Regulatory bodies turn to prime time as a time of heightened scrutiny, set to maintain a balance of interests and production formats.[45] Television formats are a manifestation of the mix of regulation, profit, norm, and novelty. An industry standard and a means to secure reception, format is therefore not only a production scheme, but an institution that balances the social, economic and cultural needs on which television is based. Programming Memorial Day's prime time schedule entails working within a consensual framework and an alert mourning conscience. The challenge for television was to conform to enhanced normative frames while satisfying regulatory demands and leaving the economic model intact.

In 2008, Channel 2 shifted from the official ceremony to the live airing of the public assembly in Rabin Square, produced by the municipality of Tel Aviv. The assembly—a sequence of live performances of popular songs by well-known singers, intermittently accompanied by spontaneous acts of audience "sing-along," and hosted until recently by the famous television-host-turned-center-right-politician Yair Lapid—has been broadcast by one of the major channels since the early 2000s. In line with the airing of the official ceremony, this programming demonstrates the extent to which television's formal idiom, especially during Memorial Day, is part of the visual and political language of public assemblies. Strategically positioned cameras extend the live event into the home, while big screens situated on both sides of the stage show short testimonials by bereaved family members in between the songs, thus bringing a television setting and aesthetics to the live performance. The live broadcast of the assembly joins those who participate by attending with those who participate by watching; the entanglement of screens conflates inside and outside. Transitioning from the official ceremony to the popular assembly juxtaposes the hierarchical choreography of the official spectacle and the spontaneous acts of singing along, the figures of state leaders and the celebrity, the official and historically charged capital and the cultural and commercial center—Jerusalem and Tel Aviv.[46]

Channel 10, which, in 2008, did not purchase the rights for the broadcast of the Tel Aviv event, has its prime time slots lined up with documentaries.[47] *Our Brother We Cried* (Shlomo Artzi and Yaron Shilon, 2008) and *See You Tomorrow, My Child* (Tzipi Bayder, 2008, rerun in 2009) both feature bereaved parents and their story of coping as a main theme. *Sparrows in the Net* (director unknown, rerun in 2011), depicts the story of an armored corps unit during the 1973 war. *The Price of the Body* (Keren Yehezkeli-Goldstein, 2007) portrays four women who deal with the trauma caused by a terror attack through a dance workshop. From a historical investigation to a personal account of disability, these documentaries pertain to Israeli memory discourse. Over the years, Channel 10's dominant features were documentaries, with a significant majority based on personal accounts of loss. *The Little Prince* (Tzipi Bayder, 2005) is structured as an episodic collection of personal "testimonials" by bereaved parents; *In the Name of the Son* (Roni Koben, 2005) tells the story of a father who follows his dead son's footsteps. In 2006 *A Line and a Half* (Nili Tal, also broadcast on 2007, and on Channel 8 in 2009) portrays eight mothers whose sons' graves are lined up in the same cemetery. The 2009 feature *Always Without Him* (Tzipi Bayder, 2009, rerun in 2010) tells the story of two women who lost their husbands, one recently and the other more than a decade ago. *We're Both from the Same Village* (Yasmin Keini, 2010) is a personal journey taken by a man who lost his dad. *Nir, You Have a Daughter* (Tzipi Bayder, 2011) documents Nir Lakrif's family, from the day he died to the birth of his first daughter. In fact, documentary was prevalent across channels,[48] privileged over other formats due to its reputation as a sober form of social contemplation.[49] The history of Israeli television and documentary is inseparable, television being documentary's main source of funding, production, and distribution. Documentaries that positioned the bereaved, rarely the injured, as social actors, producing a sentimental portrayal of loss, were the dominant mode of production in Memorial Day television of the 2000s.

Launched in 2003 as a commercial channel regulated by the state, Channel 10 had to come up to speed with producing suitable content for national days. The formula it developed satisfied the set of needs indicated earlier in the chapter by Sinai Abt: a production format that responds to both regulatory demand and public sensitivity and is economically efficient. In its first years of broadcasting, the channel purchased local independent productions that concurred with the day's spirit. Those also tended to circulate between channels over the years. In the following years, the channel shifted to in-house productions, most of them directed by the head of the channel's documentary department, Tzipi Bayder. Bayder directed at least one film per year in the years 2008–2012, evidently, and in line with her own admission, maintaining a particular interest in the personal registers of themes related to death and bereavement.[50] These documentaries follow a rather generic template in which testimonials are embellished with recurring cuts to still life—a tap dripping in the cemetery, a door sign wobbling in the wind, stones laid over the grave. These allow the viewers to be immersed in sensation or sentiment. Low-cost endeavors supported by a minimal production unit, produced over a rather short period of time, with a limited focus on research, and formally conventional, Bayder's documentaries satisfied the day's thematic specificity as well as its institutional challenges. Such a constellation, partly necessitated by the tight itinerary and the lack of revenues, explores loss as primarily an individuated experience devoid of a historical or ideological framing.

The formula of the personal account documentary forges social contemplation around a confessional, and in this case highly emotional, impulse. Shmulik Duvdevani studied the commonality of the first person account in Israeli documentary of the 2000s, diagnosing a symptomatic guilt among Israeli leftist filmmakers with the eruption of the second Intifada.[51] Duvdevani focuses on more artistically oriented documentaries that were aiming at an international viewership, in which self-examination is part of the author's artistic self-referential gesture. Here, the subject is a narrowly focused, efficiently produced television documentary aiming at national audiences. Both trends, however, indicate a narrowing of perspective, where social reality is filtered through the personal. Filmmaker Jill Godmilow describes what she terms "the liberal documentary" as "[a] useless cultural product. . . . Its basic strategy is description and it makes its argument by organizing visual evidence, expressive local testimony and sometimes expert technical testimony into a satisfying emotional form."[52] She goes on to argue that, producing "*synthetic intimacy,*" the liberal documentary's obligations are "to entertain its audience; to produce fascination with its materials; to achieve closure; to satisfy."[53] In the same vein, Louis Spence and Asli Kotaman Avci contend that an efficient testimonial formula that was established in liberal documentaries follows an aesthetically conservative path, and therefore does not challenge our politically anchored gaze.[54] In the case of Memorial Day documentaries, the fixation on the family structure as the bearer of loss centers a privatized and conformist formation as the basis for reflection, while the family's own hegemonic groundings are naturalized or obfuscated through its emotional ties. As is the case with liberal politics, its most fraught operation is its self-positioning as a transparent and "normal" social form.

The family seems to be prime time's desired social formation—both as its protagonists and its targeted audience. The assimilative, naturalizing effect of the family-form serves the principle of segmentation that organizes prime time's programming as well as content. A television review of Memorial Day programming from as early as 1983 observes: "[at] Seven, half an hour for Druze fallen soldiers, half an hour for religion [sic] [fallen soldiers]. At nine fifteen, forty minutes for kibbutz members, and the main broadcast presents eight dead from different social sectors."[55] In the early 2000s, the different social sectors were all accommodated by the documentary form. In 2008 Channel 2's documentary production *Summer Seeds* (Ilana Dayan and Gila'ad Tokateli, rerun 2009) presented a "rightist" settler, a kibbutz member, a new immigrant from the former Soviet Union, and a middle-class "leftist," brought together by a shared incident in which their sons, all members of the same tank crew, died. *Our Brother, We Cried,* Channel 10's featured documentary, introduced Druze and Jewish bereaved fathers.[56] In these examples, as well as in others, social difference is strategically organized to attract and speak to various audiences; under a hegemonic, unitizing currency, segmentation and loss become interchangeable. In 1983, when the criticism is made, the prototypical subject was the dead soldier, whereas in 2008, it is the bereaved family member, echoing commercial television's targeted audience. Through the family form, segmentation, sequencing, and seriality are synonymous with an ideological position, turning loss into that which society shares despite its internal differences, that which makes all citizens equal and subject to the same rule.

While a commonplace in 2008, in the early 1980s, the days of public television, the intimate realization of "private" family mourning through the assembly line of commercial documentary production was, for some, an obscenity. Dramatically titled "The Death of Television,"

FIGURE 11. Segmentation. Left: screenshot from *Our Brother, We Cried*, dir. Yaron Shilon and Shlomo Artzi, 2008. Right: screenshot from *See You Tomorrow, My Child*, dir. Tzipi Bayder, 2008.

a 1982 critique of the year's Memorial Day programming schedule sounds alarms against the violation of memory by its personal figuration. As the critic vehemently writes: "The presentation of the storyteller's profile, especially if he is a relative of a fallen soldier, penetrates his own private sphere of pain, such penetration feels like peeking through the keyhole, even if the person opens the door for us (and appearing in front of the camera is indeed opening the door).... Such a routine [the talking head aesthetic], especially in matters so painful and sensitive as the commemoration of the dead, is unforgivable."[57] The author goes on to argue that television should provide a more heroic and poetic evocation of memory, rejecting the close-up aesthetic of the character-driven documentary as being inappropriate and voyeuristic. Television's death, provoked by the title, is its loss of sovereignty, becoming too intimate, losing its authoritative, elevated voice, the voice of the state. Without falling back on the critic's already-nostalgic dogmatism, television's looming mortality takes place in the shift from public, state-funded television to a commercial model of broadcasting.

Pre-commercial public broadcasters based programming on the assumption that the state, and television as its extended cultural-technological form, is an emancipating authority with a pedagogical task. Memorial Day programming schedules in the 1980s revolved around what was deemed "high art": classical music, dance, poetry, prose, drama, philosophy, and theology. Television prime time aired adaptations of Hebrew literature and theatre plays such as *Zohara's Shmulik* (first broadcast in 1984), and *Akeda* (on the biblical story of the binding of Isaac; first broadcast in 1987), mixed with collections of prose and poetry, for example, *Fathers and Sons: Chapters in Hebrew Literature* (first broadcast in 1980), *In Their Memory* (first broadcast in 1982), *An Invitation to Cry* (first broadcast in 1985), and more.[58] Modern dance performances by Israel's leading dance companies,[59] and the pre-recorded broadcast of live concerts (usually in the 11:00 p.m. slot) brought performative arts into individuated households, and represented yet another manifestation of television's malleability as a medium that channels other forms and media. Thematically-oriented original compositions of dance and music had gained their nationwide television premiere.[60] These broadcasts gave an elevated, poetic, and indeed authoritative form to the already monumental themes of heroism and sacrifice. State television's broadcasting agenda was prompted by an elitist perception of art, sanctioned by the state that realized art as an emancipatory citizenry practice. Under the state program, unlike the free market, art's value was not overdetermined by singularity and exclusive access. Manifestations of original, local creativity were widely shared, replayed excessively over the following years.

A medium to disseminate national pedagogy, public television's recurring Memorial Day formats included the historical report and the sightseeing program. Sightseeing programs were a widespread format of 1980s Israeli television, with a particularly didactic inclination. Memorial Day specials manifested most directly the instrumentality of public television by the sovereign state. An episode of *Beauty Spot* was dedicated to the 1948 battle of *Yihiyam* (broadcast in 1982) and special episodes of *Middle Trail, Side Trail* toured the sites of the Battle of *Nebi Yosha* (broadcast in 1988) and the Battle of *Har Etzion* (broadcast in 1989); the history program *Stories of the Good Country* dedicated a special episode to the story of the Elders of *Tzfat* during the 1948 War (broadcast in 1990). In these instances, television's spatial and temporal formations acquire a particular ideological bent, ascribing events and places into a national narrative, geography, and language. Such programs clearly manifest what was earlier described as settler colonialism's territorial refashioning. These formats gradually disappeared from the Memorial Day programming schedule. Shifting away from its institutional ties to the state and towards a semi-private commercial form, as the 2008 schedule shows, battlefields and monuments gave way to interior domesticity, historical heroism was supplemented by personal memories, and the unified body of the state was reconfigured as the specific bodies of a series of individuals.

State television had a figurative manifestation too: the bodiless figure of the intellectual or the expert whose cultural capital, valorized by the televisual format, transcended corporeality or intimacy. Poets such as Natan Yonatan or Yehuda Amichai, artists, novelists, playwrights, publicists, and philosophers made frequent appearances on Memorial Day's TV screens. The intellectual was constantly typecast as a spiritual authority who translates national endurance into ideals of protection, redemption, and a lasting desire for a Jewish national home and historic justice, the great mottos of the Zionist regime. Over the course of the 1990s, experts, mainly from the field of psychology, took their place, concretizing national ideology by pathologizing the collective psyche. As Michel Foucault shows, the psychologization of the social body engenders the figuration of the individual as the subject of citizenship on the one hand, and the consulting and disciplining state on the other.[61] Anchoring mourning in forms of knowledge or poetics and language, these expert figures also filtered out the "noise" of occupation, colonization and non-Jewish suffering.

Moving to a commercial model, the former state television was accused of elitism, exposing the domination of television, on and off screen, by Ashkenazi (European-white), upper-class, male hegemony. In 1993, the first days of commercial broadcast, Alex Gilaadi, the first CEO of the Israeli television network Keshest, was notoriously cited as declaring that the new television would speak simultaneously to the elite and to "Massueda from Sderot." Together with Abt, whose articulation of television's "best behavior" opens this chapter, Gilaadi is another broadcaster who offers insight into a televisual ideal. Gilaadi suggested that subjects like "Massueda from Sderot"—a prototype of a Mizrahi-Jewish woman living at the periphery—were never addressed by the public channel, bringing to the fore the kind of viewership assumed, or ignored, by public television. Against the transparent and abstract body of authority and social elite, Gilaadi articulates a concrete subject. Yet, retaining a derogatory stereotype that positions the Mizrahi-Jewish woman as one who does not understand high culture, Gilaadi discloses not only the deep-rooted racism, sexism, and ageism on which television's old guard operated, but the translation of populism into fixed and narrow identity formations and bodies. While the ideological ideal of "collectivity" rendered the social body amorphous and allowed effacement, for commercial television, segmentation, synonymous here with sectorization, becomes a selling point and hinges on making bodies concrete.

In the period of transition from public broadcasting to commercial television, the most popular format was the studio talk show, topping television's ratings lists, presenting a formula for popular and commercial success, and indicating new directions for television. The studio talk show was there also in the days of public television as a prominent formation of discourse and expertise predicated on a panel of speakers staged as a theater of public debate steered by a moderator. Transitioning to commercial television, what changes is the panel, or rather the way the "publicness" of the panelists is formulated. Instead of figures of cultural knowledge, commercial television favored figures dubbed by the industry as "celebrities" or "talents" who populate social imagination by virtue of their success, networks, and glamor. They are someone to look-up-to or look-at, a ratings guarantor in the service of the network. These were paired with the "common" person with the un-common story, whose misery or fortune was utilized to trigger affect, a sympathetic figuration for the audience. The panel set-up entailed segmentation in a single space, difference processed into commercial formula, a micro-cosmos stuffed into the television's studio. A backlash to television's cultural didacticism, commercial television's studio talk show figured the social through the prism of the psychological, sensational, and melodramatic, prioritizing the story over the opinion or idea. A format of transition, the studio talk show functioned as the basis for the rise of the "character" or the individual as the motor of television's social non-fiction. Indeed, the liberal, character-driven documentary later took the lead, omitting the installation of public discourse embodied by the studio talk show's host and panel, and zoomed in on the psychological drama of a single subject.

The recourse to the individual and the economizing of life—their shaping into a commercially efficient format—is the epitome of a privatized political economy. In this new economy, the personal is at a premium, collective or national paradigms no longer hold sway, and loss changes its currency. The social body is formatted through the private habitat, an individuated experience of loss simulated within the atomized unit of the family and home. Privatization displaces social ideals into a concrete psychologized body, one that can potentially be populated by every citizen. Segmentation creates the illusion that this body transcends dynamics of marginalization and exclusion within the citizenry, that each citizen has an equal access to the political and cultural capital that comes with loss. Personalization, or the fantasy of the personal, enacts a form of withdrawal, further repressing the state's ongoing project of colonial violence. The re-economizing of loss and with it the affect of social alienation not only impacted the evolving format of the liberal documentary, but also enabled the production and programming of personal memorial videos.

Despite the transition to a free media market and the deeming of state-elicited representations as elitist, national sovereignty as a collective imaginary and as an institutional control remained intact. First, commercial television networks continued to be regulated by and accountable to an official state entity which ensured that sovereign interests were maintained. In addition, while television sought less centralized and more personalized ways to address its audiences, what emerged is what Noam Yuran has termed "the new statehood," an idiom in which the nation is commodified as an identificatory brand name.[62] Not an egalitarian authority but a personalized product circulating in the private media market, the categories of national identity were adapted to the new television language of commercialism, a selling point that secures incorporation in the face of deepening social schisms. From the perspective of prime time formats, yielding to the regulator's summoning of a local, socially oriented content to the public desired formation of privatized, personalized subjecthood and to television's economically-efficient production mode, it was ultimately the liberal, character-driven documentary that epitomized television's best behavior.

MARGINAL TIME

Late Night, Early Morning: Personal Memorial Videos

Television's temporal operations cater to what Lauren Berlant terms the "intimate public." As Berlant construes it, the intimate public is positioned in proximity to the political, constituted by the exchange of private feelings and stories, bound by a strong sense of belonging and commonality, formed through shared signs and gestures that circulate internally among its members. Berlant contends: "[the intimate public is] a space of mediation in which the personal is refracted through the general. . . . It is a place of recognition and reflection. In an intimate public sphere an emotional contact, of a sort, is made."[63] The intimate public is first and foremost a condition of temporality. According to Berlant, it is a sense of routine, shared trajectories, and the repetitive exchange of visceral and experiential transmissions that infuses intimacy. Designed as a temporal transgression with its own routines and rituals, the National Memorial Day as a whole patterns the Jewish-Israeli public through synchronized experiences: attending ceremonies, contemplating portraits of young soldiers who died, consuming particular media.[64] Beyond a formation of social and legal norms, the intimate public reproduces the state as a mediated site of shared emotions, affinities and rhythms. Television instrumentality for the formation of the intimate public is not pinned, either to its content or to its framing of a calendric happening, but it rather has to do with its transient temporal setups that crystallize precisely at the day's cusps.

Less scrutinized by the regulator or watched by the masses, marginal time slots late at night or early in the morning are where normative frameworks start to disintegrate. To some extent, this temporal niche was generated with the launching of commercial television and its extension of programming hours. Surveying programming strategies of early television, television historian Vance Kepley demonstrates how programming the margins was built with a narrower perception of audiences and content: designating night hours for young, educated singles, and morning slots for married housewives.[65] In the era of public television, broadcasting ceased at midnight and the early morning slot was occupied by educational programming directed at schoolchildren. In this programming schema, social functions and rhythms are highly defined. With commercial television, there is more room, and time, to transgress. Indeed, the content of this time slot, as it is realized in the programming schedule, is the product of disintegration—the disintegration of collective temporalities, of social hierarchies, and of historical narratives.

The privatization of the Israeli television market was one detail of a larger program of privatizing the national economy and state institutions, starting in the 1980s and culminating in the 1990s. This included the privatization of state communication infrastructure and services, technology industries, education and culture, prisons, banking and finance, construction, transportation, natural resources, agriculture, and even parts of Israel's most distinguished symbol of collective socialist utopia: the army. Economic reorganization goes hand in hand with the privatization and individuation of society. In the introduction to this book, I delineate a sequence of political crises that designate the disintegration of authority on the one hand and the emergence of (a) new political subject(s) on the other: the failed military involvement in Lebanon, a crisis of trust between political institutions and civil society, and a growing social unrest, among others. The rise of trauma discourse during the 1990s engenders a scenario of victimization that, in the Israeli context, produces a deviant interpretation, further enhancing Israeli citizens' disavowal from necessary and urgent ethical stances in the face of recurring atrocities and the ongoing occupation in Palestine and the south of Lebanon. The assimilation of the soldier, a historically and socially charged emblem, into the sphere of kinship—from a means of protection to its subject, a child—assigns the parent, and more specifically those parents whose children have died, as the ultimate utterer of a speech act. However, formed by loss, these voices stick to their singular attachment to their kin. Ubiquitous, private, decentralized, the new media landscape caters to this speech of singularization, not only by entrenching itself into hitherto domestic and privatized modes of production, but by facilitating new platforms and establishing a new visual regime.

With decentralization, marginal slots bear the potential of an excessive space that upsets the balance of power structures. This is where family-produced content, regardless of production quality, length, or cultural significance, was programmed, not as an institutional strategy, but as a gift: giving time to the families. It was a space where families could reclaim a memory not regulated by populist or national paradigms, to articulate loss in its fragmentary and destabilizing form. But as a facet of the television apparatus, a calculated shift in its temporal-ideological schema, these marginal programming niches rather emerged as a safeguard. Removed from public spectacles and public discordance, they ultimately served as a place for necropolitical sovereignty to become intimate. While the airing of family-made commemorative videos and the mere fact of their production was enabled and shaped by contingency, their programming fostered continuity. It was necessary, however, that they be situated at the margins of television operations.

For television programmers, marginal time slots dictate different audience designations. Despite not necessarily representing a scaling-down of social hierarchies, marginal time slots are the times when audiences become more concrete, no longer the amorphous "national community" or "majority of the people." The specificity of audiences impacts the mode of address, producing a sense of familiarity and intimacy with the audience. Like telling a joke among friends, a close group of members that can share the irony, when intimacy and transgression go together, their effect is affirmative rather than destabilizing. Television's marginal spaces allow things to be stirred while keeping them well within the scope of the normative.

This chapter opened with the premise that by broadcasting family commemorative videos, television gives something to the family. But does it get something in return? And what does it give up by giving away? As already indicated, with privatization, the new commercial channels faced two major issues: the constant demand to produce local, original, relevant content that will satisfy both the regulator and the public interest, and the need to do it within budget restrictions. Here lie television's "gains," a combination of time and production values that satisfies coinciding social scales. But the programming of personal memorial home videos alters a number of television's paradigmatic principles. Broadcasters consciously overlook formal standards, airing videos with poor aesthetic values and opaque or underdeveloped content. They forego exclusivity, as videos are often broadcast by different channels over the years, at times even in the same year. They air videos with no production credits, no referencing of their author, no indication of their source of funding, and occasionally with no title, which compromises standards of disclosure, creative credits, and authors' rights. Lastly, the conditions under which television is attached to the producers of content are drastically different. The broadcaster neither commissions nor buys content, and the relationship is not inscribed in any official contract-based form of attachment. Instead, programming itself becomes highly personalized, as the programmer either receives or collects the videos directly from the families.

Television's act of "giving up" is a form of transgression that applies first to its own operations. Transitioning into a new political, institutional, and technological era, it was necessary for television to loosen standards of production and authorship. Categories of labor, ownership, and quality are pushed to the limit with the broadcasting of amateur and family content. Such transgression allows a space for informality, which underscores an impression of authenticity and immediacy and associates television not with the state but with the family, the archetype of civil society in the age of neoliberalism. The transgression of professional codes demonstrated elasticity, but also, ironically, "saved" professionals from the precarity that came with the transition to a free market. The popularity of the commemorative family production, generated by its public exposure on television, opened up a new production niche in the private market and provided an additional source of income to filmmakers who, in the age of private television, mostly had to resort to freelancing. The mobility of labor in the free media market—discussed in chapter 2—translates to the mobility of content and format across the broadcast schedule. By 2008 there was already a thematic, productional, and at times aesthetic consistency between prime-time character-driven documentaries and the family-made commemorative video. Makers, stories, and the singularizing position of intimacy moved freely between the two categories.

The function of the broadcast schedule as a form of social tempo is itself transgressed. The airing of a family video further specifies the targeting of audiences, with families negotiating with the channel for a particular time slot and disseminating the airing time to all their acquaintances. By so doing families domesticate the medium, turning the programming schedule into its own calendar of internal commemoration rather than a document of the public agenda. The idea that the programming schedule can be read in a way which is specific to a single family undermines the understanding of television's programming as flow. It makes television specific, close, and intimate, and also, as if anticipating its current formation, usable, personalized, and habitual. As for viewers who are not family, they are given the lure of getting closer and being part of this intimate constituency. Once again, this can be read as a transitional phase, an epistemic precursor of user-oriented streaming and user-generated sharing platforms. What is striking in this diachronism is the fraught continuum between institution and self, especially when considering the less liberating and less optimistic utilization of habitual and personalized media as means of surveillance, everyday complicity, self-regulation, and populist authoritarianism, all symptomatic to the Israeli case.[66]

A link in an arthropodous medium, the assignment of personal homemade videos to a bracketed, specified time, removed from the time of national remembering or the articulated sequence of prime-time consensual sentiments, serves a political logic. It is a politics that displaces politics, that seeks to render certain articulations outside politics, concatenated and at the same time removed. Put at the margins, the videos are separated from the economy of production, indicative of a discrepancy of form and standards. This reflects an ideological contingency that reserves a space of intimacy that neutralizes critique or action, bracketing out violence and oppression. Television's malleability and simultaneity of scales caters to this politics of disassociation. Lastly, the margins are also the aftermath, the place where ostensibly there is nothing more to add, hence the neutralizing rhetoric. In 2008, many of the videos were immediate expressions of the 2006 Israel-Lebanon War. Tzur Zarhi, Oren Lifshitz, Yotam Lotan (*The Days of Yotam*), Oz Tzemach (*Oz*), Nissan Shalev (*Flew Away Forever*), and Shay Berenstein (*Through Me to Control*) all died during the events of the summer of 2006: a large-scale invasion by the IDF of southern Lebanon and the onset of a war against Hezbollah. These videos exist in the broadcast schedule as isolated expressions of pain. They are too close to be organized into a historical narrative, too distant to comment on some of the painful debates generated by the violent crisis of 2006, and too sporadic to be affiliated with social conventions.

RERUNS AND FILLERS

As a scheme through which time is synthesized, the schedule encompasses a complex set of temporal trajectories, or rather, it is its own temporality. A quotidian utility, the schedule records television broadcasting *now* with a very limited consideration of past and future. Drawing on television's paradigms of seriality and routine, it is concerned with reassuring the unchanging rhythm of habits, perpetuating television's ordinariness and the continuity of format, technologies, and institutional structure. Its constancy notwithstanding, as a document in and of itself the broadcasting schedule aims at the future; it foresees and precedes programming, telling us what is going to happen, at least on television. "Special days" programming adds another temporal loop, being marked by notions of rupture and exceptionalism that gesture towards past events as pertinent for, even actively shaping, a collective present. The programming schedule is the interface through which television "helps produce and render 'natural' the logic and rhythm of the social order."[67] Its gestures towards the past are imposed on television— through other timelines, such as national or religious holidays—and are also formed and neutralized through it.

Despite its empirical richness, the programming schedule, at least the one published in entertainment sections, is lacking the kind of fullness of evidence that one can find in other historical records of television conduct and production. It is coded, abbreviated, partial, ostensibly "unimportant," and enables access only to surface knowledge.[68] Initially, what brought me to the programming schedule was the absence of family memorial videos from other historical records or spaces. When broadcasters understand the videos as "a family thing"—spontaneous expressions that television features but does not *program*, with intentionality and accountability— time is indeed given away, not structured, but ephemeral. Family videos are deemed outside television's jurisdiction, thus absent from its other records. The schedule, as a quotidian appendix to television, a mundane plan (not quite a document), records their presence in the Israeli media sphere, even if as a general category of "personal commemorative videos." Indicating years, time slots, and channels in which memorial videos were aired, the schedule is therefore a reference for the emergence of form. Second, while the production of memorial videos seemed at first dispersed and individualized, each of them conceived separately by a specific family in a specific instance of loss, their situation within the programming schedule places them in a systematic diagram. Reading the programming schedule produces a chronology and anchors memorial videos on a timeline, as standardized and consistent television content, despite the institution's own exterritorialization. More importantly, it positions these articulations side by side with other memories, thus delimiting the cultural, institutional, and economic nexus in which they are made possible. This scheme not only shows the drifting of memory from an official sphere orchestrated by settler colonial state law into more intimate, trivial, and personal realms, but manifests different paradigms of television's best: a state instrument of forging the national community, a commercial tool catering to the family as an individuated consumerist entity which is a paradigmatic motor of neoliberal society, or a self-broadcasting outlet: habituated, personalized media for a self-governed subject.

The television broadcast schedule is a particularly pervasive social formation, since it is never about a single instant, but rather the fluctuation of temporalities, forms, and utterances. At the same time, it articulates these various locations and expressions of the social as a continuum, zigzagging between official narratives and other realms of experience. "It is all about assembling blocks," one television programmer explicates the art of composing the programming schedule. Then, she adds, "gluing" these blocks with 'fillers' and 'reruns.'"[69] Fillers and reruns are television's residue, leftovers that are recycled, repurposed, and inserted to maintain continuity in between heavily charged—at least in the case of Memorial Day—"blocks" of content stemming from various memory matrixes. A connective tissue, fillers and reruns are essential to ensure the continuity of the apparatus, a basis for the cohering and synchronizing rendering of televisual time.

In professional jargon, reruns stand for programs that are being shown for at least the second time, their inferiority a result of their deviation from television's actuality, its implied coalescence of the singular temporality of viewing with that of broadcasting. Fillers can be a music video clip, short episodes, or flash interviews, self-contained units that are used to literally cement cracks and gaps within the flow. As a form of utility, fillers themselves tend to be overtly rerun. Within the accelerated speed of contemporary media platforms, these formats are no longer merely an additive but content, valorized through notions of virality and immediacy. Fillers and reruns play an important role in holding together the Memorial Day programming schedule. Organized around the live broadcast of three ceremonies that produce unstable time slots due to their complex mediation of spaces and tempos, the broadcast lineup is prone to disruption. The day's banning of commercialism or entertainment, and the ensuing lack of advertisement or trailers, further enhances fragmentation.

Fillers step in to keep the flow. Memorial Day being a specifically local cultural affair that designates its own content, television networks are always short of original local productions to populate the agenda and often rerun the previous year's shows. In the days of public television and in the transition to a commercial model, broadcasters sometimes reproduced entire programming blocks, year after year. Consequently, Memorial Day programming continuously reproduces the previous year's sequence. While networks heavily rely on an economy of recycling and reshuffling, they are subject to regulation. The regulator limits the use of fillers and reruns to sustain broadcasting cultural value and safeguard novelty, originality, and relevance. While fillers and reruns are essential for television, they are perceived as something that compromises it. Beyond their adhesive functionality, reruns and fillers are markers of value, more specifically of deflated value, the low value of the repetitive, the overused, the already known. As a format, they pre-order television's always conventional, already generic mode of cultural circulation.

Existing outside production economies and regulation and with a variable length, mostly shorter than the average television format, personal memorial videos were often used as complementary items, apt to fill-in or be re-run. Here, the morbid irony of the television apparatus once again comes into play, the singularity of the subject always incongruous with the iterability of circulation. From the perspective of the family, a video produced in memory of their loved one is utterly sui generis. It is specific to their loss and their processing that loss into the visual medium. How can this be reconciled with being a *filler* or a *rerun*? While the videos insist on their subjects' irreplaceability, their successive broadcast in the course of one specific day, one day a year, sometimes year after year, creates a plurality of particular, irreducible, unrecovered singularities.

The singularity of loss remains locked within the specificity of the programming time. Through the prism of flow and sequencing, loss becomes a currency to be circulated and reproduced. This is where personal experience, ideology, and institutional practices never meet. The play of scale,

הערב יום הזכרון לחללי מערכות ישראל
לא יוקרנו סרטים בבתי־הקולנוע

FIGURE 12. Television listing for Memorial Day, *Yediot Achronot*, April 28, 1998. The title at the bottom reads: "Tonight, the evening of Memorial Day, there are no screenings at film theatres."

the concurrent mutation of an already highly fabricated construction of the public and the private enabled by television, make the homemade memorial video an intimate expression imbricated into a state formation, utterly specific and widely common. "The coupling of suffering and citizenship," notes Lauren Berlant, "is so startling and so moving because it reveals about national power both its impersonality and intimacy. The experience of social hierarchy is intensely individuating, yet it also makes people public and generic: it turns them into the kind of people who are both attached to and under-described by the identities that organize them."[70] Although born out of, and feeding into, very personal feelings of loss, being programmed means being liable to endless repetition, being imbricated in the larger frame, as a filler or a rerun.

PART TWO

Intimacy

CHAPTER 4

Figures of Speech

And quickly, like a fugitive, she goes down the steps, the very same steps up which—in a day, or a week, or maybe never, yet she knows they will, she has no doubt—the notifiers will climb, three of them usually, so they say, quietly they'll climb up those steps. It is impossible to believe that this will happen, but they will, they will climb up the steps, this one and the next, and that one that's slightly broken, and on their way they silently recite the information they are bringing her. . . . All those times she has walked to the door when the bell rings and told herself, This is it. But the door will remain shut, a day from now, and two, and in a week or so, and that notification will never be given, because notifications always take two, Ora thinks—one to give and one to receive—and there will be no one to receive this notice, and so it will not be delivered.

—David Grossman, *To the End of the Land*

For never has experience been contradicted more thoroughly than strategic experience by inflation, bodily experience by warfare, moral experience by those in power.

—Walter Benjamin, *The Storyteller*

TO RUN AWAY FROM A MESSAGE

In David Grossman's novel *To the End of the Land*, the heroine, a woman named Ora, escapes her home in order to avoid a message that will be brought to her by three messengers. The messengers will inform her, so she fears, that her son, Ofer, who joined a large-scale military operation that morning, has died.[1] Ora's escape sends her on a trip across Israel-Palestine. She visits her former lover, the shell-shocked Avram, and forces him to join her escape. She tries to silence the threat of the message of loss with a different speech, one that she believes will protect Ofer. This speech is an urgent and demanding one, functioning as a last resort, a sheltered phonetic sphere in which Ofer is kept alive, nurtured and provided for by Ora's speaking. As Grossman tells us through Ora's inner voice:

> Her entire body throbbed and exhaled his name like a bellows. . . . He was tearing her up from the inside, flailing around and beating his fists against the walls of her body. He claimed her for himself unconditionally, demanded that she vacate her own being and dedicate herself to him eternally, that she think about him all the time and talk about him incessantly, that she tell anyone she meets about him, even the trees and the rocks and the thistles, and that she say his name out loud and silently over and over again, so as not to forget him even for a moment, even for a second and that she not abandon him, because he needed her now in order to *exist*—she suddenly knew that this was what his biting meant. How could she not have realized before that he needed her now, in order not to die?[2]

The novel's triggering event, which compels Ora to escape her home and kidnap Avram, is portrayed in the book as a haunting image of three messengers approaching the doorstep. It refers to a formal procedure in the IDF in which, following a soldier's death, three military officials are sent to notify the family in its home. In the novel's world of events the arrival of the message is always imminent, yet it never materializes. Imagined, or perhaps foreseeable, the encounter not only incites Ora's escape but triggers a distinct form of speaking that attempts, with its excessiveness and excitability, to negotiate the life of the loved one, reclaim them from being carried away by the messengers' words. From its epic sanctuary, the novel provides a resonating cultural context that reveals the military's tenancy in the most trivial elements of family life. Ora's literary hysteria is painstakingly delineated through these two rituals of speech: the first, the speech brought by the messengers, is a speech that terminates. The second, a speech she carries in frenzy, is a speech that sustains and animates, keeps alive.

Recalling Ofer's course of life—childhood, adolescence, early manhood—Ora is described in the novel as going into labor, giving life through speech. For Ora, speech constitutes and acts, it ruins or recovers; through speech, life and death come into presence. This force underlies her escape, as one form of speech bespeaks the other. While the escape is irrational, it implies a refusal. By running away Ora breaches a non-written agreement that dictates family routine as always anticipating an ever-coming message. Ora refuses to wait behind the door, listening, alerted, to the messengers' footsteps, their knocking on her door. Grossman proposes an imagined, even fantastic, form of resignation: Ora turns her back to her familial and social roles, she neglects to comply with her duty to be summoned by a speech event orchestrated by the state.

To the extent that Grossman's book is about speech and its constitutive force, it is also a book about listening and being the recipient of an address. While Ora refuses the summoning power of the message, she holds to the hinging of life upon the utterance. Following such logic, if she is not there to listen to the message, the message cannot be delivered, and thus death will not take place. Accordingly, her animating speech depends on Avram to listen to it, familiarizing and remembering Ofer through Ora's stories of him. Listening is a necessary rescue not just for the possibly lost son, but for the troubled Avram. Suffering from post-traumatic stress disorder after being captured and tortured by the Egyptian army in the 1973 war, Avram is described as a ruined person. As the novel progresses, Ora's recollection of her son's life story articulates what was lost in him as well. Therefore, speech is formative and recuperative, and a necessary mode of subjugation for its utterer, its subject, and its listener. Yet, insofar as Ora, Avram, and Ofer are constituted by speaking and listening, the novel depicts them as being trapped by their stories. They speak and listen in a story that already orders and tells them. They are being seized by the violent reality that unfolds and closes in on them. Such predetermination resonates in Avram's name, Av-ra(ha)m (Abraham), in Hebrew "the father of all," the biblical figure of the originary father. By picking this name for the figure of the broken man Grossman invites an allegorical reading, implying that while the characters search for a space in which they can negotiate their demise, the thing they fear—death, loss—has already taken place.

What comes first? Speech that animates—specific, resonating, embodied—or speech that terminates, a sovereign speech that has the power to command life or death? Perhaps, as in the novel, it is the imminent listening to the knock on the door that overdetermines any form of speech. To speak of the dead, to reconstruct their life story and give them life through speech, has been conventionalized in Jewish-Israeli society through a web of channels and media: literature, journalistic profiles, television documentaries, home videos, and so on.[3] Conventionalized, this speech commissions a particular form of listening, one that is sympathetic to their pain, shares the joy of happy memories, commits itself to love and life. Inserted into the chain of life's anecdotes, one story is of a different caliber—the story in which one heard one's loved one had died. It is of a different volume, since this story encapsulates a moment in which death arrives at the family's doorstep. Here, unlike in Grossman's novel, it is not something escaped from, but something encountered, most often through a recited message delivered by military officials. This story, a story about being a recipient of a message, frames all other utterances made by the bereaved. The circulation of message stories in family videos, literature, journalism, and documentary depicts the message of death as a popular trope, a leitmotif singularized through experience. This story, told by the kin, is incorporated into their intimate mourning work. The actual formulaic locution is omitted and the exchange is marked by recalling the image of three messengers, or, even more permeating, *a knock on the door*. This is where we must question the articulated singularity of loss.

Within the personal recollection of facing loss lies an encounter with the state and the law. My argument is that the firsthand, personal experience obscures what is *de facto* a work of sovereignty; that by "giving a voice" to the one who has lost, speech renders the sovereign (the state) silent. It is not that the sovereign does not speak. It speaks in a very literal sense, announcing the death, yet the speech of intimacy sublimates the generic speech of the sovereign through a codified, gestural, echoing, and quasi-mythical sound—a knock on the door.

"Any understanding of live speech," writes Bakhtin, "is imbued with response and necessarily elicits it in one form or another: *the listener becomes a speaker*."[4] A knock on the door is a metonym for a family listening to a procedural utterance that transforms their world. Analyzing the constitutive power of speaking and listening, this chapter draws from J.L. Austin's theories of performative speech, and specifically the speech act.[5] According to Austin, certain allocutions hold a constitutive power and certain actions are performed by their mere saying: for example, "I now pronounce you married" or "I am sorry." The Austinian speech act instantaneously constitutes intentionality, kinship, and their liability to the law or the state. Yet it leaves underdeveloped the prerequisite of the position of listening. If speech acts, then listening re-acts. Such a reading understands speech as a response, a way of summoning and interpolating both speaker and listener. Here, Bakhtin's reading of "speech genre" and Erving Goffman's reading of speech through "form" provide an insightful pathway when encountering sovereign violence intimately.[6] If we think of the message story not as emanating from a foundational speaking subject, but rather a story that summons a particular listening and resonates in a listener, we locate loss not in its singularity, but its exchangeability, its status as a ubiquitous story, a genre in which speakers and listeners are interchangeable.

The chapter is organized around two sections. The first explores the figurative and constitutive power of speech, and the second analyzes message stories. In the first, speech is a scene of singularity and authenticity; in the second, driven by a protocoled military procedure, it is a means of social reproduction. The two sections are connected by a meta-critical section that tracks the genealogy of testimony within media studies, arguing that in the 1990s and the first decade of the 2000s testimony became the dominant mode through which speaking subjects were staged and analyzed. It points to a problem: originally, testimony was a tool of the law, and as such it understands the subject as a generic figure liable to the state, a citizen. The emergence, in the 1990s and early 2000s, of private media—commissioned by the private sector, from families to NGOs and private commercial entities, and in particular involving freelance videomaking—expropriated the means of production from the state and, as a byproduct, positioned the individuated subject at the center. An abstract, yet singular, signifier of humanity, such a subject, appearing in videotaped testimonies, claims global, and likewise abstract, justice, while drawing on generalized notions of pain and victimhood. Put differently, media testimonies became a social convention that personalized the address, speaking to and for "humanity" and in so doing detaching subjects from the fraught politics of sovereign violence. In the case of colonial violence, it should be noted that testimony is a tool that privileges citizens—those who speak, but also those who are in a position to listen—thus further obscuring the structured violence that dispossesses others from that very subject-position of rights, coherency, and personalization. While testimony was mobilized as a means of giving voice to a suffering subject—an important cause by itself—the complex frameworks of sovereign exclusion were too easily ignored. A similar dynamic where striving for an intimate speech overrides its liability to the sovereign happens in the tension between the two speech rituals that the chapter describes.

In the case of David Grossman, by the time the novel was published in 2008 it signified for Israeli readership an additional scale of loss and grief. At the end of the book, separated by a few blank pages, Grossman's own personal voice—not the voice of his narrator—tells the readers:

I began writing this book in May of 2003, six months before the end of my oldest son, Yonatan's, military service, and a year and a half before his younger brother, Uri, enlisted. . . . At the time, I had the feeling—or rather, a wish that the book I was writing would protect him. On August 12, 2006, in the final hours of the Second Lebanon War, Uri was killed in Southern Lebanon. . . . After we finished sitting shiva, I went back to the book. Most of it was already written. What changed, above all, was the *echo* of the reality in which the final draft was written.[7]

The fact that the author lost his son in 2006 was already well known, and Grossman—willingly or not—had become a tragic figure of Jewish-Israeli reality; tragic precisely because of the irony, that is, the tension, alternation and mutual validation of the fictive tale and real events. Like his fictional characters, Grossman, too, was figured by his allegory, his language hailed by the sovereign speech. This is not to say that the death of the author's son is merely allegorical, but to make us think about the crossing of paths, of the story and its teller, described above through the sonar metaphor of the echo.

The allegorical tension, with its rhetorical displacement—the messengers always already approaching the doorsteps, the spoken son and the perhaps already dead son—turns the dead, fictional or not, into something both singular and illustrative. Echo is an intriguing and especially rich metaphor. It is worth noting that the echo puts forward what is heard and not what is seen. As a phenomenon, the echo refers to a doubling of sound by its container, a delayed arrival of sound waves after they hit a surface. What in English was translated as "echo" appears in the original Hebrew as an "echo chamber." In the story-turned-reality there are two echo chambers in which things reverberate, the door and, as I will soon argue, the media, or a public sphere of listening and speaking. It is hard to resist the temptation of reading the knock as a signal that reverberates (publicly), when it hits a surface, a door. Yet, in an echo chamber the vibration of sound displaces its source. Could it be, then, that the knock comes from inside the door? That the story of loss was already written before reality hit? Paradoxically, in Grossman's echo metaphor, reality is the ambiguous resonation, and the story is the source.

In the print layout of the book, the story eventually hits reality—the separated paragraph at its end. The book, the fiction it contained and its non-fiction reverberation, is imbricated in a matrix of media. On Memorial Day 2008, a couple of months after the novel was published, Channel 2's Memorial Day special was a documentary about the mothers of four tank members who died during the 2006 Israel-Hezbollah war.[8] One of the mothers was Michal Grossman, David Grossman's wife. Facing the camera, she recalls the night she heard her son had died. She speaks about not being able to sleep, walking around the house, feeling she needed to prepare for something, when a thought hit her: "Oh god, I've become David's Ora." Anecdotes she tells about her family life, her son and his relationship with his siblings, uncannily reappear as part of the novel's fictional family life. In a blog entry posted on the website of the book's publishing house, Grossman, who gave no interviews when the book was released, writes about his process of writing as one that absorbs his surroundings and his everyday experiences in the process of world-making.[9] The displacement of events, from the life course of the real Uri Grossman to the fictionalized Ofer and back, echoes in these different mediations and remediations. Circulating, moving from one medium to another, across forms and formats, the media sphere becomes an echo chamber in which stories are both conventional and intimate, running along a feedback loop that creates familiarity.

Within this loop the writing voice and the speaking voice have different resonances. Undoubtedly, my question is about mediated voices as a way to convey the limits of authoritative, unicentric, and predominantly linguistic speech, and to address an enunciation that already entails a form of listening. Here I refer to Ervin Goffman's "utterance," used to analyze the complex of formal and social conventions that are summoned by the very instance of speech.[10] Rather than ascribing speech to a singular source, or reading it as an agential, formative manifestation, the utterance brings forward a relational reading, a speech that echoes an earlier speech. The utterance also accommodates what extends speech or language, but is still uttered—pauses, sighs, strangulations, weeping, speechlessness, sniffles. These prevalent utterances potentially articulate a convention of pain, and at the same time transgress the very order of language. Lastly, mediation brings with it an additional set of formal, technological, and cultural conventions that further problematize any preconception of authenticity or singularity attributed to speech. Put differently, as much as mediation "gives a voice," it also speaks by itself. The utterance is an inclusive term that allows us to think together the semiotics, poetics, technology, and performance of speech and listening, and to think them precisely through the areas in which they overlap and resonate.

Back to Grossman: when he is asked to talk to the camera about his son in the television documentary, he diverts the traditional generic convention of reminiscing that the other parents pursue. Facing the camera, the author reads out from a notebook a short fable that his son, Uri, wrote about tyranny and stupidity. Grossman favors the written fable and its implied moral over a testimonial performance. Thus, like his novel's protagonist, Ora, he refuses to accept the pre-known conventions of a ritual of speech, and the ideological position it assumes. Can one refuse the summoning of speech? If the knock comes from within as well as from outside, then one is trapped in a closed system, an echo chamber. Ora's running away from the message is depicted as an act of madness that verges on the fantastic. Grossman's resistance against the reminiscing speech comes only after the fact, and his proposition of an unbinding speech, one that resists the message, collapses into the inevitability of the events ("Oh God, I've became David's Ora").

While I argue that these utterances persist in a reciprocal system, organized by a continuous logic where loss is always imminent and all subjects are subject to the hailing speech of the sovereign, there is something necessarily uncomfortable in my reading. The chapter's exploration of speech is mostly an exploration of listening, thinking not about the intimate expression but rather about what it constitutes, or omits, when it resonates. My analysis aims not at the oppressed on whom violence is inflicted, but at the citizens who opens their doors to it. Part of the problem is the liberal assumption that through listening, we carve a moral position of truth, yet here things get complicated. My aim is neither to redeem nor to demonize the speakers, but rather to articulate the complexity in which they fail to make a speech-act.

A FIGURE, A BODY WITH NOTHING INSIDE

In one of the scenes in *From Me to Command*, a video in memory of Shay Bernstein,[11] Sivan Refaeli, Bernstein's fiancée, stands in front of a treehouse. Earlier, we see Refaeli, who also produced the video, climbing up the treehouse, peeking out of its window. Loss is mostly figured on the threshold. Refaeli says she wanted Bernstein and herself to "have a place of our own." "We worked on it [the treehouse] from sunrise to sundown, it was (her voice breaks) and he didn't get to enjoy this stuff, he was always in the army, he wasn't (sniffles) When we built this, it was a rare opportunity. He didn't have the time." She pauses and then continues: "This house was ours only. In this house I saw our children climbing. It was so much fun to see it. *This is what could have been, this is what should have been.* Our children should have climbed here and they won't." At intermittent moments her monologue is imbricated with still photographs depicting Bernstein fixing the walls inside the tree-house. Refaeli's voice breaks; she turns away from the camera, towards the treehouse. A clip-on microphone attached to her shirt continues to record her sobbing as she climbs up, creating a sound bridge over a cut that leads us inside. In the treehouse Refaeli tucks herself in the corner. We hear her quivering cry and heavy exhalations, then she recovers her speech: "Actually, he's here. I can feel him here. I feel him hugging me. I'm so happy we had [trails off]. Here I know I was lucky, honestly. I don't know how many people were ever like I was in here. You cannot describe it. There's so much joy, and now everything is so— [pause] all this joy is a tremendous pain. [crying] And I was left with nothing. I have nothing. *I'm just a walking body with nothing inside.*"[12] The camera lingers and then cuts.

The treehouse promises intimacy, privacy, a place "of our own." Is the treehouse an echo chamber? As Refaeli tells us, the tree house is a space of emptiness. A miniature model, a playful, self-conscious take on a childlike fantasy of the home, the treehouse directs towards a future that is now devoid of the projected image of reproduction and living together. It is the loss of a future that "should have been" that echoes in the empty space. The failure of a future to materialize leaves Refaeli "an empty body with nothing inside." The echo chamber directs our attention not only to the thing that is echoed, but to the space that echoes it. The scene's formal language supports the sense of hollowness; we move from the inside out and back, a move in both space and time. Refaeli's own movement inside out and in again supplements the temporal rhetoric of "what could/should have been." The images of Bernstein's past self inside the treehouse and Refaeli's present account in front of it undo the effect of time by positioning the two lovers, through the interplay of medium, in/out of the same space.

Refaeli's inability to complete her story and her lapses into crying, sniffling, and gasping similarly delimit a relationship between the external and the internal—the exteriority of language and the body's exhalation of voice and air. The clip-on microphone produces a sense of anatomic proximity that likewise traverses from the outside to the inside. The sound bridge is not a cut, but something that crosses through space and body. The lapses from outside to inside, language to crying, these formal and technical figurations delimit containers in which love and intimacy are realized through void, from "he won't" to "I feel him here."

Roland Barthes discerns three types of listening: "alert listening," oriented toward a source and applied through our animal instincts;

FIGURE 13. Screenshot from *From Me to Command*, dir. Gil and Yaniv Mezuman, 2008.

FIGURE 14. Screenshot from *From Me to Command*, dir. Gil and Yaniv Mezuman, 2008.

"deciphering listening," which is concerned with the sign; and a third mode of a "listening to me," a listening that also speaks. As Barthes writes: "Listening to the voice inaugurates the relation to the other: the voice, by which we recognize others, indicates to us their way of being, their joy or their pain, their condition: it bears an image of their

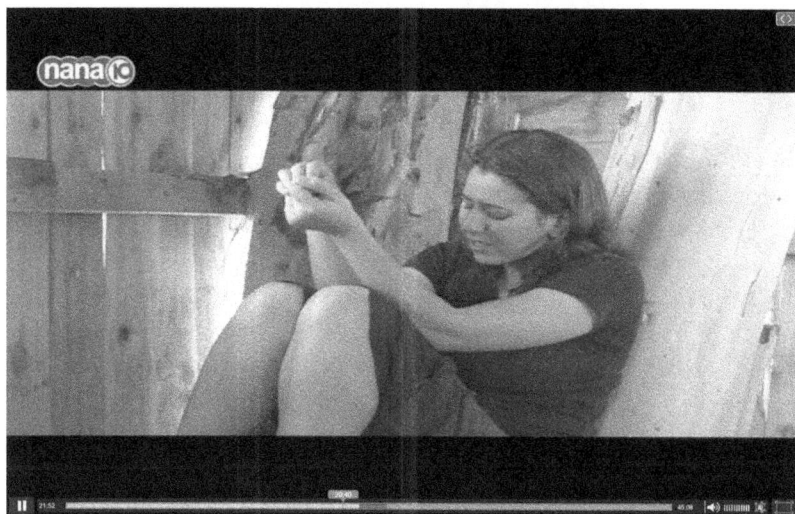

FIGURE 15. Screenshot from *From Me to Command*, dir. Gil and Yaniv Mezuman, 2008.

body and beyond, a whole psychology."[13] Refaeli's confession in the tree house, what she says, and equally what she is unable to say, are so personal and close, they manifest "a voice" in a way that places subject-hood with the organic and corporeal, a voice that, as Barthes argues in another essay, reverberates in a body with flesh and lungs.[14] Similarly, Jean-Luc Nancy situates the ontological and ethical dimension of lis-tening, a listening to the other, in reverberation[15]—Refaeli's crying and exhalations while she tries to complete the story. Drawing from struc-turalist and psychoanalytic traditions, these thinkers proffer listening as an ontological and ethical encounter with the subject. But Refaeli, per her self-portrayal, is a "body with nothing inside." What does it mean, to speak and listen from a place of emptiness, to speak and listen to a body that is here/not here? Introducing his first category of "alert listen-ing," Barthes uses two intriguing examples: Kafka listening to the noises of his own house and a baby anticipating the sound of his mother's footsteps.[16] These two scenes of listening happen in a space that reor-ganizes and attunes all of our senses—not just our ears, but our entire body—towards presence. This presence is frail, ghostly, there-not-there, but is associated with a sense of refuge and love. As Barthes seems to suggest, this mode of listening (and speaking) is highly embodied, but it also hollows the space in which it resonates, there is nothing but the absence of the figure of love. From here, we can start thinking about a semiotic of emptiness, of absence, carried out not by subjectivity as self-contained, intentional, agential entity, but a vacant container, a figure of speech.

A figure of speech is a rhetorical vessel, carrying meaning that is not bound to the literal. The figurative brings with it an artistic treatment, a representation that demands a level of abstraction and aesthetization. At the same time, the figurative insists on the figure, the body. With that it connotes the animating speech that strives to re-present a lost loved one. The dead, and so it seems those who mourn them, are figures of speech in the sense that their existence hinges on language's ambiguity and its capacity or incapacity to represent. The dead are not grounded in the literal, as they are never the thing in itself: the dead is never the living body. While the speakers insist on specificity, the notion of figurative speech as an empty container not only destabilizes subjectivity as a source of agency and intentionality, but introduces an allegorical tension, what Jonathan Kahana describes as that which is "responsible at once to the individual instance and the totality."[17] A form of figurative speech, the allegory is based on a duality of reading that pertains to both the literal and the metaphorical, a semiotic elasticity that contains the singular and the general. Furthermore, the allegory relies on displacement and projection, both of which can be found in the figurative. *From Me to Command* exemplifies a sort of emptiness that dwells in the speaking subject, uttering what is singular and yet generic, pertaining, in the same instance, to individuality and totality.

In Refaeli's video the event of Bernstein's death is recalled four times. First, Bernstein's family members recall how they were notified by the military, an account I will go back to later, when discussing the message procedure. Then, Refaeli meets Bernstein's fellow officers. One of them, Gidi, is asked to speak about his "encounter with the situation." Gidi tries to reach Bernstein through the battalion's internal radio, but does not succeed. He assumes that there are problems with the frequencies and codes, until, after a few attempts, he gets a coded transmission: "Crown. Lisbon. Oleander." He does not explain this in the video because he sits among fellow-soldiers who are familiar with the codes, and he seems to assume a similar familiarity among the viewers. Gidi insists, "I then say: 'Command to control, repeat, over.' I try to change it," but the code remains. When Gidi reaches a meeting point, he tries to find out what happened to his friend, but gets no answers: "I then noticed four covered corpses, thinking 'one of them is very tall. That's Shay.'" He hesitates but then approaches the corpse. This is when, in the video, he breaks down. He asks for water and does not succeed in carrying his story to the end where the physical fact of death—the corpse—lies uncovered. The camera frames him in medium shot while he tells the story and stays there when he gasps. A comforting arm enters the frame and rests on his shoulder. Everybody falls silent and the only thing heard is the sound of Gidi pounding on a stone with a little stick he is holding. The video then cuts and we see Gidi drifting away from the group with a bottle of water.

Gidi's story stretches over and through the technical aspect of communication, the symbolic structure of language, and the literal body. In all these, something does not quite fit. At first, death is silence on the radio channel, a misfit of frequencies. When transmission arrives, it is obscured by the cipher, an opaque system of signs designed to displace meaning. Hanging onto the opacity of language, Gidi rejects meaning; he "tries to change it." Radio codes carve a paratextual level, allowing parallel, in times secretive, channels that fuses language's professionalized and intimate markers. Ironically, Gidi's own radio name is "Certainty" (in Hebrew, "Vada'ut"), but with the splitting of language through code, certainty is hard to obtain. Lastly, when death is present as a physical fact—a covered body rather than a transmission channel or a semiotic structure—Gidi does not speak. His own body fails him in his ability to verbalize.

A third recollection takes place when Refaeli meets with those squad members whose tank neighbored Bernstein's when he was fatally hit. They stand at an observation point, wearing dark fleece and uniform, and describe their mission on the day of the strike. On that day, suffering from poor weather conditions and under fire, they were mobilizing a formation of tanks over a steep landscape. In contrast to the emotional intensity of former recollections, their language is succinct. Still conscripted, their speech is more of a debrief, a common military procedure given before a mission, to guide the soldiers through the process and in an event's aftermath. This speech, associated with the operational, is transgressed when a fellow officer recalls him approaching the tank that was hit: "It was a dark sight, *and I'm not speaking metaphorically*, the tank was black. I couldn't discern its parts, I couldn't recognize a thing."[18] To literalize speech, and demolish its metaphorical resonance, the video cuts from the talking head of the officer to an obscure image of what seems to be a destroyed vehicle, yet the image quality is too poor to convey anything recognizable. Bernstein's corpse, found a few meters from the damaged tank, is first described by the officer as a "figure" and only later identified as "Shay." The figure comes before the name, the body lies before and beyond signification. The debrief strives at linearity and coherency, banning the metaphorical; however, the strike against the tank disrupts the form's intentionality, or the ability to gain a clear view. Despite the soldier's repudiation of metaphor, the "dark sight"—the incoherency launched with the event of death—is where the literal and the figural meet.

The fourth recollection appears at the very end of the video. Refaeli is in the Golan Heights, in the north, close to her parents' home where she met Bernstein for the last time. She recalls how during the war, Bernstein came home for one night, and he asked her to marry him. In the morning, before he left, they had breakfast together, he teased her about something, a couple's joke, and then left. She describes him getting into a military vehicle, driving away, then halting, reaching his long arms out the window, waving goodbye, and vanishing at the end of the street. Here the body is not the abjection, a corpse that would cause representation to collapse. On the contrary, the body gestures, it communicates. The gesture stands for the physicality of language and invites reciprocity. By waving his arm, Bernstein says goodbye, and, implicitly, reassures Refaeli that he will return. This is where Refaeli situates her loss. While these scenes constitute speech's animating impetus, each of the attempts to recall Bernstein's death, or rather their accumulation, support the notion of a failure to convey in the face of absence. Theorizing non-fiction filmic representations of death, both Michael Renov and Vivian Sobchack, in separate essays, have reached the conclusion that death poses a semiotic failure, undermining physicality, indexicality, and representation. Reading death as a transformation from a living body to a corpse, Sobchack posits that such transformation is "in excess of representation and beyond the limits of coding and culture."[19] In that sense, the event of speech is undoubtedly animating only up to when it reaches out to the corpse. Here, speech ceases. The utterance is structured by the principle of a caesura that directs our attention to the point beyond which semiotics fail, unable to reach the dead body, only the figurative.

The semiotic failure here is necessarily a political failure, the inability to make a speech act, to recognize not only the dead body, but the structural violence in which it is imbricated. The figurative displaces the dead body for a subject of loss and longing (what should have been), and displaces the subject of ideology, for a seemingly individuated and singular agent, thereby committing itself to undiscerned reproducibility of that very structure of violence. This is not to take away from Refaeli's pain, or the pain of anyone who ever lost a loved one.

The figurative is engrained in the corporeal, yet at the same time it supplants it. In the military scenes with their group composition, speech lies in the operational—the radio codes, the debrief—yet intimacy is sustained by that very operability. The military operative language brings with it an internal logic; it draws on the common. Not only radio codes, but also slang, idiolects, songs, slogans, intonation, and specific gestures are all codified signs in an enclosed system of signification. Speech (and listening) persists in an obscure exchange available only to the intimate insider, a members-only sphere of interaction. The video cuts from scenes of military camaraderie, marked by the soldiers' idiomatic speech, to footage of Bernstein from the past, reinforcing the incorporating capacities of the utterance. Refaeli assimilates military slang and gestures, and thus gets closer. Her internalizing of language is expressed in the video's title—*From Me to Command*—a codified radio call to command. The radio code is invoked in a way that teases out the tension between the intimate and operative, reverberating as an ultimate, personal transmission from Refaeli to Bernstein. Within this setting, communication is doomed to fail. Refaeli's calling to her lover will not be answered. Nevertheless, in these scenes, speech gains its own body of gestures and affection, its figurative force with elasticity, adaptability and interiority.

Refaeli admits that "[the video] was about going through different stages up to the stage where Shay is *within me* [trails off]. When I talked of him in the video I felt as if for the first time he is coming back to me, my Shay, the loving, funny Shay."[20] In the video's opening scene, Bernstein's friends from various walks of life are gathering on the beach to prepare for a campfire. "I'm sure that through her eyes she (Refaeli) can see him passing through, as another one of the people hanging around," says one of the attendees. In another scene, Refaeli joins Bernstein's military company for a field exercise. When the soldiers come together after a day of training, Refaeli retires. Outside she tells the camera that in the tent it was as if Bernstein was there and that she could recognize him in each one of the soldiers, from the young private to the company commander. "It was too big for my little heart," she admits. Earlier, before Refaeli joins the troops, the camera depicts her at her apartment preparing for the exercise and wearing a military uniform. When the director comments that Refaeli's uniform is oversized, Refaeli responds: "it's Shay's." These scenes suggest a form of replacement, a strange kind of substitution, that uncannily renders present both the dead person and those who incorporate him. The group—of soldiers or friends—becomes a shape, primarily due to the videographic longshot, which simultaneously empties figures of their specificity and opens them to incorporate the missing person. Refaeli's physical presence populates, but cannot contain or fully fill in for Bernstein: she wears his uniform and follows his path in joining the company, but is overwhelmed by the memories. Things are "too big," and yet never enough.

In a later interview, Refaeli reflects on her process of coming to terms with loss: "I've started to redefine words. I realized that whoever it was that wrote the language did not feel what I feel. That 'difficult' is not 'difficult', that 'pain' is not 'pain', it's much more. There are words that cannot describe."[21] The problem with speech is that it is singular and generic at the same time. With the video Refaeli seeks an utterance that speaks its failure to touch or to assign meaning, and that persists within empty containers—words, spaces, and bodies defined by emptiness. Trying to articulate absence as a specific experience, beyond the communicability of language, the speakers constantly lapse on the figurative. The figure poses an ambiguity. On one hand, it is directed towards singularity, aiming at bodies that are affectively marked and specified. On the other hand, there is something empty in the figure, something that lends itself to being repopulated, re-cast. When she speaks, Refaeli's pain lies bare, her broken language lies bare, unraveled, she redefines words and the meaning she puts into loss is utterly her own.

And yet, do we listen to Refaeli specifically or do we listen metaphorically? Researching the video, I found it was uploaded on a website that Refaeli launched titled *Adam VeMefaked* ("human being and a commander").[22] In the many drafts of this book, I have kept moving this piece of information from the text to the footnotes and back, because I am not quite sure what it tells us. I was able to locate a few interviews with Refaeli and she does not read as a person subscribing to particular militant views. Her drawing on the military, it seems, refers to its everyday aspect, as something Bernstein *did*, and as a form of social organization that is commonly associated in Jewish-Israeli society with internal solidarity and commitment. The instrumentality of the military in the sovereign endeavors of occupation, injury, and death are disavowed. It seems that the military, too, is, for her, not a concrete operation but a figure of speech, an empty vessel to represent a lost loved one. There is a limit to accessing the very intimacy and singularity of Refaeli's loss; hence we are left with metaphors or figures of speech. The question is thus: What does she and what do other subjects speaking of their loss recall in excess as they recount intimate stories of love and life? What speaks through them?

AS-IF

Refaeli says: "Something happens to me whenever I hear what happened there. Every time I hear the story [of how Bernstein died], I have the feeling of suspense, I'm waiting so that this time he won't die in the end." Similarly, Gidi tells his friends that when he heard of Bernstein's death on the military radio, he "tries to change it." To narrate to the camera, and moreover, to form a sequence, to organize time, or perhaps, wishfully, to move back time, is a work done in parallel by speaking and by the media platform of the video. "He was always in the army. . . . He didn't have the time," says Refaeli in front of the treehouse. Her effort to put her loss into words is meant not only to come to terms with absence, but to make more time, to suspend, to open a gap in between "what should have been" and what is.

In *Flew Away Forever*, a video produced by the Shalev family in memory of their son Nissan Shalev, Shalev's sister, Avital, recounts the moment she heard her brother had died.[23] "A movie played in my head, of all the things that should've happened and that should've been, and won't be the same anymore. And I couldn't go home; I couldn't face my parents." In this utterance, recognition, and death itself as an ontological experience, are structured as a deferral: to refuse to listen to the message, which is also a refusal to enter the home. Avital juxtaposes the certainty of things that *"should have been"* and their cessation; a fantasy (the movie) versus an encounter which will affirm the new reality; the temptation of continuity—that things will be the same—and the knowledge of the upcoming turmoil. The video then cuts to Shalev's younger sister, who says: "it is *as if* this someone is always [/will always be] absent. He's absent on my birthday, he will be absent on my wedding, and when I have my first child. And nothing can fill this absence."[24] The notion of a permanent absence articulates a future which is abundant in presence and life, which progresses and persists negatively, always referring to a lack and to a failed promise of the things that should have been. In their speech, the sisters form a gap, a transition from presence to absence articulated through formal tensions, condensed and patterned by an *as if*.

These verbalized scenes are all about an intermediary state, a speech that stumbles over temporal arrangements characterized by deferral and displacement. Shalev's grandmother tells the camera that she keeps on thinking "*if only*" she had died that Friday, then instead of joining the operation, Shalev would have gone to her funeral and his life would have been saved. This "if only" wishes to substitute one death with another, a "more reasonable" one, according to the grandmother, since it is the young who should mourn the old. Not only a possible death, but also a life coming into being, supports the positioning of loss in-between and in-spite-of. Two weeks before Shalev's death, his brother, Yotam, had his first daughter, who is also the family's first grandchild. Shalev's father tells the camera how happy they were with the addition of a new member to the family. In a home video taken during the intimate family celebration of the new baby, the father looks at his five children, saying that he anticipates "a lot, a lot, a lot, a lot, a lot more happiness." Holding his now-older firstborn and looking at still images of Shalev with his new niece framed and hanged on the wall, the brother painfully recalls the things he will tell his daughter about the uncle she never got to know, and the joy that the first two weeks with the new baby and his brother still alive encapsulated. Shalev's death is negotiated by his loved ones in relation to the willfulness of "natural" death and the potentiality of new life, in-between a failure ("if only") and a promise ("as should have been"), between the no-longer and the not-yet.

As would have been the case *if*. . . . The phrase sustains the dead and speech itself in the in-between. In between life and loss, in between presence and representation: "as it should have been"; in between the literal and the metaphorical, the desired and what is: "if only." In that sense the as-if constitutes a state of mediation. On the one hand, the as-if bases itself on a negative semiotics, an entire system of signs preoccupied not with what is, but what was and no longer, or with what could have been. On the other hand, the as-if bears a performative weight in which the speaker puts life into the dead-one through speech ("as-if he was alive"), hence the impulse to speak. A subjunctive mode, an impossibility. A being no longer there, being in-between, being sustained only by the utterance, a memory of life is suspended in representation, called upon through another medium, *as if* alive.

Flew Away Forever provides an example of the capturing of the once-alive dead in the ambiguous referential system of the as-if. The video opens with a prologue, a series of still images of Shalev's apartment that were taken, as an intertitle tells us, right after his death. Everything is still in place, exactly as Shalev left it before he was drafted. These are casual settings: bookshelves, pieces of clothing in the closet, a biker's jacket on an armchair, a guitar laid on the sofa, left there by someone to be reused. The cuts between the still images are emphasized by the sound effect of a camera click. While the setting conveys a sense of the unintentional, the framing articulates the subjunctive, the as-if, the flow of mundane activity—what should have been but will no longer be— that is seized and captured by the camera operation, and reproduced in the video. While the still works to preserve and freeze, rearticulating the random as the monumental, the video puts things back into motion. Life and its cessation is suspended through the cut and the click. What seems to be ungraspable through speech, the gap that opens up between presence and absence, is uttered through the sounds of mechanical reproduction.

The effort to come to terms with loss and to give a form to absence repeatedly draws on different means of incorporation. In a sequence in *Flew Away Forever*, one of Shalev's brothers enters a storage space and pulls out an old t-shirt from one of the boxes. The t-shirt was made by Shalev's class in the Israeli Air Force Academy after completing a long and exhausting training regime. The t-shirt says "what is it all for?" The brother smiles bitterly while repeating the joke. The shirt eerily marks a body shaped by military training. Now crumpled and unused, it stands for the missing brother, and the irony is redolent. Shalev was trained as a helicopter pilot, and the uncanniest form of incorporation in the video is his figuration through the helicopter. A friend from the Air Force Academy tells the camera that during the war, whenever he spotted a formation of helicopters in the sky, he would tell his young daughters, "Look, here is 'Uncle' Nissan." This, too, is a figure of speech, a metonymy, in which the living person is displaced by the military device that contains them. The metonymy is repeated in a home video provided by the manager of the lychee orchard where Shalev worked for a short period while still living in the kibbutz where he was born. The farmer, a fatherly figure with a heavy Latin American accent, asked Shalev to let him know before he flew the helicopter above the orchard in the northern kibbutz. In the footage we see the helicopter up in the sky, slowly approaching the camera, while the accented rough voice of the farmer, invisible in the frame, softly speaks to the helicopter: "come a little closer, boy, come closer my child, come closer. . . ." The massive flying device and the recording technology are marked by an intimate contact, displacing what is inside or behind—Shalev for the helicopter, the farmer for the video camera.

As a figure of speech, metonymy is an instrument of expansion—lives transposed into technology, communication, and warfare. It exposes the

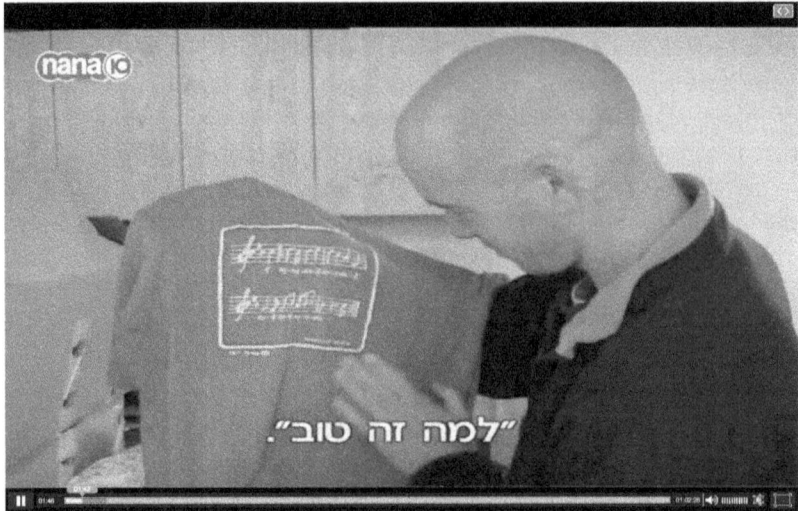

FIGURE 16. "What is it all for?" Screenshot from *Flew Away Forever*, dir. Chen Shelach, 2008.

extent to which both military and media are intrinsic to Jewish-Israeli families' everyday intimacy. This all happens while Shalev is still alive, as-if anticipating what will be seized by the devices themselves. The dead man is taken by military action, and, after his death, those who reminisce about him depend on a media form. The metonym is brought here as a form of the as-if, deferral, or the play of pretending that underlies the metonym's referential structure.

Thus, the utterance, organized by an as-if, sustains a particular temporal structure supported by media and form. Both the media and the military represent forces of amplification, prone to massification and generalization. Put differently, these are spheres of mechanical and social reproduction that work against the aspiring singularity of the listeners/speakers' as-if. In its final scene, the video, so far populated with intimate friends and family, features the famous Israeli folk singer Leah Shabbat, sitting in the family's living room, playing the riff that opens one of her most famous songs, *Always Be Waiting for You*. Shalev's two sisters sit next to her and tell her that the day before the funeral, they heard the song on the radio and felt that it talked about their brother, that "it is as if it was written about him. *It is him.*" The singer then performs the song, whose lyrics convey the anticipation of a loved one returning and the longing of the one who stayed behind. The sisters join her, singing slightly off-key while they cry and laugh. The listener becomes a singer. They sing the song's refrain: "every plane passing in the sky, every star glowing in the eyes, reminds me of you. A wagtail before it showers, crickets in the evening hours, will always be waiting for you. . . ." The video is brought to a close not by its protagonists' speech, but by reverberating, off-key musical notes. The popular song, an emblematic expression of mass media, a recitable and reproducible public address, makes the pain specific and generic at the same time. The singer and the sisters join together in between verbal speech and the melodic arrangement of the voice, in between what is constructed and what is ostensibly intuitive, in between the idiosyncratic and the broadly shared. The singer sets the tone and the sisters sing along— what should have been and what is. Mass media allows a structure of dislocation—*as-if*—projecting the much-recited lyrics into a specific, ever present, yet always-anticipated figure.

The dead is dead and not quite dead. The as-if is a counter-speech act of sorts because it constitutes something that can be constituted only through speech, yet at the same time it allows what is out of the question, a necessary fantasy impelled by the one who lost, an impossible possibility. Possible, because one was once alive and this life promised a future; impossible, because one is no longer. There is a complexity in the as-if that is worth articulating. The possible-impossible, the "perhaps," or *what could have been*, is for Jacques Derrida what allows the future to present itself. Basing a future only on the possible, he argues, amounts to conforming to a pre-existing program.[25] This position is also the source of Derrida's critique on the conventional foundation of the Austinian speech act, its being bound to a preexisting plan. Listening to the message means to submit one's self to a state apparatus that reproduces death. To undo time, to speak as-if, carves a form of suspension that counters the determining force of the death announcement. Suspension, according to Judith Butler, calls into question the very ontological and epistemo-logical webs that anchor the subject. Suspension invites critique, not as passing judgement but as a way to clearly state the principles that condition our common life.[26] As a form of imagination—as-if alive, despite the impossibility—can these utterances transgress the state program, open up other futures beyond militarism and violence? As Derrida and Butler seem to offer, it is the fictional element of the as-if, its impossibility, that opens reality to alternative possibilities, that "spins off existing narratives and seeks out new ones."[27] There is something destabilizing and genera-tive in this insistence on the as-if and its act of deferral, its impossibility.

Structuralist and poststructuralist critiques, like the one offered by Derrida and Butler as well as other critiques cited in this chapter, articulate a constant negotiation that takes place between the subject and the ideological frameworks that constitute it. Imagination is indeed a liberating mandate, and I would like to let its potentialities echo for the reader. At the same time, the ultimate reading I offer here is pessimistic. It can be assumed that families' exposure of the pain of loss, articulating it in their own terms, produces an anti-militaristic statement. This is certainly the position taken up by Jewish-Israeli liberal left of which David Grossman is emblematic.

The Shalev family were highly critical about the war, and specifically about the contestable operation in which their son died. "What is it all for?" asks Shalev's brother, and there are other instances in the video. They are critical of the state military aggression, but the video, as a formal container, does not lend itself to critique, as a way to illuminate and perhaps traverse these violent submissions. It is not about what they are saying, but rather the echo chamber in which it is said. The video's accumulating effect as a product of mass media that circulates—always echoing a prior speech, in reference to genre and conventions—complies with the narrative of enmity and security, affirms it, even if by pushing against it. The video's sticking to intimacy and kinship isolates loss from the perpetual and institutional violence that enables it. The political reality is not transgressed, but rather contained, loyal to the inner, fictional logic of the as-if.

By negotiation one also confirms the authority of the power with which one negotiates, here the dominance of militarism in every aspect of Jewish-Israeli life, including its permeation of the intimate and mundane. The home—and its metonymic form, the treehouse—invites the national fantasy of a secured haven. Tellingly, as an echo chamber the home/the treehouse is characterized by its now-emptiness, already articulating the distorted features of the kind of homely fantasy at work: a home predicated on the ghosts of expropriation and colonial violence. It echoes, if one only listened, the absolute absence of Palestinian and Lebanese life and death from every aspect of Jewish-Israeli loss, including the intimate and the mundane.[28] As an empty space of confinement, the home turned-echo-chamber is an enclosed container that enables a logic of separation. First, it privileges one form of loss over another. Then it isolates that loss from its heavily instrumental aspects and, by framing it as singular ("a place of our own"), brackets out its patterned recurrence. If imagination is already overdetermined and engendered by the speech of the state, then the as-if is also a mode of denial ("as-if he's still here," "as-if he hadn't died"). Here, the utterance works not only to indicate one's innermost desire to negotiate reality, but to singularize, bracketing an exceptional ontological condition of the not-dead dead. As a speech act it acts negatively, it disavows, rather than submitting itself to social truth.

COMING TO TERMS: THE TESTIMONIAL

Exposing the innermost registers of the price of loss could be read as calling into question the national narrative of heroic, purposeful death. But contrarily, the videos produce a muffled compliance. In the following I transition to thinking these utterances of loss not through their singularity, but through the form that organizes them, a "genre of speech," to draw on Bakhtin, that persists within a close system of codes and norms, uttered by listeners who become speakers. In this book I show how Jewish-Israeli personal commemoration is shaped by its tools of mediation, a complex of private video productions. The dominant videographic convention I want to focus on here is the testimonial, which brings with it not only aesthetic, but political, theoretical and historical dispositions. The problem with the testimonial, as I have already indicated, is that it channels politics through the narrow perspective of individuated experience. This problem applies to a wider conundrum of non-fiction speech. In Israel-Palestine, however, some losses reverberate more than others.

A genre assumes an already known set of conventions that condition, even institutionalize, its own reception. With speech genres, these conventions are set to form and reaffirm subjectivity (the order of address), sovereignty (the order of law or norm), and the order of language itself by the utterance, the "I do" or "It is me." Other linguists likewise emphasized the structural element of language. John Searle—Austin's follower—contends that to speak is to be engaged "in rule-governed form of behavior."[29] Emile Benveniste's well-known articulation that "the time at which one *is* [is] the time at which one *is speaking*" similarly ties together speech, subjectivity and the symbolic order at the very instance of the utterance.[30] Regardless of the video speakers' intentions, the convention of a personal account of loss—an iterative speech in Israeli intimate publics—affirms not only one's selfhood, but a compliance with state ideology and military norms as hinged upon the utterance, like taking an oath.[31] The conventions at stake here are linguistic as much as they are formal, medial and discursive. The way we listen to pain and loss does not persist in a vacuum. At the turn of the century, video testimonials emerge as a convention of mediated speech, underlined by trauma theory, mobilized by humanitarian discourse and propagated by private, non-governmental entities. These articulated a ubiquitous political subject formed by injury on the one hand and its mass mediation on the other.

Testimony, as a mass media phenomenon and a critical term within media studies, emerges in the 1990s and early 2000s. The shift is marked by a number of interrelated scholarly, intellectual and popular enterprises. Shoshana Felman and Dori Laub's 1992 book *Testimony: Crisis of Witnessing in Literature, Psychoanalysis and History* persists as a prominent point of reference for a growing interest in questions of historicity, representation, legitimacy and truth in light of mass trauma.[32] Although its title declares literature, psychoanalysis, and history as it spheres of investigation, the book starts and ends with media testimonies—a video testimonial from the Yale Holocaust Survivors Film Project (HSFP) in the book's introduction and an elaborate discussion of a documentary film, Claude Lanzmann's *Shoah*, in its conclusion. Lanzmann's excruciating, decade-long project, which resulted in a nine-hour film released a few years earlier in 1987, was centered on survivors' testimonies. Lanzmann openly opposed other modes of historical record, such as archival footage.[33] With a different production model, closer to the premise of accessibility afforded by video, the HSFP was a grassroots project of videotaped (despite the use of film in its title) testimonies of Holocaust survivors for the purpose of academic research.

Also in 1992, musician Peter Gabriel, the Reebok Foundation, and the Lawyers Committee for Human Rights co-founded Witness, an NGO which collects and produces testimonies from various conflict-ridden locations across the world.[34] Aiming at urgently mobilizing public opinion, Witness relied on an immediate, and probably less philosophically complex than Lanzmann's film, format of mass-produced testimonials. The trend of media testimonies found another expression with the launching of Steven Spielberg's Testimonies Project in 1994, designed as a mass production enterprise with the original aim of recording 50,000 testimonies of Holocaust survivors.[35] Witness and the Spielberg project were two exemplary and highly visible manifestations of the appropriation of media testimonies by human rights activism and archival practices—the latter reconsidering the historical record as a way to gain critical access to the past, and the former operating on the basis of immediacy and urgency in order to provoke action. Both were predicated on digital promises of instant production and mass circulation. As such assemblage shows, documentary film, archives, and human rights activism became interested in questions of record and experience as elements of social truth, prompted by technological and organizational shifts, such as the effect of digital technology on preservation and production or the utilization of media as a strategic practice in non-governmental entities.

These social institutions—documentary, the archive, and humanitarian aid—developed the testimonial into a visual form with an urge to resurrect voices that were silenced and to verbalize events defaced by history. Their aims were framed by a discursive placement of testimony as an ethical tool for social remorse that emerged out of poststructuralist continental philosophy in the second half of the twentieth century, and was addressed by thinkers such as Agamben and Lyotard. These authors positioned the witness as a liminal political subject who attests the inside and outside of sovereign power, and challenged notions of historicity and representation.[36] Felman and Laub's book, which belongs to this corpus of theoretical explorations, reads testimony through the prism of the traumatic, attempting to represent what cannot be articulated, grasped, and made meaningful through language, what speaks despite its impossibility. Testimony is thus a fragile and irreplaceable event, through which the wreckage of narrative can be restored and history's jurisdiction expanded, despite a systematic silencing or oppression. Felman and Laub conceptualize testimony as a performative instrument of social justice predicated on the relationship between the speaking subject, whose speech constitutes politics (action, intervention, claims), and the traumatic subject who is the bearer of absence and silence.

In the first decade of the twenty-first century a number of publications in the field of communication and media studies review the recent surge in testimonials. In their introduction to *Documentary Testimonies: Global Archives of Suffering,* Baskar Sarkar and Janet Walker conclude that "the vocation of documentary is testimonial," "the vocation of testimony is archival," and "the vocation of the archive is ethical."[37] In *Media Witnessing: Testimony in the Age of Mass Communication,* Paul Frosh and Amit Pinchevski state that witnessing takes place "in, through and by media" and is integrally linked with moral epitomes and social consequences.[38] Noting a growing suspicion towards images in an era of ubiquitous image-making and iconoclastic impulses, Roger Hallas and Francis Guerin implicitly undermine Felman's absence argument, contending to "illuminate how the image actually facilitates specific possibility to bear witness to historical events rather than fore-close or compromise them."[39] These collections demonstrate the indi-visible link between media and modern genocide. At the same time, as these authors observe, when documentary, or by extension non-fiction media and video activism, call upon the testimonial, they assume an ethical position, valorizing testimony as an act of truth-speaking. Mak-ing thoughtful connections between the politics of genocide and media platforms, Leshu Torchin shows the continuous mobilization of media throughout the twentieth century to create acts of witnessing and nego-tiate social justice.[40] Understanding testimony as a product of historio-graphic shift rather than a formal reflection on history is indeed key in diagnosing how it speaks to the social.

As Michal Givoni shows, in the aftermath of the First World War, personal experience became a legitimate source of historical knowledge, with the implicit qualification of psychology and sensation as a source of authenticity.[41] It is not by chance that the appearance of testimo-nial accounts of war as a form of popular historiography crosses paths with the formation of an aesthetic mode of social deliberation, namely documentary. Utilizing Walter Lippmann's ideas about the use of media as a didactic tool, enabling the masses to act consciously and intelli-gently, John Grierson conceived documentary in the 1920s and 30s as a popular art form that, combining information and sensation—Grier-son's well known "dramatic treatment" of reality—holds the potential to emancipate the audience.[42] Lippmann's 1925 *Public Opinion*, a sharp social critique of the role of mass communication in modern democracy, was itself a post-war manifestation, and so was Grierson's formation of the documentary movement. Grierson's documentary work for the British Empire Marketing Board was based on the premise that docu-mentary's power lies in dramatizing and picturing the everyday life of ordinary people as a way of presenting social reality.[43] He perceived the mediated subjects as "social actors," a blueprint and a representa-tive of social forces. Although Grierson, and by extension 1920s and 30s social documentary, accentuates everyday life and individual actors, these subjects are emblematic of the common, and the speech that the film fostered was an authoritative, bodiless, de-privatized voiceover that illustrated social conditions rather than resuscitating personalized indi-viduals.[44] While documentary depicted individual life and work, speech, instrumental in composing documentary's social subjects, articulated the voice of sovereignty—at times literally state institutions, like the post office—with its different manifestations.

The aftermath of the Second World War gave a new impetus to mediating social truth, injecting other forms of agency into documentary's speech and voicing. A juridical and historical need to register the events of the war led to a reevaluation of truth and evidence, and with it witnesses' vocalization of their own experience. As Torchin shows, the appropriation of film as evidence in the Nuremberg trials, even prior to its testimonial function, marked a shift of perspective in relation to the truth status of documentary.[45] With the establishment of new documentary paradigms such as direct cinema and Cinéma Vérité, forged through new recording technologies that were developed as part of the war effort, documentary was the bearer of a reinvigorated social truth, no longer a stylized didactic utterance but rather a multifaceted record of social reality. Documentary speech was more organically engraved in everyday life, associated with the subjects who speak, but it also emerged as a critical term to address the dialectic of subjective expression and film form. As Bill Nichols shows, both direct cinema and Cinéma Vérité are associated with a certain liberty granted to documentary and the development of a filmic language able to convey immediacy and complex social scenes.[46] While documentary in the 1960s and 70s was appropriated to give form to radical political ideals of freedom, collectivism, and anti-hegemonic struggles, it is that same motion, or rather its implicit excess, that is later fed into documentary formats that recuperate the subject as an abled agent while individuating, isolating, and personalizing patterned forms of oppression. Into the 1980s and 90s, new documentary trends affected by poststructuralist and postmodernist streams of thought turn the truth in documentary, and with it speech, into a more ambiguous, self-conscious and self-referential paradigm. This paradigm tolerated the broken, partial speech of the traumatic. In that sense, the authenticity of the record and that of speech are interconnected.

In reference to this robust interplay of agents and forms, critical takes on documentary have employed the notion of "voice" to signal the competing authority of film form and speaking subjecthood.[47] In her critique of the documentary "voice" Pooja Rangan contends that the paradigm lapses between the organic and metaphorical, situating the question of voice in "a powerful metaphysical tradition."[48] As Rangan notes, as a metaphor, "voice" assumes a particular subject, often without reflecting on it. John Mowitt argues for a recurrent problem of contextualization, urging us to think not about the discrete "voice," but what resonates with it.[49] Additionally, while the voice metaphor is meant to complicate notions of agency that might be attributed to the documentary subject, it seems to assume a distinct agency of the film itself. As Rangan suggests, the problem is precisely the collapsing of the organic into the metaphorical as it relies on a certain transparency of language, taking as its underlying assumption that voice and form are stable, autonomous categories, that they have authority. The voice metaphor indicates a documentary address that comes from a moral disposition, subscribing to an enlightened politics of truth. The testimonial is predicated on synchronicity of speech and visual form, a frame centered on a talking head that calls on proximity and attention. The speaker portrays suffering and survival, delivered in the ears of a listener who is in an elevated moral position to respond to the crisis. With the purpose of giving a voice to the subject, video testimony eliminates the dialectic tension between the voice of the speaker and the voice of the film, unifying and transcending both voice and representation through the rhetoric of crisis. With testimony the film lends a "voice" to the subject, but what is speaking through the subject and what for? What if the subject disavows its metaphysical ascription to truth and instead sticks to its own intimate hum?

The coalescing trends of global humanitarianism, hyper-mediated conflicts and discursive and socio-technological changes that brought about both the multiplicity of documentary truth, and a skepticism towards it, lead to the alliance of form with subjecthood and the collapsing of sovereign politics into the first-person singular experience. By the early 1990s, when testimony becomes a recurrent mode of documentary speech, the formal and political structures on which it relies assumes the autonomy of documentary from institutionalized truths, the autonomy of humanitarianism from the nation state (mostly through the structure of NGOs), and the autonomy of the subject as an agent. As a circulating ubiquitous format, often traveling within orbits of global suffering forged by humanitarian impulse, the testimonial abstracts sovereign politics, bypassing governmental or international politics' liability to the crisis. As critiques of global humanitarianism point out, testimony designates a global sphere made of individual agents—the witness and the receiver of testimony, the listener.[50] The canonization of trauma theory within mostly US-based humanities during the 1990s and early 2000s, Susannah Radstone tells us, was in discord with its originally aporic premises, circumventing the de-centralization and destabilization of subjectivity offered by its theoretical cradle of psychoanalysis, structuralism, poststructuralism, and deconstruction.[51] Paradoxically, while trauma theory addresses the loss of referentiality, as a recuperating tool aiming at the political, testimony was all about the concrete event, symptomatic of a Western-centric history of crisis, a teleological approach in which disaster and rupture actually reaffirm truth and its representation. As Radstone seems to suggest, by listening to testimony, the humanities' own liberal project and its calling upon ethics were reaffirmed.

When confronted with the popularity of testimony as a documentary enunciation, Felman's proposition of absence and the impossibility of testimony indicates a certain historical irony. While testimony is meant to react against a fraught sense of silence and silencing, it seems to have also enabled excessive speech and omnipresence of victimhood as a political currency.[52] The documentary staging of injured identities, to draw on Belinda Smaill, valorizes victimhood through the form of the testimonial, collapsing, according to Smaill, the political into the ethical.[53] The economy of suffering, however, leaves its geo-political formation intact. The *problem* with testimony is that as a mass mediated trend, it also leads to a univocal anesthetization of victimhood, pertaining to a narcissist politics based on injury as an exclusive framework to think the human and the ethical. Media testimony implies a voice on which political reality is inflicted or threatens, rather than a voice whose speech, or silencing, is intrinsic to this reality, a voice that echoes the rationales and regulations of the powers at work. As Smaill astutely notes, through the ethicalization of listening to this speech and its ambiguity or displacement of violence, political action is neutralized.[54]

Conceiving of Jewish-Israeli memorial videos' utterances through the category of the testimonial might come across as counterintuitive. The videos do not articulate an immediate and urgent call for action, globally conveyed through the means of mass communication, and they do not call upon a specific genocidal event, but rather exist in relation to a perpetual violence that they render obscure. In fact, what is so striking about these videos is their insistence on self-enclosure, bracketing out any context or underlining claims for truth or authority. Calling upon the testimonial here reminds us that this is a performative speech, and that as listeners we are already accustomed to the format and conditioned to its mode of engagement. On a macro-level, thinking the paradigm through its peripheral expressions sheds light on a problem that lies at its very premise. There is a thing to learn here from the Israeli case. On the micro-level, thinking memorial videos through the paradigm of testimony brings to the fore the state mechanism and its necropolitical foundations. In Felman's work trauma is a mark of a crisis of truth that erupts with the Holocaust—an event that dominates other accounts as well. At this point, the local implications need to be made explicit. Sitting in the Jerusalem courtroom during the Eichmann trial in 1961, Hannah Arendt describes the trial as a display of Jewish victimhood and a spectacle of legitimation of the state of Israel, as the sovereign representative of the Jewish people.[55] For Arendt the performance of testimony and the call upon collective injury is constitutive of Israeli sovereign politics and Israeli publicness. This juridical setting bestowed power on the witness as *the* political subject, who, rather than a reliable reporter, became a figure of collective consciousness, the one who speaks for or petitions sovereignty.[56] In the evolution of Israeli sovereign power, it is that very call on the traumatic that serves to silence and systematically efface other forms of suffering, such as that of the Lebanese and Palestinians.

These utterances of loss—resonating in private videos, the novel, and documentary—participate, without stating this and despite their intended self-enclosure, in a national convention of reckoning that ties claims to sovereignty to the claim of injury and dictates a particular subject position. However, unlike the national spectacle of the testimonial performances in the Jerusalem courtroom during the Eichmann trial, these utterances are allegedly detached from the subtextual claim for national sovereignty, wishing to speak only for their own intimate pain. Memorial videos utterances are thus the radicalization of the detachment of subjective experience and agency inscribed in one's voice from its historical, juridical, and indeed sovereign generators. The utterances of memorial videos articulate a desire for a privatized, individuated, yet public address molded in the form of a restorative speech. "Making the video was like going through therapy," reflects one bereaved video subject, positioning videographic speech as a "working through" mechanism that leads to incorporation, re-formation, and relief.[57] On the side of the listener, listening is not necessarily just a container for these feelings of excruciating loss, but, drawing on the testimonial, a space where the listeners can affirm their ethical stance through mere sympathy, neutralizing a more complex political reflection. The question is, once again, what is it that we are listening to? Speech and listening, as I have shown so far, persists in a series of displacements and negotiations on behalf of the subject. But what generates these scenes is actually much more scripted, ritualistic and cued. It opens with a knock on the door.

NEWS ABOUT DEATH

A story that repeats and is a central vantage point for memorial videos is the story of how the speaker heard their loved one had died. This is not only an utterance made by the videos' speakers, but one in which the utterance itself is the subject. In *Flew Away Forever,* the message sequence starts with a still image, a last family portrait taken when the family came together to celebrate its newborn member. "We were so happy," says the father, Amos Shalev, "and then came Saturday. . . . At ten to eleven we see a newsflash on television." The video cuts to a news item which reports the crash of a helicopter near the northern border. The succinct report, delivered simultaneously through mass media to all Israeli households, conveying an event whose affected subjects are anonymous and generic, has a different resonance for the Shalev family: it is alarming, perceived as specific and with actual consequences. The newsflash is echoed by an accelerated sequence of exchanges. First Sagi, the pilot's brother, tries to reach him by phone; he then calls his second brother, Yotam. Yotam, also a pilot in the Israeli air force, drives to the military base to get more information. There, he is informed by the base commander that his brother is dead. Yotam then calls Sagi and the two siblings drive to their parents' home to see them face to face; the parents inform other family members. Military officials, whose job was to bring the news to the family, arrive only later. The sequence has dramatically paced editing that cuts back and forth between family members. If other recollections in the video are narrated through the past tense, here, it is the present tense that dominates. In a pluri-vocal storytelling, one oc-currence leads to another, information is collected and crystallized into a new understanding of reality, a chronology that brings death to the family's doorstep. Through the interjection of mass media and of tele-communication, and through the video's formal language, the drama told is that of a family coming together, tangled, ruined, and re-formed by receiving a shattering piece of news.

The death of a soldier disturbs the parallel routines of the organi-zations of military, media, and family, and thus, from an institutional perspective, needs to be regulated and controlled. News about death involves an operation of mediation. The mass media informs the pub-lic through a prescribed, terse announcement, relying on the internal protocols of crisis and urgency that inform television genres such as "breaking news." The military has its own personnel and procedures to notify the next-of-kin and to supervise the reception of the news. But in homemade memorial videos, institutional protocols are obscured, as death is something that happens first and foremost to the family. In the purview of the family, news about death is neither "procedure" nor "newsflash." For the family the reception of the message is a moment of ontological crisis. In fact, any actual informational exchange is lacking, or, as in the Shalevs' case, the message-procedure is missed, and only comes after the fact: the media's report is too unspecified, and the military announcers arrive too late. Despite these discrepancies, recalling the colliding trajectories of different transmissions enmeshes all the entities involved. Mass media news is extended by family telecommunications, the generic report sounds the alarm for the family by insinuating a scenario through which an event becomes specific. Moreover, the narrative of the message entails a ritualistic "change of hands," the returning of the soldier to the civilian, privatized sphere of his family. Through the familial recollection, the procedural is transformed. News about death is turned from a military procedure or a mass media newsflash into a family memento to be recited and recalled, thereby keeping the family close together. Through the video, the report turns into a story, the formal utterance gains an intimate, idiosyncratic quality. It becomes a form of affective correspondence, a mode of listening.

In the video about Shay Bernstein, *From Me to Command*, the recollection of the message's delivery is provided when Sivan Refaeli, Bernstein's fiancée, visits his family. Bernstein's sister recalls: "We took the children to the zoo, but I couldn't enjoy it. . . . All of a sudden there was a gust of wind, and I remember telling my mother 'What a sad, evil wind' and we went back home . . . and then he [a soldier] said 'It's Yehuda from the municipal army headquarters, please open [the door]' and then we opened the door." Bernstein's brother: "We were paralyzed. We sat for a few minutes and didn't know what to do, and then we said, wait a minute, no one knows but us." The sister continues: "and then we started [trails off]. I don't know why, but I figured they told you [refers to Refaeli] and then I realized: they don't announce to girlfriends. In my head it was *as if* you [Refaeli and Bernstein] were already married." The move from inaction to "no one knows but us" locates the event in its knowing, framing the constitutive power of the message as a speech act. In this sense, the army and the media are not only mechanisms where one's presence is implied and maintained, but mechanisms which determine—in the actual arena of battle but also the virtual orbit of information—one's absence. In addition, the message is constitutive since it formalizes forms of proximity. In the delivery of the message, the institution (the army, the media) encounters the intimate.

Yet, as much as the family alters the message by bypassing official routes and mutating the form of the report, as in the Shalevs' case, the family itself is transfigured by it. It is transfigured by the message taking away one of its members, but moreover, in the designation of address-ees, a line is drawn between those who are "family," and those whose terms of affection are yet to be determined—for instance, the girlfriend. A prominent example of Austin's study of speech acts, the formulation of intimacy and its yielding to the law hinges on the utterance—the "I do" or the "I now pronounce you" of the wedding ceremony.[58] The death notice is the dark reversal of Austin's example: for the girlfriend there is no message, even if the video depicts her as an integral part of the family setting, and even if a marriage proposal had previously been proffered, because it was only *as if* the couple were married—the possible impossible: almost, *not-yet.*[59]

In the message procedure, "telling" is a liminal, constitutive para-digm between life and death, hence the siblings' alerted response to the fact that no one knows. Nevertheless, here, too, it seems that something had already anticipated the message. The sister mentions a gust of wind as a gut feeling that exceeded the trajectory of the formal notice. There is an implied analogy between the gust of wind and the knock on the door, both ominous signs of rupture. Earlier in the scene, while cutting salad in the kitchen, Bernstein's mother tells Refaeli about a dream she had the night before her son died. In her dream her son came home with his uniform, driving his military vehicle. She went out to the doorstep to welcome him, but "he doesn't approach me and I don't approach him." Then, the mother continues, Refaeli appears in her dream. She is dressed in black, her hair covers her face and her posture is bent. She concludes the story: "and he didn't approach me and I didn't approach him." The dream opens up a path to an unconscious realm where death is already at the doorstep, in which the knock/gust comes from within, already anticipated and listened to. In this case, the utterance itself only actual-izes, makes specific, what is already collectively known. The sense of im-pending disaster can be rationalized as the persistent collective anxiety which prevails in societies shaped by conflict. The powers at play not-withstanding, what the mother tries to convey, and what we should also try to pay attention to, is a mystic attachment, a parental love that translates into deep spiritual sensors. Once again, the procedure of the message reflects the intertwining of communication channels: in this case, the formal procedure and the kin's telepathy.

In memorial videos, the event of the message, a moment of great magnitude, is habitually repeated, slowed-down, closely dissected. Here is one more last example: in the video *Tzur Or: Memories and Longing*, Or's mother recalls the moment in detail.[60] "And then they knocked on our door. *And they didn't have to say a word.* It was enough that we saw them there. Four officers or something like that. Ma'ayan [Or's sister] dropped her glass, he [Or's father] collapsed to the floor. . . . And I just sat in the kitchen and froze. I sat on the chair and froze [insert] from that moment everything is vague [insert]." Her speech and the video's syntax provide disjunctive framings of the scene. A series of brief home-movie images of family life before and after are inserted in her speech in a disruptive way. Inserts are often spliced into testimonials to embellish the more or less static image of the talking head, and to inject dynamism into the sequence. The cuts are normally bridged by the voice of the talking head, and have the effect of extending it. However, in this specific sequence the intercuts are jumpy, intervening into the coherence of the recollection with an eerie grammar and fragmenting the video's form and the mother's speech. The temporality of the sequence is likewise disjointed: the breaking of the news about death is depicted as a freeze-frame, and at the same time, past and future collide into this very instance. Both the freeze-frame and the temporal entangling respond to and undo the concreteness of the message as a continuous event.

Or's father also recalls the message event in detail. The sequence starts with a few shots of the father in his workplace as a driver of a commercial bus, then the father recalls how he went back home to wait for the messengers.

> I remember entering Tzur's room, which faces the road. I open the blinds. It's pouring rain. And I wait for [pause] and I stand, looking out [the window], waiting for a military vehicle to pass. And it takes another nerve-wracking hour before we hear this knock on the door [trails off]. [The father starts sobbing. His voice breaks and from this point on his speech is strained.] I remember that no one moved. I walk to the door and [pause] I open the door [pause] and they stand there [pause] [sobbing] Some four faces, four shocked faces. Standing and looking at me [pause]. And I tell them 'what took you so long? [pause] Come in.' And then I run to Tzur's room and I scream 'Tzuri,' I scream, I scream like hell, I scream and my ears blow.

His recollection has a similar dramatic intensity and punctuation to the mother's. It climaxes with a sense of collapse. In neither of the two recollections is a message actually uttered or delivered. Leading from the mother's recollection to the father's is a short excerpt of a news broadcast that announces the names of the incident's casualties, Tzur Or among them. Israeli news announce the names of the casualties only after families are fully informed; for news protocols such items come as the event's aftermath. The broadcast, not the speech of the officials, stands for a quasi-formal stamp that affirms the news about death. Formality does not characterize the scene; not a program, foreseen by formal procedures, but a collapse and rampage. Structurally speaking, this sense of pandemonium and fury, shaking and screaming, contributes to a mythical formation in which death overrides social orders only to revive existing structures and rules.[61]

This outburst notwithstanding, the father's story is one of control, in which he plays a key role in preparing the scene and anticipating what is coming. In fact, those who seem "shocked" are the messengers who, as the ones holding the information, have the power to provoke the scene. The father's rushing home from work after hearing on the hourly news that something has happened, his fortification in his son's room, in front of the window, observing the road, and his words hurled in the face of the messengers—"what took you so long?"—portray him as the one who orchestrates the event. In this story, the approaching of the messengers or their knock on the door is a symbolic gesture that opens the scene. Already familiar with the ritualistic progression of the exchange, he gathers the family and awaits his cue. In the act that will soon take place he appropriates the role of the director, ostensibly retrieving mastery in a pre-defined chain of gestures. That the video reenacts the scene while re-staging the father's riding the bus in the rain only underlines how scripted the event is.

The Or family's memorial video was not the first time this father recalled his message anecdote. He contributed to a project produced for YES cable network on Memorial Day 2005 that has as its central concept the recollection of "message stories." The project is called *A Message Was Delivered to the Family* (dir. Uri Bar-On), paraphrasing a schematic expression that ends news reports in cases of military death. Commissioned to fill in schedule gaps within the day of programming, it consists of a series of highly formulaic five-minute episodes in which a family member tells their message story. Each episode starts with the speaker approaching a door or a window and gesturing towards its opening. A voice, designed to sound like a radio transmission, delivers a short report on the specific incident in which the speaker's loved one died, and concludes with the phrase "a message was delivered to the family." The speaker then takes a seat and starts their story. The project appropriates the message-story as cultural currency, a social genre. The format of the filler and the structure of the paraphrase already imply repetition with variation. If the delivery of the message provokes a mythical resonance, its circulation as a story, enacted through a set of gestures, holds a didactic purpose of predicting its possibility and training the listeners on how to react. Through the highly polished TV episode the sole encounter becomes allegorical and the message story, or rather its conventions, tell its speakers. The mobilizing of the story from the realm of family memory to mass media formats and vice-versa discloses that while loss might be conceived as intimate, its point of origin is not an idiosyncratic enunciation, but generic, an all-too-familiar scene.

Recalling the delivery of the message articulates a mise-en-abyme of speech, its infinite reproduction and echoed reoccurring, a speech about speech and semiotics. As I show in these examples, recalling news about death is always referring to a previous enunciation, even if it is displaced by the intimate recollection. The message, or its versified iteration, is a speech act. The speech act is an instance where language transcends its informative and communicative paradigms, and becomes a constitutive force. Thus, the relation of speech to actuality is not one of truth or falsehood, but of the iterative performance of speech. Admittedly, both military officials and bereaved family members locate the event not in the actual termination of one's life—what happened—but in its representation in the form of a verbal delivery. Thus, when the highly regulated message meets its addressees, it has this constitutive force. It is not that the utterance actually kills—the violence is real and should be regarded as such—but it is the utterance that constitutes ontological and social forms of recognition, reorganizing discursive relations and their subjects.

What does it mean that a singular event becomes a scene to be recited and reproduced, a convention? Ultimately, message stories function as a myth, a meta-story that society tells to itself over and over again. Certain axioms, formulas, and motifs are reiterated in message stories, and remain even with the passing of time and the enhancement of new announcement protocols or the development of new technologies of transmission. The message story, recalled in the homemade memorial video and other media formats, is brought as a dramatic transformative event, almost mystic in its precursor signals. It is often an act of collective authorship, which brings together the family, in both its narrow juridical-biological and its expanded symbolic manifestations. It leads to a critical momentum that reaffirms love and kinship. The news media play a crucial role in pre-delivering the message and/or a formal authorization of the family story of encountering death. More generally, the message story is a story of mediation, from the almost infrastructural channeling of information to its epistemic resonance. Lastly, as an event, the message is summarized by the metonymic description of three or four messengers at the door, or the sound of a knock.

These conventions are ways to sublimate what is ultimately the bureaucratization of love and life. The clairvoyance bespeaks the regulated encounter, and the terse report of the messengers is edited out by the dramatic broadcast; technocratic administration is displaced by mysticism, national annexation by media spotlighting. This moment, facilitated by a speech encounter, is recalled as what strikes an epistemological turmoil in which life and death, presence and absence, state and home, utterer and listener all disintegrate. And yet, these are all conventional leitmotifs in a reproducible allegory of social forces. Indeed, the repetition echoes not only the subjects' degree of pain and shock, but their being hailed by the state at the moment of the delivery. Nevertheless, the messengers' speech—what they are saying, to whom and how —is omitted, remains silent.

HOW DOES A MESSAGE DO, OR "WHAT TOOK YOU SO LONG?"

In his discussion of the act of interpellation—the instance in which a subject is formed as the subject of ideology—Louis Althusser illustrates the act through two speech scenes: the scene of being hailed by a policeman ("hey you!"), and the scene of a friend knocking on the door and announcing, behind the closed door, "it's me!"[62] In Althusser's model, ideology operates on and is recognized by the utterance. Per his examples, one allocution calls on obedience and the other on friendship. When, in the videos, the speakers recall the moment state officials knocked on their door and announced to them that their loved one had died, the familiarity that defines Althusser's latter scene enshrouds the procedure of power that so explicitly dominates the former. A bureaucracy of death passes as an act of mourning and a call upon loss. The knock on the door, followed by the announcement "it's (me) him!," mitigates the hailing and obscures the figure of state authority. Althusser draws on two callings—the call of familiarity, or love, and the call of compliance—when the call of power is the last and ultimate call.

Althusser's description of interpellation as a knock on the door is as follows: "we all have friends who, when they knock on our door and we ask, through the door, the question 'who's there?,' answer (since 'it's obvious') 'It's me.' And we recognize that 'it is him' or 'her.' We open the door and 'it's true, it really was she who was there.'"[63] Shay Bernstein's sister depicts a similar scene: "and then he [a soldier] said, 'It's Yehuda from the municipal army headquarters, please open [the door],' and then we opened the door." Here, too, it was "obvious." The recognizability of the knock and the obscurity of the actual speech—which is where the act of hailing is located—masks or mis-places the power it welcomes. It could also be the case, as Althusser might be suggesting, that the interpellating act of power can be an act of love, to the extent that love itself is a form of social order. As John Mowitt notes in his illuminating analysis of Althusser, interpellation, first encountered aurally, always entails a certain mis-recognition of the particular in the general that "at once presupposes and settles a certain ambiguity in the boundaries of subjective identity."[64] "What took you so long," asks Tzur Or's father when he opens the door and welcomes his position as an interpellated subject. The doorstep announcement, at once inter-personal and instrumental, renders the family imminently bound to the state. Therefore, it is an instance where the connectedness of militarized procedures, popular convention, and the familial are formed and enhanced. In fact, the message story involves a few vantage points: that of the family, which receives the message; the army, which delivers it; and the media, which disseminates and massifies it. When it comes to mediated speech, Mowitt reminds us, we should remember questions of reproducibility, amplification, and circulation that destabilize the coherency and unity of speech's subject or source.[65] If we go beyond the mythical, shattering resonance, we find a model where circulation and reproduction are *a priori* ideological acts. The gesture of opening the door strives to substitute regulated administration for intimacy, yet this is an example of administrative *mise en scène*: it is the state that makes the utterance, performing an uncanny ventriloquism in which bureaucracy speaks as fate or love.

The mythically codified figure of the three messengers and their "knock on the door" encapsulates an entire military mechanism condensed into a single image and a single sound. The message procedure is administered by a team of three: an officer, responsible for coordinating the military objectives, a physician, who oversees the family's potential responses (which may include, according to the military's own protocol, collapse, hysteria, physical shock) and an additional announcer, usually not in uniform, who serves as an intermediary between military authority and the family. According to military protocol, the team's first task is to locate the house, seal the scene, find the family members and to deliver the news to them, in person, face to face, while seated. The verbal content of the message has to be short and in simple language, and its words must be uttered and delivered. After delivering the news, the messengers obtain information from the family, accompany the family members around the house, fill-in forms, inform the family on their rights and handle the funeral arrangement while negotiating the official procedure with the family's needs. If required, they arrange a visit of one of the family members to the morgue.[66] Once they enter the house, any communication of the family with the outside world—with other family members, other bureaucratic entities, other militarized authorities, the media, or even their visit to the morgue as a last encounter with their dead—is mediated and facilitated by the announcers.

The army's objective is to manage the family and their loss while safeguarding its own mechanism and organizational function. Sociologists Vered Vinitzky Seroussi and Eyal Ben-Ari posit that while death is part of the military's routine, it also has a way of "disturbing the military's organizational order and challenging the very basis of its legitimacy."[67] They term the military announcing mechanism a "moving bureaucracy," alluding to the sensitive job description of these teams, their composition of both military and civilian officials, and the arrangement of a system of mobilized units that situate themselves and operate in the families' domesticities. While these units have a pre-defined and concrete set of tasks and functions (taking care of the burial, treating the corpse and its identification), their main role is mediating that which is a procedural and standard matter for the army to a family that experiences death as shock and devastation. Beyond the strict announcement, the messengers utilize the measurements of explanation and legitimation to make sure that the family, in its moment of devastation, is kept under military control. The family in crisis, and the family home, are transformed by the announcers and their message, turned into a closed and guarded sphere, a highly regulated military arena.

Preparing the scene, setting the tone, directing all movement, the message procedure is a carefully staged military event. In 1997, following a helicopter accident in which seventy-three soldiers died—an unprecedented number of dead in a single incident which necessitated a special organizational effort—the IDF magazine, *BaMahane'*, published two reviews of the Adjutant General Corps, the military human resources department that handles the announcement procedure. The journal is a populist outlet of the IDF organizational culture. The reviews are stories that the institution tells to itself of itself. The first review, titled "Behind the Scenes of Death," already put forward the notion of staging, of a backstage activity that manages societal and personal turmoil. The review surveys the operation of an emergency telephone center set up to provide information to the thousands of families that feared their kin might be on the helicopters.[68] According to the review, the officers who were specially recruited for the task were instructed to provide all families, even those whose kin were on the helicopters, with an ambiguous answer that was reassuring but not definite. For families whose kin were not on the helicopter the message was "as far as [we] know, the soldier is well, but things up-north are still unclear." For those whose loved one was listed as being on the helicopters, the message was "The Adjunct Corps is still waiting for the final lists to arrive in a few minutes, after a quick check, an answer will be provided to the family."[69] The task of the officers was to make sure that, by all means, the family would not hear about their kin's death on the phone or from any source other than the official announcers. The review praises the managing of the incident by concluding that the officers kept their calm, that they did not break and "respond" to the families' calls, that all orders and instructions were followed.[70] But what actually was that call made by the family, and what did it mean, on the part of the army, to respond to it? It seems that the telephone service was not about providing information, but, on the contrary, it was about obscuring it. The ambiguity of the messages provided by the phone service utilized information not as a means of transparency between the state and the public, but as a tool of regulation and control, wherein the speech act is deferred, displaced, and obscured.

The second review is an interview with the head of Tel Aviv's municipal army headquarters, Lieutenant Colonel Orna Shay. Shay recalls an incident from her former role as an announcer where she had to inform a widow that her son had died in a training accident, not a risk-generating war situation but a routine. It was early in the morning and Shay and her companions estimated that, looking through the peephole and seeing a group of three people, two of them in uniform, the woman would immediately understand what had happened. She might refuse to open the door. In order to keep the scene under control, Shay and the physician, who were in uniform, hid, while the third person, dressed in civilian clothes, stood in front of the door. In this anecdote, the announcers organize the woman's field of vision. They produce a frame, with the one dressed as a civilian functioning as camouflage for the military "targeting the house." Vinitzky-Seroussi and Ben-Ari likewise describe situations in which the civilian-dressed announcer is the one scouting the street, while the two announcers in uniform stay in the car so as not to alarm the neighbors.[71] Hiding out of eyesight, the announcers stage a play of displacement. Who is behind the door is not *obvious*. Nevertheless, insisting on the strategic face-to-face encounter establishes a very particular mode of contact, a personal one, putting the family in a state of dependency on the army. In return, the military provides it with all the needed support, pragmatic or emotional, a close care that disguises its own instrumentality, its operating apparatuses.

In this "play of displacement" another interlocutor is news media. The military's organizational logic strives at patterned reproduction performed in surgical precision, aiming at the specific kin; the media's logic is one of circulation, massively and indiscriminately disseminating a general report. As part of Israeli media's willful collaboration with the military, and in order not to upset public sensitivity in events of national casualties, the following protocol was established. In most cases military casualties are reported twice: first as a general incident, and the second time as an account of specific dead. When the media first announces an event, it maintains a certain level of vagueness in order to avoid colossal panic, and to make sure that the military maintains its authority in delivering the news to the family. Image-based live media regulates images released from the scene not to show any identifying details, such as names of soldiers marked on their belongings or body parts. Reporters are asked by the IDF to keep away from the family home until the family has been notified, so the sight of a crowd of journalists will not alert the family of the upcoming news. These protocols were often established after scandalous occurrences: for example, a television news cameraperson who, covering the scene of the helicopter accident, transmitted live a haunting image of a backpack hanging from a tree that had the name of its owner inscribed on it in huge letters, or the crowds of reporters waiting outside the house of a well-known personality after her son had died in a military training accident.[72]

In line with the consistent effacing of Lebanese and Palestinians' lives and suffering under the politics of enmity, there are no mentions of names of Palestinian or Lebanese casualties or information about incidents, unless framed as a successful elimination of a high-profile "wanted person."

There is hierarchy even within military death—the above procedures are valid for soldiers who died in action or training, not to those who were ill, or committed suicide. Media's ways of conduct resonate with strategic conduct on behalf of the military: delivering a general report that obscures and sustains ambiguity rather than informing, and controlling the field of vision, so that once a concrete transmission is delivered, it will be contained by the utterance. After the army has occupied the family's house and the message has been delivered, Israeli news provides a succinct account of names of the deceased, their pictures, and information on the time and location of the funerals. A more personal profile of the dead is aired, mostly as a short news item, in the following days.

To a certain degree, the media's operation complements the military's, but it also diverges from its orderly administration. The first news report disseminates the possibility that the general will turn specific, that the anonymous dead will be revealed as an intimate one. As the recollections above show, in the case of the Shalev family, the news report sets into motion an informal exchange. The messengers arrive later, just to announce news that had already been broken. Tzur Or's father hears a general report about an incident in his son's post, yet perceives it as a specific address and goes home to wait for the announcers. There is something excessive in the ways in which news media circulate a message, something that delivers more than is authorized. In fact, in families' message stories the institutional logics of the military and the media often crisscross each other, the obscure report in the news being perceived by families as personal and specific, and the sight of the announcers on the street often raising a general panic, following the logic that "it could be me/him." This complicates the work of both sovereign power and the mass media in articulating a speech act. According to this common sense, the news media function as a sort of Althusserian police officer, issuing an abstract call—Hey you!—unsettling and at the same time forming subjectivity while reminding us of the ever-presence of sovereignty in the sphere of intimacy. Media's mass scope and scale is somehow crossed. More broadly, as Mowitt already observes, interpellation constitutes the subject not through the concrete designation of the act of hailing, but instead its ambiguity, the ways in which it allows for a misrecognition of the generic as the specific.

The second news report, which provides casualties' names and personal information, is often re-appropriated by homemade memorial videos, inserted in a dramatic cut at the end of the message story. In a stream of family's anecdotes, appearing at the end of what is for the family a recollection of an excruciating and transformative event, the newsflash, different from the rest of the video in its source, tone, function and aesthetic, appears as what seals the scene. The citation of the "breaking news" in the videos is where the discursive event, the speech act—as something which is at the same time specific and iterable, singular and common, context-ridden and general, sudden and routinized, personal and publishable/publicized—takes place.[73] The messengers and their message, strictly speaking representatives of the state which performs the speech act in the first place, are only mentioned as a sight or a knock, their actual words never cited. Cutting from the recollection of the ominous knock on the door to the newsflash, itself a work of displacement, a referral of the speech act takes place and the procedure is passed as a story.

Interpellation, in the Althusserian sense, is an emblematic speech act. "It's obvious," writes Althusser, since interpellation, like any speech act, relies on its conventionality and iterability. Yet, in the case of the utterances of memorial videos, speech involves a series of displacements. The testimonial misrecognizes the political as the ethic of listening and displaces social address for subjective agency; a speech of truth, it fails to acknowledge its partiality and discrimination, namely its circulation of only Jewish-Israeli victimhood. The figurative speech act displaces its reference, between the literal and the metaphorical: from the real corpse to the absent loved one who now exists only as representation. To speak *as if* emanates from a temporal deferral and involves a certain disavowal, recalling the possibility of something impossible. Lastly, in message stories the procedural act is misplaced as myth, fate, or love. The procedural by itself—the mere enunciation—is too bureaucratic and banal to account for what it recalls. It thus fails to communicate, an infelicitous act.[74] When the actual announcement is absorbed into the realm of idiosyncrasy, adopted and embraced by family mementos, the hailing is displaced by its recollection, and the enunciation, the strict announcement, is displaced by the utterance, a form of speech that includes its resonances, that is, its aesthetic and social conventions, verbatim and gesture, linguistic and non-linguistic evocations, and so on. This web of displacements of meaning and subjects is essential for the non-straightforward way that ideology operates. The mere speech act, the generic formulation of a sentence announcing one's death, is not what resonates. What resonates, allegorized, duplicated, and disseminated, is a news report, a rumor, a story, a knock, a *speech re-act*.

In the first place, it is a speech re-act because its action lies in the gesture of opening the door. The speech of the announcers by itself does not kill—death took place somewhere else and by other means—but it is the opening of the door, the succumbing of Israeli society to its military metastructure, that allows death to continuously recur, and that consequently guarantees social obedience. In the gesture of opening the door, the subject conforms to the social order, the power of the sovereign over the subject is guaranteed, and the continuity and coherence of ideology is consolidated. In the second place, it is a speech re-act because its action is not in the speech that is uttered but the speech it provokes, including, but not only, its own misplacement by its recollection as a pseudo-intimate event. It is the very transformation of the announcement into a mass media genre or a personal story that conveys the act's constitutive and conventionalizing power. This excessive speech is where death is recognized and therefore social orders are formed. This is not to take away from the power of the state and dislocate it into the individual, but to understand how *sovereign power is intimated through speech, how intimacy is displaced by sovereign intimacy*. Tzur Or's father opens the door to the announcers, and before they utter a word, he says, according to his recollection, "what took you so long?" The listener becomes a speaker. Is the father controlling the scene? Has he become an active agent? No; he is a means of representation and dissemination, a figure of speech.

GROSSMAN'S TRAP: THE ORDER OF LANGUAGE

Can one disobey the message and its hailing? Can one, perhaps like the fictional heroine with whom I opened this chapter, remain within the zone of impossible possibilities? A problem with Althusser's theory of ideology is its "leaving no one outside" ideology (perhaps only the philosopher himself).[75] Throughout this chapter I insinuated a mode of refusal that attaches itself to the fictional as a way to imagine an alternative path not marked by the state's commissioning. As I noted, such refusal negotiates with the hailing mechanism but still persists within intimate sovereignty, described throughout the chapter as an echo chamber, and here, in its conclusion, as a trap.

I would like to return to David Grossman and his proposition of a refusal. In a speech at PEN's World Voice Festival in April 2007, Grossman draws on a Kafka allegory (referring to Kafka's *Little Fable*) in which a mouse is caught in a trap. With no way out, the cat already approaching him, caught in despair, the mouse says, perhaps with irony, "alas, the world is getting smaller every day." Grossman cites the fable of the trap to comment on writing in a state of perpetual violence.[76] There is, he claims, a "void that slowly emerges between the individual and the violent chaotic state that encompasses practically every aspect of their life."[77] For the author, language is "getting smaller every day." It flattens, becomes the language of conflict and hostility, a populist language of blunt clichés. As Grossman puts it, the shrinking of language is a state of despair that entraps free will. He describes writing what was back then his latest novel, *To the End of the Land,* as writing out of restlessness, urgency, and alarm, telling the story of how "the cruelty of the external situation invades the delicate intimate fabric of one's family, ultimately tearing it to shreds."[78] Indeed, Grossman writes until his writing is interrupted by a knock on the door.

It is worth stressing that the author gave this speech at a writers' convention. He speaks to those who write, to storytellers, speaking in a language (English) that is not his own, speaking about the seizing of language as free will by the violent reality around him. For Grossman, the laborious exercise of language, writing, is a way to make a world within the trap: "I write. The consciousness of the disaster that befell me upon the death of my son Uri in the Second Lebanon War now permeates every minute of my life. The power of memory is indeed great and heavy, and at times has a paralyzing effect. Nevertheless, the act of writing creates for me a *'space'* of sorts, an emotional expanse that I have never known before, where death is more than the absolute, unambiguous opposite of life. . . . When we write, we feel the world in flux, elastic, full of possibilities—unfrozen."[79]

Derrida, too, points to the rupturing force of the space within writing. For him it is not the written sign, but its deferral, literally the blank space before or between words, that points towards an alternate possibility. "Spacing which separates it from other elements of the eternal contextual chain (the always open possibility of its disengagement and graft), but also from all forms of present references . . . objective or subjective. This spacing is not the simple negativity of the lacuna but rather the emergence of the mark."[80] For Derrida there is, in writing, the possibility for something new to emerge; for Grossman, writing contains "the freedom to circulate the tragedy of my situation *in my own words.*"[81] Both articulate a space where things are yet to be determined by the order of language, or a space before language is hijacked by conventionalized violence. Grossman seeks to invert and reinvent language, defamiliarize it, make new names, expand its scope. That makes him a storyteller, but the storyteller, as Benjamin tells us, always embodies their story and is designated to repeat it, she is a figure of her story, a figure of speech.

Another intriguing instance of refusal comes from a person who seems to be using words quite minimally. In the documentary that featured the mothers of four tank members, among them David Grossman's wife, one of the fathers, the father of Adam Goren, sticks to his silence. When the announcers knocked on the Goren family's door, the father opened the door and asked them to leave. Was he too, like Grossman's heroine, refusing the message? When the father finally speaks, he relates an incident that occurred a few months after his son's death. The father was driving his car close to the local gym where Adam used to exercise. Passing by he sees the back of a young man riding his bicycle, "I said—eh [pause] Adam. [pause] [cut]." The story lapses into a reenactment of the experience, language lapses into the open airy sound of the "eh," and these lapses contain a moment of suspense, of an impossible possibility, a moment of misrecognition. Somehow, a counter hailing, the opposite of the Althusserian "obviousness" that is predicated on the possible ("it's me"). The "eh" is a faint inversion of the authoritative "hey," and rather than the sovereign mutually constituting the general and the specific by the mere act of calling, it is a delusional plea that aims only at a very intimate person. The cut leaves us in this moment before the man on the bicycle will take the 180 degree turn. The "eh" is the Derridean "space between language," what precedes a formulated knowledge of the obvious. In this brief instance, the constitutive power of the message is rejected, de-naturalized, "as if he was alive." The cut allows this moment to resonate. It is a powerful instance, but since what it exposes is not a possible future, but the ruins of a future. Ultimately, for both Grossman and Adam Goren's father, the story will always start and end with a knock on the door.

In the decade that followed the death of David Grossman's son and the publication of *To the End of the Land*, the writer became, more than ever before, the moral voice of the Israeli Zionist liberal left. He often speaks out publicly in rallies and demonstrations against war and occupation. Although I am sympathetic to the anti-violence statements in his speeches, if I leave the above analysis of a potential refusal somehow ambiguous, it is because I believe, sadly, that as the voice of the Israeli Zionist left, he attests mostly to a sense of failure. The echo chamber and the trap, two metaphors of enclosed spaces, leave Israeli society—and particularly the Israeli Zionist liberal left—entrenched in an uncanny state of sovereign intimacy, in which the knock always comes from within. Perhaps new speech-forms and new gestures are needed.

To open the door to the message does not only welcome the state into the house, but, to begin with, it assumes a space of privacy, *as-if* this were not constituted by the state. While the generative power of the imagination is something worth considering, such a scenario that situates resistance within the locus of agential subjecthood is paradigmatic of liberal politics and provides, in my view, a rather limited prospect. To assume an *a priori* space of privacy assumes a space presumably prior to and sheltered from political violence, yet it is the protection of that very shelteredness that legitimates any form of violence. As I argue here, sovereign violence already dwells in the home. Sovereign intimacy simultaneously welcomes and negates the state's ordering of life and death. It constitutes a space governed by proximity or attachment, which is at the same time—it has to be—vacuumed from the colonized other: Palestinians and Lebanese. The ghostly absence of Palestinians and Lebanese from the echo chamber that is sovereign intimacy is its most fraught formation. Zionism, we should also remember, was always armed with imagination. The Israeli liberal left perhaps rebukes sovereign politics but sticks to sovereign intimacy, empties the enmity and maintains its attachment to Zionism despite its colonial default and its history of atrocities; embraces the army, not as an executioner of state-inflicted violence but rather as an internal-facing social structure of solidarity and commonality. To listen to the message means to comply, and even to speak against it still entraps one under its force. To unravel such tight fabric means to *unlearn* what is obvious, to non-sentimentally *deliberate* that very intimate attachment, and to *eradicate* the common knowledge and shared values it brings with it in order to establish new ones.

CHAPTER 5

At Face Value

HEADS AND BODIES

In July 2014, in the midst of a belligerent military operation launched by Israel on the Gaza strip,[1] a one-minute video titled "We Don't Want You Here" circulated across social media platforms. More than 2,000 people died in that operation, the stark majority being Palestinian civilians. (According to the UN report 2,251 Palestinians and 73 Israelis died in the fifty-day armed conflict.) Both media and streets were inflamed by violence. In the video, a series of individuals—male and female, young and old, Jewish and Arab—face the camera and repeat the sentence "We don't want you here" in Hebrew and Arabic. Some of the speakers first look down or to the side and then dramatically fix their gaze on the camera. They stand against a dark grey background, some of them with head and upper torso in frame, some closely captured from the crown of the head to the tip of the chin. Each cut, from one head to another, is punctuated with a sound similar to the thrust of a sword. The video performs a multivocal provocation. Its poignant enunciation is then signed by a title, separated from the sequence of talking heads by a few seconds of black screen. "We don't want you here," reads the first title, before the ad cuts to a second: "The bereaved parents' Families Forum doesn't wish to welcome new members."[2]

The Parents Circle–Family Forum (PCFF) is a joint nonprofit anti-occupation organization of Palestinian and Jewish-Israeli bereaved

FIGURE 17. Screenshot from *We Don't Want You Here*, produced by Bauman Bar Rivnai, 2014.

families that was established in 1995. It officially started its activity in 1998 with a series of meetings between Palestinian and Jewish-Israeli bereaved families. These gatherings, some exclusive to the forum members, some open to the wider public, are based on the exchange of personal stories of loss. In addition, the PCFF takes part in organizing a joint Memorial Day ceremony[3] and initiates nonviolent protests, dialogue meetings, exhibitions, and tours. During the Gaza War the PCFF launched the "We Don't Want You Here" media campaign, produced *pro bono* by the advertising firm Bauman Bar Rivnai. It also erected a "dialogue tent" in the Cinémathèque Plaza in Tel Aviv, in which it held a daily vigil, inviting passersby to sit, talk, and share their experiences or views. In its mission statement the PCFF calls for all to "avoid the use of bereavement for further violence and retribution," maintaining that mutual acknowledgement between Palestinians and Jewish-Israelis is a necessary infrastructure for reconciliation.[4]

Anti-occupation activism in Israel-Palestine is entrenched in battles over rights,[5] narrative,[6] and images. The latter is mostly predicated on a live record of atrocities that attributes images as evidence, and relies on what Pooja Rangan in her critique of documentary's humanitarian urge has termed "immediations."[7] The media campaigns and grassroots media productions I analyze in this chapter, the PCFF's being one of them, draw on Jewish-Israeli society's filial attachment to soldiers and soldierhood, as well as its consensual, introverted, privatized language of mourning. What I have thematized throughout this book as "sovereign intimacy" places loss in the ostensibly depoliticized, private sphere of the home, making mourning an intimate pursuit that is universally shared. By excluding the loss of life from the political sphere of colonial conflict and deeming mourning private, it excludes the act of sovereign violence and its dehumanizing and obliterating effect on noncitizens. In the case of the PCFF, the organization's activity and rhetoric reject the neutralization of loss and the erasure, by this very neutralization, of the lives or deaths of Palestinians. If a sovereign intimacy is predicated on, and enhances, the denial of a politics of loss, here, loss—and mourning as a set of activities through which loss is recognized—is constitutive of political speech and action, one that articulates both Jewish-Israeli and Palestinian subjects. Moreover, the PCFF video addresses the living rather than the dead and the organization's activity centers on imagining a possible future, towards which it promotes a discourse of engagement rather than disavowal or exclusion. As a viral media campaign, calling upon mourning to articulate a social contract (or its provocative refusal—"We don't want you here!"), the PCFF video consciously participates in a political economy of the address of kinship that this chapter seeks to excavate.

In their post-9/11 collection of essays *Precarious Life,* Judith Butler proposes a political ethics based on vulnerability that questions the very means of representation through which we recognize the other as human. Like the PCFF, Butler situates mourning as intrinsic to politics, through which both life and the impact of violence on concrete bodies can be realized. Thus, for Butler, mourning over the other's life is a practice of recognition in which one is transformed by the other and at the same time becomes conscious of one's own fragility. As Butler proposes: "mindfulness of this vulnerability can become the basis of claims for non-military political solutions, just as denial of this vulnerability through a fantasy of mastery (an institutionalized fantasy of mastery) can fuel the instruments of war."[8] Butler's notion of ethics is predicated on a Levinasian theory of the face. The face, for Levinas, is not an image, but a site in which we encounter the other, where the other addresses us. Butler reviews mass-mediated images of human faces, commenting that they fail to represent an ethical encounter, an ethics constituted (per Levinas) by the mutual acknowledgement of life's precariousness.

An ethics based on mutual precarity notwithstanding, Butler cautiously introduces the fraught prerequisites of a politics of loss: the differential location of grief, the exclusive disposition of social melancholy, the realization or unrealization of life and mourning through the normative forms of the family and that of the state. Butler's theory is built along axes of proximity and distance. It is framed in the context of the "war on terror," a form of aggression that is geographically located, unevenly distributed, and technologically facilitated by means of distance. As a particular historical moment, the "war on terror" introduced a mode of operating that reattributed the very concepts of "domestic" versus "world" orders or affairs. Butler discerns grief that lends itself to the public by way of familiarity from lives rendered ungrievable due to distance and obscurity. The structural leeway they therefore offer, that of recognition, is predicated on bringing things to the sphere of the self, producing proximity, undoing distance. Placing one's own body as an attribute through which the condition of vulnerability can be understood centers injury as a political stance. While this analysis is illuminating, injury, as the geo-politics of Israel-Palestine show, is mostly self-referential and narcissistic, steering the debate towards historical victimhood rather than justice in the present. In Butler's attempts to carve representation that recognizes the other's humanity through vulnerability, they place one's own body as a vector, an index for what can and should be representable as life.

This is an ontological argument, where politics is engraved on the body, as a common property, a knowledge made available first and foremost in one's own body. As the body provides the essence for Butler's question on life recognized or unrecognized, they place this question in the domain of representation, and more specifically, the institutions of media. Throughout *Precarious Lives* Butler constantly refers to the public obituary in the newspaper, news coverage, mass circulated images and stories, all forms of US mass media where lives are either realized or effaced. Referring to the lives of 200,000 Iraqi children taken by the war, they write: "do we have an image, a frame for any of those lives? . . . Is there a story we might find about those deaths in the media?"[9] As this book has shown, means of representation are engraved in complex frameworks of production and circulation that cater to scales of proximity or pose things as formally distant or unrepresentable altogether. Can representation ever summon an encounter with the face in its deepest Levinasian sense: an address of ethics that calls for recognition of humanity as fragility? There is a foundational core both in Butler's reading of the human and the way it is mediated. It seems that for life to be realized and for bodies to be affected we need to account for both the structure of the violence and life's structures of mediation.

188 | Chapter 5

I would like to consider Butler's political ontology and their ethico-political notion of the face in relation to the figure of the body politic. The body politic is an amalgam of a metaphorical and anatomical body composed to animate political order. It brings to the fore the anatomy of power, While this premise is different than Butler's, both the overlaps and discrepancies are intriguing. Eugene Thacker traces the omnipresence of the body politic in political thought in articulating a set of relations between the ruler and the ruled.[10] The body politic, according to Thacker, makes intelligible concepts of centralization, hierarchy, and unity between parts. It gains its sentient features through corresponding notions of vitality and decomposition as well as its embodiment of the natural and unnatural. These defining characteristics, per Thacker, make the body politic both theological and medical, an attribute of order and life. The body politic is thus a biopolitical figure that brings together sovereign and regulatory powers, the much-cited Foucauldian formulation. According to Thacker, while sovereignty is often realized through the body politic's head, heart, or soul, the body itself, its overall arrangement of organs, as a carrier of diseases, infections and epidemics, is where multiplicity is expressed. The immanent decomposition of the body politic makes the body the subject of power and control as a way of sanctioning life or death.

Butler and Thacker both move from heads to bodies. They demarcate an almost opposite movement: for Butler the locus of the face opens up to the other; for Thacker, the head is the extraction of multiplicity into a unified order. For Butler, the individuated, fragile body metonymizes a human condition; for Thacker, the body as multiplicity, as a collective subject of regulation, is where individuated bodies are realized as a perilous entity, as enmity. The body, in Thacker's account of the body politic, encapsulates the collective subject of governing—not Butler's liberal entity of ethics—precisely through its medical precarity. While Butler centers self-knowledge of fragility as a basis of mutuality and relationality, and for gaining a political consciousness, for Thacker the body manifests bio-political or necropolitical power. For both thinkers the body, and more specifically the fragile body that is literal and organic as much as it is conceptual, is the crux of a political ontology of life and death: the politics of mourning for Butler, and governing by death—necrology—for Thacker.

These lines of investigation into the body politic open up new paths for thinking about the intersection of sovereign power and intimacy in a politics predicated on loss. What pertinence do they have for "We

Don't Want You Here"? In the video, there are no bodies, only heads. In fact, mostly there are not even heads but faces, framed from chin to hairline. The face is not the same as the head—not an organ of sovereignty, but an expressive, outwards-looking surface of the body politic. In the PCFF media campaign as well as the other campaigns analyzed in this chapter, the talking head or the face stands as a central image, a recurring framing of a proposition. As this chapter will show, the face articulates an address that is always complicit with the Israeli military project and the regional economy of life, even if this address comes to challenge that very ideological position. In the PCFF campaign, in videotaped testimonials of the veteran soldiers' organization Breaking the Silence, and in the hostage video of Gilad Shalit and the popular release campaign that ensued, the address is empowered through social sentiments and kinship. In each of these campaigns, all adjacent to a private media complex, the image of the face is a meeting point of a singular individuated figure with collectivity, a mutual formulation of an intimate self and sovereign order, a linkage between the head/face and the body politic. These mutual constitutions are underlined by the utterance "We don't want you here," an ironic play on the ravaging hostility, an articulation that affiliates and repudiates at the same time.

How do heads relate to bodies? The two cannot be differentiated but are, naturally, connected. In the "We Don't Want You Here" campaign the talking heads speak in the name of bodies/lives destroyed by colonial violence. The linkage of a body to a head denotes the symbiotic relationship between speech and action, singularity and unifying order, facing the other and anatomical autonomy, will and the body politic that delimits it. For Thacker it is the connection between the sovereign head and the body of population that manifests the totality of power as a means of subjugation. For Butler, however, it is the face that indicates a shared condition of vulnerability—openness, rather than totality. But does the campaign facilitate an encounter with the face? Such a reading will be predicated, indirectly, on the assumption that the image of the face transgresses the political economy of reproduction so central to the mass media image.

Butler's reading relies on a twentieth-century philosophical tradition that locates an autonomous, foundational entity in the obscurity of the face. It is a face turned against the head and its unifying power. Media and technology theorists, especially today, understand the face as a surface of biopolitical power, a sight mapped, measured, and tracked.[11] They delineate an entanglement of political and corporate agencies that turn faces into a resource for surveillance and incrimination, project-ing social malaise into individuated sites of control. For Butler, reading Levinas, the face cannot be contained by an image. For contemporary visual technology, the face *is* but an image. Later in the chapter, the face will be re-encountered as a sight of institutional policy, even a potential compromise to military modes of conduct. For now, it is important to note the liberal belief in the face's singularity versus its digital standard-ization, symptomatic to the age of private media, applied by private markets on private subjects. Are the faces in the media campaign, poi-gnantly looking at us, each a frame of their own, expelling us from their violent commons—"we don't want you here!"— singularizing each face, each loss, or rather making them indistinguishable? Is this about the face or the body politic?

The PCFF's media campaign is exceptional with respect to their rou-tine activity, which is very much grounded in interpersonal encounters as the basis for dialogue. In that sense, their employment of a politics of loss is not so much channeled through the mediated image of the face, misunderstood as an epistemic site of encounter. Although certainly calling for a mutual acknowledgement of loss, I argue that the 2014 video brings to the fore not an *ethics of recognition* predicated on mass mediated images of faces, *but rather a political economy of the face as a form of address.*

In the video the sequence of talking faces works according to the principle of metonymy. The individuated address—face and voice—ar-ticulates a condition of cohabitation. Sequenced, the address speaks on behalf of Jewish-Israelis and Palestinians who are brought together by mourning, and at the same time, speaking from and to a political condi-tion of separation. Signaling difference—mainly through language, as some say the sentence in Hebrew and some in Arabic—the head/face is an extension of the body politic. They speak from and to a society where the other, the Palestinian, is not only already dead but whose life, as I have showed throughout this book, is nullified by the inflated memory of Jewish-Israeli life. In other words, by sequencing the face and repeating the same phrase, the speakers attest their own marking by the politics of loss.

While the PCFF calls attention to the regime of separation, its cam-paign complies with the logic of privacy. The utterance is designed as a slogan, punctually cut, neatly aestheticized through composition and sound, lending itself to catchy reproduction. This rhetoric of commodi-fication makes sense given that the video is produced by an advertising firm, by professionals in the art of branding. In other chapters of this book, I noted the continuum in the private sector between the family, private media services and entrepreneurship, non-governmental agencies, and marketing. In an age of self-generating content platforms and social media, political activism and branding conflate. The archetypical slogan offers a contradictory logic: it accumulates its value through repetition, yet at the same time, repetition can also erode meaning. Perhaps the irony is well intended, as the video is meant to market an undesirable brand, and, in fact, asks its addressees not to buy into this lifestyle. Ironic or not, produced as a viral campaign where resonance is accumulated by circulation—an economy of "sharing" and "liking"—the video understands politics not through the singularity of the ethical encounter, but through branding as undifferentiated reproduction. This is not a speech of profanity, but, perhaps intendedly, the banality of the slogan. While the speakers speak for collectivity and their heads extend a body politic, the aesthetics of the close-up, the rhetoric of the commodity and their orbits of circulation taps into the individuated, privatized economy of injury. This is not to devalue the importance of the speech act, but to indicate that other things are taking place as well. I read the video as a provocation against Israeli sovereign violence not by its facilitating an ethical encounter vis-à-vis facing fragility, but by calling attention to the way life in Israel-Palestine is economized.

The economy of circulation differentiates the media campaign from other materials discussed in this book. The conduits of sovereign intimacy that I tracked in other chapters, namely personal videographic memory work, gain their value by drawing on the affective singularity and kinship that also inform its modes of production. The case studies in this chapter expand the private media complex, exposing not only the ramification of a neoliberal politics predicated on memory and death in Israel-Palestine, but the valorization of the soldier's image in the production economies of life and loss. The PCFF's "We Don't Want You Here" campaign, alongside videos produced by the Breaking the Silence testimonial project and the popular campaign for the return of the captured soldier Gilad Shalit, all demonstrate the kind of negotiations that take place while trying to break away from the national cult of intimacy.[12]

While other chapters focused on the home as a site of sovereign intimacy, this chapter engages with media productions that draw on similar currencies—loss, memory, soldierhood, violence—but tap into different production and distribution constellations. Where other chapters addressed a neutralized complicity, this chapter accounts for the complex dynamic of resistance within Jewish-Israeli society. What speaks for this difference is first and foremost the shift from the quasi-improvised homemade mode of production at the turn of the century to the well-crafted format of the media campaign a decade into the 2000s. By this time we have moved from a transitional institutional and technological object, responding to the shift from analog to digital and, in Israel, public to private television, to multimedia artifacts grounded on digital culture and platforms; from an unraveled aesthetic to an orderly coherency; from dispersed and ephemeral distribution to branding; from domesticity to the public sphere. Here, we are at the heart of the private media complex: the mutual yielding of different actors along the commodity market. In line with the argument that the homemade mode was never purely counterinstitutional in its production and content, an argument underscored throughout this book, there is no shift or break here, but rather a continuation. The media campaigns discussed here are brought up not as antithetical to intimate loss, its videographic formulation, and its bracketed and pervasive forms of complicity with state violence, but what stems from this very nexus while opening a wider referential spectrum with changing face values—values of life and death or the value of media circulation.

As already noted, in both the PCFF's "We Don't Want You Here" campaign and the Israeli sovereign intimacy, mourning is instrumentalized: in the former, to call on the recognizability of loss as a provocation against violence; in the latter, perhaps unintended and by means of exclusion, to legitimize violence. In Israel-Palestine, grief and mourning are circumscribed and unevenly economized by governmental clinical support, cultural infrastructure, and institutionalized and quasi-institutionalized media outlets. This uneven economy of life is echoed in the uneven distribution of violence, and vice-versa. As opposed to Butler's premise of unknowingness and unrecognizability predicated on distance, the region's economy of life and death can be put in a permanently unbalanced equation of life "close to me" or "like me" against "life that threatens me." In this account, the other's life is devaluing, diminished by the perception of these lives as a threat.[13] This means that certain lives—Jewish-Israeli—have priority over others—Palestinian and Lebanese.

Likewise, the media properties of rendering things close or distanced operate unevenly. Understanding media, as this book does, not just as a representational regime, but as a utility in a biopolitical system, a governing technique set to stabilize a certain managing of domestic affairs and bodies, and a market with set values, supports the shift in perspectives from the ethics of the face to the political economy of the address. Thus, this chapter is not about discerning good/ethical media addresses from bad/unethical ones—in fact, all media campaigns analyzed here are ethical in the sense that they prioritize life over death and use their address to expose the extent to which military violence had become the norm within Jewish-Israeli society. It is also not about reducing the media address to its mode of production, deeming all media forms a commodity simply because they entail a certain investment and accumulate value through circulation. Rather, it is about situating ethics in a complex media system, one that relies on institutional, discursive, and cultural constellations through which life is attributed with a certain value.

FACE US

Breaking the Silence is an organization of IDF veteran-combatants whose objective is to expose the Israeli public to the everyday atrocities of the Israeli military occupation of Palestine. Established in 2004 in the aftermath of the Second Intifada (2001), the organization's main activity centers on collecting veterans' testimonies documenting violations of rights, cruelty, and injustice endured by Palestinians. It defines this mission as inward-facing, meant to confront the Jewish-Israeli society with the immorality of the occupation. In addition, Breaking the Silence (BtS) leads tours of Hebron during which Jewish-Israeli civilians can encounter the occupation's infrastructures of separation, subjugation, and control. It arranges house meetings and lectures and keeps a regular presence in social and institutional media. In addressing Jewish-Israeli society BtS draws on the position of the military as a main social token. Questioning the ethical conduct of the Israeli soldier and probing the very norms that underlie and sustain the occupation, BtS is one of the most contested and attacked anti-occupation organizations in the Jewish-Israeli public sphere, a target of offense and silencing from the Israeli extreme and center-right. In the following discussion, I read BtS's testimonials as probing both norms and exceptions. An entanglement constituted through two sets of tensions characterizes its media work as well as its representational politics: the tension between inside and outside, and the tension between exposure and covering.

The BtS mission statement reads:

> Soldiers who serve in the Territories witness and participate in military actions which change them immensely. Cases of abuse towards Palestinians, looting, and destruction of property have been the norm for years, but are

still explained as extreme and unique cases. Our testimonies portray a different, and much grimmer picture in which deterioration of moral standards finds expression in the character of orders and the rules of engagement, and are justified in the name of Israel's security. While this reality is known to Israeli soldiers and commanders, Israeli society continues to turn a blind eye, and to deny what is done in its name.[14]

The organization both actively reaches out to and receives requests from soldiers and ex-soldiers to testify. Since its initiation, it has reportedly interviewed more than a thousand soldiers. Most of the testimonies are inscribed in text form, some in video; all testimonies are recorded by veteran soldiers and the organization researches each one of the incidents attested before publishing them.[15] Unlike the customary male-centric image of the soldier, BtS testimonies feature female soldiers, partly a result of changing gender policies inside the army since the early 2000s, partly due to the organization's own politics. The video testimonials are short, filmed in a medium shot (sitting distance) by one camera positioned on a tripod, with no cuts. It is clear from the videos that the speakers respond to an interviewer who intervenes mostly when things need clarification. The straightforwardness of format, avoiding close-ups or alternation between camera angles, eschews a videographic grammar of proximity. The testimonies are cut according to concrete incidents or actions and have been published and printed as thematic collections. They appear on the BtS website, and video testimonies can also be accessed via YouTube. In these different platforms, the testimonies are catalogued according to the incident or kind of violations to which they attest. BtS's understanding of the testimonial—manifested in the ways they are collected, cut, and stored—departs from the formation of testimony around experience and subjectivity. What leads the testimony, as a form of public record, is the act and not its agent. Humiliation, abuse, assassination, confirmation of killing, random arrests, bribery, road blocks and curfews, the use of human shields, unjust shooting, house demolition, and violence towards children are some of the divisions in BtS's catalogue of the occupation. This typological order articulates routine violence while highlighting patterns of conduct rather than subjective narrative.

In early 2000 Yehuda Shaul, then recently released from his military service and soon to become the active force behind the veterans' organization, felt the burden of communicating to the "outside" world the "inside" of the occupation routine. He started meeting with other veteran combatants, specifically looking for soldiers who had carried a

FIGURE 18. Screenshot from Breaking the Silence testimonial project.

camera during their service. His way to bridge the alienating gap of "inside" and "outside" was to collect pictures spontaneously produced by soldiers depicting their everyday military life. Perhaps intuitively, Shaul seems to locate violence not in the rupture momentum of the historical event, but the mundane. What drew his attention is the anomaly of abuse that underlines the very normalcy of habitual record.[16] Thus, the very basis of BtS's visual order is not documentation as a way to capture, and thus to prevent, violence as the exception—the dominant logic of visual humanitarianism[17]—but excavation of the routine violence that is behind the visible norm, a norm framed by amateur, personal visual practices.

Looking at something that had become quotidian and familiar to them, Shaul and his fellow veterans sought to traverse this internal common sense and to trace the political rationale that passes off violence as necessity and oppression as a means of security. They laid the ground for a visual epistemology deconstructive in its premise, calling into question the very semiotics through which the occupation as a set of routinized interactions and activities is rendered transparent, normal to the extent that it is invisible to the perpetrating society. The typological titles on the organization's testimonies platform do the same, performing the determining act of naming, and by that, questioning the

FIGURE 19. Breaking the Silence, "This is how the occupation looks like." Image: Moti Milrod, *Haaretz*, March 2016.

embedded social patterns of seeing and defining. As I will soon show, the strategy of undermining the primary set of signs that articulate the normative order can be extended to the way the organization treats the figure of the soldier and their speech.

Shaul contacted the still photographer Miki Kartzman and the filmmaker Avi Mograbi, perhaps the two best-known counter-documentarians of the Israeli occupation. With their guidance, side by side with excavating ex-soldiers' photo albums, he started a video documentation of these ex-soldiers' stories, which resulted in an exhibition presented in an art gallery in mid-2004. The conceptual work that led to the exhibition did not necessarily inform the modes of production and circulation to be adopted later by the organization, but it brings to the fore a dialectical tension between taking a picture as a way of habituating, an inward form of documentation and exchange, and displaying the very same image or record in the public sphere as a means of exposure. Here, too, the location of production and exhibition and not only the audio-visual content itself carries its own politics of re-assigning and mutually constituting social and political paradigms of the home or homemade.

BtS demonstrates a fluid and open model of media circulation and outlets that moves beyond the dichotomies of private and public, amateur and institutional—national or commercial. Starting with the appropriation of personal amateur images to attest the political reality, the mobilizing of the art show form, or, for that matter, the space of the academic art gallery in the south of Tel Aviv, the semi-professional grassroots mode of production of the testimonials themselves, the use of self-generated content platforms, and the relaying of the testimonial project to other forms such as performative happenings and feature documentaries[18]— all these assume a rhizomatic, pluri-centric, less authoritative perception of media production. By circulation I do not only refer to the travelling of the testimonials through media forms and performances, but to circulation as a force of repetition and intensification that re-organizes, even distorts, social conventions.

There is something uncanny about BtS testimonials, in their avoidance of the sensational or the popular rhetoric of exposure and instead locating recognition in naming, cataloguing, and mostly in injecting knowledge outside its habituating spheres. BtS testimonials derive from, and at the same time critically reflect on, the commonality of the soldier/ their address, as a social currency and, more concretely as what for Israelis is a familiar image. BtS testimonies are the prototypical Felmanian formulation where the witness attests from the *inside-out*.[19] They not only relay what happens in "the territories," away from Jewish-Israeli cities, to a Jewish-Israeli public, but through this very act of externalizing call the norm into question. The soldier's testimony aims not only to inform but to unravel the very terminology of security and defense, premises that are used by the Israeli political mainstream to justify the occupation, and that are embodied and implemented by the soldier. Moreover, following the organization's rhetoric, it is the position of the soldier as a representative of state power and ideology that grants them the right to social speech, the right to testify. This allocation of agency subverts the dominant social figure of the soldier either as an infantilized subject—a rhetoric that family videos circulating on the media put forward—or a traumatic one,[20] positions that subtract from the active and collective aspects of social agency. For Shoshana Felman, "inside" and "outside" refer to a demarcated space, which certainly applies to the Israeli occupation of Palestine, where space is marked through walls and blockades. The soldier testifies from the inside of the normalized language of security and to what happens behind the walls. Inside and outside have additional connotations: while inside refers to the interiority of subjective experience, outside points towards the public sphere. Appropriating an active representative position, BtS can be read as traversing the individuating, inward-facing impulse put forward by the embedded narcissism of national politics and a call for an outward-looking social accountability.

The question of inside and outside points at the geographical borders of the sovereign state on another level. From very early on, the testimonials were translated to English and circulated outside of Israel, not only through the global expansion of the internet, but through lectures given by BtS activists mostly to the Jewish diaspora. The Hebron tours are sometimes done in English as well. This distribution model supports the organization's funding scheme, legitimacy, and model for intervention. The idea that the vernacular needs to be translated and circulated elsewhere stems from the extraterritorial paradigm of humanitarian organizations' work, including media outputs as that which mobilizes international pressure to bring local crises into relief and hopefully resolution.[21] Paradoxically, the soldier as the manifestation of sovereign power and, traditionally, the one who guards the borders of the sovereign state, is the one who is calling for an international intervention, ostensibly undermining the state's sovereignty. One of the major criticisms directed at BtS inside Israel is that it is "airing the dirty laundry outside," and thus carrying out an act of betrayal. Interestingly, conservative Israeli politics evoke the intimate—rendered figuratively with the idiomatic reference to laundry—to devalue the organization's work. The accusation of betrayal centers an act that assumes the violation of a binding interiority and certainly has to do with the fact that the speakers position themselves as (ex)-soldiers, stressing their still-attached position to military order. In addition to the traversal of the inside and outside of institutional film and media production and circulation, of the intelligibility or unintelligibility of language and convention, or of national and international politics, what is traversed here is the concrete directionality of the address. The ex-soldiers speak on behalf of, but also as a way to breach social consensus around, the military. BtS provokes the norms, and at the same time reaffirms and valorizes them by re-appropriating the soldier's address, their representational currency.

The tangled logic of inside and outside comes to bear on the address itself, articulating a collective indictment but also enabling a potential exoneration, excusing the abuse of power by the sovereign state through its call for an ethical conduct of that same power. Testimony, in this instance, becomes a means of absolution, of relief. Working on the documentary tradition of soldiers' testimonials, Jonathan Kahana construes them along the lines of the excuse, a counter-performative speech act that drives regimes based on deep irony.[22] BtS is careful in framing the testimonies as done by ex-soldiers to clear their own conscience, that is, as a mode of confession, an individual act with formative and therapeutic ends. Gil Hochberg places the ethical question of soldiers' testimonies not in their self-exonerating function, but in spectatorship; thus the address is located not in the subject who makes it, but their addressees.[23] Kahana's notion of the counter-performative points at a social pattern that is constituted by a traversed logic, perhaps a speech of in-action or the excuse as a way to perpetuate the dominant order rather than change it.

Probing the convention of soldiers' testimonies, Ariel Handle distinguishes between morality and ethics: the former is the code of behavior directed towards the "inside," within one's community, while the latter is doing justice with the other, which is outside me.[24] The soldier's address to Israeli society to acknowledge the ongoing atrocities of the occupation is made, according to Handle, in order to preserve their own ethical image of themselves. Furthermore, this address is made on behalf of the soldier, not the Palestinian, asking society to acknowledge the price paid by its own representatives, living with the memory and shame of their own evildoing.

Handle's critique points at a decisive aspect of the address, and in that sense echoes other voices on the Israeli left: BtS addresses Jewish-Israeli society (the organization's appealing to the international community in that regard is an *aside* not an *address*), pleading for it to change its now corrupted ways. By extension, what is revealed is an internal social calamity rather than the norm of Palestinian death. On the one hand, Handle explicates, the ongoing reference to the mental burden carried by the traumatic perpetrator forms a clinical discourse through which individual subjects cannot be held accountable for their deeds. On the other hand, the discourse of shame associated with the atrocities secures the soldier's place as a subject of ideology, as the figure who guards a system of values. Therefore, Handle concludes, the BtS testimonies project is a mechanism meant to sustain the ethical, but it neglects the moral. Handle's insightful analysis puts pressure on the tension of "inside" and "outside" in the organization's activities, and supports the argument this book is making for an abolition of the military order, with its social attachments. However, what Handle misses is the allegorical power of media and its forms of representation.

BtS constantly legitimizes its actions while drawing on its representatives' personal history as ex-soldiers and their Zionist background, marking themselves as "insiders."[25] The military, noted one columnist, is "symbolic capital" for the organization.[26] Insisting on the ethicalization of the military and mobilizing the soldier's consensual position, BtS acts to stop the occupation, but leaves the military ethos intact, re-valorizing the agency of the soldier while defacing the Palestinian. As a representative, the soldier is the figure that reconnects (talking) heads and bodies, a carrier of a particular speech that reflects on socio-political systems and balances. This is made explicit in the organization's name "Breaking the Silence," a name that invites an audio intervention, a form of undoing the semiotics of social pattern. Here is the paradox of the address: drawing on an ethical position, a provocation against state violence in fact enables the continuation of this violence, providing an outlet through which perpetration is atoned for and excused. The problem does not form only through speech—the practice of testimony and its confessional aspect—but the channeling of these testimonies through the convention of the soldier's address. What Handle describes is an internal system of acceptance, a political mechanism that allocates, balances, and keeps under control an internal set of tensions and positions. Inward-looking, this is Israel's ethical economy of the occupation, a form of statecraft that is used to manage domestic affairs.

Speech notwithstanding, the call to break through a system of signification takes place through the visual field in the tension between exposure and covering. Many of the *BtS* testimonies are anonymous, with the actual face of the speakers obscured through various techniques. There are faces shot from behind a screen, shot from the back, overshadowed by an in-frame source of light, digitally pixelated, or circled and then blurred. One of the most striking acts of obfuscation is layering the face with a semi-opaque texture made of inscriptions of the spoken text, whether in the original Hebrew or in English translation. This last manifestation relocates the address from the image of the face into language, and more precisely, the graph that is laid over as a sort of mask.

Can the address come through if the addresser remains obscure, if their faces, as a personalizing image of singularity, are not there to encounter? How can the address expose if it engages in covering? According to Ruthie Ginsburg, "Exposure acts in a formation that runs along the lines of revealing, knowing, hiding and protecting."[27] Drawing on the discourse of human rights organizations, Ginsburg attributes exposure to the public's right to know, and yet she notices that in the case of BtS, covering is what allows for this exposure to take place, protecting those who testify from indictment and shaming. According to this logic, the testimonies are exposing the act as norm while exempting individual agency; they can be heard or publicly resonate precisely because the speaker cannot be scrutinized. Anonymity, as an attack of idiosyncrasy, lands us in the general rule. By covering the face as an image of singularity, what ends up being exposed is the body politic. The covered face invites the figure of multiplicity into the frame.

Indeed, in their testimonies BtS realizes the soldier and their address as both the rule and its exception. Back in 2004, when testimonies for the first exhibition were collected, the military police confiscated the visual materials and started an investigation against those who testified, with the charges being violation of secrecy and disclosure of sensitive information that might put human lives at risk. When BtS published their report on the 2008 Gaza invasion, known as Operation Cast Lead, the army denied the alleged events and actions that were reported. According to the IDF, the testimonies could not be taken as evidence due to their anonymity, and, without knowing the source of the testimonies, the army could not authenticate and respond to the reports.[28] These accusations are part of an ongoing public diatribe against BtS for its policy of obscuring faces, and on the side of the state, part of ongoing attempts to react to the testimonies through a discourse of criminalization.

As these incidents show, first, the army and the state used incrimination to bypass the public right to know and argued for measures taken against the state in the form of compromising secrecy. These accusations mark the soldiers who testify as an inherent part of a national, militarized collectivity—members of a secret order against which they later turn. Here, obfuscation seems to be the norm, pertaining to both the blurred face and the state's vow for secrecy. In 2008, in the name of the public right to know, the state, quite contrarily, demanded the exposure of the face as a means to account for the deeds and prosecute the doers. At first, the state called upon obscurity and collectivity, and then upon exposure and singularity. Mobilizing the juridical, either as a demand for coverage, or, on the contrary, a demand for exposure, assumes a subject to whom criminal acts can be referred, thus putting forward the singled-out individual rather than observing testimony as an indicator of an institutionalized pattern. If for the sovereign the law is the instrument through which it can respond or dismiss the address, in the popular public debate the dismissal revolved around the invisibility of the face, on the presumption that the image of the face stands for an image of truth emanating from an individuated, personalized identity.

BtS's response to these polemics highlights the stakes of exposure. In 2011 Israel's most popular newspaper published an interview with members of the organization with the title "Here We Are, Face Us."[29] In the interview the testifiers appear with their faces unveiled. One of them, Asaf Polak, explains, "When we have no face they call us 'grey people,' ones that you can't tell if they say the truth or if their words are valid."[30] The same arguments made by BtS's critics are used by its members to rationalize anonymity. First, they posit, from a legal perspective, revealing the face might lead to legal charges against specific individuals in an international courtroom for committing war crimes. This argument is problematic as, by flagging incrimination, it also assumes an exonerating speech, a speech that disavows its consequences. Therefore, in the interview the activists face the camera, stating that they are willing to bear the consequences of legal charges. Secondly, they explain the covering of the face as emanating from the fear of shaming and being rejected by one's family and friends. As Jean-François Lyotard contends, betrayal—and with it, social shame and rejection—is inherent to the act of testimony.[31] By making this argument, the activists consent with the social convention that ties military and kinship. This entanglement leads BtS to its most conclusive argument. According to the organization, the faceless testimonies circumvent the "rotten apples syndrome" that excuses atrocity as acts done by unruly individuals. From this perspective, anonymity was chosen to generalize and allegorize. The figure of betrayal—the traitor—is precisely the one who stands for both the rule and its exception or transgression. The soldier is the face of the mechanism, the voice of society, rather than a specific and singular subject of either guilt or sympathy.

This last argument highlights the address rather than the face. My use of "address" is meant to convey something that cannot be localized in speech or the image. The face is indeed a charged and unstable phenomenon. The French-Jewish philosopher Emmanuel Levinas, on whom Butler draws in their closing essay, contends that the face conveys a form of encounter rather than representation, or an image. For Levinas the face is not an image, and certainly not a mass mediated one.[32] As I already noted, in the contemporary media regime the face lends itself to disciplinary tools of uniformity and securitization. This tendency is exacerbated when the face encountered is that of the institution. Daniel Mann tracks a growing awareness in the military's strategic thinking about exposing soldiers' faces. He describes a multifaceted media economy in which the algorithmic tracking of facial images serves grassroots

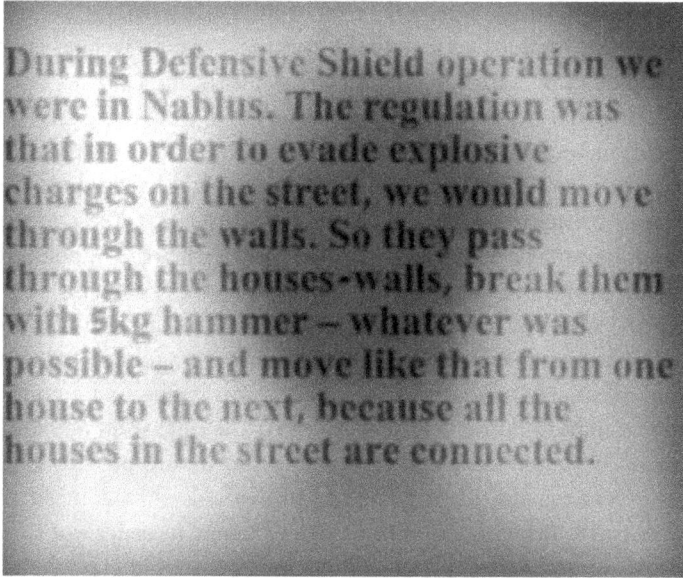

During Defensive Shield operation we
were in Nablus. The regulation was
that in order to evade explosive
charges on the street, we would move
through the walls. So they pass
through the houses-walls, break them
with 5kg hammer – whatever was
possible – and move like that from one
house to the next, because all the
houses in the street are connected.

FIGURE 20. Screenshot from Breaking the Silence testimonial project.

campaigns against soldiers' atrocities and state surveillance all at once. Aware of this economy, soldiers who participate in violent confrontations with the Palestinian population have started wearing face masks, a means of depersonalization to protect their impunity.[33] Mann writes: "Soldiers no longer hide their location or actions but their identity, not their existence but their individuality, not their bodies but their faces."[34] In the age of private media, this tendency is tied to the digital unleash: the heightened circulation of images on social media and the use of algorithm-run apps. It serves to cover impunity rather than expose it. Both in its modus-operandi and its social function as a representative, the soldier is a figure of uniformity meant to facilitate invisibility (secrecy) and indistinctiveness (collectivity), its face always referring back to the body politic. What is interesting is the different logic at play: for the military, the exposed face will also expose the action as it can be tracked down to a single agent; for BtS, the covered face exposes the action as a recurring pattern. Ultimately, the main locus of invisibility is neither actions nor specific actors, but the norm itself, the recurrence that make such violations a non-event.

Cinematic traditions of the close-up, notes Mary Ann Doane, were theorized as, first, a privileged site of individuation; second, a display of social types; and third, a primary tool of intersubjectivity, of relation.[35] BtS's video testimonials articulate the contingencies between these three theoretical positions, forming a dialectic of inside and outside, exposure and covering that hinges on the porous aspect of both media, as a form of circulation, and authority, as a form of representative power. The tension from the inside out centers a form of speech that strives to "break the silence," breaching a consensual public compliance. Yet, conforming to its own interiority, remaining attached to the rhetoric of soldierhood and kinship, this speech partly contains a disciplinary means of subjugation and exoneration that refers back to a national narcissist politics of injury. The tension between exposure and coverage puts forward the different values assigned to the face as both an image and a contradictory site of individuation and indivisibility. Claims raised against BtS's blurring of faces maintain that the testimonies should provide evidence and hence expose the identity of the individuals that committed the crimes. As such, BtS is accused of using the image in order *not to show*. Yet, targeting collective responsibility and the enabling power of the norm, what the organization is after cannot be made visible through a singular individual but through the amorphous features of generality.

"MY CHILD HAS NO PRICE"

In October 2009 the Palestinian Islamic movement Hamas released a two-minute video featuring an Israeli soldier, Gilad Shalit, who at the time had been held captive by the movement's military arm for the past three years.[36] In the video, Shalit seems skinny and pale. He sits on a plastic chair in an empty room, wearing what is meant to look like a khaki IDF uniform, holding a newspaper; the scene is shot in a medium shot, capturing his head and upper torso. A greyish undertone, a result of a source of artificial light that is positioned outside the frame to Shalit's right, merges the soldier's face and the wall behind him, underscoring his paleness. He starts by identifying himself, providing the names of his parents and siblings, his home address, and his Israeli ID number. "As you can see, I am reading from the newspaper, *Palestine Today*, the 14th of September 2009, which is published in Gaza," says Shalit, while lifting the newspaper that he is holding; he waits while the camera zooms in to capture the date, printed on the upper-center of the newspaper's first page. After the pause he continues: "I am reading the newspaper hoping to find some information about myself and about my release and my return home. . . . I'm hoping that the current

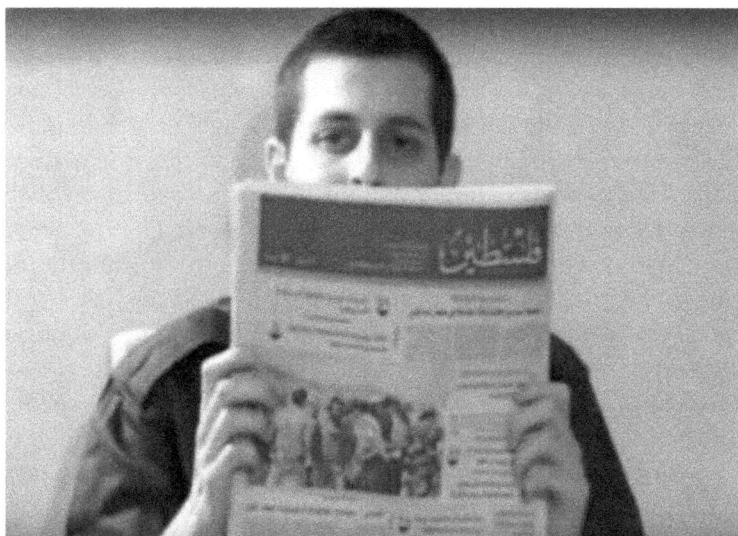

FIGURE 21. Screenshot from Gilad Shalit proof-of-life video, 2009.

government, led by Binyamin Netanyahu, will do all it can to guarantee my release." He then goes on to recall a family memory of a visit his father and siblings paid him when he was positioned in the Golan Heights and gives the Georgian and Hebrew date of the event. At this point the camera has zoomed out to frame the sitting Shalit from below the knees. Shalit reassures his family that he is in good health and is being treated well. He then pauses and looks at the camera, and, as if by a signal, he gets up from his chair, walks towards the camera, stops, and then turns around and returns to his chair.

The video was sent to the Shalit family after a delegate appointed by the Israeli government to negotiate Shalit's return had demanded proof that the soldier was alive.[37] The sending of the video was considered to be a crucial incentive in closing a deal on Shalit's release and part of a series of transactions done to retrieve information about his condition. In return for the video, the Israeli government released twenty female Palestinian prisoners. In the video, a well-choreographed series of gestures make for an eerie performance: holding the newspaper and showing it to the camera, naming names and dates, getting up from the chair, walking, pausing, turning around. The video's objective is first and foremost to show evidence. The live, captured soldier is a valuable asset; Hamas would seek to negotiate an exchange for many of its own captives held in Israeli prisons. Shalit is the leading actor in a cross-national political and juridical drama. The newspaper is meant to authenticate the date; names, dates, and intimate memories, just like the ID number, to validate the soldier's identity; the awkward walk in front of the camera to show that the soldier is in good shape. The camera zooms in and out—to a close-up on the newspaper date or on Shalit's face, to a full shot of his body, portraying a sort of autonomy—to show just enough, yet without exposing the location of the soldier or the identity of his captors. The formal language of evidence and that of the commodity are mixed, underscored with an affective notion of urgency and precariousness.

Broadcast almost immediately after it was delivered and shown incessantly on television and news websites, the video was released during the Jewish Holiday season, a time marked by its emphasis on family reunion. Family time, holidays, and Shabbat evenings were strategically used during the Shalit affair by both Hamas and the family to draw Jewish-Israeli public attention to the status of the captive. Not only the timing of the release but the way Shalit's address is formulated targets family love and memory as a way of appealing to the Jewish-Israeli public, a strategically-aimed soft spot. The state of sovereign intimacy demonstrates an affinity between family love and the figure of the soldier as well as between intimate modes of contact and Israeli mass media. In other chapters of this book, I show the affective, fetishistic status of soldiers' last signals, a transmission that assures that one is alive and well, and the media conventionalizing of such transmissions. The public sentiment that is produced around the soldier's "letter to home" haunts this video. The Shalit video is a dark reversal of this genre of contact. While the Shalits were the first to receive the video, and certainly those who were most anxiously anticipating it, family intimacy is not established by the video. Rather it is framed as what legitimates a demand. In the Shalit video, family happenings are not an amorous locus where one's memory is intimately stored, but an empirical means of verification and a strategic point of advantage before announcing the price tag. Family correspondence translates into value in the politics of loss. All the parties involved—those who took the video, the Israeli government, and not least the Shalit family—knew that family love is the most meaningful bargaining chip to show to the Jewish-Israeli public when negotiating a soldier's currency of exchange.

The video's recurring gestures towards the evidential notwithstanding, it entails a highly staged dramaturgy. This is all uncanny: Shalit's

FIGURE 22. Screenshot from Gilad Shalit proof-of-life video, 2009.

speech is overtly restrained and he seems to be reciting a written text that he holds behind the newspaper—a suspicion confirmed when, for a brief instance, the newspaper's corners slightly drop to expose a white A4 page. He often pauses and looks towards the camera/cameraperson, seemingly waiting for instructions. His clothing is meant to "look like" an IDF uniform—although real or not, uniform is always a sort of a costume, much as the soldier is always a form of a representation. He is visibly distressed, perhaps embarrassed. Nevertheless, it is this staging that enables the video to capture Shalit's ontologically fragile condition. It is precisely his awkward acting that manifests his powerlessness. The awkwardness is manifested first by the nervousness and by voicing as an act of reciting what distorts the allegedly directionality of the address. It is Shalit who utters the words, but his voice has no authority.

The video's ontology, or the proof of the soldier's well-being, is channeled through the instrumental, that is, the mere functionality of the body captured by the camera's *mise en scène*. Contrary to the convention of the testimonial, here fronting the camera is divorced from restorative agency. Likewise, the video's mediation of experience and memory as a form of authentication are framed and underlined by more basic media operations—the newspaper showing the date, the camera as merely recording, and so on.[38] On the side of the Shalit family, media, too, was often realized through its instrumental lines of communication when the family, hoping that Shalit would be allowed to watch television or listen to the radio, used mass media to send him messages. Reduced to their orbits, here broadcast media is utilized as a personal channel of communication. In the video itself, and outside of it in the broader economy of media that surrounded the captive affair, the ontological condition of captivity was constantly underscored by media infrastructure.

Indeed, on more than one level video was utilized as an extension of the operation of capturing, used by Hamas to tighten their hold on the soldier. The video was a record of the fact that the soldier was alive and his body intact, and at the same time it turned the captive into a kind of ghostly presence, devoid of free will, life hinging on the media form. Framed, manipulated, screened, spoken-through, the mere body of the captured soldier became an amplification through which an address could be channeled. Being captured means having no authority. With utterly different stakes, being addressed also puts pressure on free will. As Butler, following Levinas, contends, in being addressed one is also "taken hostage" by the address.[39] The urgency that underscores this call for help—the pressure to close a deal—and the precarious and unstable condition of the soldier captured on video, captured by Hamas, commits and interpolates the addressees. As Butler notes, this precariousness accentuates the body and resonates in our own body, it indeed takes a hold of the body, but at the same time dematerializes bodies, undoing them. Broadcast on TV, the video was perceived by the Jewish-Israeli public as a display of menacing power that potentially possesses every Israeli citizen.[40] Thus, it was not only Shalit but the entire public that was captured by the video and implicated in the frame.

To be captured and framed is isolating, an isolation that is acutely visible in the Shalit video. The captive is detached from the sphere of the common, even if, or rather since, this is done in the name of the common. Similar to the framed soldiers in the Breaking the Silence testimonials, but also different from them, Shalit too is both the exception and the rule, a singled-out someone who is, or at least could be, anyone. The captive is not the only one who has no authority, who is not at their own disposal. The metonymically extended threat is perceived as undermining the sovereignty of the state and its citizens. While the captive marks for the sovereign citizen the scandal of not being free, this image circulates within the national cult of intimacy, effacing, once again, the state's systematic oppression.

When the video was released, the Shalit family had already approached a team of media and public relations experts to help strategize its relationships with the media and garner public support. The family addressed the media (experts) because the state was non-responsive. For the captured soldier and his family, the stakes were high; the government was reluctant to close a deal as the price set by Hamas was disproportionate, and by negotiating with the organization the Israeli government unwillingly was perceived as legitimating Hamas's position as a representative political authority. For both the Shalit family and for Hamas, media was a key means for mobilizing public opinion to put pressure on the Israeli government. This is why in the video Hamas, ventriloquized by Shalit, addressed the family, and by extension the Israeli public, while framing the government's lack of action. Policymakers and international mediators working on the deal were addressed only indirectly, through the formal language of the evidence.

The soldier's life, and the video as what upheld it, were valorized slightly differently by each of the sides involved: key in determining a concrete ratio of exchange for the negotiating parties; symbolic value for the Israeli public who felt ethically compelled to the soldier acting on its behalf; and beyond value for the family. This play of values, actors, and partnerships means that the address, despite its immediacy, is complex and involves entangled channels and messages. It does not constitute a subject in the sense of a discrete agent, a representative. The video of the captive and the campaign that proceeded with its various productions relied on the media infrastructures of circulation to accumulate value and to gain a strategic advantage in the negotiation. However, while the family campaign worked according to the logic of acceleration and repetition, building on the contagious aspect of mass media, the captive video, sent after long months of anticipation for a life sign, gained its value for its very rarity and singularity.

Analyzing the captive video and the media campaign that ensued, the terminology used in the Shalit affair has ideologically loaded connotations for the political attribution of media production, intimacy, and captivity, and therefore should be noted. To start with the latter, how can the status of Shalit during the affair be defined? In US military idiom, soldiers kept by hostile states or organizations are addressed as Missing in Action (MIA). In foreign media reports, Shalit was indeed described as MIA, but in Israeli media, at least when the affair broke, he was often referred to as having been kidnapped or taken hostage, terms that stress the illegality of the action, and perhaps the illegality of Hamas itself. In that vein, referring to the captive video as a grassroots production might have the same implication, as it frames the lack of Palestinian sovereignty.

Israel argued that the fact that Shalit was denied the right to be visited by the Red Cross violated international law according to the Third Geneva Convention Relative to the Treatment of Prisoners of War.[41] Criminalizing the act not only undermined Hamas's sovereignty but lacked a self-reflective account of the conditions and rights of thousands of Palestinian prisoners in Israel, and seemed to be drawing on individuating grounds rather than the ontological condition of war.

Another expression of the infantilization or helplessness of the soldier, the terminology of kidnapping seems to disregard the fact that as a representative of state power, the soldier is a target for either killing or capturing. According to Israeli military terminology, MIA often refers to soldiers who have died and whose bodies are missing, whereas in the case of Shalit, the urgency and alertness were due to the fact that, in the words of the campaign's most popular slogans "Gilad is still alive." Lastly, the campaign leader, Tami Sheinkman, preferred not to label the viral dissemination of slogans, videos, performances, and statements made by high-profile public personas, newspaper ads, street signs, and happenings as a "media campaign," but rather as a "struggle."[42] Although problematic, I chose the terminology of capturing here because it describes the actual condition and highlights it being an exception on the Israeli side. In addition, it resonates with a kind of "capturing" made by the video itself. Associating the captive video with "grassroots production" and the series of media provocations done on behalf of the Shalit family as a "campaign" highlights modes and scales of production, although political implications are not to be ignored.

The family hired a media consultant, an advertising firm, a lobbying firm, and a crisis management consultant. It established headquarters with appointed staff, an agenda, and a managing hierarchy. The campaign team set targets, defined means, forged a strategy; it recruited celebrities and former heads of military and security bureaus and kept a constant visibility of Shalit and his family in a spectrum across the public sphere of the street and that of the media, through live-action performances and virtual and viral manifestations in mainstream and social media. To keep mass media interested, it identified main points of attraction and thematized the campaign according to them.[43] These exertions, informed by a highly professionalized insight into the craft of a mass media campaign, were themselves a means of generating and mobilizing a labor of love. The public attention that the campaign drew brought at first dozens and then hundreds to volunteer for the campaign. At the end of 2009 this led to the formation of Gilad's Army of

Friends, a non-profit that led numerous marches, performances, protests and sit-ins, initiating vigils in front of the parliament, the Prime Minister's residency in Jerusalem, or alongside main traffic crossroads, and supporting the family in all their efforts. Just by its name—Gilad's Army of Friends—the volunteers' organization once again linked love with the means of war.

In line with the argument I make throughout this book, although it presents an alternative to the commercial media industry with its insistence on production not tied to revenues, the labor of love is never an abstract or immaterial motion. To begin with, as labor, love entails in this case a massive investment of time and physical effort that the volunteers put into the campaign: they marched for miles, hung signs off bridges on the highways, handed out pamphlets, stood for hours on the sides of main roads, attended meetings, and were there for the Shalit family whenever they needed them. But also, the impetus of solidarity and giving was converted to actual currency in the form of donations that served as an important means of funding. While the labor of love was foregrounded to stress the values of commitment and obligation shared by many Jewish-Israelis, values that Shalit and his family represented, very little, if anything, was said about the actual transactions of inducing such love: not just the costs of media services but expenditures such as airtime, platform space, merchandise, printing, and more.[44] Most importantly, while the campaign was very much a public affair, neither the family nor those working on its behalf made public the actual wages of the team of professional experts leading the campaign; a few, but not all, have stated that their work was done *pro bono*, and the spirit of volunteering seemed to better serve the campaign.

The Shalit campaign is not unique in attracting individuals and firms willing to give their professional services free of charge and put their civic duties before their commercial interests, even in a profit-driven industry such as advertising. Under a thriving private media market and with a growing discourse of corporate responsibility, there is even an implied expectation that advertising firms will give their services not only to campaigns that wield profit, but to those whose causes they support. In Israel, bereavement and soldierhood are prominent arenas for such gestures of good will.[45] Mourning and memory, as I have showed throughout the book, is the business of media entrepreneurs working in the family section, individuated families, NGOs, television networks' community services, and even the technocratic arms of governmental care agencies. The *pro bono* tag encompasses its own economy, based on the perception that in the contemporary corporate world, ethics is part of the brand. Additionally, according to a branding logic, *pro bono* is a means of preemptive capital. In the case of Shalit, the campaign had become the site of media entrepreneurship and its very successful products were ultimately used by those involved to showcase their work and better their position within the advertising world. This is not to dismiss the sincerity of the effort and the emotive beliefs that motivate the labor of love, but to indicate the internal working of the *pro bono* campaign as a formation in which love and the commodity indivisibly coalesce in the private media market.

Before recruiting a team of media experts, the family's stance was to stick to a citizenship-based logic, according to which the government is mandated to secure the fate of its people, even more so its soldiers, and thus would act for Shalit's release. The family kept its intimate transmissions to itself; it did not release any pictures of Shalit before his military service, and when after one year the family received a signal from their son in the form of a letter, they did not share it with the public. This initial position was retrospectively declared by the campaign's team to be a strategic mistake.[46]

Benny Cohen from the Cohen-Rimon-Cohen lobbying firm recalls that "when we asked permission to use a picture of Gilad dressed as a clown, the family said: he's a soldier, why do we need to post a picture of him as a child?"[47] Rather than appealing to the government directly, calling upon its representative obligations, the professional campaign leaders' first strategic move was to foster an emotional rhetoric, addressing the public while leveraging popular sentiment. In interviews they describe the transition as something that was met with resistance from the side of the family. The Shalit family were reluctant to hand over their private photo albums and inclined to stick to their introverted and private family life. In line with the political thinking that underpins the state of sovereign intimacy, public familial sentiments are first perceived as challenging the logic of the state, channeled through private media; nevertheless, what this affair exposes is that love is also a strategy rather than solely an affective exchange.

In branding the Shalit affair, the family's media consultants made a few critical moves. Eran Yoels, one of the Shalit campaign's managers, explains that in order to capture public attention, "Gilad had to become a symbol of the values on which we grew up," values of solidarity and comradeship.[48] Put differently, what Yoels implies is that to raise the stakes, to make the public captivated by the captive or being willing

FIGURE 23. Gilad Shalit's Army of Friends, installation in front of the prime minister's home. Image: Emil Salman, *Haaretz*, October 2011.

to act on his behalf, his life had to become allegorical, metonymic. The format of the allegory applies a certain scaling in which the individual, being singled out, stands for the many. As cultural capital, the soldier contains this elasticity, evoking at once singularity and indistinctive multiplicity. Similar elasticity characterizes the soldier representational capital in the BtS campaigns. Benny Cohen says that the strategy was turning Gilad Shalit himself into a brand. Branding entailed establishing a typography, coining slogans, designing logos, refurbishing Shalit's face/image as iconic,[49] but first and foremost presenting Shalit as a son. The captive was referred to by his first name only—Gilad—to invoke a sense of familiarity and closeness, and the campaign capitalized on the family as a primary locus of identification, drawing on the affiliative notion of family love. Indeed, the most affective of the campaign's slogans was "Gilad is OUR son."[50] What is the son as a brand? As a slogan? The son stands for the singular, yet reproducible; it calls upon specificity— the son as a manifestation of irreplaceable, insurmountable love—and at the same time generality, claiming Shalit as emblematic kin, someone who could have been anyone's son.

Although branded, this life had to be authenticated and made real through the affect of kinship, and through a sense of urgency. Many of the iconic renderings of Shalit were based on a spectral aesthetics: turning Shalit's face image into a mask, turning his photographic image into a sketch outline, turning him into an illustrated silhouette, and then turning the silhouette illustration into the illustration of Ron Arad, an Israeli pilot who died in captivity. These visual strategies contributed to the notion of massification and multitude, but also marked the captured soldier as the living dead, the one whose life is suspended, a ghost. "Gilad is Still Alive" was another resonating slogan that consciously drew on a tension between the status of the living captive and the cultural capital of the dead soldier.

"Gilad's death would have made things easier for those who make the decisions, but he is alive and they can't leave him imprisoned there," says Aviva Shalit, the captive's mother, when interviewed by the journalist Anat Medan.[51] While the dead soldier links to an ethos of memory backed up by the state, the life of the captive cannot be contained by the same state-formulated ethos of memory. Jasbir Puar defines Israeli sovereign power as constituted through the right to maim, devaluing Palestinian lives through debilitation and slow death. The extension of that very logic, as Puar insightfully notes, is in its valorization of Jewish-Israeli life and consequently death, an economy in which debility, even within the ethno-national community, stands for a lesser subjectivity.[52] Death has a pre-arranged mechanism of "reimbursement," its remembrance is already constituted in state laws and cultural institutions. Aviva Shalit frames this very dynamic: "In this country the dead are sanctified rather than the living."[53] In other words, when it comes to the culture and politics of memory, the memory of the dead is inflated, but captivity, injury or disability, all these lives devalued by war, have no currency and no (cultural) representation, even if the captivity or injury is endured by those privileged by the state or its own representatives. Seeking to draw on the cultural capital of the dead soldier, the campaign strategists prompted other images, more ableist ones, than those that articulated captivity. The images engraved by the captive video were ones they preferred the Israeli public to forget.

When Shalit was released on October 18, 2011, the coverage of his return was made into a media event, an epic day-long span of live programing in which the media covered each and every minute of the captive's journey "back home." The terminology of family love, extended into the public sphere as a sign of commonality, had climaxed in this broadcasting event. Shalit was constantly referred to by his first name, with the adjective "child" attached to the twenty-five-year-old man.

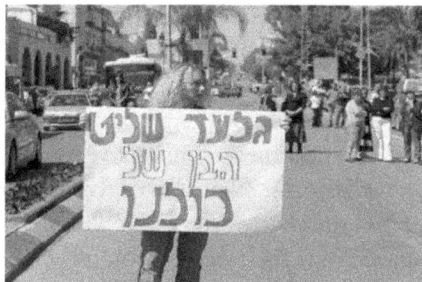

FIGURE 24. Gilad Shalit release campaign, "Our Son." Image: Reuven Castro, *Maariv*.

גלעד עדיין חי

FIGURE 25. Gilad Shalit release campaign, "Gilad Is Still Alive." February 2009.

FIGURE 26. Gilad Shalit release campaign, children wearing Shalit masks and t-shirts at a protest. Image: Daniel Bar-On, *Haaretz*, October 2011.

When the first images of Shalit arrived, one of the news presenters even said in the heat of the moment, that she, "probably like the entire public," wanted to "hug this child." Characteristically for media events, this was an opportunity for broadcast media to reflect on its own operations.[54] In a meta-representational manner, television portrayed masses of Israelis glued to television screens across the country to witness the return. It also depicted the masses of people who left their houses and screens and were waiting for the returned soldier on the side of the road leading to the Shalit family's house in the north. The collective joy for the returning soldier was manifested through media and beyond it.

But there was another manifestation of media's operations that once again aligns it with the mechanism of capturing. When transferred from Gaza to Egypt before being handed to the Israelis, Shalit was interviewed by Shahira Amin, an Egyptian journalist who seized the opportunity to get an exclusive first exchange with the captive. The interview was harshly criticized by Israeli media reporters, Shalit was described as being taken hostage by the journalist, and one newswoman even described it as "borderline torture."[55] Noam Shalit, the soldier's father, also referred to the media as a sort of capturing operation when, two weeks after the release, he asked reporters lurking outside his family home to respect the privacy of his son and family, saying that this interest by the media turned his son "into a captive in his own house."[56] Once again, media was referred to as an extension of capturing.

On the Israeli side of the border, two images depicting the captive's first hour back in Israel became synonymous with his homecoming. In one of them, he is shown talking on the phone with his parents, who waited for him in a military base in the center of Israel. In the second, he sits while three IDF officers gently surround him. The telephone and the military come together to depict care. For the Jewish-Israeli public the release of the captive was turned into a spectacle of intimate love in which family, military, and media were intertwined. As this second image reveals, as much as the return was a media operation, it was still a military operation.[57]

In return for Hamas's release of Gilad Shalit, Israel had released 1,027 Palestinian prisoners. The equation was a major point of contestation, obsessively discussed in the Israeli press. "I don't like the use of the word 'price' in the context of Gilad," says Aviva Shalit when interviewed. "A person is not a commodity that you can pay for, and my son has no price."[58] In contrast to the dark economy at work, the campaign's premise was that love rules over any economy. "Love or money?" asks

Michael Hardt, positioning love as countering an economy based on national narcissism and homophily.[59] The terminology of currencies is indeed alienating in such a painful affair, yet here too, affect and urgency abstract economic transactions and the instrumentation of love. Ultimately, in the Shalit affair and in its media campaign, the son was a form of commodity and love a means of exchange accumulated through the distributive power of media. Furthermore, while the affair was precisely about the imbalanced calculus of life manufactured by Israeli necropolitics, this was diverted into intimate love by a privatized media economy and branding. After all, love is not the language of sovereignty per se, but of privacy.

In each of this chapter's case studies, a scandal comes to bear on sovereign intimacy: in the PCFF campaign, it is the conundrum of extending intimacy to Palestinian lives as lives to be (also) mourned for; in the BtS campaign, it is by denying intimacy as singularity and familiarity; in the Shalit affair, it is the branding of intimacy that ultimately frames the necropolitical calculus. With the exception of the PCFF campaign, and perhaps in an opposite manner to it, here Palestinian lives finally equate with Jewish-Israeli ones rather than being zeroed out. To say that they equate does not mean to say that they are valued, though. In the public criticism raised by the "deal" made on behalf of Shalit, the Palestinian prisoners were tagged as a menacing threat, prisoners "with blood on their hands," meaning prisoners who are directly responsible for the killing of Jewish-Israeli citizens. As a provocation, the Israeli press was preoccupied with calculating the number of Jewish-Israeli dead—past and future—paid for an individual life. Within Israeli necropolitics, that is, the constitutive power of death in Israel sovereign politics, Palestinian lives are represented only as threat, through the numbers of lives-that-matter they took or will take, not as lives whose loss themselves we should mourn.

A similar case in which the American soldier Bowe Bergdahl, captured by the Taliban, was released after five years in exchange for five Taliban fighters imprisoned by the Americans, with no public campaign to promote the exchange, provided Israeli media and public debate with a comparative framework. It disclosed the yielding of the Israeli public to the family campaign.[60] For the Israeli public sphere neither love nor blood were means to value the deal, but rather its higher morals. Some used the deal's imbalance to present the decision as distinguished in its ethics, stemming from Israeli society's valorization of its soldiers' lives. The Shalit affair demonstrates an intriguing social system in which love passes as economy, and economy passes as ethics. The affair introduces a sense of skepticism to Hardt's premise of love and Butler's notion of the ethics of precarity. Can love as an economy, as ethics, persist outside the narcissistic paradigm?

The question of value continued to resonate. During the Shalit affair, some of the reports briefly mentioned a highly contested procedure in the IDF known as the Hannibal Directive. The Hannibal Directive is meant to guide a military force on how to react in the minutes that follow the capturing of a soldier. According to the directive, military forces engaging in action need to do whatever they can to prevent captivity, including shooting at the captors, even at the cost of the life of the captive. Named after the great Carthaginian general who chose suicide over falling into the hands of his enemies,[61] it is one of the most controversial orders in the history of the IDF, never officially confirmed by the army's command, with its license to kill still legally questionable. The few journalistic accounts of the directive stick to the partial view of its implied economy of life, stressing mainly the first moral conundrum of the directive: its implication of risking the soldier's life over risking his captivity. With this focus, Israeli journalists neglect the directive's potential permissiveness towards other lives excluded from the national community, the lives of Lebanese and Palestinians deemed collateral damage.[62] Collateral damage is yet another category through which lives are devalued, unmourned for.

In the summer of 2014, the Hannibal Directive was again a topic of debate. On August 1, 2014, also known in Israel as Black Friday, three Israeli soldiers were killed by Hamas. The body of one of them, Lieutenant Hadar Goldin, was taken by the Hamas force. At first, it was believed by the IDF that Goldin had been taken alive. The battalion which was assigned to the Rafah neighborhood in which the event took place started an aggressive attack on the ground, backed up with air strikes and massive artillery bombardment of possible escape routes. In a few hours, the IDF shot more than two thousand shells and missiles. The massive use of firepower lasted for a few days. According to Amnesty International and the London based investigative agency Forensic Architecture, more than a hundred civilians were killed (the reports range from 135 to 200), many more were injured, and many houses and civilian structures were damaged.[63] Later that year when the event was the topic of a legal investigation, commanders in the IDF were quoted as saying that the destructive measures used at the scene were legitimized under the Hannibal Directive and were meant to prevent "another

Shalit."[64] The Shalit affair had increased the value of a captured soldier to the extent that commanders "on the ground" guide their soldiers to avoid capture at any cost. While the IDF seemed to have been determined to prevent "another Shalit," being aware of the inflated value of the life of a captive, other lives were deemed as utterly disposable. Back in the summer of 2006 in the attempts to locate and rescue the captive, and on that Black Friday in 2014, the lives of hundreds of Palestinians, either eliminated or maimed, were nullified.

"I don't like the sentence 'Gilad Shalit is OUR son,'" Aviva Shalit discloses. "*He is my own private child and no one else's.* . . . Gilad is not a poster. People see him on signs, but he is my child, I know him."[65] With his face covering massive posters on highways' sides, newspaper ads, t-shirts, and even Israeli flags, a branding of the face as a call for help, Aviva Shalit insists on obscurity. For her, filial connection can provide a media campaign, but intimacy remains the sole property of the family, her own private knowledge.

Fast-forward to 2016, to a contentious grassroots campaign to condone a soldier who was convicted of killing Abed al-Fattah al-Sharif, a Palestinian who had approached soldiers with a knife, yet was lying on the ground wounded and demobilized at the time he was shot. The soldier, Elor Azaria, was referred to by the campaign as "Our Son." Once again, the soldier is positioned as an object of filial love, who is at the same time, at least by proximity, citizen X—everyone who is a specific loved one. In this affair it was the then-General Chief of Staff, Gadi Eizenkot, who drew a line, cited as saying, "a recruited 18-year-old man is not OUR son, he's a soldier."[66]

While the Israeli public, using various media platforms, pressures the government time and again to prioritize familial love at any costs, in the Shalit affair it was ultimately used to restore authority. The Shalit deal was made at a moment of civil uprising—the massive protests against austerity and economic policy that caused hundreds of thousands of Israelis to take to the streets in the summer of 2011. It was argued that the government, pushing back on family currencies, signed the deal as a way to appease the public and distract it from its newly gained collective conscious. Lastly, more than raising the stakes for the life of the captive, the Shalit affair rearticulated the security means now taken to protect the lives of soldiers in the arena of battle. Recent military operations, mostly in Gaza, demonstrate a highly crowded urban landscape raided by airstrikes and artilleries, waging war at a distance while subjecting civilian lives to collateral damage and putting "fewer boots on the ground."[67] From faces to boots, we are back to the body politic, where the calculation of Jewish-Israeli loss determines ethical considerations of Palestinian and Lebanese lives. While the value of the soldier's life—"our" son—has increased, so has the precariousness of Palestinian lives. This calculus of life is true not only to the economy of life in Israel-Palestine, but is a structural element in neoliberal, settler colonial societies in which politics of emotions, channeled through privatized media, produce a particular model of citizenship, shaped by mortality.

While in some philosophical traditions the address, incorporated and visualized through the image of the face, is used as a metaphor for an ethical encounter with the other, in the aforementioned media campaigns some faces are censored, under cover, or blurred; some faces are omnipresent and some are utterly absent. Propelled by the different currencies attributed to the soldier's address, such an image is a charged site of meaning onto which the current moral and political debates that shape Israeli culture and society are screened. There is also the notion of the face as a sphere of particularity, therefore unique in its capacity to represent. How does this resonate with the soldier's liability to the common? In writings about national memory and identity, the figure of the anonymous unknown soldier plays a crucial role. In contemporary wars there are no more unknown soldiers: technology, applied directly on bodies and their media forms, has extirpated this figure, and instead enables an anatomic, direct encounter with individuality. In contrast to this national prototype, the figure of memory and politics discussed here is the singular and irreplaceable soldier-son, *our* son. Following this line of thought, when, in the Shalit case, the people were drafted to push the government to return the captive soldier, no matter the price, Shalit had to become a figure known and loved by "us all." On the other side of the spectrum are the anonymous soldiers whose address is conscripted to break the silence. In these examples, and the example of family videos, Lebanese and Palestinian lives and losses are mostly unacknowledged and incompatible with the loss of "our sons." The addresses of the non-specified representative or the unrepresented oppressed are necessary to drag the discussion outside of the private, secretive discourse of love and the equally private/ized language of militarism and security, to break away from sovereign intimacy.

Epilogue

Answering a Call

During the 2014 Gaza conflict, an Israeli woman, Varda Pomerantz, recorded the last phone conversation she had with her son. This urge to record, to keep a trace, signals how much the Israeli family, and its use of media, is realized through the imminence of loss. What made Varda Pomerantz prepare a small tape recorder before answering her son's call? In their phone conversation, her son tells her that they were told by their commander to write a last note to their families in case something happens. The son could not find a pen and paper so he wrote something on his phone and kept it in his notes app. There have always been last notes hastily scribed by anxious soldiers before going into battle, but in this war, it is the military that orders this interpersonal transmission, and it is the phone that stores them. Upon entering Gaza, soldiers' phones were taken from them. In the 2014 Gaza conflict, it became clear that the army has assimilated the need to monitor intra-familial correspondences into its conduct, and even initiate them. The family is an arena to conquer and control. It is also made evident how entangled and interconnected habitual media has become.

The phone and phone calls, mostly unanswered, appear throughout the book. A bereaved mother who waits for a phone call from the general public; a military phone service set to spread ambiguity; the iconic image of a captive soldier speaking on the phone with his family for the first time after five years in captivity. There are many calls, and voice and text messages, not returned: "Where are you? I miss you!" "I'll be home tomorrow," "I think I saw you."[1] The unanswered call, the last call, is a synecdoche for the loss. The phone, somehow similar to the video, becomes both a domestic device of telecommunication and a performative means to represent and call on family's intimacy and family's mourning. In chapter 1 of this book, and to some extent chapter 3, I have argued that turn-of-the-century Israeli television, in its attempts at reciprocity and eagerness to answer a call, to be personal and individuated, is borrowing from the phone. As for video, throughout the book I have stressed its position as both a means of interpersonal telecommunication and representation.

Theorizing the medium-specificity of the telephone and its history as a domestic technology of communication is beyond the scope of this postscript. I use the phone and the unanswered call to think the dynamic at play from the perspective of a different, yet similar, mode of contact. The phone was never an utterly private medium of communication. As John Durham Peters notes, in its early days as a communication system, there were many anxieties about the medium's privacy, stemming mostly from the presence of an operator, a figure of technological expertise who directs the lines. According to Peters, "The telephone, like all media of multiplication (transmission and recording), was essentially a public medium. . . . The task again was to domesticate the plurality of media by the singularity of 'communication.'"[2] Mara Mills shows how since the mid-twentieth century, the phone is directed at a private and personalized point-to-point conversation—the singularization of transmission—channeling a particular form of speech and listening. Despite this common perception, its origins as an idea and its technological essence are linked with radio, as a signal and a medium of public circulation.[3] Citing the inventor H. de Parville, Patrice Flichy shows how scientists and inventors of the phone imagined it as a direct channel of power, a means of population control, commerce, and warfare. "Speech will be transmitted like thoughts, like writing. A sovereign will be able to command his armies from one end of Europe to the other," mused de Parville.[4]

Considering these histories, usages are paradigms predicated on socially and culturally framed needs and desires. In the cases I describe above, the singularized, personal call, left unanswered because one of its ends got cut off, gets lost. The cut traverses the order, turns the call public again. Instead of a trivial message anticipating the unification of bodies and hearts in time and space, the call becomes a ghostly last signal. Once there is no longer the kin to return a call to, the call is redirected for the public to listen to. The phone is turned again into a medium of representation and public circulation, and means of population control, this time by managing psychic and affective broken transmissions.

When it comes to Israeli media, calling to or calling upon soldier-related family transmissions, the lines are constantly busy. *Mother's Voice*, one of the more popular and long-running programs on the IDF radio station (a public broadcaster run by the IDF), aired every Friday since 1979, features mothers who call the show to send messages to their serving daughters and sons. Since the mid-1990s, the show has had a mobile broadcasting unit that puts the soldiers themselves live on air; thus the show becomes a public phone call between soldiers and their mothers, and the radio a channel for inter-familial correspondences.

From early days the cultural institution of memory in Israel appropriated personal notes and letters, but the phone, deemed ephemeral, private, and mundane in comparison to writing-based media, was not featured in these reappropriated displays. However, on Memorial Day 2007, a year after the 2006 war between Israel and the Lebanese militant group Hezbollah, one of the leading newspapers in Israel published a collection of text messages—an electronic, abbreviated version of the letter to a certain degree—sent by soldiers to their families. The title page featured an image of a Nokia cellphone screen with the text "Don't tell anyone, I'm entering Lebanon. Promise to come back." In line with the Nokia original setting, the bottom of the screen had the inscription "return" on its right, and "options" on the left.[5] The image is saturated with irony, not only that the messaged promise had failed, but now there are (no) returns and (no) options. The item demonstrates the reframing of habitual media and its prosaic transmissions by commercial media, and the mirroring of sovereign politics in the banal: "I'm awake," "Do you want sushi for dinner?" "If something happens to me, go on and live your life."

As part of the criticism of the 2006 war's failures it was said that soldiers' use of cellphones compromised the army's conduct both strategically and morally. This, too, is not unprecedented. When cellular technology was first introduced into the world of mass consumption, the IDF was less fixated on calls unanswered than on overexpansion and hyperconnectivity. Since the mid-1990s, the army has been campaigning for a mindful use of cellphones with the slogan "you never know who listens to you." An article from 1999 claims that the military should forbid high officers entering a meeting with their cellphones as the device can be easily tapped, even if not in use.[6] The same article also notes that the military is concerned with the use of cellphones by soldiers who serve in posts in southern Lebanon. Soldiers talking to their family and loved ones might disclose strategic information and compromise the obfuscation necessary for military action. It was not only the opening up of a channel to "the enemy," but to the home itself that was denounced as undesired and damaging to the army. An article published in 1996 addresses the introduction of cellphones into military life as what potentially "softens" the soldiers.[7] Family listening, the article argues, induces complaint and spoils the soldiers. It also made military authority more vulnerable to criticism as families became engaged in the soldiers' whereabouts. This is also where the call is redirected and the media steps in. A common joke during the 1990s was that soldiers' parents have Carmella Menashe, Channel 2's military correspondent, on speed dial—directing grievances against the army to her when the military did not respond. Similar to the dynamic described in this book, through the phone (on speed dial) the family found its ally in the media to rebuke sovereignty.

In the aftermath of the 2006 war, the military shifted its approach to habitual media, realizing that digital saturation—the idea that media is everywhere and is used by everyone—jeopardized its operations. The military response has been to both regulate the transmissions and embrace the medium. This is why in 2014 soldiers' phones were taken away from them upon entering a sphere of military action, and their correspondence with their families, especially messages that might be the last ones, were incorporated by the military.[8] As I have contended throughout this book, by incorporating mourning into its administration, the state and the army take away its destructive affect, contain and normalize it. In parallel to its war against the cellphones, the army also regulates indirect channels of information. In 2008, the IDF launched its own YouTube channel; in 2010, it opened a Facebook page; it has its own app and runs Twitter and Instagram accounts. By 2017, these various social media outlets comprised their own military section under the IDF spokesperson unit, situated in a "digital war room."[9] While the army narrows down the lines and platforms of self-expression and self-broadcast, it occupies and populates them with its own content.

Calls and text messages have been directed at Palestinians as well. In 2006, the IDF and the Shin Bet, the Israeli secret service, started sending text messages and calls to Palestinian civilians whose houses were targeted by the IDF to warn them about imminent bombings. The procedure was later termed a *knock on the roof*, and the text messages were replaced by dropping low-yield explosives on the targeted house's roof. As I note in chapter 4 of this book, in Israel-Palestine death is realized on the threshold, by a knock on the door/roof.

The notorious procedure of "roof knocking" serves as the IDF's moral "cover" in its deadly infliction of collateral damage in occupied Palestine. It performs compliance with international law and tribunals—but it is only a performance. The warning is meant to excuse the systematic destruction and civilian death, elimination passes as care and explosives are disguised as communication. The notion of moral warfare is questionable at best. In reality, the "knock on the roof" text messages and calls only generate terror, and the so-called low-yield explosives turn out to be lethal as well, not to mention their ruin of homes, livelihood, and well-being, even if lives (naked lives) are saved. Nevertheless, the *knock on the roof* was deemed a strategic success, and was adopted in 2016 by the American army in its fights against the Islamic State or ISIS. Studying Israeli sovereign power, what is striking is how asymmetrical, yet continuous and systematic it is. Necropolitics distribute death as sacred for one section of the population and life as disposable or already-dead for the other. The Israeli affecto-political power that I have sketched in this book mobilizes media on every scale, from personal to commercial, to induce Israeli intimacy and incorporate mourning. For Palestinians, meanwhile, the "knock on roof" erases not just life, but also devalues any call made on their name, since the killing was "moral." Now not only Palestinians' land and homes are invaded and expropriated, but their personal means of communication as well.

The woman who recorded her son's last call, Varda Pomerantz, is a former military officer who was the head of the military department of casualties. She is the bureaucrat turned bereaved, an emblem of Israeli sovereign intimacy. When a reporter asked her what the military announcers told her when she opened the door to them, she said: "I really don't know. I didn't let them make the announcement. . . . I guess that according to the protocol, *which I wrote*, they said something like 'it is with great sorrow that we inform you that apparently your son has been killed and we are still waiting for a positive identification [of the body].'"[10] The lines of intimacy are not ones of escape, and in this book's conclusion, what I draw is a tightening circle. Pomerantz knows that she needs to record the call because she already wrote what she is about to encounter. The army instructing soldiers to contact their families beforehand is all about managing death and its aftermath. On the other hand, following the telephone is where, through the infrastructural thread of media, things are finally coming together. A knock on the door for one, and a knock on the roof for the other; for one it is a call of recognition, for the other of elimination. They both anticipate that the sovereign is about to enter the home.

Notes

PROLOGUE

1. See Sara Hellman and Tamar Rappoport, "'These are Single Ashkenazi Women, Arabs' Whores, They Don't Believe in God and They Don't Love the Land of Israel': Women in Black as a Challenge to the Social Order," *Theory and Criticism* 10 (Summer 1997): 175–92; Daniella Mansbach, "Normalizing Violence: from Military Checkpoints to 'Terminals' in the Occupied Territories," *Journal of Power* 2, no. 2 (2009): 255–73; and Mansbach, "Crossing the Borders: The Power of Duality in the Protest of the 'Checkpoint Watch' Movement," *Theory and Criticism* 31 (2007): 77–99 (Hebrew).

2. Diana Taylor, "Trapped in Bad Scripts: The Mothers of the Plaza De Mayo," in *Disappearing Acts: Spectacles of Gender and Nationalism in Argentina's "Dirty War"* (Durham, NC: Duke University Press, 1997), 183–222.

3. The movement name originated from an article that covered the movement's first activities, published right before Passover with the title "Four Mothers." Media coverage of the movement activity demonstrates contradictory reports on how receptive the movement's core leaders were of the maternal discourse that emerged around them, or how strategic they were about it. See Eran Shahar, "Mothers at the Army's Service," *HaKibbutz*, April 4, 1997, archived at https://library.osu.edu/projects/fourmothers/mothers_service.pdf, and a set of articles archived by Four Mothers founder Rachel Ben Dor at https://library.osu.edu/projects/fourmothers.

INTRODUCTION

1. Benedict Anderson, *Imagined Communities: Reflections on the Origins and Spread of Nationalism*, rev. ed. (London: Verso, 2006 [1983]).

2. Idit Zartel, *Death and the Nation: History, Memory, Politics* (Or Yehuda: Dvir, 2002), in Hebrew.

3. I tracked these in various conversations, correspondences, and in anecdotal news items such as: Eli Ashkenazi, "Memorial Day: Commemorating Himself, Getting Over the Trauma," *Haaretz*, September 5, 2011. Accessed April 13, 2022. https://www.haaretz.co.il/news/education/1.1173444.

4. The ceremony was founded by Combatants for Peace and the Israeli-Palestinian Parents Circle-Families Forum at the initiative of Buma Inbar, a long-term activist who lost his son in Lebanon in 1995 and was one of the founding members of the Families Forum.

5. Judith Butler, *Precarious Life: The Powers of Mourning and Violence* (London: Verso, 2004). I revisit Butler's ideas, and their liberal underpinning, in chapter 5.

6. The incident was reported in both *Davar* and *Ma'Ariv* daily newspapers, May 6, 1984.

7. Amir Bochbut, "A Bereaved Father Attacked Halutz at the Ceremony: 'You Did Not Take Responsibility,'" *Walla News Online*, July 18 2011, https://news.walla.co.il/item/1841985.

8. Bochbut, "A Bereaved Father."

9. *Flew Away Forever*, a video in memory of Nissan Shalev, dir. Chen Shelach, 2007.

10. Marita Sturken, *Tangled Memories: The Vietnam War, the AIDS Epidemics, and the Politics of Remembering* (Berkeley: University of California Press, 1997). See also Jay Winters, "The Generation of Memory: Reflections on the 'Memory Boom' in Contemporary Historical Studies," *Canadian Military History* 10, no. 3 (2001).

11. See Meira Weiss, "Forensic Medicine and Religion in the Identification of Dead Soldiers' Bodies," *Mortality* 13, no. 2 (2008): 119–31.

12. See Gilli Cohen, "A Private Corner in the National Memory," *Ha'aretz*, April 24, 2012, http://www.haaretz.co.il/news/education/1.1692703. Literature scholar Hanna Nave argues that gravesites were always a dialectical space where the formal epitaph is surrounded by more private interventions in the form of gardening or notes left on the gravestone; see *Captive By Mourning: Mourning In Hebrew Literature* (Tel Aviv: Hakibbutz Hameuchad, 1993), in Hebrew.

13. See the case of Eran Vikselbaum, who died in the second Tze'elim incident, in Cohen, "A Private Corner in the National Memory."

14. See Moshe Reinfeld, "The Writing on the Helicopter Crash Casualties Will Be Changed," *Ha'aretz*, May 7, 2001, http://www.haaretz.co.il/misc/1.699255, my emphasis.

15. Ilana Shamir and Matityahu Mayzel, eds., *Patterns of Commemoration* (Tel Aviv: Ministry of Defense, 2000). See also Uri S. Cohen, "Bereavement and

Mourning in the National Library," in *Peace and War in Jewish Culture*, ed. Avriel Bar-Levav (Jerusalem: Shazar, 2006), 277–312, in Hebrew.

16. Jay Winters argues that the new technologies impacted what he terms a "memory boom" in the 1990s ("The Generation of Memory).

17. The State of Israel, Ministry of Defense, "Paths of Commemoration," 2010, http://www.izkor.gov.il/Page.aspx?pid=83 (last accessed January 14, 2018).

18. Michel Foucault, "Technologies of the Self," in *Technologies of the Self: A Seminar with Michel Foucault*, ed. Luther H. Martin, Huck Gutman, and Patrick H. Hutton (Amherst: University of Massachusetts Press, 1988), 16–49.

19. Michel Foucault, "Governmentality," in *The Foucault Effect: Studies in Governmentality*, ed. Graham Burchell, Colin Gordon, and Peter Miller (Chicago: The University of Chicago Press, 1991), 87–104; *Security, Territory, Population: Lectures at the Collège de France, 1977-1978*, ed. Michael Senellart, trans. Graham Burchell (London: Palgrave Macmillan, 2007).

20. Patricia R. Zimmermann, *Reel Families: A Social History of Amateur Films* (Bloomington: Indiana University Press, 1995). Zimmermann's critique echoes a Habermasian analysis of forms and institutions, generated by the state or the market, that articulate the public sphere vis-à-vis the private sphere of domesticity, familiality and intimacy. See Jürgen Habermas, *The Structural Transformation of the Public Sphere: An Inquiry into a Category of Bourgeois Society*, trans. Thomas Burger (Cambridge, MA: MIT Press, 1991).

21. Wendy Hui Kyong Chun, *Updating to Remain the Same: Habitual New Media* (Cambridge, MA: MIT Press, 2016).

22. Caetlin Benson-Allott focuses on how video shifted forms of viewership, making an appealing case for how videotape opened new space for the revival of "lower" genres, such as B-grade horror movies (*Killer Tapes and Shattered Screens: Video Spectatorship from VHS to File Sharing* [Berkeley: University of California Press, 2013]). Michael Z. Newman shows how video was instrumental in a new set of cinephilic methods, from distribution to remaking and citing (*Video Revolutions: On the History of a Medium* [New York: Columbia University Press, 2014]).

23. Peter Alilunas, *Smutty Little Movies: The Creation and Regulation of Adult Video* (Berkeley: University of California Press, 2016).

24. Newman, *Video Revolutions*.

25. See Michael Renov and Erika Suderburg, eds., *Resolutions: Contemporary Video Practices* (Minneapolis: University of Minnesota Press, 1995).

26. Zimmermann's book was published in 1995, the same year when Sony, JVC and Panasonic launched small digital video cameras (DV), turning digital video into the new standard of home documentation.

27. Patricia Zimmermann and Karen I. Ishizuka, eds., *Mining the Home Movie: Excavations in Histories and Memories* (Berkeley: University of California Press, 2008). In that regard, Liz Czach shows how the notion of recuperation, expropriating amateur or home footage from the recondite sphere of private life into the public sphere of scrutiny and knowledge, is central for discourses of amateurism ("Home Movies and Amateur Film as National

Cinema," in *Amateur Filmmaking: The Home Movie, The Archive, The Web*, ed. Laura Rascaroli, Gwenda Young and Barry Monahan [New York: Bloomsbury Press, 2014], 2–38).

28. See James Moran, *There's No Place Like Home Video* (Minneapolis: University of Minnesota Press, 2002). On the everyday aspect of home media see Richard Chalfen, *Snapshots Version of Life* (Madison: University of Wisconsin Press, 2008 [1987]).

29. Lauren Berlant, "Intimacy: A Special Issue" and "Sex in Public" (with Michael Warner), both in *Intimacy*, ed. Lauren Berlant (Chicago: The University of Chicago Press, 2000), 1–8 and 311–28; Lauren Berlant, *The Queen of America Goes to Washington City: Essays on Sex and Citizenship* (Durham, NC: Duke University Press. 1997). See also Ann Cvetkovich, ed. *Political Emotions: New Agendas in Communication* (Austin: University of Texas, 2010).

30. Cvetkovich, *Political Emotions*, 1.

31. See Lisa Lowe, *The Intimacies of Four Continents* (Durham: Duke University Press, 2015).

32. See Christina Sharpe, *Monstrous Intimacy: Making Post-Slavery Subjects* (Durham, NC: Duke University Press, 2010).

33. On the politics and critique of practices of care see Carlo Caduff, "Hot Chocolate," *Critical Inquiry* 45 (Spring 2019), 787–803.

34. Adi Kuntsman and Rebecca L. Stein, *Digital Militarism: Israel's Occupation in the Social Media Age* (Stanford, CA: Stanford University Press, 2015).

35. In that sense I offer an analysis that expands Benedict Anderson's much recited argument about the relationship between media circulation and the formation of a collective imagination. Intimacy does not reside in this one-way, top-down cultural formation (*Imagined Communities*).

36. Achille Mbembe, "Necropolitics," *Public Culture* 15, no. 1 (2003): 11–40; Jasbir Puar, *The Right to Maim: Debility, Capacity, Disability* (Durham, NC: Duke University Press, 2017).

37. See Adi Ophir, Michal Givoni, and Sari Hanafi, eds., *The Power of Inclusive Exclusion: Anatomy of Israeli Rule in the Occupied Palestinian Territories* (New York: Zone Books, 2009); Giorgio Agamben, *Homo Sacer: Sovereign Power and Bare Life*, trans. Daniel Heller-Roazen (Stanford, CA: Stanford University Press, 1998); Giorgio Agamben, *State of Exception*, trans. Kevin Attell (Chicago: University of Chicago Press, 2005).

38. Mbembe, "Necropolitics," 39.

39. Mbembe, "Necropolitics," 40.

40. See also Ariella Azoulay and Adi Ophir, *Bad Days: Between Disaster and Utopia* (Tel Aviv: Resling, 2002).

41. Puar connects Max Nurdau's well known "muscular Judaism" to the state's contemporary pro-natal policies. See also Neumann's phenomenological history of Zionism and the body of desire and Yosef's work on homoeroticism and homosociality: Boaz Neumann, *Land and Desire in Early Zionism* (Tel Aviv: Am Oved, 2009); Raz Yosef, *Beyond Flesh: Queer Masculinities and Nationalism in Israeli Cinema* (New Brunswick, NJ: Rutgers University Press, 2004).

42. "My Son Has No Price: An Interview with Aviva Shalit," *Yediot Achronot–Seven Days*, June 10, 2011, 20. I discuss the Shalit affair at length in chapter 5.

43. Puar's discussion of the struggle for disability rights in Israel and the status of those injured supports this notion (*The Right to Maim*). Since 2006 the marginalization of soldiers who suffer physical or mental injury is a topic of an ongoing public debate.

44. Berlant and Warner, "Sex in Public," 313.

45. Berlant and Warner, "Sex in Public," 317.

46. Elizabeth A. Povinelli, *The Empire of Love: Toward a Theory of Intimacy, Genealogy and Carnality* (Durham, NC: Duke University Press, 2006).

CHAPTER 1. TO KEEP IN TOUCH

1. This anecdote formerly appeared in a short item in the program on the community relations section of Reshet's website at http://reshet.tv/ReshetChannel2/PeopleConnection/videomarklist,103639, last accessed May 1, 2015. It was also recounted to me by Hila Barel in an interview held on January 29, 2012. It is also cited as being told by the program's first director, Gal Mor, an item that reports an event about corporate responsibility in media bodies hosted by Maala—an Israeli organization that promotes corporate responsibility—on March 11 2008: http://www.maala.org.il/he/resources/gov/view/default.aspx?ContentID=260, accessed May 1, 2015.

2. Walter Benjamin, *The Arcade Project*, trans. Howard Eiland and Kevin McLaughlin (Cambridge, MA: Harvard University Press, 1999), 846.

3. Benjamin, *The Arcade Project*, 846.

4. Peter Fenves, "Anecdote and Authority: Towards Kleist's Last Language," in *Arresting Language: From Leibniz to Benjamin* (Stanford, CA: Stanford University Press, 2001), 152–73, citation from 152.

5. Fenves, "Anecdote and Authority," 155, my emphasis.

6. Michael S. Roth, "Ordinary Film: Peter Forgacs' *The Maelstrom*," in *Mining the Home Movie: Excavations in Histories and Memories*, ed. Karen L. Ishizuka and Patricia R. Zimmermann (Berkeley: University of California Press, 2008), 62–72.

7. Roth, "Ordinary Film," 65.

8. Liz Czach, "Home Movies and Amateur Film as National Cinema," in *Amateur Filmmaking: The Home Movie, The Archive, The Web*, ed. Laura Rascaroli, Gwenda Young and Barry Monahan (London: Bloomsbury Academic, 2014) and Patricia Zimmermann and Karen L. Ishizuka, eds., *Mining the Home Movie: Excavations in Histories and Memories*.

9. Alexandra Juhasz, *AIDS TV: Identity, Community and Alternative Video* (Durham, NC: Duke University Press 1995); Richard Fung, "Remaking Home Movies," and Karen L. Ishizuka, "The Moving Image Archive of the Japanese American National Museum," both in Zimmermann and Ishizuka, *Mining the Home Movie*.

10. Various authors have further problematized the binary categories of "amateur" and "professional" or "homemade" and "institutional." Maija Howe

and Patricia Zimmermann look at trade magazines, amateur photography manuals and leisure periodicals, and their instruction on making an ideal family shot. Roger Odin observes that home videos adopted various television show's paradigms. See Patricia R. Zimmermann, *Reel Families: A Social History of Amateur Films* (Bloomington: Indiana University Press, 1995). See also Laura Rascaroli, Gwenda Young, and Barry Monahan, "Introduction. Amateur Filmmaking: New Developments and Directions"; Roger Odin, "The Home Movie and Space of Communication"; and Maija Howe, "The Photographic Hangover: Reconsidering the Aesthetic of the Postwar 8mm Home Movie," all in Rascaroli, Young, and Monahan, *Amateur Filmmaking*.

11. Lauren Berlant, *Cruel Optimism* (Durham, NC: Duke University Press, 2011).

12. Jasbir Puar, *The Right to Maim: Debility, Capacity, Disability* (Durham, NC: Duke University Press, 2017).

13. Adi Kuntsman and Rebecca L. Stein, *Digital Militarism: Israel's Occupation in the Social Media Age* (Stanford, CA: Stanford University Press, 2015).

14. Facebook correspondence with Gaya Koren, February 20, 2020. An earlier version of this subchapter appeared in Laliv Melamed, "What is a Girlfriend? Toward a Political Concept of the Girlfriend," *Discourse: Journal of Theoretical Studies in Media and Culture* 43, no. 3 (fall 2021): 421–46.

15. Colonel Yaffa Mor, The 19th Israeli Knesset, *Protocol no. 102*, "Meeting of the Committee on the Status of Women and Gender Equality," September 3, 2014, 2nd draft, unrevised and unpaginated. The protocol can be found on the committee's webpage on the Israeli parliament website at: https://m.knesset.gov.il/activity/committees/women/pages/CommitteeAgenda.aspx?tab=3&ItemID=556801. The gender specificity is in the origin. Mor's contention echoing a liability between the family and the state articulated in Pierre Bourdieu, "The Family as a Realized Category," in *Theory, Culture and Society* 13, no. 3 (1996): 19–26.

16. Bruria Aviad-Barir, "Unrecognized," *At*, July 14, 2014; and in Soldiers' Families Appeal 23478-01-10 Magistrates Court (Hi) Bernstein v. Pensions Officer, Ministry of Defense, Rehabilitation Unit (Hebrew) (February 26, 2014); Orit Kamir, "Every Woman has a Name," *Mishpatim* 29 (1996): 327–82. In the context of LGBTQ legal rights and kinship see Aeyal Gross, "Challenges to Compulsory Heterosexuality: Recognition and Non-Recognition of Same Sex Couples in Israeli Law," in *Legal Recognition of Same Sex Partnership: A Study of National, European and International Law*, ed. Robert Wintemute and Mads Andenas (Oxford: Hartt Publishing, 2001), 391–416. On the relations between love, recognition and norm see also Michael Warner, "Beyond Gay Marriage," in *The Trouble with Normal: Sex, Politics and the Ethics of Queer Life* (Cambridge, MA: Harvard University Press, 2000).

17. Mor, "Meeting of the Committee on the Status of Women and Gender Equality."

18. Hagar Kotef, *The Colonizing Self Or, Home and Homelessness in Israel/Palestine* (Durham, NC: Duke University Press, 2020).

19. Gaya Koren, "After the Fall," *Yediot Achronot*, July 6, 2005. This version also appears on the website of *The Non-Profit Organization for Emotional Support of Girlfriends (fiancées) of Fallen Soldiers of the Israel Defense Force*

(IDF) at http://www.girlfriendsidf.org.il/heb/articles/articles15.htm, accessed May 19, 2014. Another version appears in an earlier item on the girlfriends organization written by Koren in *Yediot Achronot*, November 5, 1997, and another one on Koren's Facebook in a post from February 22, 2012 (the twentieth anniversary of Elquai's death) at https://ar-ar.facebook.com/Love.Fan/posts /377093815653545, accessed May 19, 2014.

20. Throughout the years, the organization's self-representation and title have changed drastically. This is part of the institutionalization of the girlfriend that I analyze here. Its current title as of 2022 is GFIDF: The Girlfriends of Fallen IDF Soldiers. Throughout this section I address the organization either through its original title, as I encountered it in 2011, or through their own self-address as "The Girlfriends Organization," as seen on their website's about page, https://www.girlfriendsidf.org.il/about, accessed April 12, 2022.

21. Koren, "After the Fall," my emphasis.

22. See Tzvika Broot, "Bereavement is Bereavement," *Yediot Achronot*, October 5, 2005.

23. See also Michael Hardt's characterization of love in "For Love or Money," *Cultural Anthropology* 26, no. 4 (2011): 676–82.

24. Untitled videos in memory of Elad Litvak, directed by Yonatan Kanaskevich (2001), and directed by Tzvia Keren (2011). The information on the videos was delivered in personal communication with the videomakers: with Yonatan Kanaskevich, in October 2011 and with Tzvia Keren on January 8, 2012.

25. *Flew Away Forever*, in memory of Nissan Shalev, directed by Chen Shelach (2008). Personal communication with the videomaker, January 8, 2012.

26. *From Me to Control*, in memory of Shay Bernstein, directed by Yaniv Mezuman (2007).

27. Puar, *The Right to Maim*.

28. In that sense, as long as matrimony or reproduction is on their horizon, there might as well be a boyfriend. See Raz Yosef, "The Politics of the Normal: Sex and Nation in Israeli Homosexual Cinema," *Theory and Criticism* (2007): 159–87, in Hebrew; Warner, "Beyond Gay Marriage."

29. Aviad-Barir, "Unrecognized".

30. Glen Sean Coulthard, *Red Skin, White Masks: Rejecting the Colonial Politics of Recognition* (Minneapolis: University of Minnesota Press, 2014).

31. *Against All Odds*, dir. Taylor Hackford, screenplay by Eric Hughes and Daniel Mainwaring, Columbia Pictures, 1984.

32. At this time, Israeli commercial television (not including satellite channels) was based on one commercial channel in which three networks are franchised to broadcast, with each having its own regular programming days. In 2002 another channel, channel 10, was launched. In 2005 only two networks remained operating and in 2017 the commercial channel was split into two, each operated by its own network.

33. Personal communication, January 29, 2012. Freelance filmmakers who cater to family production often cite similar disavowal of the therapeutic (see the discussion of the freelance filmmaker in chapter 2).

34. This item on the project is no longer available due to a reorganization of the network and a redo of its website, but was formerly at http://reshet.tv

/ReshetChannel2/PeopleConnection/videomarklist,103639, accessed August 7, 2014).

35. http://reshet.tv/ReshetChannel2/PeopleConnection/videomarklist,103639, accessed August 7, 2014, my emphasis.

36. Shirly Mushyof, "Project that Commemorate the Fallen in Movies," *Yediot Achronot*, May 8, 2000, my emphasis. Tzanagen was Reshet's CEO from the day it was established in 1993 and until 2009.

37. For an analysis of moving limbs and affective submissions see Sara Ahmed, "A Willfulness Archive," keynote presentation at the Crossroads in Cultural Studies Conference, UNESCO, Paris, July 2, 2012.

38. I was able to access some letters at Reshet, and cite these as "Reshet files." A few letters and press items on the project were all filed in one ring binder in Barel's office; they have no catalogue or any other references. Some of the letters were anonymous, or had only the author's first name, and most had no dates. All letters are in Hebrew; the translations are mine.

39. Unknown writer, February 15, 2005, Reshet files, my emphasis.

40. http://reshet.tv/ReshetChannel2/PeopleConnection/videomarklist,103639, accessed August 7, 2014. See Odin, "The Home Movie and Space of Communication."

41. Einat (last name unknown), May 29, 2005, Reshet files, my emphasis.

42. Einat (last name unknown), May 29, 2005, Reshet files, my emphasis.

43. Einat (last name unknown), May 29, 2005, Reshet files, my emphasis. The syntax is in the original.

44. The following conceptualization of video as a medium that touches takes into consideration earlier formulations of the touching aspect of the visual form, although here I particularly emphasize the communicative and usability of video as a family medium. See Linda Williams, "Film Bodies: Gender, Genre, and Excess," *Film Quarterly* 44, no. 4 (Summer 1991): 2–13; Vivian Sobchack, *Carnal Thoughts: Embodiment and Moving Image Culture* (Berkeley: University of California Press, 2004); Laura U. Marks, *The Skin of the Film: Intercultural Cinema, Embodiment, and the Senses* (Durham, NC: Duke University Press, 2000).

45. Ora Leffer-Mintz, "A Letter from a Bereaved Mother," *Yediot Achronot*, April 26, 2004.

46. On the domestication of media see also David Morley, *Home Territories: Media, Mobility and Identity* (London: Routledge, 2000).

47. Elsewhere I refer to this as the fetishistic aspect of home movies, stemming from the untranslatability of labor and value in the face of the home movie's emotional investment and the displacement of desire into an object. The fetish is a way to think about the video through the order of love and to analyze the uncanniness and magnitude of mundane communication framed through the prism of lostness and lastness. See Laliv Melamed, "Close to Home: Privatization and Personalization of Militarized Death in Israeli Home Videos," *New Cinemas: Journal of Contemporary Film* 11, no. 2-3 (2014): 127–42. These ideas draw on Karl Marx, "The General Form of Value" and "The Fetishism of Commodities and the Secret Thereof," *Capital: A Critique of Political Economy,* vol. 1, trans. Ben Fowkes (New York: Penguin, 1990), 157–77, and

Sigmund Freud, "Fetishism," *The Complete Psychological Works of Sigmund Freud*, Vol. XXI, trans. James Strachey (London: Hogarth and the Institute of Psychoanalysis, 1950), 147–57. See also Paula Amad, "Visual Riposte: Looking Back at the Return of the Gaze as Postcolonial Theory's Gift to Film Studies," *Cinema Journal* 52, no. 3 (Spring 2013): 49–74.

48. During the Lebanon occupation soldiers were repeatedly reminded that letting their family know where they are—a trivial communication between young adults and their parents—risks disclosing sensitive information on the military movements and strategies to the enemy.

49. Ofer Shelach, "The Only Warrior Who Was Not Injured in the Naval Commando Incident Speaks," *Maariv*, September 20, 2008, http://www.nrg.co .il/online/1/ART1/788/722.html, accessed July 11, 2014; Yahya Dbouk, "The Curse of Ansariyeh Strikes Again," *Alakbar*, November 18, 2012, http://english .al-akhbar.com/node/13905, accessed February 1, 2017.

50. See also Dbouk, "The Curse of Ansariyeh Strikes Again;" Gadi Sukenik, *Men of Silence: The Whole Truth about the Naval Commando Affair,* September 5, 2012, https://www.youtube.com/watch?v=TLakkX9STPw, accessed February 13, 2017.

51. Robert Fisk, "Israel Ambushed: Double Agent Lured Soldiers to Death in Lebanon", *The Independent*, September 16, 1997, http://www.independent .co.uk/news/israel-ambushed-double-agent-lured-soldiers-to-death-in-lebanon -1239587.html, accessed April 12, 2022.

52. According to Jewish belief the body must be restored as a whole in the ground. Additionally, the common belief is that while the soldier was at the disposal of the military at the time of their service, as a corpse they are the sole property of the family. See Meira Weiss, "Forensic Medicine and Religion in the Identification of Dead Soldiers' Bodies," *Mortality* 13, no. 2 (May 2008): 119–31.

53. Ran Edelist, "The Heart Locker: Not an Ambush, Not a Drone Failure. The Naval Commando Disaster is a Result of Operative Omission," *Maariv*, April 16, 2017, https://www.maariv.co.il/journalists/Article-581416, accessed April 12, 2022). On the scandal of secrecy and coverage see Laliv Melamed, "A NonReport: The Operative image and the Politics of the Secret," *Journal of Cinema and Media Studies* (forthcoming in 2023).

54. Clare Birchall, "Introduction to 'Secrecy and Transparency': The Politics of Opacity and Openness," *Theory, Culture and Society* 28, no. 7-8 (2011): 7–25; Eva Horn, "Logics of Political Secrecy," *Theory, Culture and Society* 28, no. 7-8 (2011): 103–22.

55. The family's appeal to the Supreme Court is also mentioned in a memorial book it published: Mira Shaham-Golan, *Studio Golangrap. A Touch of an Angel* (published by the Golan Family, 2001).

56. Reut Mishor, Yinon Mils, and Alon Ben-David, "The Last Picture: Documentation of the Warriors a Moment Before The Naval Commando Incident," *Nana 10*, http://news.nana10.co.il/Article/?ArticleID=970844, accessed April 14, 2013.

57. On the incident and the following public outcry see also *Men of Silence: The Whole Truth about the Naval Commando Affair* by the alumni naval

commando warrior and journalist Gadi Sukenik, February 5, 2012, https://
www.youtube.com/watch?v=TLakkX9STPw, accessed February 13, 2017, and
a 2017 special of the investigative journalism TV show Uvda, *One Night in
Ansariyeh*, dir. Omri Assenheim, https://www.mako.co.il/tv-ilana_dayan/2017
/Article-b440ba720793b51006.htm, accessed December 5, 2018.

58. Catherine Russell, *Experimental Ethnography: The Work of Film in the
Age of Video*, (Durham, NC: Duke University Press, 1999).

59. Golan, *A Touch of an Angel*, 146.

60. Golan, *A Touch of an Angel*, 147.

61. Jacques Derrida, "Freud and the Scene of Writing," in *Writing and Difference*, trans. Alan Bass (London: Routledge, 2001 [1967]), 199; Vivian Sobchack, *Carnal Thoughts: Embodiment and Moving Image Culture* (Berkeley:
University of California Press, 2004), 110; Sigmund Freud, "A Note Upon the
Mystic Writing Pad," in *The Standard Edition of the Complete Works of Sigmund Freud*, Vol. XIX (1927–1931), trans. James Strachey and Anna Freud
(London: The Hogarth Press, 1961), 227–32.

62. Golan, *A Touch of an Angel*, 10.

63. Another possible reading presents itself toward the end of the video.
We are told that four years after Guy died, the parents gave birth to Li-Hi (in
Hebrew "she is mine"/ "she is for me"). Little Li-Hi sits in her mother's lap,
and shows the camera a heart-shape pendant with Guy's picture that Tiki wears
on her chest. She tells the camera how she often takes out the pendant, opens
it, kisses the picture of Guy, and "puts it back in mummy's heart." The video
portrays the mother as body: a source of life and continuity. I am hesitant about
this reading as this kind of representation corresponds, in my view, with a problematic tradition, highlighted in militarized cultures, of reducing the woman to
her body.

64. According to some sources, the village is partly situated on lands bought
from the people of Ma'lul. Ma'lul was occupied in 1948 and its houses destroyed.
See information gathered on Ma'lul by the Israeli NGO Zochrot that collects
and dessiminates information about the Palestinian Nakba: https://zochrot.org
/he/village/49281. Also appears in *Remembering Mal'ul*, published by Zochrot,
2011.

65. Nahum and Mina Zarhi, personal communication, January 23, 2012.

66. I discuss the selection of songs in the video in Laliv Melamed, "Learn-
ing by Heart: Humming, Singing, Memorizing," in *Silence, Screen, and Spectacle:
Rethinking Social Memory in the Age of Information*, ed. Lindsey A. Freeman,
Benjamin Neinass and Rachel Daniell (Oxford: Berghahn Books, 2014), 95–117.

67. Boaz Neumann, *Land and Desire in Early Zionism* (Tel Aviv: Am Oved
Publishers, 2009), in Hebrew.

68. Richard Fung, dir., *Sea in the Blood*, 2000, and "Remaking Home
Movies," 29–40.

69. Marianne Hirsch, *Family Frames: Photography, Narrative and Postmemory* (Cambridge, MA: Harvard University Press, 1997), 2.

70. When I contacted Zarhi in January 2012, he signed his first email as
"Nahum Zarhi, an expert in memorial videos." He did two full-length videos,
one collection of short clips, a few shorts related to his son and the farm, and

advised two families. He charged nothing for this labor and perceived it as a service to other families.

71. A similar sentiment towards the illustrative use of images in documentary evocations of eyewitness testimony was a source of a legal claim when Lt. Col. (res.) Nissim Magangi filed a suit against filmmaker Mohammad Bakri for allegedly portraying him as a war criminal. In Bakri's film *Jenin Jenin* (2002), which includes testimonies from the Battle of Jenin in 2002, an image of Magangi appears over a testimony that depicts looting in the refugee camp. See Nirit Andermann, "The Court Bans the Screening of Jenin Jenin in Israel. Bakri to Compensate the Reserved Soldier," *Haaretz*, January 11, 2021, https://www.haaretz.co.il/gallery/cinema/.premium-1.9442923, accessed April 12, 2022.

72. Nahum and Mina Zarhi, personal communication, January 23, 2012.

73. For this terminology see Roland Barthes, *Camera Lucida: Reflections on Photography*, trans. Richard Howard (New York: Hill and Wang, 1981 [1980]).

74. Barthes, *Camera Lucida*, 7.

75. Barthes, *Camera Lucida*, 27, emphasis in the original.

76. Nahum and Mina Zarhi, personal communication, January 23, 2012.

77. The Israeli-Lebanon war of 2006 lasted thirty-four days and caused the death of 1,191 Lebanese and 44 Israeli civilians, 114 Lebanese and 121 Israeli combatants. See Amnesty International, *Israel/Lebanon: Out of All Proportion—Civilians Bear the Brunt of the War*, (November 2006), https://www.amnesty.org/download/Documents/76000/mde020332006en.pdf, accessed April 12, 2022.

78. When I met Zarhi he discussed the clashes between the war's bereaved families and the army at length. He seemed to be very involved and informed, yet at the same time reluctant to clearly state his opinion.

79. For instance, in July 1993; in April 1996.

CHAPTER 2. INTIMATE PROXIES

1. State of Israel, Ministry of Defense, *Paths of Commemoration*, 2010. Hereafter, *Paths of Commemoration*. The booklet was previously accessible online, http://www.izkor.gov.il/Page.aspx?pid=83, last accessed July 2017. The link is no longer available but the text is in the author's possession.

2. Methodologically I draw here from Ann Stoler's reading of archival documents "against the grain." See Ann Laura Stoler, *Along the Archival Grain: Epistemic Anxiety and Colonial Common Sense* (Princeton, NJ: Princeton University Press, 2009).

3. *Paths of Commemoration*. The analysis of the Ministry of Defense's *Paths of Commemoration* and Foucault's notion of governmentality was previously published in Laliv Melamed, "Seeking an Advice: A Political Economy of Israeli Home Videos," in *Global Perspectives on Amateur Film Histories and Cultures*, ed. Masha Salazkina and Enrique Fibla-Gutiérrez (Indianapolis: Indiana University Press, 2021), 95–111.

4. *Paths of Commemoration*, my emphasis.

5. Michel Foucault, "The Subject and Power," *Critical Inquiry* 8, no. 4 (Summer, 1982): 777–95.

6. Michel Foucault, "Technologies of the Self," in *Technologies of the Self: A Seminar with Michel Foucault*, ed. Luther H. Martin, Huck Gutman, and Patrick H. Hutton (Amherst: University of Massachusetts Press, 1988), 16–49.

7. *Paths of Commemoration*. Gender specification in the origin.

8. At a certain point after 2017, the Office's name changed to "The Office of Families, Commemoration and Heritage." With that change of title, it cannibalized The Department of the Commemoration of Soldiers. See The Office of Families, Commemoration and Heritage, https://mishpahot-hantzaha.mod.gov .il/Pages/default.aspx, accessed April 12, 2022.

9. More information appeared on the office website under "Funding for Private Commemoration," https://www.mishpahot-hantzaha.mod.gov.il/mhn/parents /memorial/Pages/maanak_vealvaa_lemimun_anzaha_pratit.aspx, accessed September 2017. With its new organizational setting the information appears in a page titled "Information for Bereaved Parents" and list the services offers by the office. The funds are mentioned under "Memory and Commemoration," https:// mishpahot-hantzaha.mod.gov.il/Orphans/Hanztaha/Pages/default.aspx.

10. Efraim Auerbach, "Commemoration and Its Meaning," in *Paths of Commemoration* (Tel Aviv: Ministry of Defense, 1975), 3. The essay was originally given as a paper at a conference held by the Public Committee for the Commemoration of the Soldier, Tel Aviv, 1975.

11. The Paratroops Heritage Association, http://www.paratroops.org.il/% D7%93%D7%A3-1625-English.aspx, accessed July 10, 2022.

12. Noam Segev, "An Entire Life in Seven Minutes: Interview with Amir Keren," *Ynet*, April 15, 2002, http://www.ynet.co.il/articles/0,7340,L-1835630,00.html, accessed April 12, 2022.

13. Adi Katz, "The Paratroops Remembers," *Ma'ariv*, April 19, 1999.

14. Sam Gregory, "Cameras Everywhere: Ubiquitous Video Documentation of Human Rights, New Forms of Video Advocacy and Considerations of Safety, Security, Dignity and Consent," *Journal of Human Rights Practice* 2 (November 2010): 191–207.

15. Nina Laurie and Liz Bondi, eds., "Introduction," *Working the Spaces of Neoliberalism: Activism, Professionalization and Incorporation* (Oxford: Blackwell Publishing, 2005).

16. The committee members were Arik Achmon, Reuven Shoham, Vexi (Ya'akov Barnea), Gur Aryeh Israel, Amir Keren, and Yossi Gantz (some reports on the committee meetings also include Udi Armoni). The committee members were the founders of an earlier paratroops organization known as *Foundation for the Families of the Fallen Paratroopers*, or *Dad's Friends*, established in 1967 to support and accompany the paratroopers' bereaved families. On *Dad's Friends*, see "About Us," https://www.aba35.co.il, last accessed August 15, 2022.

17. Documents found in the association offices: "Members of the Movies Committee": contact information; Undated document: "Meeting Minutes", April 30, 2001, written by Itzik Nadan; "A Report on Unpaid Videos", May 6, 2001, a memo written by Itzik Nadan; "Movies Committee Meeting": summons for a meeting held on May 15, 2001, sent to the committee members, signed by Itzik Nadan.

18. "Meeting Minutes," April 30, 2001; "A Report on Unpaid Videos." See Segev, "An Entire Life in Seven Minutes."

19. Keren claims that the association initially negotiated with twenty companies; another memo, sent to the families in 1999, mentions ten. See Segev, "An Entire Life in Seven Minutes," and a memo to the families, signed by Amos Yaron, Amir Keren and Moshe Reise, May 1999.

20. "The Production of Memorial Videos—The Paratroops Association: working process." No date and no signature, document found in the association offices.

21. Both letters were found in the association offices, unfiled.

22. Unfiled letter in association offices. Gendered formulation in the original.

23. According to Foucault the idea of government is articulated as early as the sixteenth century, but established itself as a particular form of political knowledge only when the notion of population and security arose in the eighteenth century. See Michel Foucault, "Governmentality," in *The Foucault Effect: Studies in Governmentality*, ed. Graham Burchell, Colin Gordon, and Peter Miller (Chicago: The University of Chicago Press, 1991), 87–104.

24. Foucault, "Governmentality," 100, my emphasis.

25. Foucault, "Governmentality," 103, my emphasis.

26. Foucault, "Governmentality," 95.

27. "A Portrait of the Fallen Paratroopers," n.d., found in the association offices.

28. Untitled form, found in the association offices.

29. "The Paratroops Heritage Association—Video Portrait Production Agreement," no date, and a template of a personalized agreement for filmmaker Uri Harel, both found in the association offices. The personalized contract has a few additions such as the need for some flexibility when it comes to setting a time frame for an artistic project and possible scenarios in case the work incurs any additional artistic and/or professional expenses. Here too, once singularity enters the frame, in the form of the filmmaker-as-artist, concrete terms of labor and the logistics of filmmaking are diminished. A phone conversation with Harel, held in May 2015, confirmed the details.

30. "A Report on the Association's Activity—Memorial Day, 2006—Fallen Videos," May 10, 2006, document found in the association offices.

31. "A Report on the Association's Activity" asserts that the association "acted on a few levels to get the video memorials "out there," to the media." "[A]s a result of this activity [television broadcast], and the launching of the Internet [platform], we've received many responses, both of appreciation and of families who wish to apply. We will try to leverage this show of interest in an appropriate manner."

32. Aharon Gordon was a soldier in the 66th battalion who died at the Suez Canal in 1973. Ya'akov Sofer was a soldier from the 71st battalion who also died in 1973.

33. A note attached to "A Portrait of the Fallen Paratroopers," association offices.

34. Eytan Dotan and Udi Ben Dror, "A Proposal for Fallen Paratroopers' Memorial Videos Project," document found in the association's offices. The

proposal alternates the first person singular and plural. The review alternates the appointed author/s accordingly.

35. Dotan and Ben Dror, "A Proposal," 5.

36. See Marek Jancovic, Axel Volmar, and Alexandra Schneider, eds., *Format Matters: Standards, Practices and Politics in Media Cultures* (Luneburg: Meson Press, 2020), 7–20.

37. In his introduction to genre theory Robert Stam proposes two readings: a historically determined industrial category that goes back to the Hollywood studio system and is key to its economic model; and/or a cultural ritual, a structuralist reading that draws on anthropologist Claude Lévi-Straus's studies of myth. See Robert Stam, "Interrogating Authorship and Genre," in *Film Theory: An Introduction* (Malden MA: Blackwell, 2000), 123–30.

38. Dotan and Ben Dror, "A Proposal," 6.

39. Dotan and Ben Dror, "A Proposal," 7.

40. Dotan and Ben Dror, "A Proposal," 7.

41. Dotan and Ben Dror, "A Proposal," 3.

42. See Dotan's profile page on the Israeli Directors Guild website, https://directorsguild.org.il/user/eitan-dotan, last accessed August 1, 2022.

43. Dotan profile page, https://directorsguild.org.il/user/eitan-dotan.

44. Haidee Wasson and Charles Acland, eds., *Useful Cinema* (Durham, NC: Duke University Press, 2011). See also Vinzenz Hediger and Patrick Vonderau, eds., *Films that Work: Industrial Film and the Productivity of Media* (Amsterdam: Amsterdam University Press, 2009) and David Orgeron, Masha Orgeron, and Dan Streible, eds,. *Learning with the Lights Off: Educational Film in the United States* (Oxford: Oxford University Press, 2011).

45. Dotan and Ben Dror, "A Proposal," 2.

46. Dotan and Ben Dror, "A Proposal," 2.

47. Dotan and Ben Dror, "A Proposal," 2.

48. This includes research, script writing, directing, shooting (a team composed of a cinematographer, producer, lighting and sound operators, make-up, transportation, equipment, and per-diem) offline and online editing studios, sound studio, narration, music and graphics, with additional percentages for insurance and risk management. All this adds up to an estimated $6,520–12,370 US per video.

49. Examples for videos made completely outside any media institution framework are: *Rotem's Blossoming* in memory of Rotem Sharvit (Nir Chen, 1997); *Elad Litvak* (Yonatan Kanaskevich, 2001); *Yonatan Hadasi* (Arye Steimetz, Kibbutz Merhavia Video Studio, production year unknown); *Tzur Zarhi* (Nahum Zarhi and Mark Rosenbaum, 2006).

50. This was formerly available at http://www.kerenpro.com, last accessed April 13, 2015. All website information in the following pages I have translated from the Hebrew. Some cumbersome phrasing was on the original site.

51. This was formerly available at http://www.csfilms.co.il, last accessed April 13, 2015.

52. Chen Shelach, personal communication, February 2012.

53. Shelach's documentary work includes *Praise The Lard* (2016); *Partner with the Enemy* (co-directed with Duki Dror, 2014); *Photonovela* (2012); and others.

54. This was referred to as "business" and "documentary" respectively on Keren's website, http://www.kerenpro.com, last accessed April 13, 2015.

55. Tzvia Keren, dir., *The Land of Milk and Honey*, HOT, 2005; *Gamlieli-ran*, HOT, 2004; *The King of Hatzrot Yisaf*, HOT, 2005.

56. Tzvia Keren, dir., *I Was Born in Tisha'a Be'Av*, HOT, 2003; *Kol Nidre*, HOT, 2004.

57. Tzvia Keren, dir., *Tzvika Force*, HOT, 2005, *Not Just a Monument*, HOT, 2005, *Spider's Net*, Channel 1, 2007 (producer). Some of Keren's documentary productions and her inclination toward regional and militaristic themes emanates from her own biography: she was born in the Galilee in the north, into the tradition of Zionist pioneering. She is also part of what is known in Israel as "the family of bereavement." Her brother-in-law and his two daughters were killed in an attack in Nahariya, in the north of Israel. She investigates these autobiographic aspects in *Spider Net* (dir. Micha Livne, 2007).

58. "Nissan Katz," Wikipedia page, http://he.wikipedia.org/wiki/%D7%A0 %D7%99%D7%A1%D7%9F_%D7%9B%D7%A5, accessed April 15, 2015, and website for Nisansun Productions, https://www.nisansun.com, accessed November 2, 2020. Katz's work includes commissioned videos for ELM Foundation, TLV Food Festival, and the documentaries *Within the Eye of the Storm* (2011) (producer); *Choco-Banana in North Carolina* (2003); and *Thank The Lord for Goodness* (2001). His documentary work was broadcast and commissioned by Channel 8. His work on commemorative videos includes *Life According to Omer* (in memory of Omer Rabinowitz, 2010, broadcast on Channel 10) and *Nadav Neshama* ("*Nadav My Soul*," in memory of Nadav Baluah, 2011, broadcast on channel 10). According to his Wikipedia page, in addition to his film work, Katz is also an entrepreneur who founded the startup Make My Day to design user-based driving apps; see the company's website at https://www .makemydayapp.com/about.php, accessed April 12, 2022.

59. Gil Mezuman, dir., *Jenin, War Diary* (2002) and *Hanan Porat: Settled in Faith* (Ish Emunim, 2013).

60. *Taasiya* ("Industry"), https://www.taasiya.co.il/friends/14281, accessed April 12, 2022.

61. See "Major Shay Bernstein, A Man and a Commander," n.d., http://www .adamvmefaked.co.il, accessed August 15, 2022. The video itself does not necessarily follow this doctrinal tone. It is discussed in more detail in chapter 4.

62. Jacobs-Yinon's website was formerly available at http://www.aluma -films.com, last accessed July 2017. Her documentary work showcases films of poetic resonance with a Jewish-feminine emphasis. Among her directorial works are *Covenant* (2008, TV co-production with Channel 10); *Strange to be a Simple Women: Zelda* (2005, co-produced with Gil Mezuman); and *Red Sea: The End* (YES Satellite Broadcasting Company).

63. Jacobs-Yinon allocated family projects to a section of her website titled "commissioned works." However, the location of two videos challenges her typological system: *The Nature Child* (in memory of Eran Shamir, broadcast on Channel 2, 1998, Channel 4, 2001–2006, and Channel 8, 2007) and *With All Your Soul: The Story of Roi Klein* (2007, Channel 1). The latter was tagged under "documentary," funded by external sources (that is, not the family), and

has a heroic-dramatic story, yet is dedicated to a specific dead soldier and told through the lenses of his private life. I do not attempt to determine its location.

64. Steve Goodman and Luciana Parisi, "Mnemonic Control", in *Beyond Biopolitics: Essays on the Governance of Life and Death*, ed. Patricia Ticineto Clough (Durham, NC: Duke University Press, 2011), 164.

65. Fundraising page for *Eytan's Beach: A Documentary*, https://www.head start.co.il/project.aspx?id=11449, accessed July 2017.

66. Fundraising page for *Eytan's Beach: A Documentary*, my emphasis.

67. Feher develops this concept in a series of lectures, "The Age of Appreciation: Lectures on the Neoliberal Condition," which he gave at Goldsmith in 2013–2015. They are available at http://www.gold.ac.uk/architecture/projects /michel-feher, accessed July 19, 2022.

68. "About Us," *Headstart*, https://www.headstart.co.il/page-30-About_Us .aspx, last accessed August 2017. The current "About Us" page is available in English at https://headstart.co.il/page/about-us, accessed July 19, 2022.

CHAPTER 3. SCHEDULED MEMORIES,
PROGRAMMED MOURNING

1. Amanda D. Lotz argues that television remained more or less unchanged since its emergence as a popular entertainment medium in the mid-1950s up until the mid-1980s, with the move to multichannel structure. Another historical change took place in the middle of the first decade of the twenty-first century with the revolutionizing of television's platforms and screens, mainly due to digitization. In 2014 the entrance of Netflix and Amazon to the field and the emergence of streaming TV once again drastically changed television. See Amanda D. Lotz, *The Television Will Be Revolutionized* (New York: New York University Press, 2014).

2. Eviatar Zerubavel, *Time Maps: Collective Memory and the Social Shape of the Past* (Chicago: University of Chicago Press, 2003).

3. In 2002, the channel assigned the filmmaker Orna Ben-Dor to direct programming and to produce original content. In 2003–2004 it merged its programming with its affiliates in HOT, Channel 3 (the family channel) and Channel 4 (the movie channel) during special remembrance days. Channel 3 and 4 prepared the programming for the National Memorial Day, and Channel 8 covered Holocaust Memorial Day.

4. Personal communication, July 17, 2013. Abt was speaking in Hebrew but used the English phrase "best behavior."

5. This chapter is based on consistent reading of the TV listings of the National Memorial Day, the evening before and the day after, from 1980 to 2012, as published in the following newspapers and news websites: *Yediot Achronot, Maariv, Nana*, and *Walla*.

6. Mary Ann Doane, "Information, Crisis, Catastrophe," and Patricia Mellencamp, "TV Time and Catastrophe, or Beyond the Pleasure Principle of Television," both in *Logics of Television: Essays in Cultural Criticism*, ed. Patricia Mellencamp (Bloomington: Indiana University Press, 1990). See also Jane Feuer, "The Concept of Live Television: Ontology as Ideology," in *Regarding*

Television: Critical Approaches—An Anthology, ed. E. Ann Kaplan (Frederick, MD: American Film Institute, 1983), 12–22; Mark Williams, "History in a Flash: Notes on the Myth of TV 'Liveness,'" in *Collecting Visible Evidence*, ed. Jane Gaines and Michael Renov (Minneapolis: University of Minnesota Press, 1999), 292–312.

7. Mimi White, "Television Liveness: History, Banality, Attractions," *Spectator* 20, no. 1 (Fall/Winter 1999): 39–56.

8. The irony and the position of Abt as serving contradictory cultural and political systems is highlighted when taking into consideration the films he commissioned as Channel 8 director, documentaries such as *Checkpoints* (Yoav Shamir, 2004); *Waltz With Bashir* (Ari Folman, 2008); *The Law in These Parts* (Ra'anan Alexandrowicz, 2011); and *Five Broken Cameras* (Imad Burnat and Guy Davidi, 2012), all highly critical of Israeli sovereign politics.

9. Anna McCarthy, *Ambient Television: Visual Culture and Public Space* (Durham, NC: Duke University Press, 2001), 3. According to McCarthy, television's site-specific nature occurs where "the audiovisual and material forms of TV blend with the social conventions and power structures of its locale" (2).

10. Doane, "Information, Crisis, Catastrophe," 222.

11. Doane, "Information, Crisis, Catastrophe," 222.

12. Wendy Hui Kyong Chun, "Crisis, Crisis, Crisis, or Sovereignty and Networks," *Theory, Culture and Society* 28, no. 6 (December, 2011): 91–112.

13. Jonathan Crary, *24/7: Late Capitalism and the End of Sleep* (London: Verso, 2013), 30.

14. As Jonathan Crary writes: "One of the many innovations of television was its imposition of homogeneous and habitual behaviors on spheres of life that had previously been subject to less direct forms of control.... Television was the site of the destabilization of relations between exposure and protectedness, agency and passivity, sleep and waking, and publicness and privacy (24/7, 79–80).

15. In this survey I focus on the programming schedule of the two major commercial networks. Original program titles are in Hebrew, translated by me.

16. Raymond Williams, "Programming: Distribution and Flow," in *Television: Technology and Cultural Form*, 2nd ed. (London: Routledge, 1990 [1975]), 79. Jane Feuer suggests that television produces "dialectics of segmentation and flow" ("The Concept of Live Television," 15).

17. Daniel Rosenberg and Anthony Grafton, *Cartographies of Time: A History of the Timeline* (New York: Princeton Architectural Press, 2010).

18. Here Franco Moretti's work provides an interesting insight, bringing together narrative forms and discursive cartography contending that processes of reduction and abstraction lead to "a different form of knowledge" (*Graphs, Maps, Trees: Abstract Models for Literary History* [New York: Verso, 2005]).

19. Zerubavel, *Time Maps*; Orly Friedman, "Alternative Calendars and Memory Work in Serbia: Anti-War Activism After Milosevic," *Memory Studies* 8, no. 2 (2015): 212–26.

20. Danny Kaplan tells an anecdote of a playmate, who, during the 1973 war, confused the sound of the Memorial Day siren with that of the war siren, which leads Kaplan to develop his concept of social engineering ("The Songs of

the Siren: Engineering National Time on Israeli Radio," *Cultural Anthropology* 24, no. 2 [2009]: 313).

21. Chief of Staff Rafael Eytan's public address at the 1982 ceremony included the line "The bravery of the fallen is a model for us all" (*Davar*, April 27, 1982, 1).

22. Israel's president, Ezer Weizman, said "We are here with you, dear families" in his 1997 public address (Nadav Shargai, "'If They Were With Us Today, Alive, the Country Would Have Been Stronger and Better' Said Shahak in Memorial Day Ceremony," *Haaretz*, May 11, 1997, 5A.)

23. "Those who are gone are the ones who gave us this life. Their bravery opens for us a path for peace," claimed Prime Minister Binyamin Netanyahu in his 1998 address ("With the Siren this Morning Memorials in Military Graveyards Across the Country Will Open," *Haaretz*, April 29 1998, 5A).

24. Daniel Dayan and Elihu Katz, *Media Events: The Live Broadcasting of History* (Cambridge, MA: Harvard University Press, 1994).

25. The Israeli Knesset, *The Special Day Law* (1963), http://www.knesset.gov .il/laws/special/heb/chok_yom_hazikaron.htm, accessed September 30, 2013. Meira Weiss notes that since independence, prior to the passing of the law in 1963, memorial services were held across the country during Independence Day (*The Chosen Body* [Stanford, CA: Stanford University Press, 2002]).

26. The Israeli Knesset, *The Special Day Law*.

27. James E. Young, *The Texture of Memory: Holocaust Memorials and Meaning* (New Haven, CT: Yale University Press, 1993).

28. See Nadia Abu El-Haj, *Facts on the Ground: Archaeological Practice and Territorial Self-Fashioning in Israeli Society* (Chicago: University of Chicago Press, 2001); W.J.T. Mitchell, "Imperial Landscape," in *Landscape and Power*, 2nd ed. (Chicago: University of Chicago Press, 2002). For a counter-history of Israeli nationalized space see the activity of the Jewish-Israeli organization Zochrot, https://www.zochrot.org, accessed April 12, 2022.

29. Edna Lomsky-Feder, "The Memorial Ceremony in Israeli Schools: Between the State and Civil Society," *British Journal of Sociology of Education* 25, no. 3 (2004), 291–305.

30. Lomsky-Feder, "The Memorial Ceremony in Israeli Schools," 296–302.

31. On media as relating to and forming the habitual see Lynn Spigel, *Make Room For TV: Television and the Family Ideal in Postwar America* (Chicago: University of Chicago Press, 1992); David Morley, *Home Territories: Media, Mobility and Identity* (London and New York: Routledge, 2000); Wendy Hui Kyong Chun, *Updating to Remain the Same: Habitual New Media* (Cambridge, MA: MIT Press, 2016).

32. The Israeli Knesset, *The Special Day Law*. This section was not included in the citation above.

33. On April 19, 1980, *Maariv* criticized the opening of pizza places and ice-cream parlors on Dizingof street in Tel Aviv (5). *Maariv*'s weekend edition from the day before had a longer opinion piece about the closing of restaurants and entertainment venues (Talila Ben Zakai, "Magnifying Glass," *Maariv Sof-Shavua*, April 20, 1980). On April 17, 1983, *Maariv* featured a small item on the opening of steakhouses and restaurants in Ramat Gan (11). On April 24,

1985, the daily newspaper *Davar* reported that youth of the Workers Union (HaHistadrut) handed flowers to bereaved families, and mentioned that this was also a way to protest the rise of flowers' price during Memorial Day (special issue for Independence Day, item on p. 1). The moralistic genre of shaming businesses for profit-making during the National Memorial Day is continuously present throughout the 1990s and early 2000s.

34. The Second Authority for Television and Radio, "The Second Authority for Television and Radio Rules, 2009"; State of Israel Ministry of Communication, *The Second Television and Radio Authority Law* (1990), https://www.gov.il/he/departments/legalInfo/reshut2, last accessed August 15 2022.

35. See Hannah Arendt, *Eichmann In Jerusalem: A Report on the Banality of Justice* (New York: Penguin Books, 1977 [1965]); Achille Mbembe, "Necropolitics," *Public Culture* 15, no. 1 (2003): 11-40.

36. The debate was so heated that it severely disrupted the allegedly consensual sphere of Memorial Day. An item in *Ha'aretz* on May 5, 1997, reported that bereaved parents had organized to protest against the mentioning of terror attack victims in local municipalities' Memorial Day ceremonies and even threatened to boycott them. In 2000 the IDF Orphans and Widows Association petitioned the High Court and the Parliament's Committee on Symbols and Rituals to withdraw from its decision to merge the two memories, claiming that it causes the bereaved families severe mental damage and blurs the differences between those who died serving their country and those "who simply died" (untitled report in *Ma'ariv*, May 3, 2000). This is just a small sample of news items and opinion columns on the topic. The addition to the law remains controversial and a topic of discord even today.

37. The law rescinds state funding from organizations that challenge the legitimization of Israel as a democratic and Jewish state, support racism or terror, vandalize the state's flag or symbols, or mark the state's Independence Day as a day of mourning. See the Israeli parliament website, http://knesset.org/vote/3333, last accessed April 12, 2022.

38. Mbembe, "Necropolitics," 27.

39. The first approach is promoted by Dayan and Katz, *Media Events,* and the second by White, "Television Liveness."

40. Feuer, "The Concept of Live Television." According to Feuer, the televisual formation of time naturalizes Ideological structures.

41. "The televisual representation of catastrophe, on the other hand, hopes to hold onto the apolitical and attach it to the momentary, the punctual" (Doane, "Information, Crisis, Catastrophe," 237).

42. See Tom Conley, "Le Quotidien Meteorologique," *Yale French Studies* 73 (1987): 215–28.

43. The Second Authority for Television and Radio, "The Second Authority for Television and Radio Rules, 2009."

44. Charlotte Brunsdon, "Lifestyling Britain: the 8-9 Slot on Britain Television," in *Television After TV: Essays on a Medium in Transition*, ed. Lynn Spigel and Jan Olsson (Durham, NC: Duke University Press, 2004), 79.

45. Termed "preferred programs" by the regulatory appendix, quota is determined based on the broadcaster revenues. See The Second Authority for

Television and Radio, "The Second Authority for Television and Radio Rules, 2009."

46. Over the years the assembly was aired on channel 1, 2, and 10 alternately. In some years, Channels 10 and 2 have programmed live broadcasts of other municipal assemblies.

47. Channel 10 was launched in 2002. Similar to the pattern demonstrated by Channel 8, in its first year it only broadcast a flow of memorial shorts produced by the Paratroopers Heritage Association (see chapter 2). In 2003 and 2004 it did not present any programming for Memorial Day. In the following survey, the year of production is also the year of broadcast unless otherwise mentioned.

48. In 2005, Channel 3, cable television's family channel, broadcast *Not Just a Monument* (Tzvia Keren), which was rerun in 2006. In 2006 Channel 2 programmed a documentary on five women who lost their loved ones in the same suicide bombing attack and who together form an alternative family. Channel 1, the state channel, traditionally maintains a more official and less commercial programming schedule. Still, in 2006 and 2007, the main program on the channel's schedule was the channel's documentary series *A Second Look*, which presented a collection of documentary reports that focused on personal stories. In 2010 and 2011, the channel broadcast the documentary *My Young-Elder Brother* in which the director, Gil Lesnik, returns to a group of bereaved siblings who he interviewed a decade ago for a children's program.

49. See Bill Nichols, *Representing Reality: Issues and Concepts in Documentary* (Bloomington: Indiana University Press, 1991).

50. Personal communication, November 2011.

51. Shmulik Duvdevani, *First Person, Camera: Personal Documentary in Israel* (Tel Aviv: Keter, 2010) (Hebrew).

52. Jill Godmilow, "What's Wrong with the Liberal Documentary?," first published in *Peace Review*, March 1999. I am citing from a version made for the 60th Flaherty Film Seminar, June 2014, sent to me by the author.

53. Godmilow, "What's Wrong with the Liberal Documentary?," my emphasis.

54. Asli Kotaman Avci and Louise Spence, "The Talking Witness Documentary: Remembrance and the Politics of Truth," *Rethinking History: The Journal of Theory and Practice* 17, no. 3 (2013): 295–311.

55. Benny Tziper, "At First Look: Television Review," *Haaretz*, April 15, 1983, 45.

56. Mourning and bereavement in the Druze community is a recurrent theme in Memorial Day documentaries. Two recurring themes in the portrayal of the Druze community emphasize the alliance between Druze and Jewish-Israelis (constituted by blood) and gesture towards a mystic faith in reincarnation and bravery. Titles such as *Reborn* (produced by Channel 1, director unknown), *His Fate Was Determined the Day He Was Born* (first broadcast on Channel 1, 1993, director and year of production unknown), and *There Were Heroes* (first broadcast on Channel 1, 1999, production year and director unknown) recall the latter, and titles like *Fallen on the Route to Peace* (Channel 1, 1995) and *Drinking from the Same Well* (Channel 2, 1999) are informed by the former.

Beyond their use of racialized clichés, such representations deny the marginalization and discrimination of the Druze community by Jewish-Israeli society and the state.

57. Tedi Froys, "The Death of Television," *Davar,* April 26, 1982. The use of the male form is in the original.

58. Probably the most common format in the public network Channel 1's Memorial Day 1980s programming, this was based on a textual tradition titled *Parchments of Fire (Gviley Esh),* an epic volume, produced and published by the Ministry of Defense, that includes excerpts of prose and poetry edited with short biographical notes and textual ephemera left by the dead such as letters, drawings, and poems.

59. *At the End,* performed by the *Bat Dor* Dance Company (first broadcast in 1983), *Black Milk,* performed by *The Kibbutz Contemporary Dance Company* (first broadcast in 1985), and *Lamentation,* performed by the *Inbal Dance Company* (first broadcast in 1987).

60. *The Flute,* a sonata composed in memory of the musician Yadin Tennanbaum (first broadcast in 1987), and *Juvenile Sounds,* a yearly broadcast programmed sporadically since 1983.

61. Michel Foucault, "The Dangerous Individual," in *Politics, Philosophy, Culture: Interviews and Other Writings, 1977–1984,* ed. Lawrence D. Kritzman (New York: Routledge, 1988), 125–51.

62. Noam Yuran, *Channel 2: The New Statehood* (Tel Aviv: Resling, 2001) (Hebrew).

63. Lauren Berlant, "Preface," in *The Female Complaint: The Unfinished Business of Sentimentality in American Culture* (Durham NC: Duke University Press, 2008), viii. On Berlant's notion of the intimate public see also "Introduction: The Intimate Public Sphere," in *The Queen of America Goes to Washington City: Essays on Sex and Citizenship* (Durham, NC: Duke University Press, 1997), 1–25.

64. Expanding this dynamic to other broadcasting media, see Kaplan, "The Song of the Siren"; Gal Hermoni, Udi Lebel, and Batya Zuriel, "Bereavement Hit Chart and the Glocalization of Memory: Soldiering the Israeli Memorial Song," *The Public Sphere* 5 (2011): 9–34.

65. See Vance Kepley, Jr., "From Frontal Lobes to the 'Bob-and-Bob' Show: NBC Management and Programming Strategies, 1949–65," in *Hollywood in the Age of Television,* ed. Tino Balio (Boston: Unwin Hyman, 1990), 41–60.

66. See: Rebecca L. Stein, *Screen Shots: State Violence on Camera in Israel and Palestine* (Stanford, CA: Stanford University Press, 2021); Adi Kuntsman and Rebecca L. Stein, *Digital Militarism: Israel's Occupation in the Social Media Age* (Stanford, CA: Stanford University Press, 2015); Daniel Mann, *Occupying Habits: Everyday Media as Warfare in Israel-Palestine* (London: Bloomsbury Publishing, 2022).

67. Nick Browne cited in Doane, "Information, Crisis, Catastrophe," 233.

68. For all these reasons, the exercises performed by this chapter cater to what Foucault terms "archeology" (*The Archeology of Knowledge,* trans. Alan Sheridan [New York: Pantheon, 1972]).

69. Interview with Channel 10 Programming Manager Keren Kielmanowicz Freilich, December 26, 2011.

70. Berlant, "Introduction: The Intimate Public Sphere," 1.

CHAPTER 4. FIGURES OF SPEECH

1. David Grossman, *A Woman Runs Away from a Message* (2008), in Hebrew. All quotations from the book are from its English translation: *To the End of the Land*, trans. Jessica Cohen (New York: Knopf, 2010). The translation uses the word "notification" and "notifiers" respectively. "Message" better fits the Hebrew original *Hoda'a* since it emphasizes the finitude, single-sidedness, eventness and the mysticism of the occurrence.

2. Grossman, *To the End of the Land*, 167–68, emphasis in the original

3. Uri S. Cohen, "Bereavement and Mourning in the National Library," in *Peace and War in Jewish Culture*, ed. Avriel Bar-Levav (Jerusalem: Shazar, 2006), 277–312, in Hebrew; Reuven Avinoam, ed., *Parchments of Fire* (*Gviley esh*): *Anthology of Writings by Soldiers Who Died for Israel*, vols. 1–7 (Tel Aviv: Ministry of Defense, 1952–2005).

4. Mikhail Bakhtin, "The Problem of Speech Genre," in *Speech Genres and Other Late Essays*, trans. Vern W. McGee, ed. Caryl Emerson and Michael Holquist (Austin: University of Texas Press, 1986), 68, my emphasis.

5. See J.L. Austin, *How to Do Things with Words* (Cambridge, MA: Harvard University Press, 1962).

6. Bakhtin, "The Problem of Speech Genre," and Erving Goffman, *Forms of Talk* (Philadelphia: University of Pennsylvania Press, 1981).

7. Grossman, *To the End of the Land*, closing page, non-paginated, my emphasis.

8. Ilana Dayan and Gilad Tokateli, dir., *Summer Seeds* (as part of the documentaries series *Uvda*). See also Smadar Shilony, "Caught by the Message," interview with Ilana Dayan, *Ynet*, May 6, 2008, https://www.ynet.co.il/articles /0,7340,L-3540116,00.html, last accessed August 1, 2022.

9. David Grossman, "Now that the Book is Done," blog entry, The New Library website, March 24, 2008, http://www.newlibrary.co.il/article?co=14039 &BSS53=13176, last accessed September 07, 2018. In Hebrew.

10. Goffman, *Forms of Talk*.

11. Bernstein died in the summer of 2006, during the Israel Hezbollah war. The video was directed by Yaniv Mezumann. It was first broadcast on Channel 10 in 2008. The following reading of the video and its work of figuration and narration draws from Sigmund Freud, "Mourning and Melancholia" and "Remembering, Repeating and Working Through," In *The Standard Edition of the Complete Psychological Works of Sigmund Freud*, Vol. XIV (1914–1916), translated by James Strachey and Anna Freud, 243–58 (London: The Hogarth Press, 1957).

12. My emphasis.

13. See Roland Barthes, "On Listening," in *The Responsibility of Forms*, trans. Richard Howard (New York: Hill and Wang, 1985), 245–60, esp. 254–55.

14. Roland Barthes, "The Grain of the Voice," in *Image Music Text*, trans. Stephen Heath (New York: Noonday Press, 1988 [1977]), 179–89.

15. Jean-Luc Nancy, *Listening*, trans. Charlotte Mandell (New York: Fordham University Press, 2007 [2002]).

16. Barthes, "On Listening," 247.

17. Jonathan Kahana, *Intelligence Work: The Politics of American Documentary* (New York: Columbia University Press, 2008), 8.

18. My emphasis.

19. Vivian Sobchack, "Inscribing Ethical Space: Ten Propositions on Death, Representation and Documentary," in *Carnal Thoughts: Embodiment and Moving Image Culture* (Berkeley: University of California Press, 2004), 233; Michael Renov, "Filling Up the Hole in the Real: Death and Mourning in Contemporary Documentary Film and Video," in *The Subject of Documentary* (Minneapolis: University of Minnesota Press, 2004), 120–29.

20. See Hadas Shefer, "Shay, RIP, Proposed to Sivan During the War and Then Died," *NRG-Ma'Ariv*, April 23, 2007, http://www.nrg.co.il/online/1/ART1/572/500.html, accessed April 13, 2022.

21. Shefer, "Shay, RIP, Proposed."

22. *Adam VeMefaked*, memorial website for Shay Bernstein (n.d.), http://www.adamvmefaked.co.il/, last accessed November 25, 2019.

23. Nissan Shalev died in the summer of 2006 during the Israel-Hezbollah War. He was a helicopter pilot whose helicopter was hit by a missile. The video was initiated by the family, who hired freelance filmmaker Chen Shelach. It was first broadcast on Channel 10 on Memorial Day 2008 and in the following years was re-broadcast by Channel 10, Channel 1, and Channel 2.

24. My emphasis. The as-if appears here as a prosaic, common phrase (equivalent almost to the English slang use of "like").

25. Jacques Derrida, "As If It Were Possible, 'Within Such Limits' . . ." in *Negotiations: Interventions and Interviews, 1971–2001*, trans. Benjamin Elwood and Elizabeth Rottenberg, ed. Elizabeth Rottenberg (Stanford, CA: Stanford University Press, 2002), 343–70.

26. Judith Butler, "What is Critique? An Essay on Foucault's Virtue," in *The Political: Blackwell Readings of Continental Philosophy*, ed. David Ingram (London: Blackwell Publishers, 2002), 212–28.

27. I am thankful to Adam R. Rosenthal, who offered this interpretation of the as-if. The citation is taken from an email correspondence I had with Rosenthal on February 19, 2019.

28. Metaphorically, the treehouse recalls the common use of "echo chamber" in spoken English to describe a sphere in which only one kind of belief and opinion, one kind of loss, are heard.

29. John Searle, *Speech Acts: An Essay in the Philosophy of Language* (Cambridge, UK: Cambridge University Press, 1969), 12.

30. Emile Benveniste, *Problems in General Linguistics*. "Subjectivity in Language," trans. Mary Elizabeth Meek (Miami: University of Miami Press, 1973 [1966], 227).

31. See Giorgio Agamben, *The Sacrament of Language: An Archeology of the Oath*, Translated by Adam Kotsko (Stanford, CA: Stanford University Press,

2010). I am thankful to John Mowitt for suggesting this reading to me in a personal exchange, July 12, 2018.

32. Shoshana Felman and Dori Laub, *Testimony: Crisis of Witnessing in Literature, Psychoanalysis and History* (New York: Routledge, 1992).

33. Libby Saxton, "Anamnesis and Bearing Witness," in *For Ever Godard: The Work of Jean-Luc Godard 1950–2000*, ed. Michael Temple, James S. Williams, and Michael Witt (London: Black Dog, 2004); Jennifer Cazenave, *An Archive of the Catastrophe. The Unused Footage of Claude Lanzmann's Shoah* (Albany, NY: SUNY Press, 2019.)

34. *Witness: See It, Film It, Change It*, http://witness.org, accessed April 13, 2022; Sam Gregory, "Cameras Everywhere: Ubiquitous Video Documentation of Human Rights, New Forms of Video Advocacy and Considerations of Safety, Security, Dignity and Consent," *Journal of Human Rights Practice* 2 (November 2010), 191–207.

35. The Spielberg Testimonies Project is now housed at the Shoah Foundation Archive, University of Southern California. In recent years it expanded its platform to other genocidal events. See https://sfi.usc.edu, accessed April 13, 2022.

36. See Giorgio Agamben, *Remnants of Auschwitz: The Witness and the Archive*, trans. Daniel Heller-Roazan (New York: Zone Books, 2002); Jean-Francois Lyotard. *The Differend: Phrases in Dispute*, trans. Georges Van Den Abbeele (Minneapolis: University of Minnesota Press, 1988 [1983]).

37. Janet Walker and Bhaskar Sarkar, *Documentary Testimonies: Global Archives of Suffering* (London: Routledge, 2010), 5.

38. Paul Frosh and Amit Pinchevski, *Media Witnessing: Testimony in the Age of Mass Communication* (Basingstoke, UK: Palgrave Macmillan, 2009), 1.

39. Frances Guerin and Roger Hallas, *The Image and the Witness: Trauma Memory and Visual Culture* (New York: Wallflower Press, 2007), 4.

40. Leshu Torchin, *Creating the Witness: Documenting Geocide on Film, Video and The Internet* (Minneapolis: University of Minnesota Press, 2012). As Michal Givoni notes, recent treatment of testimony demonstrates the "intertwining of witnessing and testimony (the act and its discursive product, the 'saying' and the 'said')," where witnessing is validated by the delivery of testimony. See Michal Givoni, "The Ethics of Witnessing and the Politics of the Governed," paper prepared for the APSA Annual Meeting (Seattle, September, 2011).

41. See Michal Givoni, "Testimony/Witnessing," *Mafte'akh: Lexical Review of Political Thought* 2e (Winter 2011), 147–67; Givoni, "The Ethics of Witnessing and the Politics of the Governed."

42. Walter Lippmann, *Public Opinion* (New York: Dover Publications, 2004 [1922]); John Grierson, "First Principles of Documentary," in *Grierson on Documentary*, ed. Forsyth Hardy (New York: Praeger Publishers, 1966 [1946]), 145–56. See also Jonathan Kahana, *Intelligence Work: The Politics of American Documentary* (New York: Columbia University Press, 2008).

43. See Paul Swann, *The British Documentary Film Movement 1926-1946* (Cambridge, UK: Cambridge University Press, 1989); Brian Winston, *Claiming the Real: The Griersonian Documentary and its Legitimations* (London: British Film Institute, 1995).

44. This was in correlation with available film sound technology as much as an idealistic social stance. See Charles Wolfe, "Historicizing the 'Voice of God': The Place of Vocal Narration in Classical Documentary," *Film History* 9 (1997): 149–67; Jonathan Kahana, "Voice-Over, Allegory, and the Pastoral in New Deal Documentary," in *Intelligence Work,* 89–139.

45. Leshu Torchin, "Witness for the Prosecution: Films at Nuremberg," in *Creating the Witness,* 61–98.

46. Bill Nichols, "The Voice of Documentary," in *New Challenges for Documentary,* ed. Alan Rosenthal and John Corner (Manchester: Manchester University Press, 2005 [1988]), 18–19.

47. Nichols, "The Voice of Documentary." Nichols's essay is a prominent point of reference. He attributes documentary's voice to "a unique interaction of all film's codes."

48. Pooja Rangan, "Documentary Listening Habits: From Voice to Audibility," *Oxford Handbook of Film Theory,* ed. Kyle Stevens (Oxford: Oxford University Press, 2022).

49. See John Mowitt, *Sounds: The Ambient Humanities* (Oakland: University of California Press, 2015).

50. See Didier Fassin and Richard Rechtman, *The Empire of Trauma: An Inquiry into the Condition of Victimhood,* trans. Rachel Gomme (Princeton, NJ: Princeton University Press, 2009 [2007]); Thomas Keenan, "Publicity and Indifference: Media, Surveillance and Humanitarian Intervention," in *Killer Images: Documentary Film, Memory and the Performance of Violence,* eds. Joram Ten Brink and Joshua Oppenheimer (New York: Wallflower Press, 2012), 15–41.

51. Susannah Radstone, "Trauma Theory: Contexts, Politics, Ethics," *Paragraph* 30, no. 1 (March 2007): 9–29.

52. Shaped by contemporary bourgeois ideals, Radstone argues that the subject of trauma is presented as an outcome of external atrocity, failing to account for the internal complexity and instability of the concept of the subject ("Trauma Theory").

53. Belinda Smaill, "Injured Identities: Pain, Politics and Documentary," *Studies in Documentary Film* 1, no. 2 (January 2007), 151–63.

54. Smaill, "Injured Identities."

55. Hannah Arendt, *Eichmann in Jerusalem: On the Banality of Evil* (New York: Viking Press, 1963).

56. While the link between testimony and sovereign legitimacy is established in the context of the Eichmann trial, one can argue that similar evocation of justice in the service of solidifying national power took place, on a larger scale, in Nuremberg, where the trial was a primary setting at which Cold War power relations were mapped out and determined. The Nuremberg trials established a platform that exceeds the sovereignty of the nation state, and expands legal jurisdiction to persecute crimes against "humanity," articulating this category in the realm of jurisprudence. See Shoshana Felman, *The Juridical Unconsciousness: Trials and Traumas in the Twentieth Century* (Cambridge, MA: Harvard University Press, 2002). Felman is in close dialogue with Arendt, yet seems to be in disagreement with her about the role of testimony as national theatre. For her, the trial was a means to recover language, to speak back to evil, to grant

the victims agency and to "expand the space available for moral deliberation" (123). The witnesses become "authors of history" (126).

57. Shefer, "Shay, RIP, Proposed." The therapeutic aspect of the production of a memorial video is often brought up by bereaved families and official entities of support.

58. Austin, *How to Do Things With Words*. The marriage ceremony is a recurrent example used by Austin, for example, "Lecture 1," 1–12.

59. See an extended discussion of the "girlfriend" position of intimacy in chapter 1.

60. *Tzur Or: Memories and Longings* was produced by the Or family in memory of Tzur Or, who died in 2004. The video was broadcast on Channel 10 on Memorial Day, 2008. Another video that the family produced in memory of Or, *Tzur Or: The Price of Mercy,* was broadcast on Channel 10 in 2009. The family also participated in the 2005 project *A Message Was Delivered to the Families*, produced by the YES cable network.

61. In his work on myth and mourning Claude Lévi-Strauss points to the integration of the personal and the collective, producing an internal language of symbols and mythology: "Calling upon myth will reintegrate (the pain) within a whole where everything is meaningful" ("The Effectiveness of Symbols," in *Structural Anthropology*, trans. Claire Jacobson and Brooke Grundfest Schopf [New York: Basic Books, 1963],197).

62. Louis Althusser, "Ideology and Ideological State Apparatuses," in *Lenin and Philosophy and Other Essays* (New York: Monthly Review Press, 2001). The section discussed here in detail is "Ideology Interpellates Individuals into Subjects," 170–77.

63. Althusser, "Ideology and Ideological State Apparatuses," 172.

64. John Mowitt, *Percussion: Drumming Beating, Striking* (Durham, NC: Duke University Press, 2002), 46–47.

65. See Mowitt, *Percussion*; Mowitt, *Sounds*.

66. The protocol is recalled in Vered Vinitzky-Seroussi and Eyal Ben-Ari, "A Knock on the Door: Managing Death in Israeli Defense Forces," *Sociological Quarterly* 41, no. 3 (Summer 2000): 391–411.

67. Vinitzky-Seroussi and Ben-Ari, "A Knock on the Door," 391.

68. See Klil Zispal and Iris Kashman, "Behind-the-Scenes of Death," *Bamahane'*, February 1997, 46–47.

69. "Behind-the-Scenes of Death," 46. In the case of the 1997 helicopter accident there were no survivors. If an officer received a call from a family whose relative was on the list, they had to contact the municipal army headquarters and make sure that announcers were sent to the family home as soon as possible. First, families were informed that their relative was on one of the helicopters and was now "missing." Only after the identification procedure was completed were families told that their relative was dead. Here, too, the fact of death is in the formal procedure, although it is known before it is officially known.

70. "Behind-the-Scenes of Death."

71. Vinitzky-Seroussi and Ben-Ari, "A Knock on the Door."

72. While I am certain that internal memos addressing these protocols circulate within television news divisions, these are hard to access. From an exchange I had with a former official of the IDF spokesman's office, I learned that there are "gentlemen's agreements" between media entities and the IDF (personal communication with G.S., September 2014).

73. On iterability and the speech act see Derrida's critique of Austin's notion of the total context of the speech act ("Signature, Event, Context," in *Limited Inc*, trans. Samuel Weber (Chicago: Northwestern University, 1988 [1972]), 1–24).

74. See Austin, *How To Do Things with Words*, 12–25.

75. See Judith Butler, "Gender is Burning: Questions of Appropriation and Subversion," in *Bodies That Matter: On the Discursive Limits of "Sex"* (New York: Routledge, 1993), 121–42, and Judith Butler, *Excitable Speech: A Politics of the Performative* (New York: Routledge, 1997).

76. David Grossman, "Writing in the Dark," essay adapted from the Arthur Miller Freedom to Write Lecture, PEN's World Voices Festival, April 29, 2007. Published in David Grossman, *Writing in the Dark: Essays on Literature and Politics* (New York: Farrar, Straus and Giroux, 2008), 59–68. My initial access to Grossman's speech was a Hebrew transcription of it published in an Israeli newspaper ("Writing in a Zone of Disaster," Yediot Achronot, July 13, 2007, print version).

77. Grossman, "Writing in the Dark," 60.

78. Grossman, "Writing in the Dark," 64.

79. Grossman, "Writing in the Dark," 64. My emphasis.

80. Derrida, "Signature, Event, Context," 10, my emphasis.

81. Grossman, "Writing in the Dark," 67. Emphasis in the original.

CHAPTER 5. AT FACE VALUE

1. In the international press the war was referred to as "Operation Protective Edge," following the IDF's own terminology. As with other names the military uses to label its activities, the name invokes protection and endurance.

2. The Parents Circle–Families Forum's Campaign, "We Don't Want You Here," July 17, 2014, https://www.youtube.com/watch?v=Dg01MpWuwgE, accessed June 24, 2015.

3. The Israeli-Palestinian Joint Memorial Day Ceremony is an event held during the Israeli National Memorial Day that brings together Jewish-Israelis and Palestinians who wish to acknowledge losses on both sides. I briefly discuss it in the introduction to this book.

4. Parents Circle–Families Forum, "Our Vision," http://www.theparentscircle .com/Content.aspx?ID=29#.VYgc72Sqqko, last accessed April 14, 2022.

5. In this more general category I place human rights organizations that attempt to assist Palestinians gaining access and representation in their interaction with Israeli military, legal and infrastructural institutions. These include for example the Israeli branch of Doctors Without Borders; Gisha, which tries to protect freedom of movement of Palestinians (see https://gisha.org/en); and

Yesh Din, which focuses on legal representation (see https://www.yesh-din.org /en), among others.

6. For instance, the Jewish-Israeli organization Zochrot maps, narrates, and collects data on the Palestinian Nakba. "Nakba" refers to the Palestinian disaster of displacement, dispossession, and genocide. Zochrot, in solidarity with Palestinians, promotes a reading that understands the Nakba not as a historical event pinned to 1948, but an ongoing catastrophe. Their website is available in English at https://www.zochrot.org/welcome/index/en.

7. Pooja Rangan, *Immediations: The Humanitarian Impulse in Documentary* (Durham, NC: Duke University Press, 2017). On visual activism in Israel-Palestine see also Ruthie Ginsburg, *And You Will Serve as Eyes for Us: Israeli Human Rights Organizations as Seen Through the Camera's Eye* (Tel Aviv: Resling, 2014), in Hebrew, and Rebecca L. Stein, *Screen Shots: State Violence on Camera in Israel and Palestine* (Stanford, CA: Stanford University Press, 2021).

8. Judith Butler, *Precarious Life: The Powers of Mourning and Violence* (London: Verso Books, 2004), 29.

9. Butler, *Precarious Life*, 34.

10. Eugene Thacker, "Necrologies: or, the Death of the Body Politic," in *Beyond Biopolitics: Essays on the Governance of Life and Death*, eds. Patricia Ticineto Clough and Craig Willse (Durham, NC: Duke University Press, 2011), 139–62.

11. See Zach Blas, "A Cage of Information or, What is a Biometric Diagram?," in *Documentary Across Disciplines*, eds. Erika Balsom and Hila Peleg (Cambridge, MA: MIT press and HKW Berlin, 2016), 80–91; Alexander Galloway, *The Interface Effect* (Cambridge, UK: Polity Press, 2012); Kelly A. Gates, *Our Biometric Future: Facial Recognition Technology and the Culture of Surveillance* (New York: New York University Press, 2011); Allan Sekula, "The Body and the Archive," *October* 39 (Winter 1986): 3–64.

12. I'm thankful for Pooja Rangan who offered me the term in personal correspondence, May 30, 2021.

13. See also Jasbir K Puar and Amit Rai, "Monster, Terrorist, Fag: The War on Terrorism and the Production of Docile Patriots," *Social Text* 20, no. 3 (2002): 117–48.

14. Breaking the Silence, "About," n.d., https://www.breakingthesilence.org .il/about/organization, last accessed May 2, 2019.

15. Avihai Stollar, "This is How We Collected Soldiers' Testimonies After Operation Protective Edge," *Mekomit*, May 4, 2015, https://www.mekomit.co .il/%D7%93%D7%95%D7%97-%D7%97%D7%93%D7%A9-%D7%A9 %D7%9C-%D7%90%D7%A8%D7%92%D7%95%D7%9F-%D7%A9 %D7%95%D7%91%D7%A8%D7%99%D7%9D-%D7%A9%D7%AA %D7%99%D7%A7%D7%94-%D7%A2%D7%93%D7%95%D7%99 %D7%95%D7%AA-%D7%9C, last accessed April 14, 2022. In Hebrew.

16. Aviv Lavie, "Giving the Occupation a Bad Reputation," *Haaretz*, June 16, 2004. http://www.haaretz.co.il/misc/1.974927, accessed July 6, 2015. In Hebrew. The terminology of inside and outside is used by Shaul himself.

17. Such logic underlies the video practices of B'Tselem, one of the most important chroniclers of Israel's atrocities in Palestine. See their website, in

English, at https://www.btselem.org/video-channel/camera-project, last accessed April 14, 2022.

18. One example would be a testimonials marathon in Habima Square in Tel Aviv on June 6, 2014. Another five-hour event of reading testimonials was titled *Black Mirror* and took place on July 1, 2016. See videos (in Hebrew) on the Breaking the Silence website at https://www.shovrimshtika.org/medias/?cat =30, last accessed April 14, 2022. The testimonials project also instigated a number of award-winning Israeli documentaries, such as Tamar Yarom's *To See If I'm Smiling* (2007), Avi Mograbi's *Z32* (2008), and Shlomi Elkabetz's *Edut/ Testimony* (2011).

19. See Shoshana Felman and Dori Laub, *Testimony: Crisis of Witnessing in Literature, Psychoanalysis and History* (New York: Routledge, 1992).

20. See Raya Morag, *Waltzing with Bashir: Perpetrator Trauma and Cinema* (London: I.B. Tauris, 2013).

21. Thomas Keenan, "Mobilizing Shame," *South Atlantic Quarterly* 103, no. 2-3 (Spring-Summer 2004): 435–49.

22. Jonathan Kahana, "Errol Morris and the Ends of Irony," forthcoming, and Jonathan Kahana and Noah Tsika, "Let There Be Light and the Military Talking Picture," in *Remaking Reality: US Documentary Culture After 1945*, eds. Sara Blair, Joseph B. Entin and Franny Nudelman (Chapel Hill: University of North Carolina Press, 2018), 14–34.

23. Gil Hochberg, "Soldiers as Filmmakers: On the Prospects of 'Shooting War' and the Question of Ethical Spectatorship," *Screen* 54, no. 1 (Spring 2013): 44-61.

24. Ariel Handle, "Beyond Good and Evil—The Syndrome: Responsibility and Shame in Soldiers' Testimonies," *Theory and Criticism* 32 (Spring 2008): 45–68, in Hebrew.

25. Thiya Barak, "They Told Us We Should Keep a Low Profile, But This Is Not an Option. Should We Keep Quiet Whenever Someone Behaves Like a Beast?," *Mako Online Magazine*, June 24, 2015, https://www.mako.co.il /weekend-articles/Article-c47a9a942462e41006.htm, last accessed May 7, 2019.

26. See Eldad Levi, "Breaking the Silence: Sociology of Legitimization," *Haoketz*, December 22, 2015, http://www.haokets.org/2015/12/22/שוברים-שתיקה- סוציולוגיה-של-לגיטימציה/, last accessed May 7, 2019.

27. Ruthie Ginsburg, "Exposure," *Mafteakh* 7 (2014): 63–77, http://mafteakh .tau.ac.il/wp-content/uploads/2014/01/7-2014-05.pdf, in Hebrew. Citation from p. 67.

28. See Amos Harel and Gili Cohen, "A Decisive Moment for Breaking the Silence: The Court Will Determine Whether the State Can Enforce the Exposure of Witnesses," *Haaretz*, August 5, 2016, https://www.haaretz.co.il/.premium-1 .2947207, and "The Ministry of Defense: If You Have Criticism Towards the IDF, Come to Me," *Ynet*, July 15, 2009, https://www.ynet.co.il/articles/0,7340,L -3746792,00.html, in Hebrew, last accessed May 27, 2019.

29. Einat Fishbein, "Here We Are, Face Us," *Yediot Achronot*, May 20, 2011, 16–18.

30. Fishbein, "Here We Are," 16.

31. Jean-Francois Lyotard, *The Differend: Phrases in Dispute*, trans. Georges van den Abbeele (Minneapolis: University of Minnesota Press, 1989 [1983]).

32. Emmanuel Levinas, *Totality and Infinity: An Essay on Exteriority*, trans. Alphonso Lingis (Pittsburgh, PA: Duquesne University, 1969). Butler discusses Levinas's figure of the face at length in the closing essay of *Precarious Life*.

33. Daniel Mann, "I Am Spartacus: Individualising Visual Media and War-fare," *Media, Culture and Society* 41, no. 1 (2019): 38–53.

34. Mann, "I Am Spartacus," 49.

35. Mary Ann Doane, "The Close Up: Scale and Detail in the Cinema," *Dif-ferences: A Journal of Feminist Cultural Studies* 14, no. 3 (Fall 2003): 95.

36. On June 25, 2006, a few weeks before the Israel-Hezbollah war broke out, an IDF tank situated close to the border of Gaza was a target of an attack by Hamas. Two soldiers died and one soldier, Gilad Shalit, was taken captive. Between the time of his capture and that of this video, little information had been known about his location, his medical condition, or the conditions of his captivity, and international aid organizations were rarely, if at all, allowed to visit him.

37. Ronen Bergman, "The Unusual Channels," *Yediot Achronot—Seven Days*, October 21, 2011, 16–20.

38. Two decades earlier, in the case of Ron Arad, the Israeli broadcasting authority dedicated an entire broadcast to the captured pilot, officially as a pub-lic gesture towards the captive and his family, and informally with the hope that from his captivity the pilot would be listening to the radio. The highlight of the broadcast was when the pilot's three-year-old daughter, who was not born when her father was captured, addressed him directly, through the radio. When Shalit was released, as part of an inquiry into his captivity conditions it was reported that he was allowed to watch television, but only sport and nature programs. What stands behind this limitation is the assumption that sport and nature are apolitical cultural genres.

39. Butler, *Precarious Life,* 139.

40. See Jean Baudrillard, *The Gulf War Did Not Take Place* (Bloomington, Indiana University Press, 1995), especially Baudrillard's analysis of the American hostage drama during the first Gulf War.

41. Ali Abunimah, "Is Gilad Shailt a Prisoner of War?," *Aljazeera*, June 29, 2010, http://www.aljazeera.com/focus/2010/06/20106281325538018 41.html, accessed April 14, 2022.

42. See Oren Frisko, "Embroiling Emotion," *The Seventh Eye*, March 16, 2009, https://www.the7eye.org.il/25799, accessed May 16, 2019.

43. Sheinkman notes that conflict, sex and novelty, among other things, are guarantees of air time or page space. See Tami Sheinkman, lecture at the School of Communication, Ariel University, January 02, 2012, https://www.youtube.com/watch?v=ohMdk_LnBpg, last accessed May 29, 2019.

44. See Amira Lam and Amir Shoan, "The Soldier's Welfare Committee," *Yediot Achronot—Seven Days*, October 21, 2011, 22–26, and Gili Cohen, "From Silent Protest to Loud Opposition," *Ha'aretz*, October 18, 2011, http://www.haaretz.co.il/1.1525255, accessed July 2, 2015.

45. Projects covered throughout this book already support this claim: Keshet's Remember With Love project that was initiated by the network's community service department (see chapter 1) and the "We Don't Want You Here" campaign, produced pro bono by the Bauman Bar Rivnai advertising firm for the Family Forum (in this chapter).

46. Lam and Shoan, "The Soldier's Welfare Committee," 24.

47. Lam and Shoan, "The Soldier's Welfare Committee," 24.

48. Lam and Shoan, "The Soldier's Welfare Committee," 24.

49. Tami Sheinkman explains how the campaign used sketches and not a photographic image was a way to produce iconicity and urgency (lecture at Ariel University, https://www.youtube.com/watch?v=ohMdk_LnBpg). For example, a logo of the word "Help" in a special font whose design was based on Shalit's own handwriting. Responding to protectionist sentiments, another branch of the campaign featured former heads of the Shin Beit, IDF, and Mossad—Karmi Gilon, Ya'akov Peri, Amnon Lipkin-Shahak, Dani Yatom, and Ami Eylon—addressing the public, on video and in huge ads spread across the country, proclaiming "we can and we must return Gilad Shalit." In both the video and the posters, the image was that of the speakers' faces, standing for both an appeal and an affirmation—address and power.

50. Another, more literal translation would be "the son of us all".

51. Anat Medan, "My Son Has No Price: An Interview with Aviva Shalit," Yediot Achronot—Seven Days, June 10, 2011, 20.

52. Jasbir Puar, The Right to Maim: Debility, Capacity, Disability (Durham, NC: Duke University Press, 2017).

53. Medan, "My Son Has No Price."

54. See Elihu Katz and Daniel Dayan, Media Events: The Live Broadcasting of History (Cambridge, MA: Harvard University Press, 1994); Mimi White, "Television Liveness: History, Banality, Attractions," Spectator 20, no. 1 (Fall/Winter 1999): 39–56.

55. "Gilad Shalit Release: Shahira Amin Defends Interview," BBC, October 19, 2011, https://www.bbc.com/news/world-middle-east-15368819, accessed May 17, 2019.

56. "The Shalit Family Asks: Leave Mitzpe Hila," NRG, October 31, 2011, https://www.makorrishon.co.il/nrg/online/1/ART2/300/756.html, accessed May 17, 2019.

57. A large number of military units were involved, including the IDF Chief of Staff, the commander of the Southern Command, the IDF Air Force, the Southern Headquarters, the Medical Corps, the Home Front Command, the IDF Spokesperson Unit, and more.

58. Medan, "My Son Has No Price," 20.

59. Michael Hardt, "For Love or Money," Cultural Anthropology 26, no. 4 (2011): 676–82. For a longer discussion of Hardt's proposition see Laliv Melamed, "What is a Girlfriend? Towards a Political Concept of the Girlfriend," Discourse: Journal for Theoretical Studies in Media and Culture 43, no. 3 (2021): 421–46.

60. See Shay Levi, "1027 Terrorists versus 5," Mako, June 2, 2014, http://www.mako.co.il/pzm-magazine/Article-65da3f9195c5641006.htm, accessed

July 7, 2015, in Hebrew; Lawrence Wright, "Gilad Shalit: The Living and the Dead," *The New Yorker*, October 18, 2011, http://www.newyorker.com/news /news-desk/gilad-shalit-the-living-and-the-dead, accessed July 7, 2015.

61. It is said, though, that this name was randomly selected by a computer.

62. On the Hannibal Directive see Sarah Leibovitz-Dar, "The Prisoner's Dilemma," *Ha'aretz*, May 20, 2003, http://www.haaretz.co.il/1.883640; Anshel Pfeffer, "The Hannibal Directive: Why Israel Risks the Life of the Soldier Being Rescued," *Ha'aretz*, August 3, 2014, http://www.haaretz.com/news/diplomacy -defense/.premium-1.608693, accessed July 5, 2015. In Sarah Leibovitz-Dar's article, a battalion commander tells the journalist that following an abduction event his unit targeted and shot twenty-six vehicles which passed the same route suspected to be taken by the Hezbollah force which abducted the soldiers. Lebovitz-Dar goes on to interrogate the battalion commander on his decision to shoot a vehicle which might have had a captive soldier in it. The fate of the twenty-six vehicles and their passengers, some of which perhaps had nothing to do with the event of captivity, is not accounted for.

63. See Amnesty International, "Black Friday: Carnage in Rafah During 2014 Israel/Gaza Conflict," n.d., https://blackfriday.amnesty.org, accessed April 14, 2022, and Eyal Weizman, "Hannibal in Rafah," in *Forensic Architecture: Violence of the Threshold of Detectability* (London: Zone Books, 2017), 165–213.

64. Pfeffer, "The Hannibal Directive"; Yoav Zytoun, "The Government Legal Consultant: The Hannibal Directive Prohibits the Killing of a Captive Soldier," *Yediot Achronot* via *Ynet*, January 12, 2015, http://www.ynet.co.il /articles/0,7340,L-4614353,00.html, accessed July 5, 2015, in Hebrew; Yoav Zeitoun, "'Stop the Shooting I have Dead Soldiers Here': Ynet reveals the IDF Radio Transmissions After Goldin Abduction in Rafah," *Yediot Achronot* via *Ynet*, December 30, 2014, http://www.ynet.co.il/articles/0,7340,L-4609271,00 .html, accessed July 5, 2015, in Hebrew.

65. Medan, "My Son Has No Price," 24. This interview took place before Shalit's release, a fact that is crucial in considering some of Shalit's statements in the interview, which presented much ambiguity in relation to the campaign's strategies and slogans.

66. Yhonatan Bennaya and Yoav Zeitoun, "Eizenkot: An 18-Year-Old Recruit is a Soldier, Not 'Our Son,'" *Ynet*, January 3, 2017, https://www.ynet .co.il/articles/0,7340,L-4902263,00.html, accessed May 17, 2019.

67. The raids in Gaza also serve as a sort of sale display for Israeli security industry. Here biopolitics and war economy are tightly linked. See Eyal Weizman, *Hollow Land: Israel Architecture of Occupation* (London: Verso Books, 2007); Naomi Klein, "Laboratory for a Fortressed World," *The Nation*, June 14, 2007, https://www.thenation.com/article/laboratory-fortressed-world, accessed May 23, 2019; Yotam Feldman, dir., *The Lab* (Gum Films, 2014).

EPILOGUE

1. All cited in chapter 1 of this book.

2. John Durham Peters, *Speaking Into the Air: A History of the Idea of Communication* (Chicago: University of Chicago Press, 1999), 195–96.

3. Mara Mills, "The Audiovisual Telephone: A Brief History," in *Handheld? Music Video Aesthetic for Portable Devices*, ed. Henry Keazor (Heidelberg: ART-Dok, 2021), 34–47.

4. Cited in Patrice Flichy, "From Trading in Goods to Trading in Souls: The Telephone," in *Dynamics of Modern Communication: The Shaping and Impact of New Communication Technologies* (London: Sage, 1995), 84.

5. Dani Adino Ababa, Goel Beno, Eitan Glickman, Yifat Glick, Tzvika Elush, Lior El-Hai, Yael Levi, Guy Mei-Tal, Anat Meidan, Meital Moskovich, Eran Navon, Smadar Shir, and Matan Tzuri, "Don't Tell Anyone, I'm Entering Lebanon. Promise to Come Back," *Yediot Achronot*, April 20, 2007, 16–19.

6. "IDF Disrupts Cellphone Conversation in Offices of Higher Officers," *Haaretz*, April 13, 1999, 1. These concerns about the leaking of information make constant appearance over the years, for example: Gili Cohen, "New Cellphones Allow the Army to Eavesdrop on Soldiers' Conversations," *Haaretz*, April 4, 2012, http://www.haaretz.co.il/captain/gadget/1.1679007, and Lior Tzror, "All the Details about the Cellular Revolution in the IDF," *Mako* (published in the website's section of *Bamahane*, the IDF periodical), May 9, 2012 http://www.mako.co.il/pzm-soldiers/Article-bf5c3e3ae813731006.htm, last accessed Augus t15, 2022.

7. Avner Bernheimer, "Profile 96," *7 Days, Yediot Achronot*, April 23 1996, 10-16.

8. Similarly, the army lends its own operative media images, such as images taken in action by body cameras, for the purpose of family mourning. In chapter 1 I discuss a news item in which found footage taken during a top secret operation is brought to the parents as their sons' last image. A similar appropriation of operative images happened in the 2014 war with images taken from a soldier's body camera. See Yoav Zeitoun, "Footage Taken From Bnaya Sar-el RIP's Helmet Camera," *Ynet*, July 7, 2015, accessed April 13, 2022, https://www.ynet.co.il/articles/0,7340,L-4677226,00.html.

9. Tzeela Kotler-Hadari, "The Best for Digital: The IDF's War Room Takes Place in YouTube, Facebook and Twitter," *Globes*, May 10, 2017, https://www.globes.co.il/news/article.aspx?did=1001284933, last accessed April 15, 2022.

10. Smadar Shir, "Varda's War," *Yediot Achronot*, August 1, 2014, 36, my emphasis.

Filmography

This filmography contains videos' titles and directors' names, when available, as well as any information found on the circumstances of production and broadcasting. If different, year of production and year of broadcasting will appear (p)/(b). The latter refers only to the first broadcast. Some of the videos have had reruns and been played on different television networks over the years. The list is non-exhaustive and contains only videos that I could watch completely and are discussed in this study. Other videos whose circumstances of production are reviewed in the book, but that were never completed or lost, are not listed here.

A Message Was Delivered to the Family (הודעה נמסרה למשפחה), dir. Uri Bar-On, produced by and broadcast on Yes Cable TV, 2005, 55 min.

Always Without Him (תמיד בלעדיו), dir. Tzipi Bayder, produced by and broadcast on Channel 10, 2009, 50 min.

Breaking the Silence video testimonials (שוברים שתיקה - פרויקט עדויות הוידאו), dir. unknown, produced by Breaking the Silence, 2009–present, https://www.shovrimshtika.org/testimonies/videos.

Elad Litvak memorial video (לזכר אלעד ליטוואק), dir. Yontan Kanaskevich, private production, 2001/2003, 20:44 min.

Elad Litvak memorial video (לזכר אלעד ליטוואק), dir. Tzvia Keren, private production, 2011, 45 min.

Flew Away Forever (המריא לעד), dir. Chen Shelach, private production, broadcast on Channel 10, 2008, 63 min.

From Me to Command (דרכי לקודקוד), dir. Gil and Yaniv Mezuman, private production, broadcast on Channel 10/Channel 2, 2008, 45 min.

Gilad Shalit proof-of-life video, produced and released by Hamas, 2009, 3:43 min, https://www.youtube.com/watch?v=rDAsGS_gOeI&t=6s.

Guy Golan: A Touch of an Angel and His Smile (גיא גולן: מגע של מלאך וחיוכו), dir. unknown, private production/Reshet, as part of Remember with Love commemorative project, 2007, 30 min.

I'll See You Tomorrow, My Child (להתראות מחר ילד שלי), dir. Tzipi Bayder, produced by and broadcast on Channel 10, 2008, 44 min.

Life According to Omer (החיים על פי עומר), dir. Nissan Katz, private production, broadcast on Channel 10, 2010, 60 min.

Nir, You Have a Daughter (ניר, יש לך בת), dir. Tzipi Bayder, produced by and broadcast on Channel 10/Reshet, 2011, 45 min.

Our Brother, We Cried (אחינו, בכינו), dir. Shlomo Artzi and Yaron Shilon, broadcast on Channel 10, 2008, 55 min.

Since Your Light Deemed: In Memory of Avner Ron (מאז שכבה אורך (אבנר רון)), dir. Chen Shelach, private production, broadcast on Channel 1, 2008/2012, 55 min.

Smoke Grenade (רימון עשן), dir. Nahum Zarhi, private production, 2009, 8:37 min.

Summer Seeds (זרעי קיץ), Memorial Day special of the investigative journalism television show *Uvda*, dir. Ilana Dayan and Gilad Tokateli, produced by and broadcast on Keshet, 2008, 63 min.

Things I Wanted To Tell You (דברים שרציתי להגיד לך), dir. Gaya Koren, private production, broadcast on Channel 1, 1992, 41:23 min.

To See if I'm Smiling (לראות אם אני מחייכת), dir. Tamar Yarom, produced by First Hands Films/Channel 8, 2007, 59 min.

Tzur Or: Memories and Longings (צור אור: זכרונות וגעגועים), dir. unknown, private production, production year unknown, broadcast on Channel 10, 2008, 70 min.

Tzur Or: The Price of Mercy (צור אור: מחיר הרחמים), dir. unknown, production year unknown, broadcast on Channel 10, 2009, 16:49 min.

Tzur Zarhi memorial video (צור זרחי – לזכרו), dir. Nahum Zarhi, private production, broadcast on Channel 10, 2008, 18:48 min.

We Don't Want You Here (אנחנו לא רוצים אותכם כאן), produced by Bauman Bar Rivnai, 2014, 1:08 min, https://www.youtube.com/watch?v=Od5KBndY9fU.

When Jabel Fell (כשגיבל נפל), dir. Chen Shelach, produced by and broadcast on Channel 1, 2008, 56 min.

Z32, dir. Avi Mograbi, produced by Les Films d'Ici and Avi Mograbi Films, 2008, 81 min.

Bibliography

Abu El-Haj, Nadia. *Facts on the Ground: Archaeological Practice and Territorial Self-Fashioning in Israeli Society*. Chicago: University of Chicago Press, 2001.

Abunimah, Ali. "Is Gilad Shalit a Prisoner of War?" *Aljazeera*, June 29, 2010. Accessed April 13, 2022. http://www.aljazeera.com/focus/2010/06/2010628132553801841.html.

Agamben, Giorgio. *Homo Sacer: Sovereign Power and Bare Life*. Translated by Daniel Heller-Roazen. Stanford, CA: Stanford University Press, 1998.

———. *Remnants of Auschwitz: The Witness and the Archive*. Translated by Daniel Heller-Roazen. New York: Zone Books, 2002.

———. *State of Exception*. Translated by Kevin Attell. Chicago: University of Chicago Press, 2005.

———. *The Sacrament of Language: An Archeology of the Oath*. Translated by Adam Kotsko. Stanford, CA: Stanford University Press, 2010.

Ahmed, Sara. "A Willfulness Archive." Keynote presentation at the *Crossroads in Cultural Studies Conference*, UNESCO, Paris, July 2, 2012.

Alilunas, Peter. *Smutty Little Movies: The Creation and Regulation of Adult Video*. Berkeley: University of California Press, 2016.

Althusser, Louis. "Ideology and Ideological State Apparatuses." In *Lenin and Philosophy and Other Essays*, translated by Ben Brewster, 170–77. New York: Monthly Review Press, 2001.

Amad, Paula. "Visual Riposte: Looking Back at the Return of the Gaze as Postcolonial Theory's Gift to Film Studies." *Cinema Journal* 52, no. 3 (Spring 2013): 49–74.

Amnesty International. *Israel/Lebanon: Out of All Proportion—Civilians Bear the Brunt of the War.* November 2006. Accessed April 12, 2022. https://www.amnesty.org/download/Documents/76000/mde020332006en.pdf.

Andermann, Nirit. "The Court Bans the Screening of Jenin Jenin in Israel. Bakri to Compensate the Reserved Soldier." *Haaretz*, January 11, 2021. Accessed April 12, 2022. https://www.haaretz.co.il/gallery/cinema/.premium-1.9442923.

Anderson, Benedict. *Imagined Communities: Reflections on the Origin and Spread of Nationalism.* Revised Edition. London: Verso, 2006 [1983].

Arendt, Hannah. *Eichmann in Jerusalem: On the Banality of Evil.* New York: Viking Press, 1963.

Ashkenazi, Eli. "Memorial Day: Commemorating Himself, Getting Over the Trauma." *Haaretz*, September 5, 2011. Accessed April 13, 2022. https://www.haaretz.co.il/news/education/1.1173444.

Austin, J.L. *How to Do Things with Words.* Cambridge, MA: Harvard University Press, 1962.

Aviad-Barir, Bruria. "Unrecognized," *At*, July 14, 2014.

Avinoam, Reuven, ed. *Parchments of Fire (Gviley esh): Anthology of Writings by Soldiers Who Died for Israel.* 7 vols. Tel Aviv: Ministry of Defense, 1952–2005.

Azoulay, Ariella, and Adi Ophir. *Bad Days: Between Disaster and Utopia.* Tel Aviv: Resling, 2002.

Bakhtin, Mikhail. "The Problem of Speech Genre." In *Speech Genres and Other Late Essays*, edited by Caryl Emerson and Michael Holquist, translated by Vern W. McGee, 60–102. Austin: University of Texas Press, 1986.

Barak, Thiya. "They Told Us We Should Keep a Low Profile, But This Is Not an Option. Should We Keep Quiet Whenever Someone Behaves Like a Beast?" *Mako Online Magazine*, June 24, 2015. Accessed April 13, 2022. https://www.mako.co.il/weekend-articles/Article-c47a9a942462e41006.htm.

Barthes, Roland. "On Listening." In *The Responsibility of Forms*, translated by Richard Howard, 245–60. New York: Hill and Wang, 1985.

———. "The Grain of the Voice." In *Image Music Text*, translated by Stephen Heath, 179–89. New York: Noonday Press, 1988 [1977].

———. *Camera Lucida: Reflections on Photography.* Translated by Richard Howard. New York: Hill and Wang, 1981 [1980].

Baudrillard, Jean. *The Gulf War Did Not Take Place.* Bloomington: Indiana University Press, 1995.

Ben-Ari, Eyal, and Vered Vinitzky-Seroussi. "A Knock on the Door: Managing Death in Israeli Defense Forces." *Sociological Quarterly* 41, no. 3 (Summer 2000): 391–411.

Ben-David, Alon, Reut Mishor, and Yinon Mils. "The Last Picture: Documentation of the Warriors a Moment Before The Naval Commando Incident." *Nana 10*, April 14, 2013, Accessed November 1, 2018. http://news.nana10.co.il/Article/?ArticleID=970844.

Benjamin, Walter. "The Storyteller: Reflections on the Works of Nikolai Leskov." In *Illuminations*. Translated by Harry Zohn. Edited by Hannah Arendt, 83–110. New York: Schocken Books, 2007 (1968).

———. *The Arcade Project.* Translated by Howard Eiland and Kevin McLaughlin. Cambridge, MA and London, England: Harvard University Press, 1999.

Bennaya, Yhonatan, and Yoav Zytoun. "Eizenkot: An 18-Year-Old Recruit is a Soldier, Not 'Our Son,'" *Ynet*, January 3, 2017. Accessed April 13, 2022. https://www.ynet.co.il/articles/0,7340,L-4902263,00.html.

Benson-Allott, Caetlin. *Killer Tapes and Shattered Screens: Video Spectatorship from VHS to File Sharing.* Berkeley: University of California Press, 2013.

Benveniste, Emile. "Subjectivity in Language." In *Problems in General Linguistics*, translated by Mary Elizabeth Meek, 217–29. Miami: University of Miami Press, 1973 [1966].

Bergman, Ronen. "The Unusual Channels." *Yediot Achronot–Seven Days*, October 21, 2011, 16–20.

Berlant, Lauren. "Intimacy: A Special Issue." In *Intimacy*, edited by Lauren Berlant, 1–8. Chicago: University of Chicago Press, 2000.

———. *Cruel Optimism.* Durham, NC: Duke University Press, 2011.

———. *The Female Complaint: The Unfinished Business of Sentimentality in American Culture* (Durham NC: Duke University Press, 2008),

———. *The Queen of America Goes to Washington City: Essays on Sex and Citizenship.* Durham, NC: Duke University Press, 1997.

Berlant, Lauren, and Michael Warner. "Sex in Public." In *Intimacy*, edited by Lauren Berlant, 331–30. Chicago: University of Chicago Press, 2000.

Birchall, Clare. "Between Transparency and Secrecy." *Theory, Culture & Society* 28, nos. 7–8 (December 2011): 7–25.

Blas, Zach. "A Cage of Information or, What is a Biometric Diagram?" In *Documentary Across Disciplines*, edited by Erika Balsom and Hila Peleg, 80–91. Cambridge, MA: MIT Press and HKW Berlin, 2016.

Bochbut, Amir. "A Bereaved Father Attacked Halutz at the Ceremony: 'You Did Not Take Responsibility.'" *Walla News Online*, July 18, 2011. Accessed April 13, 2022. http://news.walla.co.il/?w=/2689/1841985.

Bondi, Liz, and Nina Laurie. "Introduction." In *Working the Spaces of Neoliberalism: Activism, Professionalization and Incorporation*, edited by Liz Bondi and Nina Laurie. Oxford: Blackwell Publishing, 2005.

Bourdieu, Pierre. "The Family as a Realized Category." *Theory, Culture and Society* 13, no. 3 (1996): 19–26.

Broot, Tzvika. "Bereavement is Bereavement." *Yediot Achronot*, October 5, 2005.

Brunsdon, Charlotte. "Lifestyling Britain: the 8-9 Slot on Britain Television." In *Television After TV: Essays on a Medium in Transition*, edited by Lynn Spigel and Jan Olsson, 75–92. Durham, NC: Duke University Press, 2004.

Butler, Judith. "What is Critique? An Essay on Foucault's Virtue." In *The Political: Blackwell Readings of Continental Philosophy*, edited by David Ingram, 212–28. London: Blackwell Publishers, 2002.

———. "Gender is Burning: Questions of Appropriation and Subversion." In *Bodies that Matter: on the Discursive Limits of "Sex,"* 121–42. New York: Routledge, 1993.

———. *Excitable Speech: A Politics of the Performative.* New York: Routledge, 1997.

———. *Precarious Life: The Powers of Mourning and Violence*. London: Verso Books, 2004.

Caduff, Carlo. "Hot Chocolate." *Critical Inquiry* 45 (Spring 2019): 787–803.

Cazenave, Jennifer. *An Archive of the Catastrophe: The Unused Footage of Claude Lanzmann's Shoah*. Albany: SUNY Press, 2019.

Chalfen, Richard. *Snapshots Version of Life*. Madison: Wisconsin University Press, 2008 [1987].

Chun, Wendy Hui Kyong. *Updating to Remain the Same: Habitual New Media*. Cambridge, MA: MIT Press, 2016.

———. "Crisis, Crisis, Crisis, or Sovereignty and Networks" *Theory, Culture and Society* 28, no. 6 (December, 2011) 91-112.

Cohen, Gili. "From Silent Protest to Loud Opposition." *Ha'aretz*, October 18, 2011. Accessed April 13, 2022. http://www.haaretz.co.il/1.1525255.

———. "A Private Corner in the National Memory." *Ha'aretz*, April 24, 2012. Accessed April 13, 2022. http://www.haaretz.co.il/news/education/1.1692703.

———. "New Cellphones Allow the Army to Eavesdrop on Soldiers' Conversations," *Haaretz*, April 4 2012. Accessed August 15 2022. http://www.haaretz.co.il/captain/gadget/1.1679007

Cohen, Uri S. "Bereavement and Mourning in the National Library." In *Peace and War in Jewish Culture*, edited by Avriel Bar-Levav, 277–312. Jerusalem: Shazar, 2006. In Hebrew.

Conley, Tom. "Le Quotidien Meteorologique." *Yale French Studies* 73 (1987): 215–28.

Coulthard, Glen Sean. *Red Skin, White Masks: Rejecting the Colonial Politics of Recognition*. Minneapolis: University of Minnesota Press, 2014.

Crary, Jonathan. *24/7: Late Capitalism and the End of Sleep*. London: Verso, 2013.

Cvetkovich, Ann, ed. *Political Emotions: New Agendas in Communication*. Austin: University of Texas, 2010.

Czach, Liz. "Home Movies and Amateur Film as National Cinema." In *Amateur Filmmaking: The Home Movie, The Archive, The Web*, edited by Laura Rascaroli, Gwenda Young and Barry Monahan, 2–38. New York: Bloomsbury Press, 2014.

Dayan, Daniel, and Elihu Katz. *Media Events: The Live Broadcasting of History*. Cambridge, MA: Harvard University Press, 1994.

Dbouk, Yahya. "The Curse of Ansariyeh Strikes Again." *Alakbar*, November 18, 2012. Accessed February 1, 2017. http://english.al-akhbar.com/node/13905.

Derrida, Jacques. "Freud and the Scene of Writing." In *Writing and Difference*, translated by Alan Bass, 246–92. London: Routledge, 2001 [1967].

———. "Signature, Event, Context." In *Limited Inc*, translated by Samuel Weber, 1–24. Chicago: Northwestern University, 1988 [1972].

———. "As If It Were Possible, 'Within Such Limits'. . . ." In *Negotiations: Interventions and Interviews, 1971–2001*, translated by Benjamin Elwood and Elizabeth Rottenberg, edited by Elizabeth Rottenberg, 343–70. Stanford: Stanford University Press, 2002.

Doane, Mary Ann. "The Close Up: Scale and Detail in the Cinema." *Differences: A Journal of Feminist Cultural Studies* 14, no. 3 (Fall 2003): 89–111.

———. "Information, Crisis, Catastrophe." In *Logics of Television: Essays in Cultural Criticism*, edited by Patricia Mellencamp. Bloomington: University of Indiana Press, 1990.

"Documentation: Shayetet 13's Soldiers Before the Lebanon Disaster." *Ynet*, April 14, 2013. Accessed April 13, 2022. https://www.ynet.co.il/articles/o ,7340,L-4368003,00.html.

Dotan, Eytan, and Udi Ben Dror, "A Proposal for Fallen Paratroopers' Memorial Video Projects." Israel Ministry of Defense, 2010. Accessed July 2017. http://www.izkor.gov.il/Page.aspx?pid=83.

Duvdevani, Shmulik. *First Person, Camera*. Jerusalem: Keter Publishing, 2010. In Hebrew.

Edelist, Ran. "The Heart Locker: Not an Ambush, Not a Drone Failure. The Naval Commando Disaster is a Result of Operative Omission." *Maariv*, April 16, 2017. Accessed April 12, 2022. https://www.maariv.co.il/journalists /Article-581416.

Fassin, Didier, and Richard Rechtman. *The Empire of Trauma: An Inquiry into the Condition of Victimhood*. Translated by Rachel Gomme. Princeton, NJ: Princeton University Press, 2009 [2007].

Felman, Shoshana. *The Juridical Unconscious: Trials and Traumas in the Twentieth Century*. Cambridge, MA: Harvard University Press, 2002.

Felman, Shoshana, and Dori Laub. *Testimony: Crisis of Witnessing in Literature, Psychoanalysis and History*. New York: Routledge, 1992.

Fenves, Peter. "Anecdote and Authority: Towards Kleist's Last Language." In *Arresting Language: From Leibniz to Benjamin*, 152–73. Stanford, CA: Stanford University Press, 2001.

Feuer, Jane. "The Concept of Live Television: Ontology as Ideology." In *Regarding Television: Critical Approaches—An Anthology*, edited by E. Ann Kaplan, 12–22. Frederick, MD: The American Film Institute, 1983.

Fishbein, Einat. "Here We Are, Face Us." *Yediot Achronot*, May 20, 2011, 16–18.

Fisk, Robert. "Israel Ambushed: Double Agent Lured Soldiers to Death in Lebanon." *The Independent*, September 16, 1997. Accessed April 13, 2022. http:// www.independent.co.uk/news/israel-ambushed-double-agent-lured-soldiers -to-death-in-lebanon-1239587.html.

Flichy, Patrice. "From Trading in Goods to Trading in Souls: The Telephone." In *Dynamics of Modern Communication: The Shaping and Impact of New Communication Technologies*. 82–98. London: Sage, 1995.

Foucault, Michel. *The Archeology of Knowledge*. Translated by Alan Sheridan. New York: Pantheon, 1972.

———. "The Dangerous Individual." *Politics, Philosophy, Culture: Interviews and Other Writings, 1977–1984*, edited by Lawrence D. Kritzman, 125–51. New York: Routledge, 1988.

———. "Governmentality." In *The Foucault Effect: Studies in Governmentality*, edited by Graham Burchell, Colin Gordon and Peter Miller, 87–104. Chicago: University of Chicago Press, 1991.

———. *Security, Territory, Population: Lectures at the Collège de France, 1977– 1978*. Edited by Michael Senellart. Translated by Graham Burchell. London: Palgrave Macmillan, 2007.

———. "Technologies of the Self." In *Technologies of the Self: A Seminar with Michel Foucault*, edited by Luther H. Martin, Huck Gutman, and Patrick H. Hutton, 16–49. Amherst: University of Massachusetts Press, 1988.

———. "The Subject and Power." *Critical Inquiry* 8, no. 4 (Summer, 1982): 777–95.

Freud, Sigmund. "A Note Upon the Mystic Writing Pad." In *The Standard Edition of the Complete Works of Sigmund Freud*, Vol. XIX (1927–1931), translated by James Strachey and Anna Freud, 227–32. London: The Hogarth Press, 1961.

———. "Fetishism." In *The Complete Psychological Works of Sigmund Freud*, Vol. XXI (1927–1931), translated by James Strachey, 147–57. London: Hogarth and the Institute of Psychoanalysis, 1961.

———. "Mourning and Melancholia" and "Remembering, Repeating and Working Through." In *The Standard Edition of the Complete Psychological Works of Sigmund Freud*, Vol. XIV (1914–1916), translated by James Strachey and Anna Freud, 243–58. London: The Hogarth Press, 1957.

Friedman, Orly. "Alternative Calendars and Memory Work in Serbia: Anti-War Activism After Milosevic." *Memory Studies* 8, no. 2 (2015): 212–26.

Frisko, Oren. "Embroiling Emotion." *The Seventh Eye*, March 16, 2009. Accessed April 13, 2022. https://www.the7eye.org.il/25799.

Frosh, Paul, and Amit Pinchevski. *Media Witnessing: Testimony in the Age of Mass Communication*. Basingstoke, UK: Palgrave Macmillan, 2009.

Froys, Tedi. "The Death of Television." *Davar,* April 26, 1982.

Fung, Richard. "Remaking Home Movies." In *Mining the Home Movie: Excavations in Histories and Memories*, edited by Karen L. Ishizuka and Patricia R. Zimmermann, 29–40. Berkeley: University of California Press, 2008.

Galloway, Alexander. *The Interface Effect*. Cambridge, UK: Polity Press, 2012.

Gates, Kelly A. *Our Biometric Future: Facial Recognition Technology and the Culture of Surveillance*. New York: New York University Press, 2011.

"Gilad Shalit Release: Shahira Amin Defends Interview." *BBC*, October 19, 2011. Accessed April 13, 2022. https://www.bbc.com/news/world-middle-east-15368819.

Ginsburg, Ruthie. *And You Will Serve as Eyes for Us: Israeli Human Rights Organizations as Seen Through the Camera's Eye*. Tel Aviv: Resling, 2014. In Hebrew.

———. "Exposure." *Mafteakh* 7 (2014): 63–77. http://mafteakh.tau.ac.il/wp-content/uploads/2014/01/7-2014-05.pdf. In Hebrew.

Givoni, Michal. "Testimony/Witnessing." *Mafte'akh* 2e (Winter 2011). Accessed July 6, 2015. http://mafteakh.tau.ac.il/en/issue-2e-winter-2011/witnessing testimony.

———. "The Ethics of Witnessing and the Politics of the Governed." Paper prepared for the APSA Annual Meeting, Seattle, Washington, September, 2011.

Godmilow, Jill. "What's Wrong with the Liberal Documentary?" *Peace Review*, March 1999.

Goffman, Erving. *Forms of Talk*. Philadelphia: University of Pennsylvania Press, 1981.

Goodman, Steve, and Luciana Parisi. "Mnemonic Control." In *Beyond Biopolitics: Essays on the Governance of Life and Death*, edited by Patricia Ticineto Clough, 163–76. Durham, NC: Duke University Press, 2011.

Grafton, Anthony, and Daniel Rosenberg. *Cartographies of Time: A History of the Timeline*. New York: Princeton Architectural Press, 2010.

Gregory, Sam. "Cameras Everywhere: Ubiquitous Video Documentation of Human Rights, New Forms of Video Advocacy and Considerations of Safety, Security, Dignity and Consent." *Journal of Human Rights Practice* 2 (November 2010): 191–207.

Grierson, John. "First Principles of Documentary." In *Grierson on Documentary*, edited by Forsyth Hardy, 145–56. New York: Praeger Publishers, 1966 [1946].

Gross, Aeyal. "Challenges to Compulsory Heterosexuality: Recognition and Non-Recognition of Same Sex Couples in Israeli Law." In *Legal Recognition of Same Sex Partnership: A Study of National, European and International Law*, edited by Robert Wintemute and Mads Andenas, 391–416. Oxford: Hartt Publishing, 2001.

Grossman, David. "Now that the Book is Done." March 24, 2008. Accessed September 7, 2018. http://www.newlibrary.co.il/article?co=14039&BSS53= 13176.

———. "Writing in a Zone of Disaster." *Yediot Achronot*, July 13, 2007.

———. *To The End of the Land*. Translated by Jessica Cohen. New York: Knopf, 2010.

———. *Writing in the Dark: Essays on Literature and Politics*. New York: Farrar, Straus and Giroux, 2008.

Guerin, Frances, and Roger Hallas. *The Image and the Witness: Trauma, Memory, and Visual Culture*. New York: Wallflower Press, 2007.

Habermas, Jürgen. *The Structural Transformation of the Public Sphere: An Inquiry into a Category of Bourgeois Society*. Translated by Thomas Burger. Cambridge, MA: MIT Press, 1991.

Handle, Ariel. "Beyond Good and Evil—The Syndrome: Responsibility and Shame in Soldiers' Testimonies." *Theory and Criticism* 32 (Spring 2008): 45–68. In Hebrew.

Hardt, Michael. "For Love or Money." *Cultural Anthropology* 26, no. 4 (2011): 676–82.

Harel, Amos, and Gili Cohen. "A Decisive Moment for Breaking the Silence: The Court Will Determine Whether the State Can Enforce the Exposure of Witnesses." *Haaretz*, August 5, 2016. Accessed April 13, 2022. https://www .haaretz.co.il/.premium-1.2947207.

Hediger, Vinzenz, and Patrick Vonderau, eds. *Films that Work: Industrial Film and the Productivity of Media*. Amsterdam: Amsterdam University Press, 2009.

Hellman, Sara, and Tamar Rappoport. "'These are Single Ashkenazi Women, Arabs' Whores, They Don't Believe in God and They Don't Love the Land of Israel': Women in Black as a Challenge to the Social Order." *Theory and Criticism* 10 (Summer 1997): 175–92.

Hermoni, Gal, Udi Lebel, and Batya Zuriel. "Bereavement Hit Chart and the Glocalization of Memory: Soldiering the Israeli Memorial Song." *The Public Sphere* 5 (2011): 9–34.

Hirsch, Marianne. *Family Frames: Photography, Narrative and Postmemory.* Cambridge, MA: Harvard University Press, 1997.

Hochberg, Gil. "Soldiers as Filmmakers: On the Prospects of 'Shooting War' and the Question of Ethical Spectatorship." *Screen* 54, no. 1 (Spring 2013): 44–61.

Horn, Eva. "Logics of Political Secrecy." *Theory, Culture and Society* 28, no. 7-8 (2011): 103–22.

Howe, Maija. "The Photographic Hangover: Reconsidering the Aesthetic of the Postwar 8mm Home Movie." In *Amateur Filmmaking: The Home Movie, The Archive, The Web,* edited by Kaura Rascaroli, Gwenda Young and Barry Monahan. New York: Bloomsbury Press, 2014.

Ishizuka, Karen L. "The Moving Image Archive of the Japanese American National Museum." In *Mining the Home Movie: Excavations in Histories and Memories,* edited by Karen L. Ishizuka and Patricia R. Zimmermann. Berkeley: University of California Press, 2008.

Jancovic, Marek, Axel Volmar, and Alexandra Schneider, eds. *Format Matters: Standards, Practices and Politics in Media Cultures.* Luneburg: Meson Press, 2020.

Juhasz, Alexandra. *AIDS TV: Identity, Community and Alternative Video.* Durham, NC: Duke University Press 1995.

Kahana, Jonathan, and Noah Tsika. "Let There Be Light and the Military Talking Picture." In *Remaking Reality: US Documentary Culture After 1945,* edited by Sara Blair, Joseph B. Entin, and Franny Nudelman, 14–34. Chapel Hill: University of North Carolina Press, 2018.

———. "Errol Morris and the Ends of Irony." Forthcoming.

———. *Intelligence Work: The Politics of American Documentary.* New York: Columbia University Press, 2008.

Kamir, Orit. "Every Woman has a Name." *Mishpatim* 29 (1996): 327–82.

Kaplan, Danny. "The Songs of the Siren: Engineering National Time on Israeli Radio." *Cultural Anthropology* 24, no. 2 (2009): 313–45.

Katz, Adi. "The Paratroops Remembers." *Ma'ariv,* April 19, 1999.

Keenan, Thomas. "Mobilizing Shame." *South Atlantic Quarterly* 103, no. 2-3 (Spring-Summer 2004): 435–49.

———. "Publicity and Indifference: Media, Surveillance and Humanitarian Intervention." In *Killer Images: Documentary Film, Memory and the Performance of Violence,* edited by Joram Ten Brink and Joshua Oppenheimer, 15–41. New York: Wallflower Press, 2012.

Kepley, Vance, Jr. "From 'Frontal Lobes' to the 'Bob-and-Bob' Show: NBC Management and Programming Strategies, 1949–65." In *Hollywood in the Age of Television,* edited by Tino Balio, 41–61. Boston: Unwin Hyman, 1990.

Klein, Naomi. "Laboratory for a Fortressed World." *The Nation,* June 14, 2007. Accessed May 23, 2019. https://www.thenation.com/article/laboratory-fortressed-world.

Koren, Gaya. "After the Fall." *Yediot Achronot,* July 6, 2005.

Kotaman Avci, Asli, and Louise Spence. "The Talking Witness Documentary: Remembrance and the Politics of Truth." *Rethinking History: The Journal of Theory and Practice* 17, no. 3 (2013): 295–311.

Kotef, Hagar. *The Colonizing Self: Or, Home and Homelessness in Israel/Palestine*. Durham, NC: Duke University Press, 2020.

Kotler-Hadari, Tzeela. "The Best for Digital: The IDF's War Room Takes Place in YouTube, Facebook and Twitter." *Globes*, May 10, 2017. Accessed April 15, 2022. https://www.globes.co.il/news/article.aspx?did=1001284933.

Kuntsman, Adi, and Rebecca L. Stein. *Digital Militarism: Israel's Occupation in the Social Media Age*. Stanford, CA: Stanford University Press, 2015.

Lam, Amira, and Amir Shoan. "The Soldier's Welfare Committee." *Yediot Achronot–Seven Days*, October 21, 2011, 22–26.

Lapid, Arnon. "My Own Memorial Movie." *MyNet Kibbutz*, 15 December, 2011. Accessed April 15, 2016. http://mynetkibbutz.co.il/%D7%AA%D7%A8%D7%91%D7%95%D7%AA-%D7%95%D7%90%D7%9E%D7%A0%D7%95%D7%AA/147689.

Lavie, Aviv. "Giving the Occupation a Bad Reputation." *Haaretz*, June 16, 2004. Accessed April 13, 2022. http://www.haaretz.co.il/misc/1.974927.

Leffer-Mintz, Ora. "A Letter from a Bereaved Mother." *Yediot Achronot*, April 26, 2004.

Leibovitz-Dar, Sarah. "The Prisoner's Dilemma." *Ha'aretz*, May 20, 2003. Accessed April 13, 2022. http://www.haaretz.co.il/1.883640.

Lévi-Strauss, Claude. "The Effectiveness of Symbols." In *Structural Anthropology*, ranslated by Claire Jacobson and Brooke Grundfest Schopf, 186–205. London: Basic Books, 1963.

Levi, Eldad. "Breaking the Silence: Sociology of Legitimization." *Haoketz*, December 22, 2015. Accessed April 13, 2022. http://www.haokets.org/2015/12/22/שוברים-שתיקה-סוציולוגיה-של-לגיטימציה/.

Levi, Shay. "1027 Terrorists versus 5." *Mako*, June 2, 2014. Accessed July 7, 2015. http://www.mako.co.il/pzm-magazine/Article-65da3f9195c5641006.html.

Levinas, Emmanuel. *Totality and Infinity: An Essay on Exteriority*. Translated by Alphonso Lingis. Pittsburgh, PA: Duquesne University, 1969.

Lippmann, Walter. *Public Opinion*. New York: Dover Publications, 2004 [1922].

Lomsky-Feder, Edna. "The Memorial Ceremony in Israeli Schools: Between the State and Civil Society." *British Journal of Sociology of Education* 25, no. 3 (2004): 291–305.

Lotz, Amanda D. *The Television Will be Revolutionized*. New York: New York University Press, 2014.

Lowe, Lisa. *The Intimacies of Four Continents*. Durham, NC: Duke University Press, 2015.

Lyotard, Jean-Francois. *The Differend: Phrases in Dispute*. Translated by Georges van den Abbeele. Minneapolis: University of Minnesota Press, 1988 [1983].

Mann, Daniel. "I Am Spartacus: Individualising Visual Media and Warfare." *Media, Culture and Society* 41, no. 1 (2019): 38–53.

———. *Occupying Habits: Everyday Media as Warfare in Israel-Palestine.* London: Bloomsbury Publishing, 2022.

Mansbach, Daniela. "Normalizing Violence: From Military Checkpoints to 'Terminals' in the Occupied Territories." *Journal of Power* 2, no. 2 (2009): 255–73.

———. "Crossing the Borders: The Power of Duality in the Protest of the 'Checkpoint Watch' Movement," *Theory and Criticism* 31 (2007): 77–99 (Hebrew).

Marks, Laura U. *The Skin of the Film: Intercultural Cinema, Embodiment, and the Senses.* Durham, NC: Duke University Press, 2000.

Marx, Karl. *Capital: A Critique of Political Economy.* Vol. I. Translated by Ben Fowkes. New York: Penguin, 1990.

Mbembe, Achille. "Necropolitics." *Public Culture* 15, no. 1 (2003): 11–40.

McCarthy, Anna. *Ambient Television: Visual Culture and Public Space.* Durham, NC: Duke University Press, 2001.

Medan, Anat. "My Son Has No Price: An Interview with Aviva Shalit." *Yediot Achronot –Seven Days,* June 10, 2011, 20.

Melamed, Laliv. "A NonReport: The Operative image and the Politics of the Secret." *Journal of Cinema and Media Studies* (forthcoming, 2023).

———. "Close to Home: Privatization and Personalization of Militarized Death in Israeli Home Videos." *New Cinemas: Journal of Contemporary Film* 11, no. 2-3 (2014): 127–42.

———. "Learning by Heart: Humming, Singing, Memorizing." In *Silence, Screen, and Spectacle: Rethinking Social Memory in the Age of Information,* edited by Lindsey A. Freeman, Benjamin Neinass and Rachel Daniell, 95–117. Oxford: Berghahn Books, 2014.

———. "What is a Girlfriend? Towards a Political Concept of the Girlfriend." *Discourse: Journal for Theoretical Studies in Media and Culture,* 43, no. 3 (2021): 421–46.

Mellencamp, Patricia. "TV Time and Catastrophe, or Beyond the Pleasure Principle of Television." In *Logics of Television: Essays in Cultural Criticism,* edited by Patricia Mellencamp. Bloomington: University of Indiana Press, 1990.

Mills, Mara. "The Audiovisual Telephone: A Brief History." In *Handheld? Music Video Aesthetic for Portable Devices,* edited by Henry Keazor, 34–47. Heidelberg: ART-Dok, 2021.

"The Ministry of Defense: If You Have Criticism Towards the IDF, Come to Me." *Ynet,* July 15, 2009. Accessed April 13, 2022. https://www.ynet.co.il/articles/0,7340,L-3746792,00.html. In Hebrew.

Mitchell, W.J.T. "Imperial Landscape." In *Landscape and Power,* edited by W.J.T. Mitchell, 5–34. Chicago: University of Chicago Press, 2002.

Morag, Raya. *Waltzing with Bashir: Perpetrator Trauma and Cinema.* London: I.B. Tauris, 2013.

Moran, James. *There's No Place Like Home Video.* Minneapolis: University of Minnesota Press, 2002.

Moretti, Franco. *Graphs, Maps, Trees: Abstract Models for Literary History.* London: Verso, 2005.

Morley, David. *Home Territories: Media, Mobility and Identity*. London: Routledge, 2000.

Mowitt, John. *Percussion: Drumming Beating, Striking*. Durham, NC: Duke University Press, 2002.

———. *Sounds: The Ambient Humanities*. California: University of California Press, 2015.

Mushyof, Shirly. "Project that Commemorate the Fallen in Movies." *Yediot Achronot*, May 8, 2000.

Nancy, Jean Luc. *Listening*. Translated by Charlotte Mandell. New York: Fordham University Press, 2007 [2002].

Nave, Hannah. *Captive By Mourning: Mourning in Hebrew Literature*. Tel Aviv: Hakibbutz Hameuchad, 1993. In Hebrew.

Newman, Michael Z. *Video Revolutions: On the History of a Medium*. New York: Columbia University Press, 2014.

Neumann, Boaz. *Land and Desire in Early Zionism*. Tel Aviv: Am Oved, 2009.

Nichols, Bill. *Representing Reality: Issues and Concepts in Documentary*. Bloomington: Indiana University Press, 1991.

———. "The Voice of Documentary." In *New Challenges for Documentary*, edited by Alan Rosenthal and John Corner, 18–19. Manchester: Manchester University Press 2005 [1988].

Odin, Roger. "Reflections on the Family Home Movie as Document: A Semio-Pragmatic Approach." In *Mining the Home Movie. Excavations in Histories and Memories*, edited by Karen I. Ishizuka and Patricia R. Zimmermann, 255–71. Berkeley: University of California Press, 2007.

———. "The Home Movie and Space of Communication." In *Amateur Filmmaking: The Home Movie, The Archive, The Web*, edited by Laura Rascaroli, Gwenda Young, and Barry Monahan, 15–26. London: Bloomsbury Academic, 2014.

Ophir, Adi, Michal Givoni, and Sari Hanafi, eds. *The Power of Inclusive Exclusion: Anatomy of Israeli Rule in the Occupied Palestinian Territories*. New York: Zone Books, 2009.

Orgeron, David, Masha Orgeron, and Dan Streible, eds,. *Learning with the Lights Off: Educational Film in the United States*. Oxford: Oxford University Press, 2011.

Peters, John Durham. *Speaking Into the Air: A History of the Idea of Communication*. Chicago: University of Chicago Press, 1999.

Pfeffer, Anshel. "The Hannibal Directive: Why Israel Risks the Life of the Soldier Being Rescued." *Ha'aretz*, August 3, 2014. Accessed April 13, 2022. http://www.haaretz.com/news/diplomacy-defense/.premium-1.608693.

Povinelli, Elizabeth A. *The Empire of Love: Toward a Theory of Intimacy, Genealogy and Carnality*. Durham, NC: Duke University Press, 2006.

Puar, Jasbir. *The Right to Maim: Debility, Capacity, Disability*. Durham, NC: Duke University Press, 2017.

Puar, Jasbir K., and Amit Rai. "Monster, Terrorist, Fag: The War on Terrorism and the Production of Docile Patriots." *Social Text* 20, no. 3 (2002): 117–48.

Radstone, Susannah. "Trauma Theory: Contexts, Politics, Ethics." *Paragraph* 30, no. 1 (March 2007): 9–29.

Rangan, Pooja. "Documentary Listening Habits: From Voice to Audibility." In *The Oxford Handbook of Film Theory*, edited by Kyle Stevens. Oxford: Oxford University Press, 2022.

———. *Immediations: The Humanitarian Impulse in Documentary*. Durham, NC: Duke University Press, 2017.

Rascaroli, Laura, Gwenda Young, and Barry Monahan, eds. *Amateur Filmmaking: The Home Movie, The Archive, The Web*. London: Bloomsbury Academic, 2014.

Reinfeld, Moshe. "The Writing on the Helicopter Crash Casualties Will Be Changed." *Ha'aretz*, May 7, 2001. Accessed April 13, 2022. http://www.haaretz.co.il/misc/1.699255.

Renov, Michael. "Filling Up the Hole in the Real: Death and Mourning in Contemporary Documentary Film and Video." In *The Subject of Documentary*, 120–29. Minneapolis: University of Minnesota Press, 2004.

Renov, Michael, and Erika Suderburg, eds. *Resolutions: Contemporary Video Practices*. Minneapolis: University of Minnesota Press, 1995.

Roth, Michael. "Ordinary Film: Peter Forgacs' *The Maelstrom*." In *Mining the Home Movie: Excavations in Histories and Memories*, edited by Karen L. Ishizuka and Patricia R. Zimmermann, 62-72. Berkeley: University of California Press, 2008.

Russell, Catherine. "Archival Apocalypse: Found Footage as Ethnography." In *Experimental Ethnography: The Work of Film in the Age of Video*, 238–74. Durham, NC: Duke University Press, 1999.

Sarkar, Bhaskar, and Janet Walker. *Documentary Testimonies: Global Archives of Suffering*. London: Routledge, 2010.

Saxton, Libby. "Anamnesis and Bearing Witness. Godard/Lanzmann." In *For Ever Godard: The Work of Jean-Luc Godard 1950–2000*, edited by Michael Temple, James S. Williams, and Michael Witt, 364–79. London: Black Dog, 2004.

Searle, John. *Speech Acts: An Essay in the Philosophy of Language*. Cambridge, UK: Cambridge University Press, 1969.

Segev, Noam. "An Entire Life in Seven Minutes: Interview with Amir Keren." *Ynet*, April 15, 2002. Accessed April 12, 2022. http://www.ynet.co.il/articles/0,7340,L-1835630,00.html.

Sekula, Allan. "The Body and the Archive." *October* 39 (Winter 1986): 3–64.

"The Shalit Family Asks: Leave Mitzpe Hila." *NRG*, October 31, 2011. Accessed April 13, 2022. https://www.makorrishon.co.il/nrg/online/1/ART2/300/756.html.

Shamir, Ilana, and Matityahu Mayzel, eds. *Patterns of Commemoration*. Tel Aviv: Ministry of Defense, 2000.

Sharp, Christina. *Monstrous Intimacy: Making Post-Slavery Subjects*. Durham, NC: Duke University Press, 2010.

Shefer, Hadas. "Shay, RIP, proposed to Sivan during the war and then died." *NRG-Ma'Ariv*, April 23, 2004. Accessed April 13, 2022. http://www.nrg.co.il/online/1/ART1/572/500.html.

Shelach, Ofer. "The Only Warrior Who Was Not Injured in the Naval Commando Incident Speaks." *Maariv*, September 20, 2008. Accessed April 13, 2022. http://www.nrg.co.il/online/1/ART1/788/722.html.

Shilony, Smadar. "Caught By the Message." *Ynet*. Accessed January 1, 2014. http://test.ynet.co.il/articles/0,7340,L-3540116,00.html.

Shir, Smadar. "Varda's War." *Yediot Achronot*, August 1, 2014.

Smaill, Belinda, "Injured Identities: Pain, Politics and Documentary," *Studies in Documentary Film* 1, no. 2 (January 2007), 151-163.

Sobchack, Vivian. *Carnal Thoughts: Embodiment and Moving Image Culture*. Berkeley: University of California Press, 2004.

Spigel, Lynn. *Make Room For TV: Television and the Family Ideal in Postwar America*. Chicago: University of Chicago Press, 1992.

State of Israel, Ministry of Defense. *Paths of Commemoration*. 2010.

———. *Paths of Commemoration*. Tel Aviv: Ministry of Defense, 1975.

State of Israel, The Israeli Parliament. The *Second Authority for Television and Radio Rule 1990*. https://main.knesset.gov.il/Activity/Legislation/Laws/Pages/LawPrimary.aspx?t=lawlaws&st=lawlaws&lawitemid=2000577.

Stam, Robert. "Interrogating Authorship and Genre." In *Film Theory: An Introduction*, 123–29. Malden, MA: Blackwell, 2000.

Stein, Rebecca L. *Screen Shots: State Violence on Camera in Israel and Palestine*. Stanford, CA: Stanford University Press, 2021.

Stoler, Ann Laura. *Along the Archival Grain: Epistemic Anxiety and Colonial Common Sense*. Princeton, NJ: Princeton University Press, 2009.

Stollar, Avihai. "This is How We Collected Soldiers' Testimonies After Operation Protective Edge." *Mekomit*, May 4, 2015. Accessed April 13, 2022.

Sturken, Marita. *Tangled Memories: The Vietnam War, the AIDS Epidemic, and the Politics of Remembering*. Berkeley: University of California Press, 1997.

Swann, Paul. *The British Documentary Film Movement 1926–1946*. Cambridge, UK: Cambridge University Press, 1989.

Taylor, Diana. "Trapped in Bad Scripts: The Mothers of the Plaza De Mayo." In *Disappearing Acts: Spectacles of Gender and Nationalism in Argentina's "Dirty War,"* 183–222. Durham, NC: Duke University Press, 1997.

Thacker, Eugene. "Necrologies: or, the Death of the Body Politic." In *Beyond Biopolitics: Essays on the Governance of Life and Death*, edited by Patricia Ticineto Clough and Craig Willse, 139–62. Durham, NC: Duke University Press, 2011.

Torchin, Leshu. *Creating the Witness: Documenting Genocide on Film, Video and the Internet*. Minneapolis: University of Minnesota Press, 2012.

Tziper, Benny. "At First Look: Television Review." *Haaretz*, April 15, 1983, 45.

Tzror, Lior. "All the Details about the Cellular Revolution in the IDF." *Mako* (published in the website's section of *Bamahane*, the IDF periodical), May 9, 2012. http://www.mako.co.il/pzm-soldiers/Article-bf5c3e3ae813731006.htm. Accessed August 15, 2022.

Warner, Michael. "Beyond Gay Marriage." In *The Trouble with Normal: Sex, Politics and the Ethics of Queer Life*. Cambridge, MA: Harvard University Press, 2000.

Wasson, Haidee, and Charles Acland, eds. *Useful Cinema*. Durham, NC: Duke University Press, 2011.

Weiss, Meira. "Forensic Medicine and Religion in the Identification of Dead Soldiers' Bodies." *Mortality* 13, no. 2 (May 2008): 119–31.

————. *The Chosen Body.* Stanford, CA: Stanford University Press, 2002.

Weizman, Eyal. "Hannibal in Rafah." In *Forensic Architecture: Violence of the Threshold of Detectability*, 165–213. London: Zone Books, 2017.

————. *Hollow Land: Israel Architecture of Occupation.* London: Verso Books: 2007.

White, Mimi. "Television Liveness: History, Banality, Attractions." *Spectator* 20, no. 1 (Fall/Winter 1999): 38–56.

Williams, Linda. "Film Bodies: Gender, Genre, and Excess." *Film Quarterly* 44, no. 4, (Summer 1991): 2-13.

Williams, Mark. "History in a Flash: Notes on the Myth of TV 'Liveness.'" In *Collecting Visible Evidence*, edited by Jane Gaines and Michael Renov, 292–312. Minneapolis: University of Minnesota Press, 1999.

Williams, Raymond. "Programming: Distribution and Flow." In *Television: Technology and Cultural Form*, 77–120. 2nd ed. London: Routledge, 1990 [1975].

Winston, Brian. *Claiming the Real: The Griersonian Documentary and its Legitimations.* London: British Film Institute, 1995.

Winters, Jay. "The Generation of Memory: Reflections on the 'Memory Boom' in Contemporary Historical Studies." *Canadian Military History* 10, no. 3 (2001): Article 5. https://scholars.wlu.ca/cmh/vol10/iss3/5.

Wolfe, Charles. "Historicizing the 'Voice of God': The Place of Vocal Narration in Classical Documentary." *Film History* 9 (1997): 149–67.

Wright, Lawrence. "Gilad Shalit: The Living and the Dead." *The New Yorker*, October 18, 2011. Accessed April 13, 2022. http://www.newyorker.com /news/news-desk/gilad-shalit-the-living-and-the-dead.

Yosef, Raz. "The Politics of the Normal: Sex and Nation in Israeli Homosexual Cinema." In *Theory and Criticism*. Jerusalem, 2007. In Hebrew.

————. *Beyond Flesh: Queer Masculinities and Nationalism in Israeli Cinema.* New Brunswick, NJ: Rutgers University Press, 2004.

Young, James E. *The Texture of Memory: Holocaust Memorials and Meaning.* New Haven, CT: Yale University Press, 1993).

Yuran, Noam. *Channel 2: The New Statehood.* Tel Aviv: Resling, 2001. In Hebrew.

Zartel, Idit. *Death and the Nation: History, Memory, Politics.* Or Yehuda: Dvir, 2002. In Hebrew.

Zerubavel, Eviatar. *Time Maps: Collective Memory and the Social Shape of the Past.* Chicago: Chicago University Press, 2004.

Zimmermann, Patricia R. *Reel Families: A Social History of Amateur Films.* Bloomington: Indiana University Press, 1995.

Zimmermann, Patricia R., and Karen I. Ishizuka, eds. *Mining the Home Movie: Excavations in Histories and Memories.* Berkeley: University of California Press, 2007.

Zispal, Klil, and Iris Kashman. "Behind-the-Scenes of Death." *Bamahane'*, February 1997, 46–47.

Zeitoun, Yoav. "Stop the Shooting I Have Dead Soldiers Here": Ynet reveals the IDF Radio Transmissions After Goldin Abduction in Rafah." *Yediot*

Achronot via *Ynet*, December 30, 2014. Accessed April 13, 2022. http://www
.ynet.co.il/articles/0,7340,L-4609271,00.html.

———. "The Government Legal Consultant: The Hannibal Directive Prohibits the Killing of a Captive Soldier." *Yediot Achronot* via *Ynet*, January 12,
2015. Accessed April 13, 2022. http://www.ynet.co.il/articles/0,7340,L
-4614353,00.html.

———. "Footage Taken From Bnaya Sar-el RIP's Helmet Camera." *Ynet*,
July 7, 2015. Accessed April 13, 2022. https://www.ynet.co.il/articles/0,7340,L
-4677226,00.html.

Index

Founded in 1893,
UNIVERSITY OF CALIFORNIA PRESS
publishes bold, progressive books and journals
on topics in the arts, humanities, social sciences,
and natural sciences—with a focus on social
justice issues—that inspire thought and action
among readers worldwide.

The UC PRESS FOUNDATION
raises funds to uphold the press's vital role
as an independent, nonprofit publisher, and
receives philanthropic support from a wide
range of individuals and institutions—and from
committed readers like you. To learn more, visit
ucpress.edu/supportus.